ONE PEOPLE, ONE BLOOD

Jewish Cultures of the World

Edited by Matti Bunzl, *University of Illinois, Urbana-Champaign*,
and Jeffrey Shandler, *Rutgers University*

Advisory Board

Yoram Bilu, *Hebrew University*
Jonathan Boyarin, *University of North Carolina*
Virginia R. Dominguez, *University of Illinois, Urbana-Champaign*
Susannah Heschel, *Dartmouth College*
Barbara Kirshenblatt-Gimblett, *New York University*
Jack Kugelmass, *University of Florida*
Riv-Ellen Prell, *University of Minnesota*
Aron Rodrigue, *Stanford University*
Mark Slobin, *Wesleyan University*
Yael Zerubavel, *Rutgers University*

ONE PEOPLE, ONE BLOOD

*Ethiopian-Israelis and the
Return to Judaism*

Don Seeman

RUTGERS UNIVERSITY PRESS
NEW BRUNSWICK, NEW JERSEY, AND LONDON

First paperback printing, 2010.

Library of Congress Cataloging-in-Publication Data

Seeman, Don, 1968–
    One people, one blood : Ethiopian-Israelis and the return to Judaism / Don Seeman.
      p. cm.—(Jewish cultures of the world)
    Includes bibliographical references and index.
    ISBN 978–0–8135–4541–7 (hardcover : alk. paper)
    ISBN 978–0–8135–4936–1 (pbk. : alk. paper)
    1. Jews, Ethiopian—Israel. 2. Jews—Ethiopia—History. 3. Judaism—Ethiopia.
4. Feres Mura. 5. Ethiopia—Ethnic relations. I. Title.
    DS113.8.F34S44 2009
    305.892'4063—dc22   2007037880

A British Cataloging-in-Publication record for this book is available from the British Library.

A previous version of chapter two appeared in the *Journal for Religion in Africa*. A previous version of chapter six appeared in the journal *Culture, Medicine, and Psychiatry*.

Copyright © 2009 by Don Seeman

All rights reserved

No part of this book may be reproduced or utilized in any form or by any means, electronic or mechanical, or by any information storage and retrieval system, without written permission from the publisher. Please contact Rutgers University Press, 100 Joyce Kilmer Avenue, Piscataway, NJ 08854–8099. The only exception to this prohibition is "fair use" as defined by U.S. copyright law.

Visit our Web site: http://rutgerspress.rutgers.edu

Manufactured in the United States of America

For Debra, and to the families whose lives I have shared.

כַּמַּיִם הַפָּנִים לַפָּנִים--   כֵּן לֵב-הָאָדָם לָאָדָם.

משלי כז

(Proverbs 27:19)

Loss, mourning, the longing for memory, the desire to enter into the world around you and having no idea how to do it, the fear of observing too coldly, or too distractedly or too raggedly, the rage of cowardice, the insight that is always arriving late, as defiant hindsight, a sense of the utter uselessness of writing anything and yet the burning desire to write something, are the stopping places along the way. At the end of the voyage, if you are lucky, you catch a glimpse of a lighthouse and you are grateful. Life, after all, is bountiful.

—Ruth Behar, *The Vulnerable Observer: Anthropology That Breaks Your Heart*

CONTENTS

Acknowledgments ix

Introduction 1
1 A Death in Addis Ababa 12
2 The Question of Kinship 41
3 Purity of Heart 62
4 Returning to Judaism 84
5 Absorption 109
6 Blood and Terror 150
7 The "Feres Mura" Dilemma 180

Notes 213
References 215
Index 233

ACKNOWLEDGMENTS

An ethnographic study of this nature can only succeed as a work of friendship. My warmest and most profound thanks go to the many individuals and families who have opened their homes and lives to me over the years, and who continue to do so today. This book could not have been written without each of you, although I cannot for your own sakes mention you by name. Those whose pseudonyms appear in this book—Desta, Rachel, Meles, Yossi, Yitzhak—you know who you are, my brothers and sisters. My fieldwork was also greatly facilitated by many other individuals whose role in these events is more public. Thanks to former member of Knesset Addisu Messele and founders of the South Wing to Zion organization Avraham Neguse and Yafet Alamo for many enlightening conversations; to Rabbi Menahem Waldman for allowing me to observe the "Return to Judaism" program up close without precondition; to Joseph Feit and Barbara Gordon at the North American Conference on Ethiopian Jews for access to the compound in Addis Ababa; and to Andy Goldman and Dr. Rick Hodes for their views of the situation in Addis. The controversy surrounding the policy of return to Judaism made my research uncomfortable for many, and I am grateful to those whose generosity overcame other considerations.

    I have had the privilege of membership in several academic communities of high quality and true collegiality. The medical anthropology group at Harvard built by Arthur and Joan Kleinman, Byron Good, and Mary-Jo Delvecchio Good remains a moral and intellectual touchstone for many who have been trained there. Arthur Kleinman's voice has conditioned my own writing and teaching in ways subtle and profound—the model of interdisciplinary scholarship and humanity he set is why I became an anthropologist in the first place. Colleagues in the department of sociology and anthropology at Bar-Ilan University and later at the Hebrew University of Jerusalem taught me how to live as a scholar in a place where the ivory tower of academia is not so tall that research and teaching can be neatly separated from the desperate existential dilemmas of the surrounding society. Special thanks to Sam Cooper, Harvey Goldberg, Don Handelman, Tamar El-Or, and Yoram Bilu. Thanks also to Ethiopian Jewry specialists Steven Kaplan, Chaim Rosen, and Shalva Weil, whose insights and collegiality have benefited me at every stage. Thanks finally to all of my colleagues in the Department of Religion, the Graduate Division of Religion, and the Tam Institute for Jewish Studies at Emory University, where I now teach. Together, you have helped me to see what ethnography can offer the study of religion, and how thinking in a sustained and critical but sympathetic way about religion can make me a better person as well as ethnographer. Laurie Patton, Gary Laderman, Joyce Flueckiger, Deborah Lipstadt, David Blumenthal, Michael Broyde, Liz Bounds, Vince Cornell, Edward Queen, Dianne Stewart, and others have all gone above and beyond the call of duty in friendship and collegiality. The decision to use part of the Tam Institute's generous endowment from the Blank Foundation to create a position in the Ethnography of Jewish Communities is one that I hope will be emulated widely at other campuses. The ethnography of Jews and Judaism seems finally to be coming of age in American anthropology, and I want to thank Matti Bunzl and Jeffrey Shandler for inviting me to inaugurate their new *Jewish Cultures of the World* book series with this volume.

My many really extraordinary students at all levels are the main reason I keep writing and teaching. In the time it took this project to reach completion, some of you have gone on to become friends and scholars in your own right—Sarah Willen, Anat Rosenthal, Tsipy Ivry, Elly Teman, Wasfi Kailani, LeRhonda Manigault—thank you for your questions and critiques, and for becoming a really important part of my intellectual community. Thanks also to scholar-friends Tim Lytton, Erica Lehrer, and Sue Kahn. The Wexner Foundation and my fellows in the Graduate Fellowship program supported me not just financially at an early stage, but also spiritually and emotionally, helping to reinforce the message that scholarship should benefit the many interlocking communities to which we belong. In a book about kinship and the questions it raises, I must acknowledge the steady, ongoing support of my parents, in-laws, and family.

In the end, I cannot conclude without telling the truth—that my wife Debra and our two daughters, Racheli and Hadara, own the lion's share of credit for helping me to carry this project through to fruition while remaining human in the process. Bringing my newest family members with me to the field to meet some of the people whose lives I have shared has been a profound joy and accomplishment. My blessing to them as a parent is that they always remember our common humanity in diverse settings, learn to laugh in many languages, and work to find the divine spark that can sometimes be seen on the faces of other people.

ONE PEOPLE, ONE BLOOD

INTRODUCTION

> Before we proceed further, it would be well to note that there are ambiguities in the ordinary notion of understanding another person.
>
> —Alfred Schutz

Qäs be-qäs—we ought to proceed with caution.

Or to cite the whole familiar Amharic proverb, *Qäs be-qäs, ənqulal be-əgərou yehedal*, which means, "Little by little, an egg will come to walk upon its own leg." Ethiopian Jews in Israel are fond of quoting this bit of folk wisdom whenever they talk about their own history and the slow, difficult process by which they came to fulfill their destinies so far from the Horn of Africa where they were born. In context, *qäs be-qäs* can serve either as admonition or as reassurance, as in "Have patience, defer the pleasures of the moment, and make careful plans. One day, you will prevail." It is an apt summary of how Ethiopian Jews, or Beta Israel, have perceived themselves and their history in modern times. The early waves of immigrants during the middle 1980s, who trekked by foot across hundreds of miles of deadly wilderness in order to reach the refugee camps in Sudan from which they hoped (sometimes incorrectly) that they would be whisked surreptitiously to Israel, applied this aphorism to themselves quite literally. But it also continues to resonate with later waves of Ethiopian migrants—including the so-called Feres Mura immigrants of the 1990s and beyond, the descendants of Beta Israel whose ancestors converted to Christianity but who now wish to "return to Judaism" and who consequently face very different obstacles and threats.

"Feres Mura" immigrants of the 1990s and early 2000s have not had to trek across hundreds of miles of dangerous desert terrain in order to reach Israel. But they have frequently been forced by circumstance to spend years in conditions of extreme poverty and displacement while they await decisions about their right to emigrate by successive Ethiopian and Israeli governments. Since the conclusion of my fieldwork, many thousands of people have come forward to claim their heritage as Beta Israel, and there are said to be some ten to twenty thousand still clamoring in Ethiopia for the right to emigrate and return to Judaism. Between fifteen and twenty thousand have already migrated to Israel, where they face a different set of problems related to their need to demonstrate religious and ethnic authenticity both to Israelis in general and to the Ethiopian immigrant community that preceded them. *One People, One Blood* is the first ethnography to focus sustained attention on the lived experience of these "Feres Mura" and on the deep cultural, political, and epistemological conundrums aroused by their desire to return to Judaism at this time.

The very existence of "Feres Mura" who desire to return to Judaism poses uncomfortable questions for many contemporary Jews—not least Israeli policy makers—about how to determine the measure and limits of belonging in the national and/or religious Jewish collectives. The alleged apostasy of parents or grandparents might easily be thought to render such people outside of any possible consensus about "who is a Jew" in today's fractured Jewish world, but their assertion of penitence and return to Judaism also complicates this exclusion. Should the descendants of converts who say they wish to return be eligible to immigrate with their extended kin under Israel's expansive Law of Return (in this case, geographical return is meant), which normally is extended to anyone who is descended from at least one Jewish grandparent and would therefore have been considered Jewish under Germany's infamous Nuremberg laws? Or does the original sin of conversion to Christianity render any such attempt by later generations inherently suspect and ineffective? How should the roles of rabbis, bureaucrats, or even ethnographers and historians be defined in making that decision? And what, if any, are the special burdens of "punishment" or suffering that those who say they wish to undo their ancestral apostasy be asked to bear? These are questions that define not just a group of immigrants or potential immigrants, but the communities that seek to decide their fate as well. It means that this book cannot serve as the ethnography of some bounded ethnic and religious group without also engaging in critical observations of Israeli society as a whole.

One of the major theses of this ethnography is that interpretations of religious agency lie at the heart of this crisis. State policy makers, religious authorities, media analysts, humanitarian advocates, and earlier waves of Ethiopian immigrants are only a few of the social actors who have been struggling to determine—each in accord with their own canons of interpretation and analysis—why and under what circumstances the ancestors of "Feres Mura" converted to Christianity, and why so many of their descendants have been returning to Judaism in the here and now. For some of the participants in this ongoing social drama, it has become important to determine whether the original conversions to Christianity by ancestors of today's "Feres Mura" should be considered "forced" or "voluntary," because so-called forced conversions might free their descendants from the strong social stigma borne by apostates. Yet other relevant questions include the extent to which these converts came to think of themselves as fully Christians over time and the extent to which they also retained ethnic and religious allegiances to their Beta Israel kin that might be viewed today as evidence of ongoing links with Jews and Judaism. Most important to Israeli policy makers, however, has been the question of agency in the contemporary return to Judaism, and whether this should be viewed as mere economic opportunism, as many of its opponents have claimed, or as the pure-hearted, penitential campaign portrayed by its supporters. The question itself entails an important but possibly insoluble methodological dilemma, which is how the religious agency of other people can be evaluated in a way that transcends the ideological concerns of the viewer. Or to put the question in its most concrete ethnographic form: is there no more plausible alternative to the stark and highly polemical opposition between penitence and opportunism that seems to define the public discourse on contemporary "Feres Mura"?

The overwhelming cultural and political salience of these questions, combined with their refractoriness to clear and objective resolution, forms the major theoretical backdrop to this ethnography. I locate myself comfortably within the broad "phenomenological" or "experience-near" school of anthropological writing, championed by writers like Kleinman (1995), Wikan (1990), and Jackson (1998), among many others. Like them, I believe that the scholarly focus on "culture" or on religious belief and practice alone, without a rigorous theoretical and methodological approach to lived experience, can lead to significant misunderstandings of the distinctive life-worlds in which human habitation and meaning occur. In chapter 5, for example, I argue that abstract accounts of what are taken to be the rules of kinship in Beta Israel society sometimes mislead researchers away from the strategic and malleable uses of kinship in real social life, and compound the tendency of Israeli bureaucrats to view Ethiopians as "liars" or cheats who use kinship categories in a manipulative way to gain what they need from the welfare state. In chapter 6, similarly, I argue that Israeli politicians and public health experts allowed a discourse of "Ethiopian culture" shorn of its lived experiential context to mask the real meaning of a violent public controversy over donated blood. The Blood Affair, as it came to be known, was portrayed as a contest between traditional beliefs and objective science rather than as a revelation of the fraught and painful relationship between Ethiopian immigrants and the state. In each of these cases, "Feres Mura" have been especially vulnerable because of their potential double exclusion, as Beta Israel as well as people whose hearts are widely thought to be tainted with infidelity. This book focuses, in fact, on the "Feres Mura" experience of three separate but closely related spheres of state policy and bureaucratic practice that impinge upon them in mutually reinforcing ways: state immigration policy, public health practice, and the power of Israel's religious establishment.

Yet this ethnography also insists that an "experience-near" approach to the "Feres Mura" dilemma must focus upon the epistemological limitations of this project, and the dangers—theoretical for us, but sometimes very real for our informants—attendant upon failure to do so. Assertions about the moral and religious experience of people who are undergoing religious change are at the very heart of the "Feres Mura" dilemma, yet the interpretive grounds upon which such assertions can be made are often deeply contested and poorly understood. How does one determine, for example, whether penitence or economic salvation is really uppermost in the minds and hearts of refugees, whose motivations for radical change may actually include both these and other factors that policy discourse has yet to privilege? And how do we take account of imponderables like remorse or ambivalence in human experience, which are frequently deleted from simplistic social scientific accounts of religious agency, even though philosophers like Charles Taylor (1985) insist that these second-order experiences bear witness to the crucial self-interpretive dimension of human subjectivity?

For me it is axiomatic, following the great sociologist Alfred Schutz (1967), that social scientists are really nothing but specially trained and well disciplined analysts of interpretive materials that all people who live in society are forced to analyze and interpret every day of their lives. Schutz's breakthrough was to combine Max Weber's interpretive sociology of meaning (Weber 1963) with Edmund Husserl's phenomenology of the experiencing subject (Husserl 1970), in order to bring analytic focus to bear on lived experience without denying the fundamentally hermeneutic nature of this enterprise. Experience and interpretation go together on at least two levels for Schutz: First, because each of us is constantly forced to make an interpretive evaluation of the agency and motives (which is to say the experience) of the people around us in our social world. And second, because our own direct experience is already partly constituted by second- and third-order interpretations of what we have experienced in the past. Like ethnographers and historians, social actors are always engaged in the construction of *plausible narratives* about their own and other people's agency, based on clues and interpretive dispositions that yield only imperfect clarity. By insisting on the interpretive or hermeneutic contingency of such narrative construction, writers like Schutz and Taylor remind us that lived experience is never merely transparent to the observer, any more than it is to the experiencing subject, and that there is no realm of pure experience devoid of the need for interpretation. That is why "there are ambiguities," Schutz tells us, "in the ordinary notion of understanding another person" (1967, 107).

What Is at Stake in This Ethnography?

The anthropologist of Indian religions T. N. Madan (1975) once described ethnography as the art of "living intimately with strangers." Of course this is only the first stage in an analytic process that uses the relationships developed with informants through participant observation to generate insights about the nature of social life, culture, and human experience. Ethnography for this book was collected by living intimately with different groups of strangers who became friends and confidants over an unusually extended period of change and growth for both of us. Some of their stories are included in the pages that follow, but for me these years included the time of my student apprenticeship in anthropology at Harvard, my first academic jobs at Bar-Ilan and Hebrew universities in Israel, and later my move to a newly created position in the ethnography of Jewish communities at Emory University. Each of these intellectual communities has left its mark on this work and deserves my heartfelt appreciation. In addition, it should be emphasized that although this book focuses on the "Feres Mura" dilemma, it is enriched by previous fieldwork that I conducted in the Beta Israel community in Israel starting with student research in Upper Nazareth in 1989, where I developed an intimacy with several families that continues until this day; that community also makes frequent appearances in this book. I conducted preliminary research for this ethnography in Addis Ababa during the summers of 1992 and 1993, then spent two years conducting full-time research in Israel between 1994 and 1996. I lived and taught in Jerusalem between 1998 and 2003, conducting research at immigrant absorption centers in Haifa and Jerusalem, at the university where I taught, and in the towns and cities where some of my earlier informants had by then settled in an attempt to begin their lives anew.

This kind of multisited ethnography (G. Marcus 1995) was all but necessitated by the desire to investigate the lived experience of migrants, whose lives were heavily defined by the need to move from villages to transit camps in Addis Ababa, then from Addis Ababa to Israeli immigrant centers, and finally to permanent housing in their new country. The people whose experience I have tried to capture in this book do not live in a circumscribed village or neighborhood, in the classical anthropological model, but move increasingly in a whole *country* whose politics and culture, including periods of violent strife, constitute the necessary backdrop and context to this story. One of the key arguments of this book is that the "Feres Mura" must be viewed as an integral part of the larger Beta Israel or Ethiopian Jewish community whose center is today in Israel. There are currently more than 100,000 Ethiopians living as Jews in Israel, a country whose total population is around 7.2 million (almost 20 percent of whom are mostly Muslim and Christian Palestinian-Israeli citizens). Given these numbers, the 20,000 or so "Feres Mura" who have already immigrated to Israel and are my central concern in this book may seem insignificant. I insist, however, that the "Feres Mura" dilemma cannot be divorced from the wider spectrum of problems facing the Ethiopian immigrant community, and is in fact an important window upon many of them, just as Ethiopians constitute a window upon social and cultural processes in the State of Israel.

Issues of religious gatekeeping and social integration that are endemic to the situation of all Ethiopians in Israel face their sharpest formulation in the "Feres Mura" dilemma, just as the stereotyping of cultural and religious identities concerns the shape of the state as a whole. It is important to remember that even "Feres Mura" who have already immigrated and undergone a formal return to Judaism face their own special challenges that may compromise their ability to get on with their lives, and that this imposes a heavy sense of responsibility upon a writer who is sensitive to the ways in which researchers both participate in and help to shape the social fields they study. Departing from the focus on thick description and interpretation of cultures that was defined as *the* anthropological project by writers like Clifford Geertz (1973), the experience-near or cultural-phenomenological approach to ethnographic writing presumes that our first obligation is to the thick and detailed description not of culture but of what is at stake for real people in local settings—stakes that are patterned in important ways but never wholly defined by cultural considerations. This is a departure from previous work in the field of Ethiopian Jewry studies, although this book benefits in innumerable ways from work that has preceded it.

Many fine historians and anthropologists have already written about different aspects of the Beta Israel or Ethiopian Jewish reality. The historical context of Beta Israel (Abbink 1990; S. Kaplan 1992b; Quirin 1992; Summerfield 2003; Shelemay 1989; Seeman 2003; Trevisan Semi 2005), their linguistic and cultural context (Rosen 1985, 1994; Anteby-Yemini 2004; Weil 1991; Salamon 1994, 1999; Ben-Dor 1987), and the challenges of adjustment to life in Israel (Ashkenazi and Weingrod 1987; Shabtay 1999; Schwarz 2001; Hertzog 1999; Wagaw 1993; BenEzer 1992; Seeman 1999b, 1999c) have all been treated extensively by these and many other scholars. Indeed, two full volumes of bibliography on the study of Ethiopian Jewry have already been published (S. Kaplan and Ben-Dor 1988; Salamon and S. Kaplan 1998), and even these lists are now both outdated. More recently, Malka Shabtay (2007) has written about the problems of immigrant absorption faced by descendants of Beta Israel converts, while Brhane (2000), Goodman (2008a, 2008b), and Cohen (2006) have expanded upon specific aspects of the ethnography presented here. I am indebted to all of my predecessors and colleagues in research, not all of whom can be appropriately cited or thanked in the confines of this volume.

One People, One Blood is the first book-length ethnography to focus on the "Feres Mura" dilemma, or to subject their formal return to Judaism to any kind of sustained, empirical analysis. It is also the first work to insist that understanding the Beta Israel in modern times requires an analytic framework broad enough to include not just the Jewish descendants of historical Beta Israel (that is, Ethiopian Jews) but also the descendants of those who converted to Christianity and are now "returning," as well as more recent converts to (mostly Pentecostal) Christianity, who continue to identify in paradoxical ways with Judaism. This breadth of focus will no doubt be controversial in some quarters, because it challenges the popular assumption that "Ethiopian Jews" can be neatly separated in analytic and historical terms from those Beta Israel who did not, so to speak, keep the faith. The politics of authenticity that worked to exclude "Feres Mura" politically have also helped to ensure their near absence from contemporary ethnography, as evidenced in the comment by a senior colleague who warned me in 1992 before I traveled to Ethiopia for the first time that my trip was pointless because "there are no Jews left there anymore." It should be clear that one of my goals in this book is to fundamentally shift the conversation about Beta Israel and Ethiopian Jews in a more analytic direction, both by including the study of converts and returnees to Judaism and by leveraging this data to drive theoretical reflection about religious and moral experience in this context.

It might be too much to ask that a scholarly work such as this one should also play a role in the ongoing public conversation about "Feres Mura" immigration and their return to Judaism. Yet the focus on moral and religious experience that underlies this project does lend itself to a broader conversation about the real-world consequences of the themes raised by ethnography. Lived experience in a setting like the one I am studying forces ethnography to grapple extensively with the political implications of how experience is constituted and interpreted in the social world, which is the very essence of the "Feres Mura" dilemma. How we talk about experience in political and analytic contexts *shifts* the possibilities for future experience, for liberation from suffering, and for cultural and political change. That does not mean that ethnographers are necessarily activists, or that this ethnography purports to solve a political problem in any immediate sense—indeed, it may cause more problems in the short run than it seems to solve, by raising intractable questions about how the "Feres Mura" dilemma ought to be framed. But this is only an indication of the fact that cultural politics, which are so often excluded from purely cultural accounts of people's lives, enter here with a vengeance. Knowing what is at stake for informants must include the political contexts of their lives, as well as the Heisenberg-like effects of participant observation, which turns the observer into a part of the social scene.

This book is not written primarily for a policy-oriented audience, yet it is my hope that those who make claims about the religious agency of other people—which in this case includes not just academics, but also journalists, bureaucrats, and rabbis among others—may take pause from this ethnography at least so far as scrutinizing the grounds of their interpretive choices more closely. A humane social science, like a humane immigration policy, requires frank acknowledgment of the interpretive difficulties and limitations we face, and a willingness to live with the terror of the opaque rather than rushing to fill it with comforting but finally misleading certainties. Resisting the pressure to conclude with a definite and factual conclusion ("Are they really Jewish?"), but calling instead for a more informed, more nuanced, and more ethically responsible kind of public debate—one that includes the voices of those whose fates are being decided—may be the best service that any ethnography of the "Feres Mura" dilemma can hope to provide.

What's In a Name?

There is one additional issue that must be raised at the outset for the sake of reader comprehension. A great deal has been written about the many different names by which Ethiopian Jews and Beta Israel converts to Christianity have been known over time (Rosen 1985; S. Kaplan 1992b, 53–78; Quirin 1992, 11–27; Weil 1995a; Salamon 1994). Only a small portion of this terminology is directly relevant to this ethnography, but I ought to take responsibility for the terminological choices I have made, some of which will certainly prove to be controversial. Three terms that are of special significance to this ethnography are "Beta Israel," "Ethiopian-Israeli," and "Feres Mura."

Beta Israel

"Beta Israel" is an indigenous Ethiopian term that literally means "house of Israel" in both Amharic and Ge'ez. It refers to the ancestral ethnic and religious group from which all contemporary Ethiopian-Israelis (including Ethiopian Jews, "Feres Mura," and recent Christian converts) derive. Today it is the most commonly used term for Ethiopian Jews in academic and historical contexts; it lacks the negative connotations associated with the term "Falasha," which was until recently the term of choice in academic writing. "Falasha," as we shall see, was sometimes associated with landlessness and social inferiority in highland Ethiopia, as were pejorative epithets like "Kayla" (metalworker) or "Buda" (possessor of the evil eye), which obviously have no place in an ethnography such as this one unless they are quoted from other sources. The ancestors of today's Beta Israel did not commonly describe themselves as "Jews" (*Ayhud*), which makes the term "Ethiopian Jews" inaccurate in many historical contexts. They did, however, describe themselves as "Israelites," so I use the term "Beta Israel" whenever possible for the period preceding immigration to Israel, as well as in contemporary contexts when I am referring to the whole historical ethnic and religious group. "Beta Israel" is a term frequently used by Ethiopian-Israelis themselves when describing themselves to outsiders.

Ethiopian-Israelis

One stylistic departure from tradition in this ethnography is my emphasis on the term "Ethiopian-Israeli" in many contemporary ethnographic contexts. The virtue of this term is that it has fewer primordial connotations than either "Ethiopian Jews" or "Beta Israel," which allows me to skirt the whole question of cultural and religious authenticity when necessary. Since it primarily designates citizenship without prejudging other kinds of social arrangements, it is broad enough to include Ethiopian Jews, "Feres Mura" seeking to return to Judaism, and recent Beta Israel converts to Pentecostal Christianity who now live in Israel. Moreover, "Ethiopian-Israeli" helps to promote comparisons with other Jewish ethnic groups in Israel (like the Yemenite-Israelis discussed in chapter 6) and calls attention to the weighted political and bureaucratic contexts in which this ethnography takes place. It is as citizens rather than as cultural objects that today's Ethiopian-Israelis make themselves heard on the issues that concern them, and this ought to play a larger role in analysis than it has in most previous works.

Feres Mura

By far the most significant and problematic term I will use throughout this ethnography is "Feres Mura," which I intentionally mark off by "scare quotes" everywhere in appears. This term has sometimes been applied in bureaucratic contexts to the suspected descendants of converts who are today seeking to return to Judaism. The term itself has no obvious meaning in the languages spoken by contemporary Beta Israel, nor is it directly attested in Hagar Salamon's 1994 study of the terms used by traditional Beta Israel to describe converts to Christianity in different regions of Ethiopia. It is phonetically similar to regional variants that she does describe, like "Faras Moqra," which may, it has been suggested, have been used as private epithets by Beta Israel religious leaders who wished to speak disparagingly about converts. Be that as it may, "Feres Mura" was the unchallenged term used by Israeli embassy workers and foreign volunteers in Addis Ababa when they wished to speak about the suspected descendants of converts during the early 1990s when I began fieldwork. It was also the term used quietly by members of the community themselves when they wished to discuss their distinctiveness and unique vulnerability. It is not, however, a term that is generally welcomed by the people to whom it has been applied, and they often take special pains to reject it in public settings. My decision to use the term anyway is therefore taken advisedly, because its use is itself a social and bureaucratic fact of considerable significance. My hope is that friends and colleagues in the Ethiopian community will understand that this ethnography strives to call attention to the unique burdens and dilemmas faced by those who have been asked to bear the name "Feres Mura" in recent history, and to construct a more honest analytic and ethnographic record of their experience, so that the term and what is signifies might ultimately be transcended.

Late one Friday night in 1999, I sat with Yossie, a young man born in Gondar Province in Ethiopia who had become one of my dearest friends. Yossie knew all about my research, and asked me offhandedly what good could possibly come from people always telling me about their problems. Problems were not to be talked about in Yossie's worldview. They were to be actively but quietly overcome, or else borne with almost infinite patience. He had spent part of his childhood concealing his Beta Israel identity in a Sudanese refugee camp during the middle 1980s, and he knew better than I did from his own family's experience what suffering meant. So I told him that he had asked a fair question, for which I had no easy answer. Then I suggested that better understanding of the problems faced by Ethiopian immigrants could only be of help, and that his future children might one day want to be able to read an honest and sympathetic record of their parents' generation. These are relatively insubstantial benefits for pragmatic people like Yossie and many other Ethiopians I have come to know, but he was too generous to point this out. After over a decade of friendship, certain things did not, in any case, need to be stated explicitly.

For me, the goal in ethnographic writing must certainly be to lighten rather than exacerbate the burdens of those who can least afford to be weighted down. To avoid imposing additional burdens on any of the specific individuals represented in this book, I have followed standard ethnographic practice in changing the names and identifying details of individual informants, except where these are public figures who understood that they were speaking to a researcher and whose anonymity could not in any case have been easily protected. I would like to ask readers who may know the Ethiopian community in Israel to respect this scholarly convention and resist the temptation to speculate about the identities of individual informants. All of us who are deeply involved in scholarship concerning the Ethiopian-Israeli community have been engaged at one point or another in research or other involvements that were designed to address practical problems in some immediate way, and I have great respect for such research. The starting point of this book, nevertheless, is that sometimes social science must raise difficult questions and work to expand the sphere of moral imagination within which they can be understood without presuming to offer definite solutions. This is especially true where the problems faced by our friends and informants may themselves be partly caused by limited vision or empathy and clarity of understanding.

I have tried to think hard in this ethnography about the moral and political implications of representation, particularly where questions of agency and religious experience are involved. The theoretical tasks this monograph undertakes are themselves related to the formulation of a moral and political problem, posed initially not for abstract scholarly reasons alone but also in the hope of making sense of the world in which my friends and informants have been struggling to make their way. I can make no claim to a conclusive and inarguable word on any of the problems addressed here, and I know that other observers may well interpret aspects of the "Feres Mura" dilemma differently than I have interpreted them. My point is not that all accounts are equal—the reader will see that I am quite willing to make evaluative distinctions among different narratives on empirical grounds—but simply that no ethnographic account can ever be considered final. Too much is riding on the "Feres Mura" dilemma, even today, for anything less than the sympathetic and critical engagement that I believe this kind of ethnographic scholarship is uniquely situated to contribute.

CHAPTER I

A DEATH IN ADDIS ABABA

> The *content* of experience. One would like to say, "I see red *thus*." "I hear the note you strike *thus*," "I feel pleasure *thus*," I feel sorrow *thus*," or even "*This* is what one feels when one is sad, *this* when one is glad," etc. One would like to people a world, analogous to the physical one, with these *thus*es and *this*es. But this makes sense only where there is a picture of *what is experienced* to which one can point as one makes these statements.
>
> —Ludwig Wittgenstein, *Remarks on the Philosophy of Psychology*

ADDIS ABABA, JULY 1992

We arrive in a white pickup truck with the plain wood coffin of an eighteen-year-old girl—I learned her name was Tigest Mekuriaw—smaller than life, loaded on back. The corpse of an older man who died the same day in an unrelated incident is also being returned from the shed outside Menelik Hospital where rough autopsies and some semblance of *taharah*—the cleansing of the bodies before burial—have been performed. My attention is transfixed by the girl though, because she was, like me, a relative newcomer to this place, and because I had witnessed the accident that took her life the previous morning; had struggled in the company of others to commandeer a passing car for the stop-and-go trip across Addis Ababa to the hospital; and had pleaded with the overworked, lackadaisical emergency staff at Menelik Hospital to examine her ahead of her place in the queue while she died. "She is one of yours," a bystander had said to me at the roadside where she was struck, before adding that she might have a better chance of being seen quickly at the hospital if a foreigner—a *farenge* or white person in local usage—accompanied her there. *She is one of yours.* The stories we tell ourselves about belonging and kinship are at the very heart of the story that this book aims to tell, as are the differential life chances that accrue to those who manage—or who fail to manage, in varying degrees—to make the right social connections, or to craft socially and bureaucratically compelling narratives about who they are and where they are going in the world. Ethnography is not just another way to gather sociological data or to embellish social theory with provocative and sometimes heartrending anecdotes. Ethnography is, at its core, always about the relationship of the theoretical to the lived and existential heart of social life—to the *content* of social experience.

In the context of Tigest Mekuriaw's death, this means that ethnography must inevitably grapple not just with the difficult politics of refugee life in a city like Addis Ababa but also with all of the local and not-so-local constraints that contributed to her refugee status in the first place, including disputes over religious identity and the tensions between contemporary Ethiopian and Jewish-Israeli nationalisms. Perhaps most importantly though, this ethnography invites us to reflect on the forms and nature of human subjectivity—including religious subjectivity—and on the ethical and epistemological difficulties faced by those who wish to describe or to categorize the subjectivity of other people. Tigest's presence in Addis Ababa during the summer of 1992 was conditioned by long-standing and far-ranging disputes in places like New York and Jerusalem over the quality of the religious experience of people in her community, who all had been designated "Feres Mura"—a designation to which we shall return. Had the ancestors of these "Feres Mura" *really* been Beta Israel (that is, Ethiopian Jews) who converted to Christianity, and, if so, why and under what circumstances had they done so? Even more urgently, what was the real nature and motivation for their clamor to "return to Judaism" starting in the late 1980s? Was the so-called return-to-Judaism movement sufficient in scope and authenticity to oblige an open-ended political and economic commitment from Jews around the world, and from the State of Israel in particular? What does it mean to be a Jew or a Christian anyway, in a context of ongoing, transnational religious transformations, in which citizenship and other pragmatic benefits as well as historical trajectories are all very much in question? And finally, what should religious designations like these have to do with the substantive political concerns of modern governments or other agencies in the Middle East or the Horn of Africa? These are questions that may seem painfully specific to the dilemmas faced by Ethiopian Beta Israel in modern times, but they also point toward methodological and analytical conundrums that are central to the whole project of the ethnographic study of religion. Ethnography depends more than any other discipline on the construction of narratives about agency and constraint through which the lived experience of its subjects may emerge. But what counts as agency or as constraint in a setting where people's motives for religious change are complicated by both desperate need and narrative frameworks imposed upon them by others? Telling Tigest's story—by which I really mean the story of her funeral and of the community that survived her—forces a confrontation with all of these issues and imbues them with moral as well as analytic concern.

The question of religious experience was not propelled to the heart of this story primarily by my own research proclivities. It was propelled, rather, by the fact that innumerable journalists, religious functionaries, state bureaucrats, and immigration officials as well as academic researchers and immigrants themselves have made their pragmatic evaluation of the "Feres Mura" dilemma dependent upon a set of complicated and often problematic assertions about the religious experience and agency of these potential immigrants. Before her death, Tigest was one of several thousand people who had been left behind in Addis Ababa during the State of Israel's historic airlift of approximately 14,500 Beta Israel during the final hours before the Ethiopian communist regime known as the Dergue fell to rebel forces in 1991 (Spector 2005). The State of Israel had disavowed the responsibility that it asserted for tens of thousands of other Beta Israel because these "Feres Mura" were considered to be the descendants of more-or-less sincere converts to Christianity, and more-or-less insincere Jewish penitents. Even more damning from the official point of view was that they were often portrayed as self-interested "economic refugees," believed to be manifestly incapable of sincere and lasting attachment to any religion or people, and deserving of help from none, either.

Had she lived, Tigest would likely have made it to Israel eventually, like most of the other people I encountered in Addis Ababa that summer. Not, however, without considerable hardship and grief. In Israel, moreover, she would have been forced to prove and to prove again in differing contexts that her heart was not tainted by the complications of religious history and ambivalence to which she had been born. She would have had to adopt some strategy for living with taintedness anyway, however, because the allegation of tainted hearts—my own gloss for a complex cultural construct of spoiled agency and suspect religious history—is perhaps the most constant cultural and political theme defining the social experience of all "Feres Mura" in the two homelands (Ethiopia and Israel) that continues to shape and constrain their lives. Over a decade since her funeral as I write, the contested immigration of so-called Feres Mura from Ethiopia to Israel continues and even increases today, because of political arrangements that I will describe in later chapters. But attempts by immigrants to overcome the taint of impure motives or incomplete religious change continue as well. Failure to speak in a sophisticated way about the nature of religious experience and its transformation, among both academics and policy makers, and more broadly throughout the societies in which we live, does not prevent these issues from figuring closely at the heart of public controversy, or from exacting a heavy, sometimes debilitating human cost.

The central theoretical problematic of this book is, therefore, that we can neither do justice to nor can we avoid the discussion of other people's religious experience; social science research—ethnography in particular—bears a heavy burden for thinking through this conundrum. Ultimately, the necessity of describing moral and religious experience despite the opacity of its surface drives a research agenda that seems well suited to an anthropological methodology but ought also to be supported by history and other related disciplines. This is an argument that must be built slowly, at the leisurely pace of an ethnographic monograph, and already I have gotten ahead of myself. Back in the summer of 1992, all I knew was that I had stumbled upon a controversial funeral whose ripples would be noted in Addis Ababa and beyond. Tigest's contested bureaucratic status ensured that the disposition of her body would be perceived by all as a shot across the bow in an ongoing struggle over the disposition of her living relatives and neighbors, who had gathered at her funeral to wish her—and themselves—well. It is apparently not enough, in our highly segmented society, to win a place to live and endure in this world, a phenomenon that nationalist writers have sometimes overoptimistically described as "winning a place under the sun" (Netanyahu 1995). For many, and especially for those who are poor and marginal, or who fail to meet the bureaucratic criteria established by the more secure and powerful, winning a place in the ground can be challenging enough.

The "Falasha Cemetery"

At roadside, local children chirp *farenge, farenge!* as they chase our pickup. At a fork in the path, one of them asks whether we are looking for the "Amhara cemetery" or the "Falasha cemetery," and points us on our way. These are ethnic designations in the Ethiopian context, but they also carry strong religious connotations, since the Amhara are the historic bearers of the Orthodox Church in its spiritual and material conquest of the Ethiopian highlands—a conquest that still strongly shapes Ethiopian culture even though the majority of the population and many of its ruling caste today are Muslim. "Falasha" is a slightly outdated and frequently pejorative term for a highland religious and ethnic group now known in polite company as "Beta Israel." Still, I have learned not to take offense where none was offered, and here in Addis Ababa most of the refugees insist on being called "Falasha" because of the Jewish legitimacy that they think the term implies. Better Falasha, at any rate, than "Feres Mura," which is a designation bearing with it no promise of aid or support, and no clear hope of leaving Ethiopia. During an earlier period of fieldwork in Upper Nazareth, in Israel, I once saw a young Ethiopian boy standing tensed and ready to fight because some other boys (the children of immigrants from Russia and Romania) had taunted him by calling him "Falasi." He had stood there with his hands at his sides, fists balled, an expression of barely masked humiliation and surprise upon his face. In America, an illustrated children's book titled *Falasha No More* (Kushner and Kalina 1986) tells the story of Ethiopian

Jews through a lens of triumph over oppression and the desire to leave the hated name "Falasha" behind. The book was written far from the realities of Addis Ababa though, where a Jewish physician working for one of the North American aid organizations told me frankly that he would not participate in Tigest's funeral because "*they* [his emphasis] are not true Falasha."

The term "Falasha" probably is related to the decree of the fifteenth-century emperor Yeshaq, who used Portuguese weapons to crush regional ethnic revolts that involved the ancestors of today's Beta Israel. "May he who is baptized in the Christian religion inherit the land of his father," Yeshaq is said to have decreed; "otherwise, let him be uprooted from his land and be a stranger (*falasi*)" (S. Kaplan 1992b, 58). That this epithet of landlessness and disinheritance should come to constitute a mark of honor and hope for land—even for a plot at a local cemetery—is perhaps not so surprising. To be buried in the "Falasha cemetery" even at a young age was in some sense a stroke of peculiar good fortune for someone in Tigest's position, because it meant both a final resting place among "her people" as well as a tacit recognition of her claims to kinship with other Beta Israel and by extension with Jews outside Ethiopia—kinship ties that her surviving relatives would eventually use to good advantage if they were both lucky and persistent. Beta Israel are in no way unique in the profound concern they show for the disposition of their dead, nor for the way in which burial seems to ground social ties for them in an aura of pure finality that can be elusive during life, but these emerged as especially painful and explicit tropes during the course of my research. Despite their grief, relatives expressed satisfaction that Tigest had at least been buried *ki'inya wogen*, "among our people."

The cemetery itself was modest and neatly laid when I first visited in 1992, but was recently overgrown. The grounds had been purchased in 1924 and registered as the property of "the Jewish Community of Addis Ababa," an entity that had never before existed in any institutional sense. The historian Izhak Grinfeld (1986) wryly notes that this purchase of ground for a cemetery could actually be described as the birth of the Addis Ababa Jewish community, but it was also a foundational event for the whole modern history of Ethiopian Jews, because it was the first formal cooperation between Beta Israel and foreign Jews on Ethiopian soil. Signatories to the transaction included the Polish-born Jewish researcher and activist Jacques Failovitch, who dedicated his life to frustrating Christian missionaries and fostering the connection between Beta Israel and international Jewry, along with his Beta Israel protégé Taamrat Emmanuel. The deed was also signed by five members of the local Jewish mercantile community, most of whom were traders from the British protectorate of Aden on the Yemeni coast (Shelemay 1991) who had come to Addis Ababa for business but stayed.

A few aging Adenite men are in fact the only permanent Jewish presence left in Addis Ababa outside the Israeli embassy, now that even Beta Israel pass through Addis Ababa only on their way to someplace else. The Adenites are more numerous in the cemetery at this point than elsewhere in the city. Their relatives have left behind elaborate stone monuments in the Sephardic style, with lengthy Hebrew inscriptions. Many have gone on to Israel or to England, while those who remain carry multiple passports, speak multiple languages, and try to hedge their bets. *They* certainly do not consider this to be the "Falasha cemetery," and they are ambivalent about the refugees being buried here. Every time a refugee burial takes place, it is subject to a protracted negotiation between the Adenite community, a group of North American NGOs who portray themselves as the representatives of the remaining Beta Israel in Addis Ababa, and various officials attached to the Israeli embassy who vigorously dispute that role. Faitlovitch and Taamrat Emmanuel might have been pleased about Tigests's burial despite the controversy, however, because this is exactly the kind of exchange across groups that they sought desperately to encourage when they helped to establish the cemetery.

Faitlovitch came to Ethiopia in 1904 to follow in the footsteps of his teacher, the French-Jewish semiticist Joseph Halévy, who visited in 1867 on a fact-finding mission funded by the Alliance Israélite Universelle after British missionaries reported that they had discovered a lost Jewish community in Ethiopia (S. Kaplan 1994a; Trevisan Semi 1994, 2007). The significance of these missionaries to the subsequent history of Beta Israel is the subject of the second chapter of this book, but here it is important to note simply that Faitlovitch devoted much of his life to the proposition that the Beta Israel, who had been singled out for missionary attention, were in fact Jews who needed the support of international Jewry to resist evangelical inroads. His arrival did indeed slow the pace of conversions by missionaries, but perhaps his most lasting accomplishment was in choosing dozens of young Beta Israel men, several of whom were already deeply influenced by the missionaries (today we would call them "Feres Mura") to study under Jewish auspices outside Ethiopia. Simon Messing (1982) has called those individuals who later returned to the land of their birth as leaders and educators "culture-brokers," and Taamrat Emmanuel was possibly the most important among them. He was a sixteen-year-old student at a Swedish missionary school when Faitlovitch persuaded him to accept Jewish patronage instead.

Ultimately, Taamrat became a major Beta Israel communal leader and was appointed principal of the first Beta Israel school established under Jewish rather than missionary auspices in Ethiopia (see Summerfield 2003; Weil 2005; Trevisan Semi 2005, 2007). His signature upon the deed of title to the cemetery, alongside those of Faitlovitch and the Adenite merchants, bears witness to Faitlovitch's long-term goal of integrating Beta Israel and foreign Jews socially and religiously. It was one thing, after all, for important European rabbis to sign letters of support for fund-raising efforts on behalf of the Beta Israel as

Faitlovitch had convinced them to do (see Corinaldi 1988), or even to accept an occasional young student into their schools and homes. But the creation of a joint Beta Israel, European, and Adenite Jewish cemetery would signify the first time that Beta Israel and world Jewry had ever shared significant ritual space—or recognized one another on a practical religious basis—in any permanent way. This really was the birth of the Ethiopian Jewish community in the modern sense of the term, forging ties of destiny to an international Jewish Diaspora of which the Beta Israel had scarcely heretofore been aware. Burial in the same earth constitutes a visceral and deeply evocative act of practical kinship for Beta Israel and other Jews, even if it is not without complications, as the contested burial of people like Tigest Mekuriaw shows.

The cemetery bore witness when I visited to complications of time and circumstance that are systematically effaced from most popular (and many scholarly narratives) about Beta Israel. Amid the sprawling Adenite tombs, for example, I was struck by the appearance of a few upright headstones in the Western Jewish style, sporting long Amharic inscriptions complete with engravings or photographs of young Ethiopian men. My eye was caught by one that carried the image of a young man dressed in a striped suit who died in 1989 and probably worked with the Israelis or one of the North American NGOs here. He must have been a man of relative means, judging both by the photo and by the elaborate grave in which he was buried. The contrast between his grave and the dozens of simple earth mounds, many of them ringed with stones, that had recently begun to dot the landscape of the cemetery, was extreme. These were the graves of migrants and refugees from the countryside who were among those who had sought to pass through Addis Ababa on their way to Israel, but arrived at extended and finally permanent waiting here, instead. Their graves bespoke a whole different economy of memory and power than the more impressive tombs that seemed at first to define the landscape. Several had oddly shaped tree limbs or hunks of scrap metal thrust upright into the earthen mounds that covered them, which seemed odd to me until my new acquaintance Desta—he would soon become a fast friend—knelt next to what he told me was his father's grave and asked me to photograph him there, "so that I will remember." The flotsam that these refugees had gathered were the memorial tools of the *bricoleur* (Lévi-Strauss 1966), who uses what comes to hand, tangible reminders of loved ones that might soon be erased. Many of these refugee graves had already been covered by the Israeli embassy with concrete slabs that enforced a cold, if hygienic, anonymity. Space had been left on the slabs for inscription of names, but by the time these were laid here, it seemed as if most names had been forgotten as relatives moved on.

Everyone, it seemed, was moving on. All but twenty-eight hundred of the Beta Israel who had gathered in Addis Ababa before the 1991 airlift had gone to Israel, and even Ethiopia's strongman, General Hailie Mariam Mengistu, had fled to Zimbabwe when the mostly Tigrean rebels he had been fighting for over a decade finally closed in on his capital. The Israeli government had pushed the airlift forward during the confusion because of fears that Beta Israel refugees living in shanty towns in Addis Ababa might become targets of resentment or even random violence during the chaos of an inevitable rebel takeover. The U.S. State Department had negotiated with the groups approaching Addis Ababa to hold off their final assault until the airlift could be completed. It was reportedly the largest civilian airlift in history, completed in just less than two days, and it was kept secret from the Israeli public until it was finished (Spector 2005; Bard 2002; Feldman 1998)—no doubt in recognition of the tragic role played by news leaks in bringing the airlift of Ethiopians from Sudan crashing to a halt in 1985. When I mingled with new immigrants in Jerusalem in 1991 I heard their first hushed whispers and cautious explanations about why a cousin or a brother had been left behind, their clipped rebukes and anxious glances when someone used the term "Feres Mura" in front of outsiders. Many of those whose first-degree relatives remained in Ethiopia might well have been designated "Feres Mura" themselves had it not been for some accident of bureaucratic practice, and it was the felt unfairness and arbitrary quality of their families' fate that constituted the core experience of being "Feres Mura" during that time.

Even the eventual arrival of a loved one or family member in Israel might not be enough to heal the wound of a parent or spouse left behind permanently at the "Falasha cemetery" in Addis Ababa. When Desta finally made it to Israel with the first wave of "Feres Mura" in 1994, he blamed the immigration authorities not just for his father's untimely death in Addis Ababa but also for the humiliating abandonment of his father's grave there. Theodore Herzl once quipped that attachment to the old cemeteries of Europe would doom the modern return to Zion because Jews would never leave the graves of Europe behind, but here the cemetery itself stood testament to Desta's frustrated desire to leave Ethiopia and to reconfigure his life around a different set of coordinates and memories in the Jewish State. Frustrated desire was in fact the primary emotion in evidence at Tigest's funeral outside the small immediate circle of grief-stricken mourners (her mother and sisters) and those who tried to comfort them. Most of the "Feres Mura" in Addis Ababa worked at small handicrafts to help defray the costs of subsistence support provided by the North American Conference on Ethiopian Jews (NACOEJ), the aid organization that had taken responsibility for their care once the Israeli embassy and other foreign organizations pulled out after the conclusion of Operation Solomon. NACOEJ had given all of the workers a few hours off to attend the funeral, and several hundred people had already arrived when we showed up with Tigest's coffin.

While we milled about waiting for the burial to commence, a young man asked me in a tone that left me feeling more than a little defensive if I had "come to watch" (*le-ma'et metah*?), to which I could only shake my head and mutter the Amharic consolation, *Igziabher yetnewot* (May God strengthen your heart). It seemed to forestall his question, but the problem from my point of view was that I *had* come to watch—*also* to watch, as I told myself—and could feel myself begin to blush with embarrassment. I was relieved by the approach of a young Ethiopian-Israeli who was intent on speaking with me in Hebrew, our mutual acquired tongue. Two years since emigrating, he had returned to seek an immigrant visa for his mother—a losing proposition as it turned out—and he was proud to show off his new language and connection with outsiders. His desire to demonstrate a connection with the outside world dovetailed nicely with my own desire to demonstrate friendship with local mourners. A few people knew that I had been asked to help organize the preparation of the corpses for burial and were appreciative. When someone asked if I would also be willing to read a few psalms in Hebrew at the graveside though (few people in Addis could read Hebrew well), I was glad to do it, if only to escape the sensitive charge of being merely a spectator at other people's funerals. What I had apparently misunderstood—but which local participants would not allow me to forget—was that witnessing this event was also a form of participation in its own right.

As the mourners dispersed, a cousin of Tigest who had helped me to wash the bodies at Menelik hospital pulled me aside to chastise me in terms that I did not at first understand. "Don't think that I don't know the rules!" he shouted, pointing his finger at me while a small crowd gathered. The young Christian student I had hired as a translator had refused to come to the funeral because she was uncomfortable intruding, so I was on my own and it took a few moments to understand what he was saying. "Don't think that I don't remember! If this had been the village, I would have spent seven days outside the house and then gone to the river. But here, what can I do? There is no place . . . What can I do?" It was not just the language however that required parsing. By failing to isolate himself for seven days after participating in the funeral, this cousin of Tigest had broken with one of the best-known of all Beta Israel purity rites (see Trevisan Semi 1985). Christian neighbors used sometimes to call their Beta Israel neighbors *ya-ouha Falasha* or "water Falasha" because of the smell of water occasioned by their constant immersions, and Tigest's cousin wanted to make sure I understood that his abrogation of discipline was not to be understood as a sign of his laxness or apostasy. Through me as witness, he wanted to communicate with the wider world of judgment and power to which I had access, but he himself did not, that the collapse of the Beta Israel purity regime in Addis Ababa was occasioned by recent trauma and displacement rather than infidelity or failure of moral will, and by extension that he never should have been classified "Feres Mura" at all.

The facts of the matter, such as whether Beta Israel villagers (let alone the descendants of converts) regularly observed these rites in the years preceding Operation Solomon interests me less here than does the deep moral import of this exchange. Observers already noted in the 1970s that the Beta Israel regime of purity and pollution was in decline (Schoenberger 1975), and there is no reason to think that this process reversed itself in the 1980s or '90s. Yet purity remains a powerful touchstone of contemporary Beta Israel self-understanding (Trevisan Semi 1985), with which "Feres Mura" returning to Judaism also frequently identify. The meaning of this man's protest, therefore, was simply that he was a "true Falasha," and that while his body may now have been tainted with an indelible stain of corpse-impurity, the same could simply not be said about his heart.

Framing the "Feres Mura"

The "Feres Mura" dilemma burst onto Israeli public consciousness in 1991. I was riding on a Jerusalem city bus when I first heard reports of the dramatic Operation Solomon airlift on the evening news, accompanied by an outburst of joy and clapping among my fellow passengers. Their reaction was real enough, the pent-up frustration of people who had seen too many of their ideals and idealism ground away through the tireless accumulation of scandals and catastrophes that characterize Israeli public life. Operation Solomon was depicted—and was experienced by many—as a heroic intervention, like the daring Israeli raid on Entebbe or the Six Day War. It reunited suffering families, was cited by some as refutation of the UN's longstanding "Zionism is racism" calumny, and, best of all, it had nothing whatsoever to do with peace talks, border disputes, or the overwhelming weight of the Palestinian question. Even the novelist and left-wing social critic David Grossman got drawn uncharacteristically into the romantic national fervor of the moment. "Soon enough," he wrote for the *New York Times* op-ed page on May 21, 1991, "the newcomers will be part of the Israeli potage, rising again to its surface in caustic newspaper accounts of the vagaries of absorption, and in bitter reports of despair. But for a brief 24 hours, no mean amount of time to us, we knew a forgotten joy amid our cynical, cantankerous, rapacious existence. . . . Plane after plane landed around us: 14,000 refugees. Even underneath the veil of torpor their beauty was apparent." For Grossman and many other observers, these were not just refugees; they were "little Queens of Sheba" and King Solomons, "majestic" in their "biblical" appearance. On the Jerusalem bus I was riding, however, a different yet equally powerful imagery was invoked by a young American who stood at the back and shouted gleefully in English, "Ethiopia is finally *Judenrein*!" The dissonance of the outburst earned him irritated glances from some of the other passengers, yet this was an early sign of a much broader confluence of themes relating to suffering and authenticity that would eventually come to dominate the "Feres Mura" dilemma in Israeli discourse, and it indicated to me as an ethnographer that now would be a good time to begin taking notes.

It took a week or two for the "Feres Mura" issue to rise to the level of explicit public conversation. I spent the first few days after Operation Solomon traversing the Galilee with Ethiopian friends in stretch Mercedes outfitted as taxis, driven by entrepreneurial Nazareth Palestinians. My friends needed to make the rounds of all the immigrant absorption centers searching for newly arrived relatives, and their reunions when they found someone they loved were sometimes spectacularly emotional. For the family of the patriarch Teshome, with whom I had begun my fieldwork as an undergraduate anthropology major in the summer of 1987, Operation Solomon was a dream come true. He and his family had mostly immigrated during the difficult days of Operation Moses in 1984–85, traveling under cover of darkness across the dangerous war-torn wilderness of northern Ethiopia to refugee camps like Gudareff across the Sudanese border, from which they had heard that they would be spirited to Israel. When the tottering Sudanese president Numeiri withdrew his tacit permission for the airlift after a news leak brought the wrath of the Arab world down upon his head, anyone who had not already made it to Israel was either cut off in the camps or left behind in Ethiopia.

Teshome and other 1980s immigrants had suffered horrifying losses of their own from thirst and bandits, or predation by military and rebel groups along the way. The journey they called *Derekh Sudan* ("the way to Sudan," in Hebrew) became a watchword for Beta Israel suffering and fidelity as well as intractable traumatic wounds (see BenEzer 2002). "Like the Shoah [Holocaust]," Teshome's wife Balaynish said to me one day in 1987, grasping for words with the help of her sixteen-year-old immigrant son Yossie to describe the enormity of her experience on the road and in the camps. And then she added quietly—asking me not to repeat this in front of other Ethiopians who had suffered their own losses—"My head hurts all the time for my daughter," who had been left behind. After Operation Solomon, I began to hear subdued whispers among these 1980s immigrants (sometimes in wonderment and sometimes in resentment) about the way the newcomers had flown directly from Addis Ababa, avoiding the dreadful travail of the *Derekh Sudan* generation, and in some quarters I also began to hear whispers about additional relatives who had been left behind once more.

The first explicit discussions of the "Feres Mura" situation in Israeli public media were, not surprisingly, somewhat tentative and confused. Within a few days of the airlift, some of the newest immigrants had already begun complaining about the unfinished exodus. Discussions on the nightly news began to include hesitant references to *anusim* who had been left behind in Addis Ababa, invoking through that one word a whole archetype of the modern Jewish imagination. *Anusim* is a plural term that refers specifically to Jews who have been forcibly converted to Christianity, and it self-consciously evokes the controversies surrounding Iberian conversos of the fifteenth through seventeenth centuries. The word itself is derived from a root that means "coercion" or "violent compulsion," and it is commonly used in modern Hebrew in its feminine form to connote the victims of rape. Without assuming too much forethought on the part of television newscasters, the implications of that term being used in this context were unmistakable. It meant that the refugees remaining in Addis Ababa were forced converts, who should enjoy prima facie support from the State of Israel to emigrate and reclaim their Jewish heritage.

Medieval responsa literature shows that Iberian conversos who sought to rejoin Jewish communities at many years' remove from their initial conversions were not always welcomed and were subject to hard questions about why they had chosen conversion rather than flight or martyrdom when the choice was available (Y. Kaplan 1989a; see Fram 1996). Similarly complicated cultural and religious negotiations were compounded in the "Feres Mura" case by lingering doubt about the Jewishness of the Beta Israel as a whole (see chapter 2), as well as uncertainty about the nature of conversion to Christianity in Ethiopia—was it really "forced"? The "Feres Mura" case was also complicated by a set of pervasive secular considerations deriving from many Israelis' attachment to a sense of national authenticity and belonging defined by tropes of shared historical suffering from which the ancestors of these "Feres Mura" had ostensibly excluded themselves. The designation of "Feres Mura" as *anusim* was difficult for many of their advocates to accept, because it involved open acknowledgment of a history of conversion to Christianity that they had long denied. Yet it had the advantage of at least framing that history in a way that pointed strongly toward "Feres Mura" Jewishness and rights to immigrate. This was not the only frame available to Israeli pundits and newscasters, however.

Within a few days after the initial story of refugees left behind in Addis Ababa became public, *mitnatzrim* began to overtake *anusim* in journalistic usage. *Mitnatzrim* is a verbalized form of the Hebrew *Notzri*, or Nazarene (that is, Christian), and thus means something like "Christianizer." It is used in modern Hebrew only for willing (as opposed to forced) converts to Christianity, and its public application to the new immigrants pushed "Feres Mura" claims to Jewishness much further into question. The fact that modern Hebrew maintains a distinction not just between converts to Christianity and other religions but also between willed and forced converts is perhaps remarkable, pointing as it does to a very long and troubled history of religious persecution. But the public *anusim-mitnatzrim* debate also helps to underline one of the central analytic themes of this book, which is the thorny question of agency in religious transformation that the Hebrew usage—and its Israeli political context—forces inexorably to the foreground. Was conversion to Christianity in Ethiopia a forced or a voluntary process, and what was the quality of the religious experience that it engendered? Hiding behind this question is always also the corollary and in some sense much more significant question of why some converts would later seek to return to Judaism and whether they can be taken at their word when they do so, or should instead be treated as merely "economic refugees" whose return to Judaism is assumed to be ulterior and inauthentic.

In principle, these two questions—the questions of agency in conversion to Christianity and of agency in the return to Judaism by subsequent generations—are quite separable. Yet those who portray the original conversions as voluntary also tend to assume that the later return to Judaism is also a matter of mere convenience, while those who portray baptism as forced tend to portray the return to Judaism as an act of heartfelt penitence. These are binary choices in the cultural logic of contemporary Israel, rather than careful assessments of Ethiopian reality. The thorny question of religious and social agency in conversion is always at least in part a matter of interpretation by those who hold political and classificatory power, and whose decisions ought to be subject to analysis alongside the ostensible subjects of ethnographic research. To their credit, Israeli journalists quickly understood the rhetorically loaded nature of terms like *anusim* and *mitnatzrim* and began to seek more ostensibly value neutral terms. "Feres Mura" was only one variation in a rhetorical field that also included corruptions like "Felasmura," "Felasha-mora," and the version that finally gained ascendancy in most Israeli media accounts, "Felashmura"—to which one enterprising television journalist even appended the fanciful Hebrew etymology (fanciful because Hebrew was not spoken in Ethiopia) *Falasha shehemir et-dato*, "a Falasha who has exchanged his religion." Hagar Salamon's (1994) study of narratives about conversion among Beta Israel found evidence for a wide variety of local terms to designate converts in Ethiopia, including the well-attested *maryam wodet* (lovers of Mary) and *Felasmukra* (no translation given), but she does not mention "Feres Mura," which was the term used by Ethiopians and Israeli aid workers in Ethiopia during the early 1990s.

This conflict over terminology was not just an argument about historical facts; it also expressed a degree of cultural anxiety over a group of people whose history and contemporary social position resisted assimilation to some of the most binary categories of Israeli Jewish cosmology. As I will describe in more detail over the next two chapters, Beta Israel converts often retained a distinctive middling status in the social order of the Ethiopian highlands, not really Christian nor yet Beta Israel, and this betwixt-and-between status is, ironically, what allowed many to retain and later reclaim a sense of ancestral Jewishness when historical circumstance allowed. Yet it is this same set of qualities that is, paradoxically, tainted in the eyes of their new society, a society that is committed among other things to the binary structural opposition of Jews and Gentiles (especially Christians, but also in a somewhat different way Arabs, as I will explore in chapter 6). This makes taintedness into more than just a social and bureaucratic ascription; it becomes a set of basic experiences, a whole cultural phenomenology of taintedness that needs to be addressed in analytical as well as moral and political terms. The epistemological disquiet that being betwixt and between raises for both "Feres Mura" and their interlocutors goes well beyond the choice of nomenclature. It evokes diffuse symbols and rhetorical strategies whose meanings are often contested but that help to shape the contours of daily life, including contested interpretations and visceral experiences of longing, belonging, and rejection.

A good example of what I am trying to convey here took place at one of the first public demonstrations on behalf of those who had been left behind in Addis Ababa, which was held in Jerusalem several weeks after the conclusion of Operation Solomon. It appeared from television accounts as if the demonstration was attended by no more than a couple of dozen people who were probably all close relatives of the Addis Ababa refugees, but it received prominent coverage on the nightly news because of its novelty at the time. Interviews featured a young Ethiopian man who had obviously been in the country long enough to speak a clear but still accented Hebrew. His anger (still infrequently identified with the "shy and quiet Ethiopians") shone clearly through. "The government is performing a *selectzia* in Ethiopia," he said with quiet bitterness, "and you shouldn't think I don't know what that word means. I know *exactly* what it means." Through emphasis and choice of words he had managed to portray the "Feres Mura" languishing in Addis Ababa as Jews arriving on the trains to Auschwitz, where Nazi guards (that is, Israeli immigration officials) would "select," or separate, those who would be sent to work from those who would be sent to their immediate deaths instead. This was pretty strong stuff for an Ethiopian immigrant on the nightly news, and non-Ethiopian Israelis with whom I spoke over the next few days were not especially amused. "Did you notice," a fellow academic asked me indignantly, "that he had a cross tattooed on this forehead?"

Tattoos are certainly prohibited by Jewish law and are seen even by some secularists as somehow "un-Jewish," but my impression was that in this case implied criticism cut much deeper than the allegedly secular cast of much Israeli public culture would have seemed to allow. In his anger, this young man had chosen to portray his suffering kin as icons of Jewish persecution at the hands of Israeli policy makers, and in response his critic chose to focus instead on the tangible stigmata of his spoiled and inauthentic identity—the sign of the cross. Contests over authenticity and the play of competing symbols in the "Feres Mura" case were not in any way limited to the 20 percent or so of Israelis who typically define themselves in polls as being "religious" (*dati*) or even the much larger number (many of North African or Middle Eastern descent) who portray themselves as "traditional" (*masorti*) but not strictly Orthodox (Leibman 1997; Leibman and Katz 1997; Leibman and Susser 1997). Indeed, as I hope to show, the "Feres Mura" dilemma created uncomfortable and sometimes surprising bedfellows in Israel's fractured political landscape—right-wing Zionist rabbis planning pro–"Feres Mura" events together with far-left civil rights activists, while other representatives of the Chief Rabbinate joined forces with militantly secular politicians and bureaucrats in an effort to foil their plans.

This is no simple tale of ideological blocs or even parliamentary horse trading. It reflects, rather, the fact that the "Feres Mura" dilemma opens an especially painful window onto some of the deep fissures that have helped to shape contemporary Jewish and Israeli cultural life: debates over different understandings of what it means to join a community of shared suffering, for example, and the contested relationship between religious and secular criteria of national belonging and authenticity. These issues do not always map neatly onto the expected social cleavages. Consider the response of an Israeli aid official named D. whom I interviewed in Addis Ababa during the summer of 1993, a year after Tigest's funeral. I wanted to know why there had been so much opposition to "Feres Mura" being buried at the "Falasha cemetery," and why he thought that the Beta Israel refugees remaining in Addis Ababa should be denied entry permits to Israel. "I am secular [*hiloni*]," he told me with heavy emphasis on that word, "and if my daughter one day wants to marry an Ethiopian [despite the Chief Rabbinate's formal doubts about Beta Israel Jewishness], that's fine with me—but not with one of *them* [that is, not with a 'Feres Mura']. All over the world it was difficult to be a Jew," he said. "*They* became Christians." This was one of the first, but certainly not the last, time I would be impressed by the deep emotive significance of the "Feres Mura" issue for many Israelis, including some who had been active in promoting other waves of Ethiopian immigration and who took pains to make it clear that their scruples were not primarily religious in nature. For D. and others like him, the original sin of the "Feres Mura" was not essentially a religious failure but an act of betrayal toward the community of shared suffering that amounts to a kind of "secular apostasy" for which no religious or ritual strategy can possibly atone.

Another way of saying this might be that since Jewishness is now often defined in the absence of any explicitly religious content or meaning among secular Israelis, the burden of belonging has fallen entirely to the historical and affective plane, or to what one twentieth-century Jewish theologian has called "the covenant of fate" (that is, shared suffering) as opposed to the shared theology and ritual practice implicit to the "covenant of Sinai" (Soloveitchik 1968, 2000). But this kind of nationhood, which is in some ways radically inclusive of people with many different kinds of or no religious identity, can also be harsher and more exclusive to those who are interpreted as having dropped their share of the difficult burden. This was only one of several reasons that some of the most consistent and effective—but also problematic—allies of "Feres Mura" immigration to Israel have been Orthodox rabbis like R. Menahem Waldman, who holds open the possibility of ritual rectification for past failings, in the form of a government-sanctioned return-to-Judaism program that will be described in greater detail in later chapters. For officials like D., Waldman was an annoyance when he visited Addis Ababa not just because he publicly disputed what was then official government policy toward the "Feres Mura" but also because he and the organizations he worked with (such as NACOEJ) held up an alternate vision of Jewish national and religious belonging, in which gaps in both history and shared suffering could ultimately be repaired through ritual means.

Unlike many other pro–"Feres Mura" activists, Waldman did not deny the history of conversion to Christianity in Ethiopia, and he specifically insisted in his Jewish legal rulings (see Waldman 1996) that the generation of converts were to be considered willing apostates rather than *anusim*. Yet, unlike D., he also held open the possibility for efficacious ritual procedures that could effectively wipe out the vestiges of a troubled past. "Ritual," as Claude Lévi-Strauss (1966) once remarked, can be viewed as "a machine for the suppression of history." But this does not mean, even in traditional societies, that the attempted suppression will necessarily succeed, and this difficulty is what gave rise to the whole ethnographic setting of this book. What are the circumstances under which a return to Judaism—any return to Judaism—can be said to have truly succeeded? This is not an idle question, because there was more than one possible form of return available, and success was never guaranteed. D. didn't like the idea of NACOEJ and Waldman's involvement in Ethiopia, but he found it even easier to dispute the activities of Beta Israel religious leaders who took an interest in the "Feres Mura" case on their own terms. Beta Israel priests known as *kessotch* who had already arrived in Israel by 1991 expressed themselves in sharply divided ways on the "Feres Mura" issue but tended to agree that renegades could in theory rejoin the community through the agreement of local religious leadership and the imposition of a seven-day purifying fast (like that occasioned by contact with a corpse). My Ethiopian friends in Upper Nazareth were not pleased when I told them I would be going to Ethiopia to investigate the "Feres Mura" issue. "We don't like them," one of Teshome's grown daughters told me, "because they didn't help us when we were trying to leave Ethiopia." The local priest, Kes Imharan, was more sympathetic, saying only that he opposed their immigration until they had received the appropriate *'onesh* (punishment) for their transgression, by which he meant some penitential regime that included fasting and purification.

Beta Israel priests in Addis Ababa before 1991, like Kes Malki and Kes Meheret, actually began applying the traditional model of purification to "Feres Mura," allowing over a hundred of those purified to be registered for immigrant visas before Israeli officials decided to ask them to stop. I asked D. why the Israelis had interfered in the traditional Beta Israel process of reincorporation, and his answer was enlightening. "We have to protect our own society," he told me. "We have our own leaders and our own society to protect.

It's not up to them [the Beta Israel priests]." Yet when I asked him to justify the formulation of the category "Feres Mura" upon which Israeli bureaucrats were basing their immigration decisions, D. and others told me it was the Beta Israel priests and elders themselves on whose testimony the designations of people as "Feres Mura" were often based. Thus, while immigration authorities used oral testimony by priests and elders to help establish lists of eligibility for immigration, non-Ethiopians insisted upon their own control of the interpretation and application of those lists and worked hard to prevent Beta Israel leaders like Kes Malki from intervening once bureaucratic designations had been made. The need to "protect our society" meant that a locally meaningful category for managing communal membership among the Beta Israel had been appropriated by the Israeli state in its constitution of the "Feres Mura" as a bureaucratic designation, while Beta Israel themselves were systematically excluded from the subsequent application of that category. Those who had been designated "Feres Mura" were left with no ritual solution, and nowhere to turn. The importance of this transformation cannot be overestimated, because it meant that a fundamentally flexible *ritual* response to questions of social and religious exclusion had been exchanged for a rigid and sometimes seemingly arbitrary *bureaucratic* apparatus that depended upon the assertion of fixed and unchanging categories of social and religious identity. While Kes Imharan and others that I interviewed repeatedly insisted that a person might have been branded "Feres Mura" for transgressions ranging from the consumption of impure meat all the way to formal baptism, one of the core assumptions behind Israeli policy at this time was that all Beta Israel who had been estranged from their communities were necessarily full converts, as D. insisted: "There was no 'secular Judaism' in Ethiopia," he told me. "You were either completely Jewish or you joined the church." Period.

It can be tempting for sympathetic outsiders to assume that any opposition to Ethiopian immigration on the part of Israelis must be due to some kind of racial animus, but it is important to emphasize that "Feres Mura" opponents were often far more scandalized by the taint of Christianity than by the color line. D. himself maintained vociferously that previous waves of immigration from Ethiopia (including the one he had helped to facilitate in 1991) included many *barya*, the Amharic term for descendants of lowland Ethiopians who were often kept as household slaves by Beta Israel (as well as by Christians and Muslims) on the Ethiopian Plateau. Ethiopian-Israelis interviewed by Salamon during the 1980s insisted that *barya* were "pagan" (that is, without religion) as well as racially distinctive, showing darker skin and woollier hair than highland Ethiopians (Salamon 1999). D. echoes these depictions when he tells me forcefully, in the course of our conversation that "I know who they [the *barya*] are. You can tell by their noses, their complexions." He claimed to have no difficulty acknowledging that many of these individuals immigrated to Israel together with the Beta Israel families to which they had been assimilated, and insisted that this—by contrast with the presence of the "Feres Mura"—did not bother him. Another aid worker who, like D., had served for a time in Ethiopia, later went to work for a Jerusalem-based civil rights organization and took the unprecedented step of trying to convince her organization, in advance, to forswear involvement in any cases having to do with the civil rights of "Feres Mura" immigrants, as I learned when a confounded coworker turned to me for advice. Clearly, this immigration and the process of return to Judaism had touched an emotional cord that calls out for explanation.

In addition to taxonomic anxieties, I have also become convinced that some of the special intensity of emotion that has tracked the "Feres Mura" issue can be traced to feelings of personal betrayal felt by some officials because of the politics of mistrust engendered by the cultural focus on questions of religious agency and authenticity. Indeed, taxonomic anxieties helped to create the conditions under which immigrants and potential immigrants were made subject to impossible expectations. Mistrust is, in fact, endemic to nearly all interactions between refugees and state authorities the world over (Daniel and Knudsen 1995), but here it was particularly acute because of the way the immigration debate was framed around issues of religious experience, which are by their nature largely opaque to the observer, inviting speculation, poorly grounded assertions, and a hermeneutics of suspicion. Mistrust is thus compounded by the opacity of religious experience and by the lack of universally agreed upon ritual mechanism for "Feres Mura" reincorporation. Potential immigrants and their interlocutors often simply spoke past one another in ways that gave each side ample reason to suspect that the other was acting dishonestly, or with malevolent intent.

One of the reasons that this ethnography resists the pressure to address the historical questions posed by the "Feres Mura" dilemma in purely factual terms (*Are* they Jewish? Why *are* they returning to Judaism?) is that these questions are hardly ever soluble in the positivistic frame in which they are typically posed. Neither the question of genealogy and origins nor the question of agency in religious transformation can be reduced to merely factual matters without a much broader analysis of the cultural, political, and phenomenological contexts in which they continually arise. We need to understand why these questions are being posed in particular ways in the first place, and what kinds of answers are even possible within the overlapping frameworks presented by Ethiopian, Israeli, and Diaspora Jewish realities that intersect or collide at critical events (Das 1995) like the funeral of Tigest Mekuriaw. This is not a popular stance, because it frustrates the widespread desire for technical and taxonomic fixes to what ought to be described as social and philosophical problems. Scholars and policy makers bear a special responsibility to tread carefully in the absence of a clear and adequate epistemology for the resolution of claims about religious experience. When we acknowledge that we work *in* social settings rather than *on* particular groups or cultures, we may finally begin to write more expansively about the conditions of discourse in which realities like the "Feres Mura" dilemma take root, and more earnestly confront the principle of our own entanglement in the cultures and politics of the fields we study.

Suffering Impurity

On July 29, 1992, several hundred refugees gathered not far from the Israeli embassy in Addis Ababa to appeal to Zimna Brhane, an Ethiopian-Israeli who worked for the Ministry of Immigrant Absorption and was currently serving in the capital. The refugees were all newcomers to Addis Ababa, from villages in the Dembeya region like Chilga, Quokora, Chewahit, and Aberja, and they claimed that they had been chased from their land after Operation Solomon by Christian neighbors who coveted their property. They had been turned away by the Israeli embassy and even by NACOEJ (the organization was under considerable pressure not to do anything that might encourage the further exodus of "Feres Mura" from their villages). Thus twice rejected, they subsisted on street sweeping and begging and, incredibly, on small donations from the "Feres Mura" who had arrived in Addis before the airlift and were receiving subsistence rations through NACOEJ. A man named Takeleber from the village of Ateke told me that he had come to the capital because his neighbors in the village would not let him live in peace. He also suggested that another ten thousand individuals from the Dembeya region probably found themselves in similar straits. He later added that those who had come to Addis Ababa were warning others to stay where they were until the situation could be stabilized, but it wasn't clear to me how much he thought he was telling me what I wanted to hear. He acknowledged in the end that he thought others would come to Addis Ababa searching for sustenance no matter what the Israelis or NACOEJ said, and offered that they would probably die if they found none. "If we die though," he concluded, "we want to die with our people [*ki'inya wogen*]."

Together, the refugees had chosen a representative to deliver their plea to Zimna at the embassy. They allowed me to preview the text, written by Melki Jember, and read aloud by a member of the group:

> God of Israel, please help us!
> Make Zimna's heart kinder,
> We chose elders and sent to him:
>
> "The wind and cold are killing us all—
> Please forgive us,
> We carry stones [in supplication] and beg you,

Make [D.] give us the afternoon meal
And you give us dinner!"

"We people of Israel are suffering in poverty,
We are weeping every morning
So Zimna, please help us!
Please be kind to us by smiling
And reach out your hand to us."

"What a father and a mother Zimna has!
He is a sharpshooter—
Most of our people have gone [to Israel] because of your kindness,
Don't you feel sorry for those of us remaining here?"

"While some of us are hungry here
Some of them are eating there;
Seeing this, we are dying of envy [*siset*],
We don't want a feast, just something to eat."

"Hunger is making us suffer,
Hunger is killing us like bullets kill.
We are begging help from your organization;
It would be very sad if even one person dies."

"Please Zimna, Ox of Aramacheho, Pillar of Quarra,
You'll regret it if someone dies—
Is there anyone who can make you understand?"

These refugees had personified their crisis by drawing upon traditional Ethiopian-highland models of patronage and support (Levine 1965). They employ subtle imagery that might imply penitence in the religious sense, like carrying stones upon the neck in a supplication for forgiveness that never specifies any particular transgression. Yet the dominant trope of the appeal to Zimna was of rightful expectation based on shared identity ("we people of Israel are suffering in poverty"), coupled with a barely implied threat of guilt or retribution ("seeing this, we are dying of envy"—*siset*, a term sometimes associated with evil-eye attacks). Not just suffering, but the manifest unfairness of suffering ("while some of us are hungry here, some of them are eating there") cries out for resolution. "Hunger is killing us like bullets kill—is there anyone who can make you understand?"

Claims to shared kinship and patronage are central to the whole "Feres Mura" story that this ethnography seeks to tell. Zimna Birhane declined to be interviewed, so it is difficult to know what if any consequence these demands had upon his view of the situation, but they certainly did not affect government policy in any immediate way. Refugees appealed their suffering to anyone who would listen, but their pleas fell mostly on deaf ears. Unlike officials such as D., who viewed the refugees' relationship to suffering as just one more sign of their deep estrangement from Jewishness—"all over the world it was difficult to be a Jew—but *they* converted!"—refugees themselves deployed accounts of suffering that would distance them from what might otherwise have been read ungenerously as signs of a tainted and problematic past. We may be impure, Tigest's cousin insisted at her funeral, but that is only because of how much we have suffered; we bend our necks in penitence, Melki Jember wrote, but our suffering and need outstrips whatever complications of history may separate us from you. Suffering, kinship, and purity are the shifting rhetorical coordinates of an ongoing conversation about belonging and relatedness that ought not be artificially reduced to the spare sociological and bureaucratic language of "identity" conceived as relatively fixed and self-explanatory categories. The "Feres Mura" dilemma is above all a moral discourse, in which themes of suffering and purity can be played against each other as claim and counterclaim in any number of different configurations depending on the needs of the immediate setting or conversation.

Immigrants from the *Derekh Sudan* generation, for example, often invoked implacable suffering and impurity together as complexly interrelated features of a lifeworld in varying stages of moral and physical collapse. Some, like my adoptive mother Balaynish in Upper Nazareth, attributed their own chronic sickness and sense of unease—the literal inability to remain at home in their own skin—to the pervasive effects of the new Israeli climate, together with regularized impurity and the disorientation of open-ended grief. One of Balaynish's grown daughters and a son had been left behind in Ethiopia when the airlift was called prematurely to a halt in 1985, and another daughter had died along the road to Sudan without receiving a proper burial, when it would have been too dangerous for the group to tarry and observe the rites. Balaynish was not alone among the 1985 immigrants in fearing that her own breaches of purity discipline during the long trek from Gondar to the UN camps at Gudareff may have had something to do with her family's terrible misfortune. Impurity is more than just "matter out of place," or an interruption in the cognitive schema as Mary Douglas (1966) and other anthropologists have sometimes argued; it may also carry the weight of an experienced failure to uphold the most important of shared values, like the collapse of maternal responsibility for household well-being, which are felt viscerally upon the flesh.

Without pushing too far afield, my point is that perceptions of loss and trauma were pervasive in the Ethiopian-Israeli community I came to know in the years preceding the "Feres Mura" immigration, and these were frequently related to feelings of sickness, of widespread dissatisfaction with medical services they received (Reiff 1999; Reiff, Zakut, and Weingarten 1999), and of malaise brought on by forced breaches of purity discipline (Trevisan Semi

1985; Anteby 1997; Seeman 1998). In the 1980s and again in 1991, immigration workers expressed consternation and wonder at the sight of immigrant women sleeping in hallways or in elevator shafts during their menses to avoid polluting family quarters, and teachers in some religious schools had to remonstrate with their female Ethiopian students to attend class (and religious services) during their periods. Balaynish slept in a different room from her husband for part of each month, but this was clearly a departure from the Beta Israel custom of dwelling under separate roofs and led to a perception that the whole house was irredeemably *requs* (impure).

This embodied idiom, extending to medical, political, and religious contexts, is also part of the context of subtle competition over moral prestige that has sometimes divided different groups of Beta Israel from one another. As happy as they were to be reunited with friends and loved ones after Operation Solomon in 1991, for example, earlier immigrants sometimes perceived the new arrivals as less ritually austere and more assimilated than the immigrants of Operation Moses (1984–85) had been. Those who had sacrificed so much to leave Ethiopia through the early Sudanese route spoke about the purity of faith and religion that made them different from those who had waited until leaving might be made simpler through the opening of an Addis Ababa route, and this was merely a foreshadowing of the much more strenuous objections raised by some veterans of both waves of immigration to the later influx of "Feres Mura" beginning in 1994. It is not possible to accurately assess the resistance of some Beta Israel to "Feres Mura" immigration without understanding the moral continuum of both purity and suffering that had long been invoked by Beta Israel immigrants in earlier contexts.

Some of the most powerful and resonant signs of belonging for Beta Israel reside in or upon the body and its habits of practice and posture, rendered visible and thereby supposedly incontrovertible. To know a thing "upon my flesh" (*'al bisari*) is a Hebrew expression for the kind of knowledge that comes with visceral certitude of lived experience (especially the experience of suffering) and that cannot be ignored or gainsaid. This is "experience" in the sense of trial or undergoing, which is related in English to the word "experiment" (see Desjarlais 1994), and when anthropologists talk about experience, this is usually what they have in mind. Experience is irreducibly moral in this sense, because it refers to that which is at stake for actors in the social world (Kleinman and Kleinman 1991), and to the patterns that help to shape agency and constraint in concrete social settings. When we speak in this sense about "the experience of American women" or "the 'Feres Mura' experience of immigration" we are not referring to ineffable inner states like those sometimes invoked by scholars of religion such as William James—something that stands out from the horizon of the lifeworld ("to have" a religious experience, for example)—but to the structured limits or "horizon" of the lifeworld itself, to which ethnographic observation can give us privileged though imperfect access. In modern Hebrew, "having an experience" is expressed by the word *havvayah*, but "being experienced," learning by trial and suffering, or by habit and experiment, is expressed by the old biblical word *nisayon*, which also means experiment and is derived from the biblical term for a trial or test, as in "God tried [*nisa*] Abraham" (Genesis 22:1). *Nisayon*-experience thus refers both to the structuring features of the lifeworld and to the embodied patterns of inhabiting that world, the way we say of an "experienced" tailor that his or her hands have been conditioned to act through training over time. Together, these constitute the essential backdrop to the "picture of what is experienced" (Wittgenstein 1980, 158e), to which one needs to point when making empirical claims.

Nisayon-experience is what helps me to understand what some Beta Israel mean when they say, usually in moments of great rhetorical pathos, that they are "Jewish in their bones" (cf. Salamon 1999): that this is one of the reasons that the disposition of their bones through burial among kin imposes such a deeply felt moral burden. At a meeting of heads of Ethiopian Jewish organizations in Israel in 1995, which I describe at greater length in chapter 3, I was treated to an angry soliloquy by the head of one small Ethiopian-Israeli organization who wanted me to understand why he was opposed to "Feres Mura" immigration. "I am Jewish in my bones," he said to me with a great deal of heat, "and no immersion in a *mikveh* [one of the requirements of both conversion and the return to Judaism required of 'Feres Mura'] can give that to someone." He was not making a point about race or genealogy, still less telling me something that could have been restated in a distanced, ethnological vein, such as "Beta Israel believe that their Jewishness resides in their bones." On the contrary, I understood him to be saying (and I will defend this interpretation in subsequent chapters) that Jewishness rhetorically accretes to one's bones through years and generations of fidelity—through shared ritual practice or through suffering and undergoing together with others over time—and that he had no patience for those who had failed in his estimation on both of these counts. The bones are simply the most firm and internal, the most hidden and intimate of bodily parts, and this helps to convey a sense of what is real and solid in human affairs. For "Feres Mura" and other Beta Israel I encountered, perceptions of social and moral solidity were often desperately at stake in questions of kinship and belonging.

One of the first mistakes I made as a an inexperienced field-worker was to ask very direct questions about the nearly ubiquitous tattoos that marked many of the refugees in Addis Ababa; I did not fully grasp how what had once seemed like a mere curiosity in the context of previous Ethiopian immigrations to Israel had become dangerous signs of estrangement that bore real-world policy implications for "Feres Mura" in Addis Ababa. Displaced people in Addis Ababa knew better than I did what this potentially dangerous sign might mean, and immediately resisted my questions on the topic. Some tattooing in rural Ethiopia is aesthetic or medicinal—like tattoos on the neck serving as a prophylactic against goiter (Young 1973). But there is also a long history of religious tattooing that is associated in Ethiopian history with the reign of the pious emperor Zara Yaqob (literally, "Seed of Jacob"), who ruled from 1434 to 1468. Zara Yaqob's religious nationalism was grounded in the long-standing anxiety of Christian rulers who saw their country surrounded by "pagans and Muslims in the east as well as in the west" (Tamrat 1972, 219). Tattoos helped solidify the impression of a uniform national-religious identity and may have helped to impose a degree of actual religious uniformity upon his subjects. He insisted that the names of the Father, the Son, and the Holy Ghost be tattooed on servants' foreheads and that the sign of the cross be emblazoned upon clothing and even farm implements—a set of practices that he compared favorably with the Egyptian custom of tattooing the cross only upon the hands of believers.

The inscription of religious symbols upon the flesh in highland Ethiopia outlasted Zara Yaqob and continues today primarily through the tattooing of crosses upon arms and heads. Beta Israel did not historically tattoo for primarily religious purposes, yet the most powerful and unexpected example of this practice I ever encountered was in Jerusalem, where my new friend Solomon showed me two small Stars of David tattooed on each of his wrists. The Magen David was not a symbol endemic to Beta Israel life; rather, it had been introduced by Western Jews during the course of the twentieth century, when it came to adorn many synagogues and Beta Israel ritual objects, including pottery and woven articles produced for tourists. Solomon had been a teacher at the embassy school for Beta Israel children before the 1991 airlift, and though his father and father's family were left behind as "Feres Mura," he had come to Israel as a Jew under the Law of Return during Operation Solomon. "I got the tattoos," he told me, "so that if I die far from home people will know where to bury me." Many Jews in Israel and North America share the folk belief—though many rabbis deny it—that possession of a tattoo renders a person ineligible for burial in a Jewish cemetery, but Solomon had adapted the prevailing Christian custom for a decisively Jewish enactment of belonging and moral solidarity. While this was in some ways a uniquely personal statement by a remarkable individual, the experience also made it harder for me to accept the claims I later heard from those waiting in Addis Ababa, who almost uniformly insisted that their tattoos—including many crosses upon foreheads—were really just decorative in nature.

During my first weeks of fieldwork in Addis Ababa, middle-aged Dawit answered my questions about tattoos while he worked at sewing in the NACOEJ compound one afternoon, but he was twice interrupted by other workers who tried to change the subject. Finally, with his neighbors watching, he told me an elaborate story about how young girls in his home village of Deberke had regularly been seized by local Christians to be tattooed with the sign of the cross against their will. I was unsure what to make of this story, but no one present took issue with it. Later though, when I asked an eleven-year-old orphan from Kewalla Duba about her village childhood, she told me among other things that it was her brother's wife who had inscribed her forehead with the sign of the cross a few years before. At the end of a fifteen-minute conversation (which was not by any means devoted primarily to tattoos) I unthinkingly gave her half a *birr* (a little more than ten cents) for candy, and by the end of the day a story had been circulated throughout the compound that I was paying children to lie about the community. A delegation of elders asked the NACOEJ administrator to have me banned from the premises, and even though he helped to calm the situation and vouched for my motives, I wasn't sure how to proceed. It was Addisu, the young man I had chatted with in Hebrew on the day of Tigest's funeral, who helped me avoid taking the rejection by my would-be informants too personally. He had returned to Ethiopia, as I have mentioned, in order to arrange for an immigrant visa for his mother to accompany him back to Israel, and we would meet in the evenings sometimes to share our individual frustrations. "Don't be angry with them [the refugees]," he told me. "They are suffering and they don't understand what you are trying to do."

In retrospect, of course, they had every reason to be cautious and defensive about this topic. During the 1990s, Ethiopians in Israel frequently went to the trouble and expense of having their tattoos surgically removed in order to fit in, or to avoid the stigma of "primitivity" and Jewish inauthenticity in a society where boutique tattooing and voluntary body piercing were still a few years away from the trendy teenage circuits of Haifa or Tel-Aviv. Two Israeli dermatologists who performed more than four hundred tattoo removals for Ethiopians at their laser unit in Herzelia note laconically that their patients' decision to remove tattoos was important for "improving the quality of life of Ethiopian immigrants in Israel" (Lapidoth and Aharonowitz 2004). Ridding themselves of tattoos was an act of liberation from the signs of deep estrangement that might trouble even the relatively affluent and culturally legitimate "Jewish" Ethiopians, but it was not an option available to poor and contested refugees in Addis Ababa. They understood the social costs of even talking about tattoos in a way that I did not yet grasp. In the end I convinced many (probably not all) of the people with whom I spoke that my intentions were honorable, but an especially hard lesson had been learned about the importance of understanding what research means in the broad social contexts where it inevitably occurs.

Directly and indirectly, I am indebted to the phenomenological sociology of Alfred Schutz (1967), who was the first to combine the phenomenological perceptions of Edmund Husserl with the meaning-centered *verhesten* of Max Weber. Schutz insisted that the only way to study lived experience was by attending to the interpretations of lived experience by means of which informants as well as social scientists navigate. Informants who push back against analysis are actually doing ethnographers a favor by reminding them that there is no clear and absolute distinction between the interpretive work of social scientists and that of people who must constantly analyze the agency and motivations of other people with whom they come into contact through everyday life: Is my friend sincere about wanting to help, or self-interested? Are there more agendas here than meet the eye? These are questions that can have life-or-death consequences outside the research setting, and their informal adjudication is a central and almost reflexive component of all social life. The social scientist in this view is really just a specially trained and attentive observer of human affairs, generally seeking a somewhat broader, more comparative, and less ideologically overdetermined sort of analysis than that which interests the average person involved in social dynamics. This realization should be both humbling and liberating, in the sense that anthropological work occurs along a broad continuum with other sorts of vernacular perception and interpretation of the social world. Yet it is well to remember that the costs of mistaken or inadequate analysis on the part of social scientists will almost always be borne disproportionately by those who are already most disadvantaged, like the "Feres Mura" waiting in Addis Ababa.

Pushing my research relationship with people at the NACOEJ compound to a near breaking point also served, paradoxically, to drive my research agenda forward by breaking up the local status quo in such a way that certain halting and delicate friendships—including some that have now lasted for well over a decade—could begin to be built. Shortly after the debacle of the tattoos, for example, I made the acquaintance of an earnest young man named Ageru, who served as one of the prayer leaders in the makeshift synagogue that had been built in the midst of the NACOEJ compound. He had once angered the other refugees by speaking with a Canadian journalist, and now he agreed to speak with me as well, if only quietly and outside of the spotlight. It was the first time that anyone from the community had spoken with me openly about life before the return-to-Judaism program. He had come to believe that only truthfulness about the past would help to advance his people's cause. I was touched by his bravery, and also by his pathos. His position on the need for painful truth telling was one I came to espouse strongly as well, once I understood the tangled web of expectation and disappointment that had helped to make the "Feres Mura" dilemma into such a tortured subject in Israel. Yet what most surprised me was when he took me by the sleeve at the end of our first interview and surprised me by saying, "I know that you [that is, non-Ethiopian Jews] have suffered more than we have, but you have to understand that we have suffered too."

Ageru had never been outside Ethiopia and had met only a handful of foreign Jews in the time since he arrived in Addis Ababa, but he had already come to understand something of the overbearing practical relevance (Kleinman 1997) not just of suffering but of perceptions of suffering in determinations of kinship between Beta Israel and foreign Jews. Frequently, people like Ageru understand the things that their lives depend upon better than disengaged scholars ever can. He told me that he knew about modern Jewish history from an exhibit the Israeli embassy had recently sponsored at a local museum, focusing on the traditional *me-shoah le-tekumah* (from the Holocaust to the creation of the State) theme, and from his own reading. He showed me an Amharic language paperback about World War II and the Holocaust that he had bought at a local market. "We have suffered too" was a rebuke aimed at me as the apparent representative of a Jewish world "out there" that had still to make up its mind about the level of recognition to be granted to people like Ageru and the others waiting in Addis Ababa. It was an assertion of kinship in suffering despite the manifest signs of impurity or taintedness through apostasy, and a call for hermeneutic generosity (Farmer 1992) that might yield sympathetic interpretation and solidarity despite the rare acknowledgment of religious and historical difference.

Part of the problem for "Feres Mura," but also, paradoxically, their only hope, has been the ways in which powerful outsiders tend to read the history and circumstances of the Beta Israel in light of their own powerful tropes of longing and memory In his paean to Operation Solomon on the op-ed page of the *New York Times*, Israeli novelist David Grossman called the immigrants "little Queens of Sheba" not just as a rhetorical device, but as part of the deep significance of the Ethiopian immigration for many thoughtful secular Israelis:

> Apparent, too, was the majesty of these new Israelis: little Queens of Sheba; children of almond, of olive; adolescents without the arrogant glare of our teenagers; old men and women angular and black as coal, only their eyes ember.... A Judaism that strayed 2,500 years through the thicket of history, that rose and fell, that was separated, yet survived. Perhaps what survived is what we seek with our eternal question: who is a Jew? Perhaps, it is they in their remoteness, in their longing, who bring us the answer. Perhaps this is why we scrutinize them so closely—to see, in the blazing blue light, the photographic negative of our history. (Grossman 1991)

"Olive" and "ember," "almond" and "black as coal" are not just colors in this account, they are ciphers: visceral clues to the play of difference and sameness that makes Ethiopian Jews so "good to think with" in Jewish and Israeli society. Lévi-Strauss (1966) wrote that animals were "good to think with" in the context of totemic societies of the American Northwest and Ethiopian-Israelis or Beta Israel have also been reduced to a kind of totemic image for some Jews. Reduced to being a "photographic negative of *our* [emphasis added] history," how can Beta Israel not suffer a certain flattening, a corresponding loss of their own color in the "blazing blue light" of photo-negative appropriation by others?

Ageru was finally allowed to immigrate in 1994, and to participate in the return to Judaism program outside Haifa that I will describe in later chapters, but he remained concerned about the fates of all those "Feres Mura" who still remained in Ethiopia. In 1998, he was part of an Ethiopian-Israeli team that returned to Ethiopia to help teach the newer groups of refugees who were now squeezed into the NACOEJ compound awaiting visas. On his return to Israel, he wrote a thirty-five-page English-language report entitled "The Black Jews Describe to their Fellow White Jews About the Hardship and Suffering They Have Had to Face" (Kassa 1998). It completely eschewed the term "Feres Mura" or any discussion of the religious complexity of his community's history. His earlier preoccupation with the Holocaust and with comparisons between Beta Israel and non-Ethiopian Jewish suffering, however, remained strong:

> As we all know, our forefathers had suffered a great deal. For example, in Germany around 6 million people were burnt. . . . Similarly in Ethiopia, the Jewish people are thought to have evil eyes that could kill others, and as a result some have been badly beaten up, some others were shot down, and still others have been forced out of their villages. All those things have happened to us since we are Jews; there is no other reason . . . The Beta Israelis who are victims thus leave their villages and come to Addis Abeba in order to save their lives. There are now around 2,122 family heads and around 7, 125 people as a whole. (Kassa 1998, 5–6)

He goes on to describe fifteen different cases of Beta Israel families who came to Addis Ababa during the 1990s, including stories of shootings and house burnings, intense pressure by neighboring landholders to vacate land, and socioeconomic collapse faced by those who remained in regions that most of their near and distant kin had already evacuated upon leaving for Israel. These accounts were corroborated in the main by a Refugees International Report from the same year (Thompson 1998). Ageru also describes the attempts by displaced people in Addis Ababa to develop a coherent communal structure while awaiting permission to emigrate. He concludes the report in a manner that recalls Tigest Mekuriaw's contested funeral, however, in a chapter he calls "The Burial Place Problem for the Beta-Israelis Living in Addis Abeba."

"In any society," Ageru writes, "a person would feel sad and mourn when a close relative or friend dies." But for the people he calls "Beta Israelis" living in Addis Ababa, the situation is worse because "people get worried when one gets very sick, not because he/she is sick, but because they would not have a place to bury him/her if the unfortunate happens and the person dies" (Kassa 1998, 29). He describes the case of Mr. Gobeze Besuneh Tessema, "who was 50 years old and had come from Durge." He died on December 8 1998, but because the family could not find a place to bury him, the body remained in their rented lodgings for two days, until the landlord complained, after which he was buried "at a place where people with no religion get buried." Later, when permission was finally arranged for him to be buried in the Jewish cemetery of Addis Ababa, the man's brother was unwilling to disturb the corpse. Ageru blames this situation squarely upon those who should ostensibly be responsible for the welfare of displaced Jews in Addis Ababa:

> Since the A.J.D.C. and the Israeli government have not given recognition to these people, the Committee members of the Beta-Israeli Association told me that there were previously . . . 7 other Beta-Israelis who died and were buried at the place where people with no religion get buried. In general, the Israeli people and the government should know that the Beta- Israelis are facing a great deal of hardship and suffering that is too difficult to imagine. (30)

The situated account that ethnography provides can help sharpen the picture of what is experienced not just by calling attention to the special cultural significance of an issue like burial among one's kin but also by sharpening the analysis of what is at stake for people in some specific and irreducible set of circumstances, which includes the competing discourses through which they define themselves and others describe them. It is not just the depiction of cultural specificity that makes an ethnography convincing, but also the human empathy that can only be evoked by adequate description. This is an act of moral imagination not in the sense of "becoming the other" but in the more modest attempt to think oneself into the other's predicament as best one can.

"One would like to say," with Ageru Kassa and with Wittgenstein (1980, 158e), "I feel sorrow *thus*." Yet this makes sense, we must insist, "only where there is a picture of *what is experienced* to which one can point as one makes these statements." I have written this chapter as a broad and sometimes impressionistic introduction to some of the primary cultural and rhetorical themes that have come to define the "Feres Mura" dilemma: purity, authenticity, suffering, and a sense of belonging to a people and a nation. We will need to examine these themes in a variety of concrete ethnographic settings. Before going any further, though, it is necessary to examine some of the historical complications of the claims to kinship between Beta Israel and foreign Jews without which the "Feres Mura" dilemma could never have emerged.

CHAPTER 2

THE QUESTION OF KINSHIP

> But the joy, which was excited in him by the comprehensiveness of that Gospel which he had been commissioned to preach to all . . . did not extinguish . . . a tender and affectionate regard for his own countrymen: on the contrary, the grief which pierced his soul when viewing the sad consequences of their rejection of the Gospel, seems to have added warmth and fraternity to his fraternal love. . . . *I could wish myself separated from Christ, for my brethren, my kinsmen, according to the flesh* (Romans 9:3).
>
> —Charles James, London Jewish Society (LJS) Annual Sermon, 1843

At some point during their first year in Israel, most Ethiopian immigrants are taken from their schools and absorption centers on a field trip to the *kotel,* or Western Wall, in the Old City of Jerusalem. The wall has both national and religious significance for many Israelis since it represents the last of the ancient retaining walls of the Temple destroyed by Rome after a Jewish revolt in 70 CE. One of the things that Ethiopian Beta Israel shared with Jews elsewhere in the world was the strong cultural and liturgical focus on Jerusalem not just as a destination for religious pilgrimage but as an imagined homeland. So it is no surprise that Ethiopian-Israelis have chosen Jerusalem for their annual *Sigd* festival, a unique holiday that has also become the most important regular gathering for Ethiopians from around the country. But Jerusalem also maintains a strong Ethiopian Christian presence through its ancient Orthodox monasteries and occasional visits by Ethiopian evangelicals who come to study or pray. The confluence of Judaism and Christianity in Jerusalem has special significance to the history of Beta Israel because Protestant missionaries with a strong interest in Jews and Jerusalem were the first to make a sustained claim about the relatedness of Beta Israel and other Jews in modern times.

Black and white photographs from the 1920s reveal that today's Christian Information Center near Jaffa Gate in Old Jerusalem once flew a banner identifying itself as the Palestine office of the London Society for the Promotion of Christianity Amongst the Jews. It was a small but influential organization, also known—ironically—as the London Jewish Society or LJS. LJS agents opened the first hospital in Jerusalem, much to the consternation of local rabbis, who begged and threatened their followers to eschew its services, and it was instrumental in the appointment of the first Anglican bishops in Palestine. But the LJS also maintained an active missionary profile throughout the Jewish Diaspora, and its Palestine office was responsible for operations throughout the Levant, including Ethiopia. The spiritual successors of the LJS still operate in Ethiopia as well as Israel; a bookstore near the Jaffa Gate distributes free missionary literature and Amharic-language Bibles to anyone who says they will distribute them among Ethiopian-Israelis. But a century and a half ago, at a time when the mass immigration of Beta Israel to a sovereign Jewish state could scarcely have been imagined, these missionaries were also the first to pose what I have called the question of kinship between Beta Israel and other Jews in a sustained and articulate way. Their influence was so profound that it is difficult to imagine the subsequent history and emigration of the Beta Israel unfolding without them.

The Beta Israel in Their Ethiopian Context

The first LJS missionaries to set foot in Ethiopia for the specific purpose of proselytizing Beta Israel arrived in 1860. Historians set the stage for their arrival in 1855, however, with the rise to power of Tewodoros II as Emperor and King of Kings of Ethiopia (S. Kaplan 1992b; Quirin 1992). Kaplan has characterized the Beta Israel in 1855 as "politically powerless, economically impoverished, and socially marginalized" (1992b, 114). While they had probably never been unified into a single political or geographical unit, Beta Israel in some regions had continued to exercise military and social resistance to incorporation by the Ethiopian state well into the seventeenth century, representing over three hundred years of intermittent conflict, as Kaplan cautiously argues, "between Judaized groups and the Christian emperors of Ethiopia" (94). Their defeat by the Christian emperor Susenyos in 1620 marked the end of any real hope for political autonomy, forcing the survivors into reliance upon the economic and political patronage of strong central rulers. This made them especially vulnerable during the period that preceded Tewodoros's reign, which became known as the Era of the Princes, or *zemana mesafent* (1769–1855) because of the breakdown in central authority that took place during those years. Tewodoros's unification of the state under central authority was in some ways beneficial to Beta Israel, who could more easily count on the peace and protection of the monarch, but this certainly did not put an end to their troubles.

James Quirin (1992, 55) has argued that the Era of the Princes marked a stage of final consolidation for the Beta Israel as a low-status occupational caste group working largely as blacksmiths, potters, weavers, or tenant farmers. They had been banned in most regions from owning agricultural land since the fifteenth century, when Emperor Yeshaq (1414–1430) famously declared, "May he who is baptized in the Christian religion inherit the land of his father; otherwise let him be uprooted from his land and be a stranger [*falasi*]" (ibid.). In effect, this meant the end of hereditary title over plots of land (*rist*), which were otherwise the mainstay of rural economy. During the *zemana mesafent*, the disenfranchisement was further extended to include patronage (*gult*) lands that had been granted to individual Beta Israel in return for outstanding service or loyalty to ruling monarchs. As Donald Crummey (1983) has shown, the Era of the Princes was associated with the emergence of hereditary nobles who increasingly asserted their independence of royal authority. The seizure of *gult* lands by these new elites was merely one aspect of their overall assault on centralized power in Ethiopia. For Beta Israel who had historically resisted conversion to Christianity, however, this coincided with an extended process of isolation and marginalization that pushed them into even greater reliance on the same noble patrons who were seizing land and authority from more marginal groups.

The economic decline that accompanied these developments was a significant factor in the rapid acculturation of Beta Israel to the dominant society during this period (Quirin 1992). Thus, Beta Israel in the Gondar region moved rapidly during the nineteenth century toward the adoption of Amharic as a secondary and then primary language. By 1860, when the LJS mission arrived in Ethiopia, even rural Beta Israel were reported to speak Amharic fluently, and by the early twentieth century only a few elders near Gondar were said to recall their ancestral Agau dialect, even though missionary records indicate that Agau may have been preserved longer in some regions (*Jewish Records*, August 1862, 31). By the time most Beta Israel emigrated from Ethiopia in the late twentieth century, Amharic had emerged as the undisputed mother tongue of the Gondar region Beta Israel. The process of "Amharization" has also been studied among other groups in Ethiopia, like the "pagan-Hebraic" Kemant, who historically spoke an Agau dialect similar to that of the Beta Israel but have been adopting Amharic (and in many cases Christianity) throughout modern times (Gamst 1969). Until recently, most Ethiopian regimes strongly supported this tendency on the part of both non-Amhara and non-Christian groups, but Beta Israel are probably unique in having undergone a process of significant religious and cultural change twice in two hundred years—first to the Amharic culture of the Ethiopian state and later (though it is still ongoing) to the Hebrew culture of modern Israel. This at least should give pause to those who still want to portray Beta Israel history as one of static and unchanging tradition.

Change was not of course uniform, and may have varied from region to region, but by and large the *zemana mesafent* was accompanied by both linguistic acculturation and the attenuation of certain ritual disciplines. Poverty made it difficult for Beta Israel to maintain their sacrificial system intact, and there is evidence that penalties for the infringement of some dietary laws were also relaxed during this period (Quirin 1992, 154). One Beta Israel document refers to the Era of the Princes as a time of spiritual decline and heavy proselytizing by the Orthodox Christian majority, in which "the religion of Israel disappeared again, and this decline lasted twenty years." Quirin also reports an oral tradition that "our religion was lost for forty years," and this assessment is echoed by the French travelers Combes and Tamisier, who wrote in the 1830s that "[e]xposed to continual harassment, the Falasha are rather disposed to abandon their faith" (see Quirin 1992, 153–154; S. Kaplan 1992b, 108–110). At the same time, this apparent decline in religious fervor was accompanied by an intensification of social separation between Beta Israel and Amhara that was often justified in supernatural terms. *Buda* (evil eye) accusations against Beta Israel increased during this period, leading to social ostracism and in some cases to violence against those who had been accused. As blacksmiths and potters, it was perhaps inevitable that Beta Israel who engaged in such trades would be associated with occult powers (see Reminick 1974; Herbert 1993). In many regions of Ethiopia, however, the mythic association of blacksmith-Falasha-*Buda* became nearly seamless, further helping to block social mobility (Quirin 1992, 141–145).

For their part, Beta Israel drew on earlier cultural and religious themes to solidify their social separation and sense of religious or moral superiority to the dominant society. Their consolidation as an occupational caste group facilitated the observance of increasingly strict avoidance rules, including the famous *attenqun* (literally, "don't touch me") practices, which rendered all physical contact with non–Beta Israel contaminating. European visitors to Ethiopia during the 1860s mention observance of these rules repeatedly, but ritual piety seems to have waned during the twentieth century, prior to the beginning of mass emigration (Messing 1982, 34; Schoenberger 1975). Ethiopian immigrants to Israel during the mid-1980s and early 1990s repeatedly invoked *attenqun* when I asked them to describe their relationships with Christians in Ethiopia, assuming that this one word was enough to explain everything I might want to know. This does not mean that social and physical contact between religious groups was in practice impossible (as the number of people I have met who were avowedly born to unions between individuals from the two groups testifies), but it does signify that an ideology and ethos of separation has had deep and long-lasting effects on Beta Israel self-perception.

Patterns of avoidance and competition over religious prestige between Beta Israel and highland Christians utilized what S. Kaplan (1992b, 112) has called "a small number of interconnected key symbols" that betrayed their cultural similarity as well as their structural opposition to one another. While Orthodox Christians accused Beta Israel of transforming themselves into *Buda*-hyenas in order to consume the blood and corpses of their victims, for example, Beta Israel mocked the transformative ideology of the Eucharist, in which the blood and body of Christ were said to be consumed. Beta Israel looked askance at both the consumption of blood by Christians—raw meat cut from the haunch of a living animal was considered a delicacy in some regions (Salamon 1993)—and at the failure of Christians to insist upon physical separation and segregation from the blood of menstruating women. Yet despite these differences, Beta Israel were unique among Jewish communities in maintaining an elaborate monastic system that was almost identical in structure to that of their Christian neighbors.

Ascetic monks had been crucial to the formulation and maintenance of religious and communal structures of Beta Israel society ever since the fourteenth century, when this tradition seems to have crystallized in its final form. A number of renegade Christian ascetics, like the famous monk Qozmos, are known to have joined with the ancestors of the Beta Israel in the region of Lake Tana during this period. S. Kaplan (1992b) has shown that some of these renegade Christians were people who joined the ancestors of the Beta Israel precisely because of their disputes with the dominant church over "Judaizing" practices like the Saturday Sabbath and their commitment to an extremely demanding purity regime. The importance of cultural and religious proximity between Beta Israel and Orthodox Christianity should not in any case be underestimated, even though there are important and perhaps determinative points of divergence as well. Shelemay's 1989 study of Beta Israel liturgy goes so far as to argue that this liturgy is derived from fourteenth- and fifteenth-century Christian practice, although it was self-consciously purged of Christological and Trinitarian references. This raises the thorny theoretical (but also political) problem of how distinctive but related religious traditions should be compared with one another and how lines should be drawn. How, in other words, do we evaluate whether the Beta Israel rejection of Trinitarianism ought to count for more or less than the existence of a nearly identical monastic system in determining how its relationship with Orthodox Christianity should be conceived? Quirin (1992) has argued strongly that it was the marshalling of essentially Christian social institutions like monasticism that allowed the Beta Israel to forge their own cultural and religious autonomy for five hundred years in the shadow of an aggressively expanding Christian state.

The ascetic and monastic character of Beta Israel religious tradition certainly shaped the religious lives of the Beta Israel during the *zemana mesafent* and their subsequent encounter with European missionaries beginning in the 1860s. In the 1840s, a monk named Abba Wedaje from the Qwara region was said to have "brought his people back to their religion" (Quirin 1992, 156), which probably involved a renewal or strengthening of concern with various ritual and ascetic practices. Liturgical fasting was, for instance, a constant feature of religious practice among both Beta Israel and Orthodox Christians in highland Ethiopia, much in excess of what many Christian or Jewish groups practiced elsewhere. As early as the seventeenth century, a traveler named Jerome Lobo, who was a Jesuit missionary, noted with ambivalence that the Orthodox monks "carry austerities and mortification much farther than the most rigorous of our hermits" (Lobo 1789/1978, 381). The Ethiopian Church prescribed more days of fasting for lay Christians (an average of 180 days per year) than any other Christian denomination (Isaac 1995; R. Pankhurst 1990, 6), and traditional Beta Israel practice was comparable, with at least 150 days of fasting per year (Quirin 1992, 50; Shelemay 1989, 131–179).

Beta Israel fasts were often somewhat stricter than those of their Christian counterparts, in that usually no food of any kind was permitted from dawn to dusk. Reports by foreign observers during the 1840s indicate that many Beta Israel fasted every Monday and Thursday and on the last days of every moon. Most of these fasts were explained to observers in terms of their connection with biblical directives or personalities (Quirin 1992, 146–150). Nearly every important change in status, like those accompanying the investiture of monks and priests, rituals of incorporation for those who had come into contact with a corpse, or the return home of travelers who had been forced to spend time among Christians, was accompanied by seven-day abstentions from all food except for lentils or chickpeas, which were considered purifying and purgative. Just like their Christian neighbors, Beta Israel also attributed healing power to pilgrimage sites associated with the names of famous ascetic saints; they made efforts to visit these sites during periods of drought or other calamity (Tamrat 1972, 112; Leslau 1975; Ben-Dor 1987). The missionary J. M. Flad (1869, 29) reported that he had heard of ascetic saints healing directly through the laying on of hands, but he did not witness this practice during his sojourn in Ethiopia during the 1860s, and it is not well attested.

Asceticism also played a competitive political role in both religious communities. Beta Israel and Christians competed with one another for ascetic and genealogical prestige as the true embodiments of biblical religion (see Abbink 1990) and marshaled the prestige they won within their own communities into positions of leadership and influence. Donald Levine (1965, 232–235) has referred to the Christian monks of highland Ethiopia as literal "heroes of oral renunciation" to indicate the honored place they held in their community's religious imagination. Beta Israel monks who succeeded in emulating the ideal of ascetic piety were also able to translate that approbation into loose charismatic authority over communal affairs, which was not seriously challenged until the arrival of Western Christians and Jews, who forced all the religious communities of highland Ethiopia to contend with new models of authority and practice. Europeans called the monks' ascetic ethos radically into question by interpreting local ritual models in light of their own quite different concepts and concerns. But along with the diminution of monk's authority, which they fostered, Europeans also marshaled new historical narratives and racial taxonomies to pose a new and surprising set of questions to the Beta Israel they encountered. I have called the most important of these the "question of kinship," because it was centrally concerned with the question of spiritual and genealogical or even racial relationship between Beta Israel and Western Jews. The monks and other leaders of Beta Israel society were able to accommodate, appropriate, or resist the transformative project imposed upon them by the question of kinship, but they were never able wholly to evade the implications of its having been asked.

The Aesthetics of Conversion

Henry Aaron Stern arrived in Ethiopia on March 10, 1860. The London Society for Promoting Christianity Amongst the Jews was preceded in Ethiopia by a number of other evangelical groups, most notably the Church Missionary Society (CMS) of England, whose agents Samuel Gobat and Christian Kugler had, in 1830, been the "first Europeans to establish a firm and continuous link with Ethiopia" (Crummey 1972, 29). Gobat, in fact, had worked periodically among the Beta Israel himself, and it was he who later encouraged the London Society to undertake a dedicated mission to the Beta Israel. In 1846, however, Gobat left Ethiopia to be ordained Anglican Bishop of Jerusalem after the untimely death of his predecessor, Michael Solomon Alexander, who was himself a converted Jew and agent of the LJS. Society members had hoped that Alexander would make inroads among the Jews of the holy land by virtue of his "racial affinity" to other Jews, and this was very probably also the reason that they chose a converted Jew like Henry Aaron Stern to lead the mission to the Beta Israel.

It is worth emphasizing that neither the LJS nor the Church Missionary Society had set out initially to establish a mission to the "pagan" peoples of Africa, and that the CMS did not begin proselytizing the non-Christian Oromo population until twelve years after its arrival in the country, in 1842 (Crummey 1972, 12, 53–54). Instead, the CMS viewed Ethiopia as a Levantine outpost for the "reawakening of the Eastern Churches" under Protestant influence. For members of the London Jewish Society, it was not surprising that the proselytism of Jews would be treated as perhaps *the* foundational project, but even this was often described by the society's agents as a means for "regenerating the Churches of Asia."[1] This mission had both a religious and a modernizing-economic dimension, as Henry Stern emphasized:

Hitherto neither the sovereign [of Ethiopia, that is, Tewodoros] nor his subjects have had much opportunity for forming a correct estimate of the various sources of wealth that lie within their reach, or of what is of far greater import, of becoming acquainted with the beauty of that Gospel in which they so loudly profess to believe; but let the missionary quietly and judiciously pursue his evangelistic work; let the fostering hand of trade develop the hidden treasures of the land, and an impulse will be given to industry, a stimulus to civilization, and a salutary power to law; and the only nation in Central Africa bearing the name Christian and now, alas, notorious for vice, may yet become famous for "whatsoever is honest, lovely, and of good report." (Stern 1862/1968, 322)

A topos that informs Stern's whole *Wanderings in Abyssinia* is in fact his juxtaposition of the wild and unruly but still-pristine setting of "Africa's garden" (ibid., 80, 121) with the infectious pestilence of African habitations, bodies, and healing or religious practices. On his visit to the famous healing spring at Wanzagie (see R. Pankhurst 1990, 123–133), for example, he writes that the baths vividly reminded him of nothing but Bethesda's pool. "There were men and women, youths and maidens, all more or less branded by the indelible curse of depravity and vice." Stern had no inclination to protract his stay in what he called "this lazar spot of disease and ill-famed home of savage harpies" (Stern 1862/1968, 91–93).

Stern reserved special condemnation, however, for local ascetic practice. On his first visit to the important Beta Israel monk Abba Mahari in Dembeya—which would later become an important center of Beta Israel conversion—Stern and his party were obliged to wait outside the village because of the purity discipline the monks enforced. "Being Christians, we were obliged to keep a respectful distance from the home of *Aboo Maharee* and his monks," Stern wrote, but added that he preferred this to the "foul and reeking hut" (ibid., 248). Stern had hoped that the meeting would develop into a formal disputation, but what happened in the end was even more enlightening. By keeping his party waiting and at a distance, the monks may well have sought to reinforce their own authority and prestige by subjecting European missionaries to a series of ritual indignities. "The *kibur* [honor] of the monk," notes Alan Hoben " . . . is derived from the direct contact he has with heaven by virtue of his rigorous ascetic piety" (1970, 214). Yet even Stern was impressed by Abba Mahari's "dignified gravity" when he finally appeared "in front of the heaving and undulating mass" of common villagers (Stern 1862/1968, 247–248).

Stern's first impression of Abba Mahari is worth citing for what it reveals about the cultural anxieties underlying the missionary project:

He is, I should think, about sixty years of age, of a noble and commanding figure, high and expressive forehead, melancholy, restless eyes, and a countenance once no doubt mild and pleasing, but to which self-imposed penances and a repulsive practice have imparted an expression most strange and unearthly.... There sits the old monk ... with the brown skin hanging in loose folds around his wasted features, his eyes sunk and lusterless from long mortification, or bright and sparkling with the mad fire of fanaticism. (Ibid., 248–250)

Without putting too fine a point on it, this is a neat encapsulation of the whole mission to the Beta Israel in poetic and aesthetic terms; the fate of the degenerate old monk is one that must befall all those who substitute world-denying forms of ascetic rigor for the vigorous spiritual and economic engagements that Stern has come to Ethiopia to promote. Yet despite the loyalty of the Beta Israel who surrounded their saint, Stern convinced himself that he could detect "some secret apprehension, some latent fear, that, after all, these proud and secluded anchorites might be in error, and, instead of the substance, grasp a mere shadow—instead of revealed truth, cling only to a mere self-created fancy" (ibid., 250–251). His proof was that many of the villagers had "healthy looks and smiling expressions" visibly at odds with the appearance of the "mutilated, dissatisfied, and unhappy" Beta Israel priests.

The importance of this medical-theological trope can best be understood by contrasting it with the nearly contemporaneous evaluation of Beta Israel bodies by the Jewish writer Joseph Halévy, who had come to Ethiopia in 1867 on a fact-finding mission for the French Alliance Israélite Universelle and who merely noted in passing that "the priests are fairer than the other Falashas because of the benefits of working indoors, out of the sun" (Halévy 1877, 255). For Halévy, Beta Israel ascetic practice was a positive expression of their commitment to "ancient Mosaic observances" (ibid., 217), so it is hardly surprising that when Halévy met the important Beta Israel priest Abba Menassie at a village near Walkait in 1867, he described him simply as "a man of mature age, with a majestic mien, and a light complexion" (ibid.). Narrative aesthetic and religious ideology are here almost indistinguishable, reflecting the different ways in which Western Jews and Christians began to perceive Beta Israel bodies over time. Stern was not well liked, even by some of his fellow missionaries, because of his strident tone (Crummey 1972). But his overwhelming concern with the aesthetic and health consequences of ascetic practice was far from merely idiosyncratic. His sometime colleague J. M. Flad wrote that ascetic monks come to look "like the very old women of the country, so wrinkled and haggard and unnatural do their faces become under the privations they endure" (1869, 33).

The modernizing vision of LJS missionaries like Henry Aaron Stern was informed by a powerful Victorian ethos of moral balance, emotional reserve, and purposeful mastery of the natural world (see Danahay 1993, 117–145). The health of individuals and societies was conceived as a "state of constitutional growth and development ... under the direct motive power of vital energy, or the indirect power of the moral will" (Haley 1978, 21). Asceticism and hedonism, by contrast, could both be described as "diseases of the mind leading to the fatalist ruin" because they are the "concentration of man upon himself, whether his heavenly interests or his worldly interests matters not ... while every healthy state of nations and of individual minds consists in the unselfish presence of the human spirit ... energizing over all things" (ibid., 48). In reading these narratives for their cultural import, we must make ourselves aware of the "basic forms, imageries, and rhetorical frames that make up the fictions of a body" (Desjarlais 1995, 210) in the specialized moral discourse employed by self-conscious agents of change like Henry Aaron Stern. The aesthetic and moral dimensions of religious life cannot always be easily distinguished, and for LJS missionaries the abject failure of Beta Israel religion to provide health for body and mind amounted to a call for radical conversionary rebirth that only European Christians could facilitate. Religious change is often organized around the transformation of modes of attention through which bodies are perceived, ordered, and even experienced subjectively over time (see B. Turner 1980; Kleinman and Kleinman 1987; Csordas 1990), and nowhere has this been truer than with respect to Beta Israel transformations in the modern world.

Contesting Ritual

There is no Beta Israel chronicle of Abba Mahari's first meeting with Henry Stern. On the basis of missionary narratives alone, however, it is possible to piece together some outlines of a Beta Israel response. It is telling, for instance, that while Stern consistently describes Beta Israel habitations as a source of disease and pestilence, Beta Israel sometimes reversed the accusation, as they did during an epidemic at Genda in 1852. "No Abyssinians came near our abodes," complained the missionary Bronkhurst, "everyone saying that there was *Beshitta* [plague] in the dwellings of the Europeans" (*Jewish Records*, January 1862, 2). Similarly, at the end of their first meeting, Stern presented Abba Mahari with a gilt-edged Bible and a white dress, in honor, he said, of "Abyssinian custom" (Stern 1862/1968, 251). These gifts, however, were far from customary. The distribution of vernacular (Amharic) Bibles, together with public disputations such as the one Stern had hoped to instigate with Abba Mahari, were key tools in missionary efforts to diminish the charismatic authority of monks and priests, who were typically unskilled debaters and held a monopoly on the comprehension of traditional Ge'ez language texts used by Beta Israel. It is telling, therefore, that while Abba Mahari is said to have received these gifts with a great show of gratitude, even Stern acknowledged that he refused to accept them from the missionary's polluted hand, thus effectively reversing the symbolic amplitude of the exchange. Stern may have recognized the contingency of this first encounter; he writes that Abba Mahari turned to him and proclaimed in a "halting and tremulous voice" that "[e]ither you shall become one of us, or I shall become one of you" (ibid.).

Abba Mahari became one of the most outspoken opponents of the missionary endeavor and took part in more than one attempt to foil the missionaries by leading Beta Israel in migration away from the areas frequented by evangelists. In 1874, J. M. Flad reported that an announcement had been made in Beta Israel houses of prayer that "Abba Maharee invites all those who wish to die as Falasha to leave West Abyssinia, and to follow him to a place of refuge" (S. Kaplan 1992b, 137). More famously still, Mahari was among the leaders of a disastrous exodus toward the Holy Land in 1862, when he became convinced that "the time is near when God will gather the Jews from among all the nations into the land of their fathers" (S. Kaplan 1992b, 135–138; Quirin 1992, 156–160; Ben-Dor 1987). It was no doubt partly a reflection of these efforts by Abba Mahari and other monks that no more than perhaps .01 percent of the Beta Israel population are estimated to have converted to Christianity in any given year during the nineteenth century (S. Kaplan 1992b, 218). By 1894, after over thirty years of effort, missionaries reported only 1,470 Beta Israel converts (ibid.). Those who did convert were drawn disproportionately from certain marginal groups, including poor youths attracted to the promise of free education.

Another group that seems to have converted in disproportionate numbers were deacons, or *debteroch*, who were known for their proficiency at magical and potentially heterodox forms of healing, including divination and amulet writing (Levine 1965, 170; Young 1975, 1977). Many *debteroch* were in fact men who had trained for the priesthood but been disqualified because of defects, including physical deformities. Flad (1869, 32) noted that "the [Beta Israel] *Debtera* for the most part attend the Christian schools," and Shelemay (1992) has shown that this allowed *debteroch* to become important conduits of information and social exchange between the two religious communities. Some of the most prominent Beta Israel converts to Christianity were in fact *debteroch* like Neguse, who had been appointed as guide to Henry Stern by none other than Abba Mahari himself, and Beru, who went on to become an important "native agent."[2] There is reason to think—and Stern certainly thought—that one of the features attracting *debteroch* to the evangelists was their rejection of the monk's bodily and ascetic ideal, with which they had been unable to compete:

> *Debterah Negousee*, an honest and candid *Falasha*, told me he knew a priest who threw himself into a boisterous river flowing through *Armatgioho*, but as the current was very strong . . . he was drifted ashore in a state of stupor. The self-immolating ascetic, when consciousness returned, felt deeply afflicted at this escape from premature death . . . Those who inflict on themselves all the tortures and wasting agonies that frail humanity can endure,

are regarded by the common people with great veneration; although others, and particularly the *debterahs*, or learned class, consider them proud, arrogant, and self righteous fanatics. (Stern 1862/1968, 196)

By framing their attack on Beta Israel religious life through the prism of a contested *technique du corps* (Mauss 1935/1979), LJS missionaries attempted to provoke a crisis in leadership that would favor the ideals of individualistic faith, literacy, and modernization that were essential to their own embodied worldview. The attack was directed not just at Beta Israel but also at Orthodox Christianity, and Stern was delighted when he provoked the Emperor Tewodoros himself to call the priests who attended him "simpletons and blockheads" for trying to teach the king about fasting while inadvertently demonstrating their ignorance of Scripture (*Jewish Intelligence*, September 1, 1869, 219).

Tewodoros resonated sympathetically with the missionaries' evangelistic and modernizing program but also tried to harness them to his own purposes, including the quest for military technology from Europe (Crummey 1969, 1972; Zewde 1991, 31–35). The result was an unstable alliance, and in 1863 Tewodoros took Stern and his party captive during a dispute over their inability to deliver on the king's expectations of substantial British military aid (Stern 1869). They were held until 1868, when a British-Indian military force under Lord Napier was dispatched to free them. Tewodoros committed suicide at his stronghold, Magdalah, rather than submit to capture, and left a note bewailing his people's failure to modernize along European lines (Rubenson 1966, 83). Modernizing and rationalizing disciplines and perspectives promoted by missionaries in religious contexts often had political or military applications. The tragedy of Tewodoros was in some sense that he grasped too clearly the inner relationship between the two and sought to use the offer of one as leverage to achieve the other. The mission to the Beta Israel may not have been the largest or the most numerically successful of the European missionary projects in the Horn of Africa at the time, but it quickly managed to upset and transform conditions for life among the Beta Israel while inadvertently also serving as a wedge for the European conquest of this proud African kingdom. Britain did not attempt to hold Ethiopia as a colony at this time, but the crisis engendered by Stern and the LJS helped to promote a complicated restructuring of political and religious relationships between Europe and Africa that continued well into the twentieth century.

"Kinsmen According to the Flesh"

LJS opposition to ascetic practice and the promotion of modernizing bodily and economic conceptions were not the only ways in which contests over the meaning and interpretation of bodies came to define the European encounter with

Beta Israel during this period. Like many other missionaries, Stern depicted Christian Abyssinians as racially superior to the darker-skinned "pagan" Africans found elsewhere on the continent (Stern 1862/1968, 310–314). Because they were considered taxonomically intermediate between black Africa and white Europe, Stern also encouraged Ethiopians to approximate European cultural and hygienic models that might offset the infirmities of their race (cf. Bratlinger 1985). But Beta Israel were subject to a far more intimate discourse of bodily recognition than most Africans because Stern insisted on portraying them racially as kin:

> In physiognomy, most of the *Falashas* bear striking traces of their Semitic origin. Among the first group we saw at *Gondar*, there were some whose Jewish features no one could have mistaken, who had ever seen the descendants of Abraham either in London or Berlin. Their complexion is a shade paler than that of the Abyssinians, and their eyes, although black and sparkling, are not so disproportionately large as those which characteristically mark the other occupants of the land. (1862/1968, 197)

This was an extraordinary statement for a European evangelist in Africa, especially when we recall that Stern himself was a "descendant of Abraham" who was thereby claiming an unprecedented degree of racial affinity with this community. And unlike the process of "aryanization" to which some communities elsewhere in Africa may have been subject during the colonial period (Barnes 1997), this racial logic was grounded primarily in theological models of the relationship between race and Jewishness.

Writers for the London Society for Promoting Christianity Amongst the Jews had been preoccupied for decades with the problem of Jewish religious and racial distinctiveness. Charles James's 1843 *Annual Sermon* argued that "the existence of the Jewish nation, intermingled with all other nations, yet entirely distinct from them, is justly spoken of as a standing evidence for the truth of Christianity."[3] The distinction of Jews on a metaphysical plane was, moreover, mirrored in a perception of distinctive physiognomy validated by scriptural interpretation. The distinction between "Jew and Greek" wrote the Reverend F. Goode in 1835, is true "in a spiritual view," since although "both [Jews and Greeks] are equally precious," nevertheless "the Jew may have his particular privileges as a Jew. . . . All the members [of the Lord's family] united in one body, and yet not every member capable of sustaining the same office" (Goode 1835, 16). Did Stern recognize himself in the 1843 sermon describing the grief of the converted Jew Paul over the continuing disbelief "of his own countrymen?" Indeed, LJS sermons emphasized the pathos of converted Jews who had found the true faith yet sought to maintain the moral solidarity of their racial or national Jewishness: "I could wish myself separated from Christ for my brethren, my kinsmen according to the flesh" (ibid., 4).

This model of the relationship between Jewish religious and national distinctiveness had important practical ramifications for missionaries in Ethiopia, because LJS writers believed that the single greatest impediment to conversion was the long history of Christian anti-Semitism that lent support to the Jewish view of converts as traitors. "Our agents go to work to win the hearts of the Jews," wrote W. T. Gidney in 1914, "and to persuade them that we do not want them to cast off their national and race distinctions, but that we wish them only to be Christian Israelites" (69–70). The opening of a critical space between racial and religious Jewishness was at the very heart of the LJS project. Thus, in July of 1861, Stern introduced himself as kin in a racial sense to one of the first Beta Israel groups he encountered. "The announcement that we were Felashas," Stern wrote for readers back home, "afforded them ineffable delight, and with their dark eyes riveted on me they gazed and gazed, till at last their silent amazement vented itself in the ejaculation, 'He looks indeed like a son of Israel, like a true child of Jacob!'" This is Stern's only report to claim that Beta Israel themselves asserted the existence of a shared Israelite physiognomy, and the veracity of this claim may be questioned. He also asserts, however, that Beta Israel emphasized their racial difference from other Jews by referring to his party as "white Christian Felasha from beyond Jerusalem" (*Jewish Intelligence*, July 1, 1861, 174).

At a time when prevalent anti-Semitic discourse in Europe often portrayed Jews as Negroid (Gilman 1991, 99–101), it is perhaps significant that the philo-Semitic evangelism of Henry Stern identified the Beta Israel as relatively—but only relatively—white (cf. Goldstein 2006; Brodkin 1999; Azoulay 1997). Stern employs a shifting racial discourse that sometimes claims identity with the Beta Israel and sometimes highlights his own whiteness for a white, evangelical audience. When "one or two querulous priests" from Defatcha claimed that they were Levites descended from biblical Aaron, Stern "merely told them that their black faces contradicted their pretensions. This was considered a conclusive argument, and for more than an hour we uninterruptedly expounded to them the great scope of Divine revelation" (*Jewish Intelligence*, July 1, 1861, 182). This whole theme is missing from similar accounts by Stern's non-Jewish missionary colleague J. M. Flad, who assumes the Jewish descent of the Beta Israel (Flad 1869, 1) but assimilates them racially to "black" Ethiopia (ibid., 25). It is possible that the racial discourse of Jewishness was especially attractive to missionaries of Jewish extraction—just as it was to highly secularized French Jews—because it gave them a way of talking about their sentiments of attachment to other Jews without denying their radical religious alienation from Judaism.

Race provided a convenient but not uncontested alternative to religion as a language of Jewish solidarity throughout the nineteenth century. The Alliance Israélite Universelle (AIU), which sponsored Joseph Halévy's fact-finding mission to the Beta Israel in 1867, has been described as the first Jewish organization in Western Europe to argue for transnational solidarity between Jews on what amounted to a modern ethnic or racial (rather than traditional religious) basis, expressed through its philanthropic concern for "distant brothers" (Albert 1982, 260). The mission of the AIU was to defend Jewish interests around the world and, like the LJS, to work for the "regeneration" of co-religionists in the East. Post-Holocaust discomfort with the idea of a racialized Judaism ought not blind us to the effects of this rhetorical convention among many nineteenth-century Jews. Indeed, race has been called the "only semantic framework" in late nineteenth century France "within which all Jews [including the highly acculturated] could express their feelings of Jewish identity" (Marrus 1971, 26). Yet unlike Henry Stern, the AIU assumed that the racial basis of Jewish solidarity would mediate against the missionary claim of Beta Israel Jewishness, and it expected Halévy to support the contention that Beta Israel were not in fact Jews. Halévy surprised and chagrined his sponsors by quietly insisting instead that the Beta Israel were "brothers" who should be thought of primarily as "co-religionists" rather than racial compatriots. A careful reading of his 1877 *Travels to Abyssinia* makes it clear that apparent *ritual* embodiments of shared commitment and memory supplant race as the single most important field of signs in which a profound sense of Jewish kinship between Beta Israel and other Jews might be discerned.

Halévy was careful to conceal his own Jewishness from the Christians and Muslims he met in Ethiopia because of the danger he perceived in revealing his true identity (1877, 213). Ironically, his first encounter with Beta Israel was with two mission converts, only one of whom, he said, could be described as "slightly resembling the Jewish cast of countenance," while the other was "altogether black" (ibid., 196). This did not deter him, though, and when he next chanced upon a group of unconverted Beta Israel at a public market, he whispered to avoid being overheard:

> "Are you Jews?" They seemed not to understand my question, which I repeated under another form—"Are you Israelites?" A movement of assent, mingled with astonishment, proved to me that I had struck the right chord. . . . I resolved to visit, as soon as possible, the quarter where they resided. (Ibid.)

So much effort has been spent debating the Jewishness of the Beta Israel over the past hundred years that we sometimes forget what a tentative thing it was for foreign Jews to be accepted as kin or even allies by Beta Israel during these early, tentative meetings. Like Stern, Halévy was subjected to a veritable choreography of strangeness and impurity:

> Men and women cried out in astonishment at the sight of my complexion and of my dress. I was politely asked to go back and enter a hut where several men were sitting together. On my arrival, they saluted me and surrounded

me, though at a considerable distance. They seemed uncomfortable, and when I wished to go near them, they drew back. Only two persons ventured to grasp my hand in a friendly manner, while the others called out "Atedresbeni!" (Touch us not!). A man attired in a long tunic, and holding a small dish containing water, examined me from head to foot without uttering a single word. This cold reception was beginning to be unpleasant to me; I could not understand their strange ways, but I determined to be patient. (Halévy 1877, 214)

Unlike Stern, Halévy ultimately concludes not with repugnance at the false asceticism of Beta Israel but with pleasant surprise that "these ancient Mosaic observances [are] still in force in Abyssinia" (ibid., 217).

Halévy's identification with Beta Israel religious practice came to occupy a roughly equivalent place in his narrative to the one occupied by racial identity in Stern's. When some of the gathered Beta Israel refer to him as "a European," he corrects them: "You must know, my dear brethren, that I am also a Falasha! I worship no other God than the great Adonai, and I acknowledge no other law than the law of Sinai!" (ibid., 215). Where Stern reassures his readers that Beta Israel "looked Jewish," Halévy pauses to dwell on their incredulity that there could ever be a "white Falasha," and his own response that "all the Falashas of Jerusalem and in other parts of the world were white . . . [and] could not be distinguished from the other inhabitants of their respective countries." Yet the erasure of racial identity from Halévy's narrative only serves to highlight the religious dimension that takes its place:

> The name of Jerusalem, which I had accidentally mentioned, changed as if by magic the attitude of the most incredulous. . . ."Oh, do you come from Jerusalem, the blessed city? Have you beheld with you own eyes Mount Zion and the House of the Lord of Israel, the Holy Temple?" . . . I must confess that I was deeply moved on seeing those black faces light up at the mention of our glorious history. (Ibid.)

My suspicion is that Halévy was familiar with missionary accounts and sought to counter them directly in these passages. The very point in the narrative where racial affinity appears in Stern's account of first contact with Beta Israel is here substituted by a specific dismissal of missionary claims. Halévy's Beta Israel specifically call the rhetoric of lost brothers into question, because "They [the missionaries] also said that they were Falashas and brethren; but as soon as they won our confidence, they began to preach to us of the Trinity according to the belief of the Amharas, and sought to turn us from the commandments of the Lord" (ibid., 216).

In the end, Halévy spent only a brief time in Ethiopia, and his importance to the history of the Beta Israel was largely in setting the stage for his student

THE QUESTION OF KINSHIP   57

Jacques Faitlovitch's later, more extensive efforts. Neither he nor Faitlovitch was ever able to put the question of Beta Israel Jewishness decisively to rest among the Jews of Europe or America, and Halévy soon began to complain that his onetime funders at the AIU had turned on him because of his assertion that the Beta Israel really were Jews (S. Kaplan 1992b, 141–142). But Faitlovitch, who came to Ethiopia for the first time in 1904, succeeded to a great degree through sheer perseverance and political organization. Groups like NACOEJ (the North American Conference for Ethiopian Jews) and AAEJ (the American Association for Ethiopian Jews) are the modern successors to the "Pro-Falasha Committees" that he founded in various European and North American cities. A great deal has, justly, been written about Faitlovitch, but I want to restrict myself here very briefly to those aspects of his career that relate most directly to the question of kinship. Faitlovitch surpassed his teacher in defending the thesis that Beta Israel were Jews who deserved support and solidarity from Jews abroad. Unlike Halévy, however, he did so by marshalling religious as well as racial arguments.

Like Stern, Faitlovitch affirms the taken-for-granted racial Jewishness of Beta Israel, but like Halévy, he also must contend with the mistrust engendered among many Beta Israel by Christian missionaries claiming on the basis of racial affinity to be Jews:

> I first came into contact with Falashas at Axoum, the ancient capital of Ethiopia. What struck me first when I told them that I was one of their brothers was their sentiment of extreme reserve, I might even say the distrust and incredulity, with which they received my statements. "Every time a European comes to see us," they declared, "he proclaims himself a Jew; but that is only in order to act on us the more surely and to convert us." . . . Gradually, however, I succeeded in inducing them to abandon their reserve, and at length I dissipated their distrust.(*Jewish Chronicle*, October 27, 1905)

Faitlovitch was an Orthodox Jew, identified with the *mizrahi* (religious Zionist) movement, and although he did attempt to reform aspects of Beta Israel religious practice (I will have more to say about this in chapter 3), he shared none of Stern's automatic antipathy to indigenous ritual. Indeed, he called this practice—including its strongly ascetic dimensions—"hygienic" because it purportedly protected them from the deleterious effects of the African climate as well as miscegenation among local people. "These Jews are distinguished from their neighbors," he wrote, "by the persistence of the character of their race, visible in the refinement of their features and the vivacity of their intelligence" (Faitlovitch 1928, 2). It is striking that Stern and Faitlovitch, who each committed themselves to the religious transformation of the Beta Israel during this period, also insisted on Beta Israel foreignness to the racial and religious orders of highland Ethiopia. They differed, however, in that Stern couched his worldview in a call for radical change while Faitlovitch almost always portrayed religious change as a "return" to historical connection and integration with the Jewish people outside of Ethiopia.

Disturbed by Faitlovitch's success at promoting the idea of Beta Israel Jewishness in Ethiopia and abroad after 1904, the AIU responded heavy-handedly by sending its own representative to Ethiopia on a more-or-less predetermined mission to debunk Faitlovitch's claims. This time it chose a Sephardic Jew named Haim Nahum who, though born in Smyrna, had been educated under AIU auspices in Constantinople and groomed for future high office. In fact, Nahum later went on, with AIU support, to serve as chief rabbi of the Ottoman Empire's Jewish *millet* (Quirin 1992, 196) and was the last person to hold that office before the empire's collapse.

Nahum did not arrive in Ethiopia until 1908, and like all of his predecessors, he was impressed by the discipline of purity to which he was subjected at his first meeting, when Beta Israel leaders were unwilling to touch or be touched by him. Lacking Halévy's tolerance for "ancient Mosaic practices" or even Stern and Faitlovitch's sense of racial identity, however, Nahum soon wrote that the experience left him feeling no sense of religious or racial kinship with the Beta Israel (Nahoum 1908). While denial of any and all claims to kinship set him apart from most other European visitors to the Beta Israel at the time, however, it was in his methodological rhetoric that Nahum's uniqueness emerges most clearly. Unsatisfied with the largely impressionistic discussion of race on the part of both Jewish and Christian predecessors, he sought to impose a more scientific racial taxonomy to adjudicate the Jewishness of Beta Israel. He was not, he admitted, qualified to take a position on the contemporary debate between monogenetic and polygenetic accounts of human origins (the question of whether all human beings really do share a common genetic origin). Instead, he wrote laconically from the field on January 9, 1908, his method would involve the much more straightforward comparison of "the two [racial] types, the Ethiopian and the Falasha, and the latter with the Jewish type" (Benbassa 1995, 105).

Despite his appeal to science as the final arbiter of Beta Israel identity, however, Nahum had to admit that he had no special training or tools for the one truly "objective" measure of racial identity that was available: craniometry, or the measurement and comparison of skulls. All that was left, he said, was to settle for "the most practical method suggested by anthropologists, namely the *impressionistic* study of external racial features and anthropometric characteristics" (ibid., 130; emphasis added), by which he meant the methodical measurement and comparison of bodily proportions. Nahum's retreat to the "impressionistic" study of racial features only highlights the comic pretensions of scientific race classifications, and Nahum, predictably, failed even at this improbable goal. "Because of interbreeding," he finally declares in overwrought self-justification, "it is difficult to establish an absolute Falasha type" (ibid., 30). His recommendations to the AIU were to offer limited support for Beta Israel migration to more prosperous regions of Ethiopia, and to avoid the establishment of any schools except trade schools, which would "upset the mental balance of the Falasha race" (ibid., 142). This view was later echoed by the American Reform rabbi George Zepin, who wrote in 1912 that only "industrial education" of the type Booker T. Washington had been advocating for African Americans would be appropriate to the Beta Israel's "primitive state" (Quirin 1992, 197).

All the major Jewish and Christian visitors to the Beta Israel during the late nineteenth and early twentieth centuries were thus consumed by the ultimately insoluble question of kinship, which for Europeans revolved around observations of Beta Israel bodies and bodily practices. Racial ideologies, scientific and otherwise, were especially crucial to this discourse not just because of their general salience in Europe at this time but also because they helped to provide a discursive link between morally weighted social and religious ideologies and their "objective" confirmation in observable bodily reality. In the Beta Israel encounter with Westerners, this was nothing less than the spirit made flesh. But the discursive field was also underdetermined, in the sense that individual writers could manipulate the juxtaposition between race and ritual in a variety of different and apparently contradictory ways. For Faitlovitch, the racial Jewishness and ritual/religious Jewishness of Beta Israel seamlessly reinforced one another, while his teacher Halévy invoked ritual and memory to affirm a Jewishness that was decidedly unracial. At the other extreme, Henry Stern emphasized the racial Jewishness of Beta Israel even as he attacked their inauthentic and to his mind syncretistic religious practice, while Haim Nahum denied the Jewishness of Beta Israel on both racial and religious grounds. What all of these writers shared were the symbolic and metaphoric terms—focusing on interpretations of the Beta Israel body—within which the question of kinship could be formulated. Their disagreement over the correct answer to that question should not blind us to the common cultural project in which they all were engaged.

We have yet to consider the Beta Israel response to religious transformation during this period, but it is worth concluding this chapter with a nod to the American linguist Wolf Leslau, who revisited some of these themes during a visit to Ethiopia in 1949. Leslau visited a number of Beta Israel villages during his stay and later wrote about them for the bimonthly journal of the American Jewish Congress, *Commentary*. "When I first saw the Falashas," he writes, "I asked myself whether I would be able to distinguish them from other Ethiopians, whether they possessed distinctive physiognomical features of their own." The questioning tone of this account distinguishes it from those of predecessors like Stern or Faitlovitch, who were all more or less convinced of the outcome before they started. Leslau said he was unsure whether he thought that the Beta Israel he met resembled their immediate Amhara neighbors or an "Agau tribe" he had encountered in Eritrea, but he certainly never invokes "the sons of Jacob in Berlin or London" as Henry Stern did. More interesting is that Leslau may have been the first visitor to ask the Beta Israel themselves what they thought about the question of physical distinctiveness from their neighbors and countrymen. "The Falashas themselves," Leslau writes, "believe that they look like the rest of the Ethiopian population; indeed, one Falasha informed me that Ethiopians say that they can recognize a Falasha only by the heavy mineral odor of water which clings to him as a result of his incessant ritual ablutions" (Leslau 1949, 217). Yet such "ritual ablutions" could only be transformed into marks of visceral difference (the characteristic smell of *ye-ouha Falasha*, or "water Falashas") through a presumed intimacy of local social relations that Stern and Faitlovitch were each eager to deny.

To the extent that Beta Israel have been rendered "Ethiopian Jews" in the distinctively modern sense of that word, it has been through the choice of specific interpretive frames that were to some extent contingent, like subjective and culturally influenced measures of race or of ritual and religious similarity and difference. This is in no way to belittle claims of kinship that hold life and death significance for those who make them and are often fiercely defended. On the contrary, it is to understand something of their force and power that we must also understand in what ways they were, and may remain even today, contested. Certainly the attempt to make clear and objective distinctions between "true" and counterfeit "Falasha" (as I described in chapter 1) looks different when we realize just how complex and problematic the assertion of kinship between *any* Beta Israel and their Western Jewish counterparts has been. Missionaries and counter-missionaries to the Beta Israel were almost all deeply moved by doctrines of transcendent Jewish distinctiveness and by the modernizing redemptive projects of colonizing evangelism on one hand and Zionist "ingathering of exiles" on the other. Neither of these projects has ever been brought to completion, of course, and their respective instabilities have served as the shifting platforms upon which other cultural projects—like the "Feres Mura" return to Judaism—have also been imperfectly superimposed. My attempt to frame the history of the Beta Israel in these terms, rather than in the chronological and inductive style of most historical accounts, has both theoretical and political motives.

First, it is my hope that focusing analytic concern on the social constructions of bodies and bodily practices through conceptions of race and ritual practice may help us to formulate questions that bring us closer, as Werbner (1997, 324) has suggested, to "underlying problems of identity, the self, and the nature of subjectivity" that will be more useful than the constant wrangling over contentious oppositions between traditional and modern, or authentic and inauthentic cultural and religious expressions. Explicitly, I want to shift the conversation about Beta Israel away from the perplexing question of origins, with its immediate and perhaps inevitable leakage into the bureaucratic question of "true identity," and toward a greater appreciation of contingency in the history of the present. I am less interested as an anthropologist in establishing the past than I am in trying to trace the contours of that past in the crystalline structures of the ethnographic here-and-now, where the Ethiopian Jews, "Feres Mura," and Beta Israel Pentecostals that I have come to know all struggle to define themselves—and also struggle just to get by. The frantic "Feres Mura" debate that has colored Israeli public life over the last two decades is just one instantiation of a much broader set of cultural dilemmas occasioned by the encounter between Beta Israel and other Jews. It is not possible to understand the "Feres Mura" dilemma without first locating it as a single point in a broad continuum of debates over kinship and belonging that have taken place in earnest over the past 150 years since missionaries dedicated to evangelizing Jews first arrived in Ethiopia.

CHAPTER 3

PURITY OF HEART

"Purity of heart is to will one thing."
—Søren Kierkegaard, *Purity of
Heart is to Will One Thing*

The question of kinship could not, by its nature, be answered once and for all by men like Jacques Faitlovitch or Henry Aaron Stern. Both men invoked the fragile certainties of race but also demonstrated by their own example just how delicate an interpretive construct "race" can be. The question of kinship between Beta Israel and foreign Jews derives its hard moral edge precisely from the fact that here an epistemological difficulty meets a moral conundrum. In the absence of truly objective and unqualified criteria, how should different communities decide how far to extend the bonds of solidarity and affiliation, when this is conceived to be much more than a merely strategic decision for mutual aid? These questions were often framed in racial terms when they concerned the relationship between Beta Israel and European Jews, but where Beta Israel converts to Christianity were concerned, matters of the flesh often gave way to matters of the soul, which is to say questions of agency and desire. Instead of focusing on the alleged similarity of racial or ritual patterns, in other words, the question of kinship for Beta Israel converts and their descendants has been inflected by the even more delicate matter of intentionality in religious conversion, which amounts to a quest for "purity of heart."

THE ANXIETY OF SUCCESS

The first foreigners to concern themselves in a sustained way with the intentionality of converted Beta Israel were, of course, the Christian missionaries from Western Europe who evangelized them. Beginning in the 1860s, missionary and counter-missionaries brought about what Quirin (1992, 165) has called a "splintering of the Beta Israel," which is an aptly violent metaphor for the hard choices that all Beta Israel were now forced to face. They could affiliate with Western Judaism, convert to Christianity or reject both options out of fidelity to their ancestral religious practice. All three trends can still be found among today's Beta Israel, although it seems fair to say that the traditionalist option has lost the most ground. Although there are Beta Israel priests and others today who reject the authority of the Israeli rabbinate or who encourage the maintenance of Beta Israel ritual patterns, even they have for the most part accepted the idea of their membership in a global Jewish community whose practical center is in Israel. Indeed, the only workable alternatives to accommodation with global Judaism over the past century have proven to be either some form of conversion to Christianity or else passive assimilation to the dominant (and diffusely Christian) Amharic culture of modern Ethiopia.

Conversion to Christianity was not rapid during the early days of missionary work. It took Stern and his party fully two years to achieve their first baptisms of 22 Beta Israel. In 1868, the missionaries still claimed only 65 converts, a number that rose to 1,470 (out of a total estimated population of between 50,000 and 100,00) by 1894 (S. Kaplan 1992b, 128). Rather than laboring to overcome Beta Israel resistance to conversion in large numbers, however, Stern and his colleagues set out to create separate and self-sustaining, but necessarily small communities of "Falasha Christians," whose intercourse with nonconverted brethren could be more easily managed, and whose commitment to the true faith could be constantly monitored and strengthened. Paradoxically, this also made it easier for those converts who later returned to Judaism to gain acceptance as Jews, because of the presumption by some rabbis that converts had tended to marry only among themselves. Missionaries were, however, more concerned with ideological than genealogical purity.

"At Genda itself," Stern wrote as early as 1861, "three of the best informed Jews we met on our whole tour candidly avowed their solemn conviction of the truth of the Gospel, and their determination to secede from their *mesgeed*, as their synagogue is called; in fact, I feel fully persuaded that that if our agents act diligently in faith ... they will ere long be able to collect around them a congregation of believing Felashas" (*Jewish Intelligence*, April 1, 1861, 91). "Solemn conviction," "separation," and "secession" from broader kinship and religious networks are the watchwords of missionary zeal, together with "diligent" and "faithful" action by converts in evangelizing their unconverted brethren. These were urgent objectives for the missionaries, both because of their continuous need for inspirational stories that would spur their readers in Europe to increased generosity and because these themes were central to the evangelical model of intensive religious change. Early missionaries wanted to create an ongoing and permanent religious revolution among missionized Beta Israel, just as later Pentecostal advocates (see chapter 5) would do. This was a marked departure from the ethos of traditional Beta Israel and other Jewish communities, which tended to place a greater emphasis on notions of ritual fidelity than on the "solemn conviction of truth" and spiritual rebirth championed by men like Stern.

Keeping the new flock together was not always easy. "Many of the Falasha converts work for cattle and sheep owners," lamented Reverend T. L. Gidney (1914, 121), "and as these move about a great deal they are hard to be traced and followed up." The London Jewish Society (LJS) had by this time established three different mission stations at which converts could support themselves through traditional Beta Israel occupations like weaving and could be "settled down, so that one can work amongst them with greater regularity" (ibid.). Gidney estimated there were between 1,700 and 1,800 converts at the time. We have already seen that the idea of controlled settlements combining subsistence work with religious instruction was also adopted by Jewish organizations who took responsibility for the return to Judaism of "Feres Mura" starting in the early 1990s. Like the evangelists whose work they sought to undo, these twentieth-century Jewish groups were also concerned with potential "backsliding" and anxious to demonstrate the authentic sincerity of their Beta Israel protégés to religious and financial backers in North America. This is probably the result of "convergent evolution" rather than any self-conscious attempt to emulate missionary strategies. Missionaries themselves were continually preoccupied with the periodic loss of converts to competing denominations as well as the return of converts to their unconverted Beta Israel communities, and insisted that their teachings be continually reinforced to avoid this problem (Trevisan Semi 2002).

Early evangelists were seized by what might be described as an "anxiety of success," so eager were they to show that those who converted were only the most sincere and single-minded of individuals, whose personal self-transformation was rooted in a highly abstract notion of free and unhindered moral will. "In places where we passed the night or stayed some days on account of the numbers assembled," wrote J. M. Flad in the 1860s, "we were so overwhelmed with visitors that even Mr. Stern's large tent could not contain them all.... It was a blessed thing for us to be able to satisfy the spiritual hunger and thirst of our numerous visitors with the Word of Life." Yet not all visitors were motivated by the same austere spiritual motives, and some begged for "clothing, mules or money." Such requests were apparently a source of embarrassment to Flad, who insists that they were invariably refused: "we only relieved those who were really poor, sick, blind, or suffering" (*Jewish Intelligence*, September 1, 1869). True suffering and true religious motivation were occasionally conflated in missionary narratives, but this is not surprising given the persistent missionary theme of religious rebirth as the only answer to human suffering and anguish.

Another and possibly less obvious reason for missionaries to focus upon the purity of will among proselytes was the need to refute Beta Israel claims that missionaries exercised malignant agency, coercion, or even witchcraft in winning converts to the new faith. Like Jews in Europe (Carlebach 2001), Beta Israel often responded to the conversion of their kin with an almost reflexive attribution of ulterior motives and spoiled agency to both the missionaries and their acolytes. Debterah Neguse, whose conversion I discussed in chapter 2, visited Henry Stern before his conversion in 1861 with disturbing news about how the missionary message was being received:

> After some sighs and vacant glances, Negousee narrated that there was a rumour among the Felashas, that although we spoke kind and comfortable words, our object was to force them to become Christians; and that if this was really our intention, he had been instructed by his people to inform us, that all, young and old, women and children, would resist such an attempt even to the death; but if, on the contrary, (and they would believe us if we said so,) we had come to instruct them in the Word of God, and to teach them our faith, they would welcome us to their villages, listen to our instructions, and joyfully believe every truth contained in the revelation of God. (*Jewish Intelligence* July 1, 1861, 175–176)

Willingness to suffer martyrdom or suicide rather than submit to religious coercion has been a long-standing theme of Beta Israel self-representation, which continues today in Israel. Stern responded to Beta Israel fears at the time by rehearsing the fundamental missionary commitment to free-willed religious transformation and by attributing any fears the Beta Israel might harbor to the nefarious machinations of "bigoted, intolerant and lying" local Christians, "who delighted in creating distrust and suspicion." The missionaries would never administer baptism, Stern insisted, without "previous instruction and unmistakable evidences of conviction and conversion" (*Jewish Intelligence* July 1, 1861, 175–176).

Stern did not succeed in allaying all the fears of many Beta Israel, and relations between Beta Israel and missionaries soon worsened. In 1862 a group of Beta Israel priests excommunicated a boy named Kindy Fanta along with his parents when the boy acknowledged that he was planning to be baptized under missionary auspices.[1] Kindy Fanta responded to insult with insult, uttering an oath on the life of the Emperor Tewodoros—*be-Tewodoros yemot!*—abjuring the Beta Israel from offering their animal sacrifices. The whole matter was eventually referred to the governor of Dembeya Province, who called for a public disputation between missionaries and Beta Israel, in Tewodoros's presence. Accounts of the disputation vary, but it is not surprising that missionaries focused on their critique of Beta Israel ritual while Beta Israel (with some necessary circumscription) disputed the belief in the Trinity (Leslau 1947).

Although both sides claimed a measure of victory, even Beta Israel admitted that theirs was somewhat pyrrhic. Tewodoros gave them a period of four years to reconsider their refusal to convert, after which their sacrificial worship would be proscribed by law. Tewodoros's later defeat and suicide prevented the decree from being fulfilled, but this episode led to a considerable degree of fear and upheaval in Beta Israel life and marked the end of whatever tolerance they may have shown for missionary activity in their midst (S. Kaplan 1992b, 128). There is no evidence that the missionaries themselves supported efforts to curtail Beta Israel religion by force of law, but the real-world implications of their attempts to divide the traditional community on the basis of religion could no longer be ignored.

Although the missionary commitment to a model of free-willed and independent religious agency would naturally tend to emphasize the conversion of individuals, missionaries tried to convert whole family groups in practice whenever possible, because of the difficulty they would otherwise face in separating individuals from their kin groups. Indeed, the Beta Israel priests who excommunicated Kindy Fanta were supported in doing so by his uncle, and Beta Israel resistance to conversion was most effective when the kin of converts could be mobilized to ostracize them in this way (S. Kaplan 1987). Given the gender biases that Europeans brought with them to Ethiopia, the rhetoric of individual self-transformation made most sense when it was applied to male heads of household, and missionaries were sometimes hesitant to accept the conversions of women whose husbands did not want to join them. Near the town of Tshanker in 1904, missionaries encountered a woman who came to them asking for baptism, who said that her husband wished to "die in the religion in which we were born" (*Jewish Missionary Intelligence*, July 1904, 102). She complained that if she converted, her husband would curse her and keep most of their property as well as their children, so evangelists recommended that she go back to him unbaptized in the hope that one day she might transform his heart.

In another account, the native agent Gochu Beleta encountered a woman who had fled to the lowlands to escape fighting between Ethiopians and Sudanese dervishes during the 1880s. She became estranged from her husband, who did not wish to embrace Christianity, but Beleta encouraged her to reconcile and return to him (ibid., January 1900, 12). LJS agents may well have been concerned about the financial strain that unmarried female proselytes would place upon their already stretched resources, but neither should we underestimate the power of bourgeois European gender norms to inform or even constrain the evangelical project. Stern (1869, 316) himself wrote with open frustration about the failure of his efforts to force the Ethiopians in his employ to obey European norms of gendered work.

As communities of converts spread across the countryside, missionaries began to rely increasingly upon "native agents" or converted Beta Israel who had been trained for the hard work of opening new areas to proselytism or keeping contact with scattered communities of converts. While they were inevitably less well educated than their European counterparts, native agents often could relate to fellow Ethiopians in ways that their European counterparts could not. In chapter 2, I described Henry Stern's assessment of the traditional healing spring at Wanzagie as an "ill-famed home of savage harpies," but the converted debteras Ain Alem and Negusei brought their own sick children there in 1904, using it as an opportunity to combine familiar Beta Israel tropes of healing through purification and cleansing with missionary emphasis on literacy, Bibles, and purity of heart:

> Early we went down to the hot spring; some of the proselytes went with us. There we found a great many people from far and near.... Some did honor to us, others scolded us. We made the best use of our time. We took our Bibles, invited every one who likes to hear the Word of God, and day after day, the number of our listeners increased.... It was sowing in hope. (*Jewish Missionary Intelligence*, July 1904, 102)

Sites of religious pilgrimage and healing have frequently been sites for religious mixing and transformation in Ethiopia (A. Pankhurst 1994; Ben-Dor 1985), and here we see mixing of a particularly robust kind between Beta Israel proselytes, native missionaries, and unconverted Beta Israel that Stern himself could not have imagined. Yet native agents were not immune to problems of their own, including rejection and displays of anger or violence by former neighbors and kin.

In 1908, two converted *debteroch* named Sanbatu and Beleta undertook a round of preaching in the Tshelga region from which numerous "Feres Mura" of my acquaintance would later emigrate. Peripatetic visits to the scattered Beta Israel converts by both missionaries and their native agents helped to reinforce religious transformation and provided the backdrop for many of the adventure-filled narratives that were constantly being published in missionary journals in Europe. On this occasion, Sanbatu and Beleta visited the village of Debterah Ishanaw, who had converted three years earlier with his family of seven. Since converting, Ishanaw had continued to make his living through the traditional Beta Israel weaver's craft, but he had also begun to preach without charge to the Beta Israel on Saturdays and local Christians on Sundays. He was estranged from his unconverted mother and sisters, however, who lived in poverty that was undoubtedly exacerbated by the loss of a son and brother who might otherwise have supported them. They did not respond well when Ishanaw brought his native agent friends on a visit to his mother's village:

> We had a very bad reception ... The mother began to scold us in very bad language, her daughters and other Falasha women joining her. In a short while the entire Falasha village was in an uproar. The mother cried, "You have stolen my only son from me, and now you come to bewitch us also. None of us will listen to you; we obey our priests, who are living at Goorala." So our dear Ishanaw said that we had better leave them alone. We then left, being cursed and abused with all the bad words our language contains. (*Jewish Missionary Intelligence*, October 1908, 153)

Like the missionaries they emulated, native agents always portrayed themselves as loving and tolerant of their unconverted brethren despite provocation, but the pandemonium caused by the mere presence of native agents in this Beta Israel village helps to illustrate the level of suspicion they engendered.

Accusations of witchcraft against native agents were far from mere hyperbole. They were in fact a direct refutation of the missionaries' core theological assertion of good will toward "Israelites according to the flesh" and an attempt to undermine their portrayal of converts as autonomous individuals who made free-willed redemptive choices. Beleta and Sanbatu knew that they were being insulted but failed to articulate for readers in Europe the true import of this attack on the most basic missionary assertions about converts' pure and uncontaminated hearts. The women's tirade was both a rejection of missionary claims and a skilled reversal of the traditional Christian polemic that portrayed Beta Israel as agents of witchcraft and malevolent transformation. Of all the rhetorical frames available to Beta Israel who resisted conversionary pressure, signs of malevolence among missionaries and ambivalence among converts would have been among the most devastating rebuttals to the missionary focus on purity of heart. I will argue that ambivalence was ultimately more significant to the course of converts' lived experience, but malevolence was certainly the theme more easily assimilated to religious polemics on the Ethiopian plateau.

Malevolence, Ambivalence, and Double-Mindedness

The "splintering of the Beta Israel" into different religious camps was neither neat nor unequivocal. Conversations about conversion and resistance to conversion were part of a much broader cross-religion (and cross-ethnic) discourse on the nature of agency and transformation in which conversion was traditionally invoked alongside witchcraft, evil eye accusations, and the exercise of structural violence that sometimes emerged into open conflict. Although many writers have touched upon this subject, none has shown better than Hagar Salamon (1999) just how central the attribution of malevolent transformation was to relations between Beta Israel and Ethiopian Christians, and it is worth dwelling on this point because I will argue that this culturally overdetermined theme remains central to relations between "Feres Mura" and the state of Israel today.

Salamon argues on the basis of her interviews with Ethiopian-Israelis during the 1980s and early 1990s that an expectation of "malevolent transformation" was at the heart of social relations between Beta Israel and Christians in highland Ethiopia. It was manifest most powerfully in the Christian belief that Beta Israel had the ability to transform themselves into hyenas to attack Christians and eat their corpses. In conditions of deep structural inequality, Christian landholders often acted as patrons to particular Beta Israel families or villages, allowing them to sharecrop the land or to serve as local blacksmiths and potters for Christian farmers. But blacksmithing and pottery making were also closely associated in the cultural imagination of rural Ethiopia with magical transformation of the elements, and this contributed to a sometimes dangerous confluence of social vulnerability and local suspicion (see Reminick 1974; Hoben 1970, 204). Accused of wielding the evil eye (*buda*) against their Christian neighbors, and also long associated with tropes of heresy and Christ killing, Beta Israel were subject to considerable stigma and sometimes physical violence (see Messing 1957; Young 1973). "The kindly Jewish blacksmith who forged your scythe might well turn out to be the hyena who dug up your family funeral plot last night" (Salamon 1999, 8). To this day, Ethiopian Jews I have met describe *buda* accusation as one of the greatest difficulties they faced in Ethiopia, and they distinguish between regions in which the phenomenon was particularly harsh, like Dembeya, and others where it was less consequential. Even in relatively recent times, there have been incidents of *buda* accusations leading to lethal violence against Beta Israel (Quirin 1992, 144; Kessler and Parfitt 1985).

Yet central as these accusations may have been to the experience of insecurity among Beta Israel, they were part of a broader anxiety around issues of transformation and its social consequences. While Christians expressed their anxiety about Beta Israel neighbors through an idiom of malignant agency in self-transformation into hyenas, Beta Israel mocked the transformative pretensions of local Christianity. Thus, the Christian sacrament of communion was especially distasteful to Beta Israel not just because of the ritualistic cannibalism it implied if taken literally—a beautifully symmetrical reversal of the *buda* allegations directed by Christians against them—but also because of the "magical" transformation of persons it seemed to promise. Salamon's informants (1999, 59) complained about the holiday known as *Temqat*, or "baptism," on which Christians would sprinkle holy water on themselves, and sometimes on Jews as well. "This water is a sign of conversion," her informant told her, "that someone was once a Jew or something, and then became Christian." This is similar to the tone of derision I have heard from my own informants describing the *temqat* ritual, but I am convinced that part of the reason for the derision is that baptism is simply incomprehensible to many Beta Israel, because it flouts the strong Beta Israel norm of transformation through slow disciplines of purity and ritual separation over time.

Differing logics of transformation were an explicit component of the angry polemic over "symbolic conversion" that arose for Ethiopian immigrants to Israel during the 1980s, when the Israeli chief rabbis insisted that Beta Israel should clear up lingering doubts about their Jewishness by undergoing a conversion ritual constituted of immersing in a ritual bath or *mikveh* and allowing a drop of blood to be drawn from the men's penis. The requirement for drawing blood was soon dropped under heavy protest, but the demand for immersion remained, and still remains today for those Ethiopian immigrants who want or require the Israeli chief rabbinate's imprimatur. Steven Kaplan (1988b) has already noted that thanks to this controversy, the mythic image of the black-coated ultra-Orthodox rabbi has now replaced the mythic image of the black-frocked Ethiopian priest or Protestant missionary as the agent of malevolent and magical-religious transformation for contemporary Beta Israel. Although a considerable minority of Ethiopians in Israel actually acquiesced to the rabbinate's decree, a majority responded through refusals and protests, through the establishment of their own separatist religious services, and even through threats of violence against fellow Ethiopians. They also became almost obsessively suspicious of supposed rabbinic strategies to trick them into converting.

This was all that many Ethiopian-Israelis were willing to talk with me about during fieldwork in the north of Israel in 1989 (see Seeman 1990). Parents anxiously refused to let their children attend public swimming pools during the heat of the summer and denied them permission to go on class trips out of a nearly universal panic that rabbis would forcibly immerse them without consent. In fact, the parallel between *mikveh* use and baptism was quite direct, because Ethiopian-Israelis routinely translated the Hebrew word *tevilah*, which for Orthodox Jews can mean only ritual immersion in a *mikveh*, with the Amharic word *temqat*, which refers only to Christian baptism. The rhetorical power of the association was obvious, but it was only a few years later, during the intense protest over the "Blood Affair" (see chapter 6), that I came to understand the full import of this usage. One of the leaders of that 1996 protest reminisced with me that he had also been a leader of the protest against the Rabbinate ten years earlier, when he was, paradoxically, working as a government translator for new immigrants. I asked him on a hunch about the confusion of *temqat* with *tevilah* and was only a little surprised when he matter-of-factly took credit for intentionally choosing a translation that he knew would help to inflame the Ethiopian-immigrant population. He was a political operative of substantial sophistication who knew very well how to motivate his base, yet it would be a mistake to ignore the cultural logic that he manipulated to make this translation into such an effective and incendiary strategy.

The *temqat* accusation resonated deeply with many Beta Israel not only because they experienced the Chief Rabbinate's demand for conversion to Judaism as deeply hurtful and humiliating (they already considered themselves to be proud Jews), but also because it came to be perceived as an offensive imposition of foreign sacramental logic. When I pushed my informant on how he justified such an inaccurate translation, he countered without hesitation, "*Temqat* and *mikveh* are the same thing. You think you can change a person by sprinkling water on them like this [he makes a sprinkling gesture with his hand]? The water in the *mikveh* is not pure [Hebrew, *tahor*], it doesn't flow." The scandalous association of baptism and Jewish immersion was premised for him not just on the fact that neither *mikveh* nor baptism made use of clear flowing water but on the absurdity of personal transformation divorced from physical purification and washing of the body, or purity of soul without the slow work of ritual disciplines over time. This is less about the infringement of discrete rules of religious practice, in other words, than it is about the violation of deeply held and culturally reinforced intuitions about the nature of personhood and change. Very few people can articulate such intuitions in the abstract, and that is why concrete social controversies like the one over *mikveh* immersion can be so important for analysis. They provide an important context for investigating the nature of transformative logic that is also at the heart of the "Feres Mura" dilemma.

Earlier, I described an episode in which the head of an Ethiopian-Israeli immigrant organization told me heatedly at a community meeting that "*we* [unconverted Beta Israel] are Jewish in our bones," implying that "Feres Mura" seeking to immigrate are not. So it was striking for me that Salamon's informants told her that Beta Israel could not really convert effectively to Christianity because their bones remain Jewish. Indeed, the indelible Jewishness of bones can be contrasted with the inability of mere *temqat* baptism to effect real and lasting transformation of Beta Israel, even in Christian eyes:

> The Christians wanted us to do *temqat* so that we should marry Christians and then we'd have land too. In Wogera they use land three times a year because the soil is very rich.... But their children won't be allowed to marry Christians. If you are *felasmuqra* [Beta Israel converts] ... then you have to find another *felasmuqra* to marry.... In the beginning they tell you that they will let you marry them. Then they finish with the baptism and they don't let you. If someone says "you ate someone" it's remembered for all the coming generations. (Salamon 1999, 67)

This account is typical, in that unconverted Beta Israel tended both to attribute only mercenary rather than sincere religious motives to converts and to insist that even these motives were ultimately frustrated by Christian duplicity. "The Christians still suspect them of eating people's flesh. They think that maybe the converts are worse than those who stayed in their own religion, because those who remained in their own religion are known, so their destructive power doesn't work if you're careful and watch them" (ibid.). The result, according to Salamon's analysis, is that Beta Israel converts were often stuck in a kind of "permanent liminality" (ibid., 65), because they were unable to shed either their Jewish bones or their malevolent hearts, and were often excluded from burial in Christian as well as Beta Israel cemeteries (ibid., 99).

The discrepancy between Salamon's informants, who insisted that converts have Jewish bones, and mine, who insisted that they do not, was not ultimately a result of personal disagreement or alternative cultural traditions, but it did reflect the sometimes neglected importance of context in the conduct of ethnographic fieldwork. My conversations about Jewish bones took place during the middle 1990s or later and were all explicitly related to the problem of "Feres Mura" immigration, which had by then become a major source of controversy within the Ethiopian community. Salamon's interviews were conducted during the previous decade and had no relationship to the potential immigration of former converts; they did focus, however, on the issue of *barya*, the former household slaves of some Beta Israel who immigrated as members of the extended families of their former owners. While *barya* were routinely converted to the religions of their masters in highland Ethiopia, they were also disparaged as marriage partners for *chewa*, or well-born members of those communities; even today it is a deadly insult to refer to a person as *barya* or the descendant of one. Ethiopian-Israelis I knew joked sometimes that Ethiopians who married whites (*farenge*) must have been the descendants of former slaves who could therefore not find acceptable partners within their own Ethiopian community. By insisting that that even converted Beta Israel shared "Jewish bones," but that *barya* did not, they were making a context-dependent assertion about the distance that separated them from low-status former slaves, not an abstract and context free statement about the nature of Jewish bones and identity.

The denial of Jewish bones to "Feres Mura" by a community leader opposed to their immigration is now comprehensible, as is Avraham Neguse's sharp retort to all challengers: "[T]hese people are our flesh, our blood, and our bones" (quoted in Butcher 2007). The Jewishness of bones is, in other words, an idiom of kinship rather than an abstract "cultural belief" or code that can be applied without attention to the interpretive context. Salamon suggests, not without merit, that the Jewishness of bones and the liminal status of Beta Israel converts to Christianity are both evidence of a distinction between religious and ethnic foci of identity, because one remains Beta Israel no matter what one chooses in religious affiliation. The religion/ethnicity distinction is attractive not least because of the theoretical abstraction and cross-cultural comparisons it suggests. Yet making this distinction too neat also constitutes a subtle departure from what Beta Israel themselves have to say about the grounds of belonging and carries unintended analytic consequences that ought to be explored.

While missionaries worked to drive a wedge between what they perceived as distinct religious and racial components of Jewishness, many Beta Israel and other Jewish communities resisted not only conversion itself but also the analytic splitting that makes these categories seem like structural oppositions to a social science schooled in the habits of Protestant taxonomies (Asad 1993; Seeman 2003). Even in today's highly secularized and culturally fractured Jewish world, I am aware of no significant Jewish community that regularly accepts the claims to participation of "Christian Jews" in the Jewish community on purely ethnic grounds. The Israeli High Court decision that Jewishness for purposes of immigration should be limited to those born or converted to Judaism who are not members of another religion (Shaki 1978) is clearly not without problems, but it does seem to reflect what has so far emerged as a rough consensus of modern Jewish communities, including that of mainstream Beta Israel, who still presume that Jewishness is simultaneously a religious and a national, or ethnic, position.[2]

Rather than distinguishing between religion and ethnicity, highland Ethiopians engaged in a more complicated set of conversations about intentionality in social change. Just as Beta Israel frequently were unable to gain full acceptance as converts because of the malevolent power that helped to mark them indelibly as "Falasha" in Christian eyes, so too Beta Israel often claimed that converts remained "Jewish in their hearts" or "in their bones" either because their agency in conversion was said to be shallow—the hope of material gain or of escaping pervasive structural violence—or because no single act of will could hope to undo the long accumulation of communal identity through shared history and kin networks, through shared suffering, and through the slow training and shaping of ritual habitus. This kind of intentionality, inherent to bones and hearts, is fundamentally different from the kinds of articulate intentionality—contained in statements of faith or doctrine—that are described in missionary sources. Like the will to be buried among one's brothers, or the self-explanatory call to "die in the religion in which we were born," the religious intentionality of Beta Israel who resisted conversion is almost always expressed in images of visceral permanence (like "bones" or cemeteries, or visions of bodily martyrdom) that offset the observed instability of some people's hearts. But whether to emphasize these features of the interpretive landscape or to adopt the hermeneutics of suspicion that views converts fundamentally through the prism of malevolence—like the desire to defraud the state of its resources through unjustified immigration—remains a choice that is not given to purely empirical resolution.

From "Wax and Gold" to "Willing One Thing"

Like ethnographers and historians, members of religious communities are constantly making complex interpretive assertions about the agency of other people—including religious converts—in a variety of contexts. Protestant missionaries who longed for "unmistakable evidence of conviction and conversion" were not long in finding it, which does not mean that they were operating in bad faith, but only that the decision to portray religious agency in certain ways tends to shape what can be observed in human subjectivity. Missionary discourse promoted an ideal of clear, declarative statements about faith that could easily be measured against behavior, and this approach offers a strong promise of epistemological transparency in making judgments about the true motivation for conversion. Despite the heavy ideological shaping of narrative in works like Stern's autobiography or the columns of the *Jewish Missionary Intelligence*, these works present themselves to the reader as straightforward and objective accounts in which both theological and mundane truths shine clearly through the text. Nothing could be more distant from the pervasive "wax and gold" model of double entendre and hidden meanings (Levine 1965) that characterize so much of Ethiopian highland culture.

The practice of "wax and gold" speech (*semana worke* in Amharic) implies that the "wax," or outer meaning of an utterance, is designed to mislead, or to create a plausible counterstory to the real, deep meaning that can only be understood by someone who possesses the right tools or the requisite advance knowledge. In some cases, this takes the form of a highly developed poetic style, but the term "wax and gold" also stands for a pervasive cultural aesthetic that applies equally to a form of prose in which meaning is elusive and masks are common. It can take a real virtuoso to crack the code of *semana worke* when it is well performed, because the surface meanings themselves contain multiple levels to confuse or misdirect those who lack the perspicacity to see what lies beneath. This may be one of the reasons that both native Christians and Beta Israel tended much more than missionaries to assume that the real story of religious transformation must often be contrary to appearances, deep in the "bones" or in the secret motivations of those who exchange religions. The "gold" of intimate understanding requires special insider knowledge, and an almost constant premium is placed upon new and clever ways to speak by indirection, or to hide deeper meaning in webs upon webs of subtle language. My Beta Israel informants recognized *semana worke* as a technical art and could sometimes recite classical examples that they had learned in school, but they also prized complicated word plays and humor based on double entendres, and almost always assumed that people's motivations were more complicated than those people acknowledged.

Much has been said about "wax and gold" as a typical Ethiopian culture trait, but it might also be viewed more expansively, as a variant on patterns of communication that are widespread throughout the Levant and have their more vulgar instantiation in the propensity to see conspiracies everywhere. Despite Western biases to the contrary, this style of communication is by no means opposed to high levels of linguistic and intellectual virtuosity. Many of the religious philosophers of the Middle Ages thought that something like "wax and gold" was key to the interpretation of Scripture as well as their own highly erudite and esoteric reflections. In the twelfth century, Moses Maimonides famously described the language of Scripture as "apples of gold in a filigree of silver," by which he meant that the same words could be read by the elite and by the masses, with each deriving from them only the meanings appropriate to their intellectual station (Diamond 2002). Indeed, Scripture is written this way precisely in order to hide its true meaning from those who cannot properly understand, and Maimonides emulates this style in his own philosophical writing. Against the modern Western preoccupation with intelligibility in religious discourse, here is a style that reflects the perceived danger of inappropriate or premature knowledge in the wrong hands, and subsequently revels in the ability to communicate as well as misdirect.

If this juxtaposition of "the great eagle" Maimonides with Ethiopian peasant villagers seems jarring, that is in part because we are unused to seeking cultural continuities and structural patterns across such widely varying contexts. I would argue, however, that this juxtaposition is potentially important because it helps free us from the alienating and dehumanizing view of Ethiopians or Ethiopian culture as somehow inherently dishonest or dissembling. It also speaks to the need for greater subtlety in how we approach such questions in a context where expressions of clarity may be perceived as threatening. In the sociopolitical context of the Ethiopian Plateau, private information about the self was very often treated as potential leverage for an enemy or competitor. My informants in Israel frequently shared stories about the Ethiopian folk hero Abba Gabra Hana (an Orthodox monk, although contemporary Beta Israel sometimes treat him in their stories as if he were a Jew), who bests his adversaries through clever wordplays and double entendres that leave them guessing. "Wax and gold" is both a defensive strategy and an art form, a literal poetry of the opaque, and this only compounds the difficulty—because this is part of its purpose—of attributing clear and unambiguous motivations to social actors. Ethiopians themselves must struggle with the implications of a landscape in which agency is only partly ever revealed to outsiders, and this is a reality with which the ethnographer too must learn to cope.

Thus we come to what I believe is an important crux in the understanding of the "Feres Mura" dilemma as well as other problems relating to Ethiopian immigrants in Israel. Salamon has argued that the Beta Israel encounter with Israeli society has been a fundamental confrontation between what she calls "two different and basically opposed models of thinking: the Western idea of the constancy of objects, and the Ethiopian transformative model" (1999, 122). While Ethiopians assume the possibility of different kinds of categorical and even bodily transformation, her argument goes, Israeli debates about the Jewishness of Beta Israel "implied a non-transformative Judaism bound by uniform criteria and fixed boundaries" (ibid., 123). Therefore, when Ethiopians came to Israel expecting to be thoroughly transformed and incorporated into society (some even talked about becoming "white Jews"), the reality according to Salamon was that they were treated as fixed entities whose exclusion and perceived inferiority could not be overcome. I would argue by contrast that the state apparatus is deeply invested in the transformation of people and things across certain kinds of taxonomic boundaries and is not necessarily wedded to the "constancy of objects" that Salamon posits. Michael Herzfeld (1992) has described the whole project of immigration bureaucracy, from a cultural point of view, as the "spinning of straw into gold" through a precarious legal and taxonomic alchemy in which stateless migrants or refugees are transformed into solid citizens of the state. This is a deeply transformative venture, in which Israel is perhaps even more deeply invested from an ideological point of view than most other contemporary states, as manifested by the return-to-Judaism program. The choice, in other words, is not between a logic of transformation or one of "constancy" but between different kinds of transformative logic, and differing conceptions of what makes transformation seem authentic or efficacious in particular cases.

One of the things that "wax and gold" virtuosos tend to share with modern immigration bureaucrats, for example, but which sets them apart from missionaries like Henry Aaron Stern, is their regular and almost reflexive attribution of hidden and malevolent motivation to those who undergo religious and social change. Evangelical rhetoric forces Stern and his missionaries, after a certain vetting process, to assert "unmistakable evidences of conviction and conversion" among proselytes and to speak of them as quite literally reborn in single-minded dedication to the new faith. This means that converts are granted a certain presumption of transparency and trustworthiness by missionaries that they are rarely if ever granted by their fellow villagers, or by the complex bureaucratic apparatus of the state immigration services. The logic of radical rebirth and sincerity that informs missionary discourse may, however, do violence to the converts' experience of ambivalence or the regret that can also accompany religious change. This turns out to be a major lacuna, because ambivalence and regret characterize so much of the Beta Israel convert experience. One of the few reliable accounts of Beta Israel converts between the time of Jacques

Faitlovitch's arrival in 1904 and the emergence of the "Feres Mura" controversy during the early 1990s is a brief account by the anthropologist Simon Messing, who visited Ethiopia during the 1950s and again during the 1960s. "The *Oritawi* (Torah-true) Falashas whom I first met in 1953–54," he wrote, "did not like to talk about their kinsmen who had changed their faith prior to the 1904 appearance of Faitlovitch. It seemed an embarrassing topic" (1982, 94). Messing's first impulse was, like Salamon, to think in terms of a distinction between ethnicity and religious affiliation, even though he wondered aloud about whether this might be the right model: "Had kinship ties, so powerful in Ethiopia," he asked, "been ruptured by the split in religion?" (ibid.). Messing allowed the reticence of the people he met to set the limits of inquiry and did not press them for more information than they seemed willing to provide.

It was only when he returned to Ethiopia for a medical survey in 1962 that Messing chanced upon one of those serendipitous ethnographic encounters that sometimes change a person's view of a field he had thought was familiar. A survey respondent had listed the village of Jenda in Dembeya Province as his place of birth, and Messing, who was himself a Jew, recalled reading that Jenda had been the headquarters of the Protestant mission run by the LJS in Ethiopia. He therefore paid special attention to the next question on his list:

> When asked his religion, the respondent looked away when he softly replied "Christian." This was quite different from the proud manner in which Coptic Amhara Abyssinians responded to the question on religion. (Ibid.)

A certain unexpected quietude; a quick, embarrassed glance and a hint of ambivalence in response to a standardized question about religion—all would have been ignored by most researchers in Messing's position. He had not, after all, come to this village between Gondar and Lake Tana in northern Ethiopia to study the Beta Israel or the phenomenon of Beta Israel conversion to Christianity, but had taken a personal interest in Beta Israel because of his own biography. Ethnography of Jews by Jews so often has the feel of whispered conversations among strangers who meet in transit, eager to make some familiar contact but also not wanting to be overheard. Messing's encounter recalls Joseph Halévy's first whispered conversation with Beta Israel converts almost a hundred years earlier in 1867. Like Messing, Halévy too had been anxious to establish his own Jewish kinship credentials while avoiding the possibility that any outsider might hear him say, "I am an Israelite, like you." Like Halévy, Messing proceeded cautiously, aware of the potential electricity of this moment, in which he might be accepted as distant kin, or maybe even as *balnister*, the Amharic word for a confidant and sharer of secrets. "I asked him casually whether there were still any Falasha in Jenda," Messing writes. "He replied that Jenda was all Christian, but the question had startled him" (ibid.).

Messing must have been encouraged by this beginning, because he continued to hint indirectly at his own knowledge of the Beta Israel community and its luminaries. "I asked whether he knew Taamrat Emmanuel, Tadesse Yaquob and Yona Bogale"—all public figures who had been students of Faitlovitch, then culture brokers in their own rights during the course of the twentieth century. This was apparently sufficient, as Messing reports, for "[h]e was eager to have someone from the outside world to tell the story of his family and kin group. He belonged to this group of New Christians who had converted prior to 1904, who had given themselves the name *Maryam Wodet*, short for *Maryam Wodedoch* (Lovers of Mary)" (ibid.). Like a secret password, the names of famous kin help to establish a degree of trust and rapport for Messing, and I cite the incident here at length here because I want to demonstrate how, as late as the 1960s, descendants of converts from the period before 1904 were still capable of being portrayed as not quite at home in their skins as Christians and still eager to make the acquaintance of foreign Jews. This uncertainty, the piecing together of clues by both sides, and the joy of a first meeting that is framed as a kind of reunion are persistent tropes in modern Jewish writing about the Beta Israel, which have helped to structure their entire modern history as "lost Jewish tribes." Personal relationships are the very medium of knowledge for anthropology, and there is no reason at all for surprise that the existential position of the researcher—here a Jew, tentatively seeking contact with another Jew—made a crucial difference to what he was able to learn about this topic.

Messing's account of the people he calls "Falasha Marranos" accords in most respects with the memories embedded in oral history narratives collected by Salamon several decades later, with the important exception that Messing had some direct contact with converts themselves; perhaps for this reason he found it more difficult to make clear and categorical distinctions between "ethnic" and "religious" aspects of converts' experience. All the inhabitants of the town in which he was working had been "nominally listed as Christians," he reports, but he nevertheless soon discovered that converts made up a significant and distinctive element of the local population:

> Saturday was the big market day, and most of the Copts and Muslims had gathered at the market as the biggest event of the week. But a walk through the Maryam Wodet section of town evinced an unusually large number of able-bodied men and women who seemed to lounge in and around their huts. By contrast, on Sunday afternoon, when the Old-Christian Amhara were resting after Sunday dinner, the backyards of the Maryam Wodet were humming with activity. Plows were being repaired, homespun cotton was being wound on bamboo reeds, and weavers were working on looms as if making up for lost time, which was considered hard work. They had

refrained from work on Sunday morning in order not to offend their Old-Christian neighbors returning from church. (Ibid., 95)

Sabbath observance would later prove a major test for those "Feres Mura" who returned to Judaism, and even in 1962 it was apparently one of the primary ways that some descendants of Beta Israel converts continued to express a degree of unwillingness to wholly conform with their adopted religious surroundings. Yet it would probably also be wrong to think of these people merely as victims of religious persecution who had been forced to maintain a charade of Christian existence. Messing finds evidence of mixed motivations and what he calls "soul searching" among the descendants of Beta Israel converts, compounded even in 1962 by the rumor that Taamrat Emmanuel had chosen Beta Israel students to travel to Jerusalem; the promised return to Jerusalem had touched a chord for them.

Despite their apparent ambivalence over the Sabbath, these descendants of converts took pains to emulate their Christian neighbors in a variety of other ways. Women allowed their hair to grow long rather than shaving it like traditional Beta Israel women and also wore crosses on dark cords (*matab*) around their necks just like Christians. Both women and men avoided the common Beta Israel professions of pottery making and iron smithing "in order to escape the suspicion of lycanthropy-sorcery in which Falasha artisans were held." Yet despite these accommodations, Messing thought that few converts were able to "pass" in the end as Christians, because "in Abyssinia, a person is always identified by the ancestral village and district, and as soon as kinship relations are discovered to contain former Falashas, the one who tried to pass is treated to a knowing smile and raised eyebrow" (ibid., 96). Knowing smiles and raised eyebrows are the very stuff of social relations in Ethiopia, and among Ethiopian immigrants to Israel, too. Converts trying to pass as Christians are in a difficult position, as Messing notes, because those who succeed in obscuring their own origins might be thought to be descended from *barya* (slaves), whose taint is even worse because they are thought to be "without kin" of their own.

That is why I suspect that "passing" in this context may really mean downplaying certain kinds of potentially damaging information so that it remains merely implicit, rather than truly concealing it from public knowledge. "When asked about the Maryam Wodet," Messing acknowledges, "the Old-Christians responded with a smile. This turned out to mean, 'These people are not fooling us'" (ibid., 98). Sometimes, in the "wax and gold" ethos, both parties realize the secret meaning of an exchange but agree for mutual convenience to pretend that they do not. "Though the superficial sharing of the same religion allowed them to interdine [eat together]," Messing concludes, "the Old-Christians, on leaving the house of a Maryam Wodet host, would say to each other, 'I have just come from the house of a Falasha,' or even use the offensive word *kalya*" (ibid.). It seems from all accounts, moreover, as if the descendants of Beta Israel converts knew that this was the kind of thing that many of their neighbors said about them but were glad enough to have it not said publicly.

What would Henry Aaron Stern have said about these descendants of converts, still living furtively betwixt and between Christianity and the religion of their ancestors, exchanging whispers and smiles with foreign Jews, and wondering whether one of their children might perhaps be chosen to study at a Jewish school in Jerusalem? This clearly was not the model of "conviction and conversion" that Stern had insisted upon. Faitlovitch too would have been disappointed that these people had been unwilling or unable to make the choice to identify clearly and unequivocally with the Jews of the Diaspora and of Israel—although it should be said that in 1962 the State of Israel was still mostly unwilling to seek or to acknowledge such identification from any Beta Israel, let alone the descendants of converts. Somehow, in a way that would please proponents of neither Western faith, these people had constructed a life at the interstices, where mixed motivations and ambivalence seemed to rule. Records for the Church Missionary Society during the 1950s betray ongoing concern that converted Beta Israel would leave for other missionary denominations or even "apostasize" back to their ancestral Beta Israel communities if their commitment to Christianity was not continually reinforced (Trevisan Semi 2002). Indeed, the contemporary return-to-Judaism phenomenon indicates just how real a possibility this may have been. Anthropologists tend to romanticize liminal and hybrid states, but we should remember that the "permanent liminality" Salamon (1994) posits brings permanent danger and powerlessness too. A "wax and gold" existence of partial concealment and partial revelation ensures that secrets will be kept well enough most of the time, but it is always accompanied by a threat of dangerous exposure when circumstances change.

The ambivalent Beta Israel Christians that Messing describes said that they or their ancestors converted during the early missionary period, before Faitlovitch, but some activists, like Faitlovitch's student Taamrat Emmanuel, insisted on reaching out even to much older groups of converts. Taamrat became the principal of the first Beta Israel school under Jewish auspices in 1920. In an angry 1935 letter about funding, which he sent to one of his sponsors at the American Pro-Falasha Committee, Taamrat defended his decision to maintain the "Falasha school" in Addis Ababa rather than move it to the populous Beta Israel center in Gondar Province, because he said that he wanted to reach out to the descendants of seventeenth century converts living near the capital:

> Furthermore, it should not be forgotten that at a distance of 40 to 50 kilometers from Addis Ababa we have Falashas who have forgotten, or almost forgotten, that they are Falashas. They long to be like the society that surrounds them, but they are cast off by it, and live a worse life—from a spiritual

perspective—than the Falashas or the Spanish Marranos. That is why the foundations of the school in Addis Ababa were well intended, so that now the Marranos of Ethiopia can benefit from our school, since the means have been provided to cross the divide (S. Kaplan 1994c).[3]

It is worth noting how important Taamrat thinks these converts are to his project of drawing Beta Israel closer with world Jewry. Did his own experience of religious complexity and change render him more open to the complicated religious history of Beta Israel converts than the Europeans who typically framed these issues? And could this have been one of the reasons that his call to focus attention on long-lost kin and co-religionists never really gained steam the way "pro-Falasha" advocacy more generally did until recent times? Modern "Feres Mura" advocacy has tended to eschew depictions of ambivalence like those recorded by Messing or failed assimilation described by Taamrat.

I opened this chapter with the philosopher Søren Kierkegaard's famous assertion that "purity of heart is to will one thing." More than any other single statement in the history of Western religion, this epigraph captures the dilemma for anyone (immigration bureaucrat, religious gatekeeper, or ethnographer) who is charged with making determinations about the religious agency of other people. Like "wax and gold," purity of heart is not just a theological watchword but also a style of discourse and a set of interpretive expectations that help to shape how agency is plumbed and evaluated in social life. Yet there is a singleness of purpose behind this encapsulation that seems to me inadequate to almost any part of the Beta Israel encounter with Western religion. Most Beta Israel converts and their descendants, for example, simply *will many things*, as befits a community living close to the edge of subsistence and trying to strategize for its own survival. The potential benefits of joining a dominant religious group or of association with a powerful and wealthy community of foreign patrons cannot be easily or neatly separated from the truth claims made by foreign religious authorities, or the painful question of loyalty to one's ancestors. There is something decidedly counterhistorical in the strident demand for singleness of purpose made by the Protestant mission and, as we shall see, by certain advocates and opponents of the return to Judaism by "Feres Mura" today. Kierkegaard himself emphasized that "willing one thing" means a willingness to "suffer all in order to be and remain committed to the Good" (1956, 160). But is this perhaps more than we can demand in good faith from a people who find themselves so often on the receiving end of history's dangers?

This moral question is related to one of the central epistemological dilemmas of this ethnography. We have seen that for Beta Israel, religious purity was above all a visceral sensibility bound up with ritual disciplines of separation and cleansing over time, and with an embodied sense of loyalty unto death—"Let us die as Falashas!" The missionary aesthetic of intentional purity was by comparison relatively abstract and cognitive—a thing of the mind—and here we should recall Talal Asad's 1993 critique of modern anthropology for uncritically accepting the post-Reformation claim that authentic religious practices must be bearers of symbolic meaning that could, in principle, be expressed in verbal terms outside the ritual context (see also Seeman 2003). By focusing so hard on thick descriptions of the symbolic meanings that allegedly underlie practice, Asad argues that anthropologists have popularized a secular version of the Protestant devaluation of ritual life. Medieval flagellants may have been less concerned, in other words, with the meanings that could be abstracted from their practice than with the inculcation of religious virtue through bodily experience and institutional power.

This discrepancy was crucial to the devaluation of Beta Israel practice by religious modernists like Henry Aaron Stern, but the insistence upon a clear correspondence between external action and an inner core of articulate meaning is also part of the philosophical and religious background to the framing of the "Feres Mura" dilemma by both advocates and opponents in Israel today. Purity of the body has been subordinated to a characteristic modernist emphasis on purity of heart, which is a "figure of speech that compares the heart to the sea" because "the depth of the sea determines its purity, and its purity determines its transparency" (Kierkegaard 1956, 176). Transparency in this sense also implies stability and changelessness:

> Shall a man in truth will one thing, then this one thing that he wills must be such that it remains unaltered in all changes, so that by willing it he can win immutability. If it changes continually, then he himself becomes changeable, double-minded and unstable. And this continual change is nothing else than impurity (Kierkegaard 1956, 60).

These are the core concepts of an epistemic regime that systematically devalues the kinds of multiple motivations and ambivalence that seem to accompany the "Feres Mura" dilemma at every stage. It defines purity as self-consistency under scrutiny, the avoidance of what Kierkegaard calls "double-mindedness," and the pristine sovereignty of a detached observer's gaze.

This kind of intentional purity is exceedingly different from the ritual purity imposed by Kes Malki or Kes Meheret in Addis Ababa, as they sought to return "Feres Mura" families to the fold. The formal return-to-Judaism program that I describe in chapters 4 and 5 requires formal observance of the Jewish religious commandments rather than statements of faith, but the real test to which descendants of converts are put almost always involves questions of intentional purity. This may seem like a fairly abstract set of concerns, but it contributes directly to the most basic features of the lifeworld that the descendants of Beta Israel converts inhabit today. The optics of transparency associated with "pure hearts" discourse resists interpretive contingency and sees religious change over time as the loss of what is pure. "Is this not the sole certainty," asks the philosopher, "that one's so-called conviction is not altered from moment to moment as a result of the different things that happen to one?" (Kierkegaard 1956, 111). What would he make of people who had exchanged their religion not once but twice in changing circumstances, and whose decision to do so cannot be separated from—even if it is not exclusively dependant upon—the quest for a better life? If there is another way of thinking about the moral coherency of Beta Israel converts' experience, it will emerge only from a more situated account of their lives in historical and ethnographic context. Yet this account must reckon with the "wax and gold" realization that language and experience are often teasingly opaque, and that there is no avoiding the uncertainty that accompanies interpretive labor of any kind.

CHAPTER 4

RETURNING TO JUDAISM

Have mercy Lord, for from myself I flee . . .
To gain the glory to belong to Thee.

—Daniel Levi de Barrios, a seventeenth-century
"crypto-Jew" who returned to Judaism

Tazza Gember was reputed to be upwards of ninety years old when I encountered her on a rainy summer day in 1993 near the gated entrance to the "Feres Mura" compound in northern Addis Ababa. She was with a group of older women, all regal in their clean white *shamma*s, sweeping past me on their way to market. Tazza paused just long enough to recite a verse she had recently written:

When Israel reigns,
When [white] foreigners [*farenjoch*] come,
Then wisdom is enhanced,
And my children grow strong.

She recited the verse again more slowly so that I could record it, but then declined to be interviewed and strode off on business of her own. It had been over two years since almost fifteen thousand Beta Israel were dramatically airlifted from Addis Ababa to Tel-Aviv, and those who remained here were all designated "Feres Mura," the descendants of Beta Israel converts to Christianity who now wanted recognition of their "return to Judaism" and the chance to emigrate. Tazza was brusque, but I was sure that her public acceptance of me had opened doors that might otherwise have remained closed. She was the matriarch of a large extended family that included some of the primary leadership of the "Feres Mura" community in Addis Ababa, and some of her relatives would go on to become my close friends and informants. I could not have guessed, of course, that in less than two years I would stand at the foot of her grave on a hillside just south of Haifa, witness at last to the fulfillment of her wish to die and be buried among the people she described as her own. Cemeteries and the hope of cemeteries punctuate this tale at every stage.

Agency and Authenticity

"Returning to Judaism" is an exceedingly delicate matter. The descendants of Beta Israel converts who chose to affiliate as Jews at the end of the twentieth century were forced to leave behind not only their modest property and possessions (and in a few cases their civil service positions), but also the whole social and ritual context in which their lives had been embedded until then. The Israeli Judaism to which they "returned," furthermore, was in many ways foreign to the Beta Israel Judaism of their ancestors and was dependent for its legitimacy in the modern context upon decision makers far removed from Gondar or Addis Ababa. Some "Feres Mura" were able to draw for support upon kinship networks that already had been transplanted to Israel, but others had to deal with estranged kin who viewed them as merely opportunistic, or worse. Above all, the descendants of converts who wished to return to Judaism had to convince an entrenched and almost uniformly antagonistic political and administrative establishment in Israel to take their change of heart—and their request for immigrant visas—seriously. That they did so from a position of extreme and life-threatening poverty with only a few external allies makes their success over time somewhat remarkable.

For Tazza and many of her closest relatives, "return to Judaism" meant something much more than merely a change of heart. It meant gaining registration in "the program," administered in Addis Ababa by NACOEJ (the North American Conference on Ethiopian Jews) and by Rabbi Menachem Waldman from Israel, then persevering in that program long enough to convince Israeli policy makers to change the immigration policies that had excluded them. Those who did eventually reach Israel had to undergo yet another formalized process of education and scrutiny so that their friends and relatives who still remained in Ethiopia might one day be allowed to follow in their footsteps. Several different facilities for the return to Judaism have been operated in Israel and in Ethiopia since 1991, but the compound in Addis Ababa was the first and in many ways paradigmatic example of what was to follow. Whatever one may think of that program and its ambiguities described in this chapter, it is well to acknowledge at the outset that this was the only proposal—and that NACOEJ and Rabbi Waldman were among the only allies—available to "Feres Mura," who faced intransigence and hostility from many other quarters. The deal offered to these displaced people was a relatively simple one. In return for their demonstrated "purity of heart" and penitential return to Judaism (*hashavah le-yahadut* in Hebrew), Rabbi Waldman and a small group of North American and Israeli advocates would work tirelessly to see that their aspirations for immigration and acceptance were ultimately fulfilled.

The most urgent immediate goal of the program in Addis Ababa was simply to keep the displaced "Feres Mura" alive. The official position of the Israeli government in the aftermath of the 1991 airlift was that they had not wanted the "Feres Mura" to come down from their villages in the first place and now bore only the most tangential responsibility for their future. It was hoped and believed by many that the unwanted migrants would simply return to their home villages if they failed to find needed support in Addis Ababa, so pressure was exerted on nongovernmental organizations like NACOEJ and the much larger IJDC (International Joint Distribution Committee) to limit aid for "Feres Mura" in the capital. The Joint Distribution Committee (JDC), which had been founded after World War II to care for displaced Jewish refugees and survivors in Europe, largely accepted this decision, although it did continue to provide medical care for "Feres Mura" in Addis Ababa. NACOEJ, by contrast, took the unpopular position that the people designated "Feres Mura" by the Israeli embassy had indeed come to Addis Ababa in good faith, believing that they would be included in the eventual evacuation of Beta Israel from Ethiopia, and that their decision to leave their homes signaled a clear desire to throw in their lot with the Beta Israel and Jewish people. The reason they faced an immediate humanitarian crisis, according to this view, was that they could not or would not return to their villages in the north.

Land that had been farmed by "Feres Mura" before they left their villages had now in many cases been taken over by other local people, and there was even some evidence—including refugee testimony (Kassa 1998)—of forced eviction of "Feres Mura" in some areas. A report commissioned by the JDC (Motzen 1998) disputed both the Jewishness and the forced dispossession of "Feres Mura" from their land, but a nearly simultaneous report by the group Refugees International (Thompson 1998) affirmed some of these accounts and did not hesitate to refer to the "Feres Mura" as refugees despite the fact that they had not yet crossed any international boundary. By late September 1998, a journalist for the American periodical *Jewish Week* reported that the JDC was "no longer denying persecution reports in Ethiopia" and was looking for ways to help support "15,000 destitute Ethiopians who want to go to Israel" (Cohler-Esses 1998, 37). The irony is that by failing to quickly evacuate some three thousand refugees in 1991 or four thousand in 1992, the government allowed for the creation of a relatively permanent "Feres Mura" nucleus in the city, which continued to grow exponentially through migration from the countryside even as some individuals were gradually granted immigrant visas starting in 1994. This history of shifting policies and truth claims by the Israeli government and by other organizations working in Addis Ababa has merited separate treatment (Spector 2005), so I will confine my description here to those issues that have had analytic or theoretical importance in defining the nature of the "Feres Mura" dilemma over time.

Israeli officials and representatives of the Joint Distribution Committee frequently expressed bitter resentment of both NACOEJ and another small American Jewish organization, known as the American Association for Ethiopian Jews (AAEJ), which they blamed for precipitating the 1990–1991 exodus of Beta Israel. The influx of refugees to the capital caught aid and immigration officials unprepared and also brought several thousand "Feres Mura" whose immigration rights were in doubt. Representatives of the American organizations have claimed in their own defense that they were worried about the possibility of violence in remote areas once it became clear that the Mengistu government would soon fall; that no clear criteria had been established that would exclude those who came to be known as "Feres Mura"; and, most damningly, that the Israelis themselves had used American organizations as informal proxies to bring the Beta Israel down to Addis. Spector (2005, 53) also seems to support this argument. My interest here is not to adjudicate the facts of the matter but rather to elucidate some of the claims and counterclaims that have helped to make the "Feres Mura" dilemma so exceptionally bitter for many of its main protagonists.

Once AAEJ closed its Ethiopian operations in 1992, it fell to NACOEJ to meet the needs of "Feres Mura" families remaining in Addis Ababa. The Israelis were not happy that NACOEJ had stayed in the city, and they were adamant that no actions be taken to increase the number of refugees seeking international Jewish and Israeli support. Under pressure, NACOEJ agreed to fund only those families who had arrived in Addis Ababa before the 1991 airlift in the hope that this at least would help to stem the tide. The compound that NACOEJ administered was not really a residence for "Feres Mura," but a walled property that had been transformed into a protected space for religious and social life as well as bureaucratic functions. This is where a synagogue and school for "Feres Mura" children was located, where the administration of the return-to-Judaism program got its start, and where aid recipients were expected to work on "traditional" handicrafts (mostly needlework and basket weaving) to help defray the considerable costs of maintaining them. In addition to demonstrating their commitment to life as Jews, participants in the program were expected to undertake different kinds of educational and modernizing disciplines, like showing up on time for work and meetings. Discipline was applied in many different ways during this early period and was unapologetically justified both by the exigencies of the moment and by the claim of preparing future migrants for life in modern Israel. One day a sign was posted in English and Amharic to the side of the public outhouse: "*Shint Bet* [Outhouse]: Fine of 5 *Birr* for Poor Aim." There was a great deal of good-natured banter among the program participants around such interventions, but sometimes they also rankled.

Program participants knew that they could be removed from the rolls of "the Program" for failure to show up to work or for serious behavioral infractions like domestic violence, and some also complained of being pushed or kicked for failing to follow the compound's rules, but what they feared most was being accused of religious backsliding or duplicity, which had the potential to derail the whole return-to-Judaism program. A committee of elders and notables (known simply as "the Committee") was formed to adjudicate disputes, represent the community to the outside world, and organize the collection of funds for those "Feres Mura" who had lately come to Addis Ababa and were therefore ineligible for NACOEJ funds. Most of all, however, the committee was responsible for coordinating strategy with Rabbi Waldman, who was their most visible non-Ethiopian ally in the fight for recognition and the primary architect of the return to Judaism. During his frequent visits to Ethiopia, Waldman preached about ritual and religious issues like the importance of holidays and dietary laws, and the Committee worked with him on implementing these directives. In the vicinity of the "Feres Mura" compound, one could find men wearing colorful homemade skullcaps (*kippot*) and ritual fringes (*tzitzit*) that had been brought to them by visitors like Avraham Neguse, an Ethiopian-Israeli advocate of "Feres Mura" immigration. At public gatherings, committee members would speak about the importance of acting in ways that demonstrated the truth of their claims to the outside world.

Local controversies that helped define people's day-to-day lives were frequently related to the broader problem of convincing people in Israel and North America to accept their religious and ethnic claims. The Adenite-Jewish merchants who still frequented the old synagogue across the city from the "Feres Mura" compound frequently failed to achieve a quorum of ten adult men for public prayers, but they were unwilling to count the twenty-five or thirty men from the compound who made the trek across Addis Ababa to join them each Saturday. Most of the Ethiopians knew little or no Hebrew and would stand crowded together in a corner of the synagogue praying, or just watching and listening, with their prayer books sometimes noticeably upside down. While the Adenites were not willing to count them for the quorum as individuals, they were sometimes willing to count them as an aggregate, under the theory one member shared with me: "You cannot tell me that amidst all of them there is not at least one or two who really is Jewish!" From the Adenites' largely pragmatic point of view, the Jewishness of "Feres Mura" was not so much a categorical problem as an issue of individual genealogies and personal religious histories. These mostly well-off merchants and import-export traders had made relative peace with the burial of "Feres Mura" refugees in "their" cemetery, but synagogue participation still seemed inappropriate. It was probably not surprising under these circumstances that most of the refugees preferred to attend the small white synagogue that they had built at the center of the NACOEJ compound. Here they appointed their own prayer leaders and prayed from Amharic translations of the standard Israeli prayer book commissioned by NACOEJ.

It is important to recognize that the return-to-Judaism program that began in Addis Ababa was tailored to address three very different kinds of doubt concerning "Feres Mura" Jewishness. The first was a generic doubt about the claims to Jewishness of all Beta Israel; that doubt has remained a subject of dispute among halakhic authorities, even though the broad consensus of Israeli policy makers today is that Beta Israel should be treated as Jews. The second was a specific concern about the genealogical purity of the matrilineal line, given that at least some Beta Israel converts would be expected to marry Christians of non–Beta Israel descent. Each of these doubts could have been settled through formal conversion to Judaism, which "Feres Mura," unlike their non-convert counterparts living in Israel, had declared themselves ready to embrace. Indeed, when one of the Adenite business leaders in Addis Ababa decided that the children he had with an Italian expatriate should be made Jewish, the Israeli embassy helped facilitate this by arranging for a conversion court of three Israeli rabbis who had to fly to Ethiopia for this purpose. When I later asked an embassy official why the same solution couldn't work for "Feres Mura" refugees, he answered without hesitation that it was "because *they* [the 'Feres Mura'] want to immigrate to Israel!" The real crux of the "Feres Mura" dilemma from a political point of view was not genealogical so much as it was intentional; doubt over the motives of potential converts or returners to Judaism combined with the clear assertion of their desire to immigrate en masse, which created a cultural impasse whose solution was uncertain.

This is why testimony collected from a wide range of academics, activists, and religious experts that was collected in 1992 by the Inter-ministerial Committee charged with crafting a response to the "Feres Mura" dilemma tended to focus on the question of motivations. One group of respondents basically dismissed the return to Judaism as irrelevant or incredible and classed the "Feres Mura" as essentially "economic refugees" for whom the state bore little or no responsibility. From media accounts, this seems to have been the position of the minister of immigrant absorption at the time, but he was certainly not alone (Gorenberg 1995). "As I see it," testified a professor of Middle East and Islamic studies at the Hebrew University, "this is part of the wider global phenomenon of search by the Third World, or the starving south, for a solution to its suffering in the northern world. Therefore a dividing line must be set on the question of the Falash Mura, not according to religion or who is of Jewish descent, but according to our strength and our capacity to absorb them."[1] She acknowledged that this solution "sounds very brutal," but insisted along with several others that any responsibility Israel had in the resolution of the "Feres Mura" dilemma was purely humanitarian, and should be handled in Ethiopia, rather than by bringing tens of thousands of problematic new immigrants to Israel.

Another group of witnesses did, however, frame its response to the "Feres Mura" dilemma "according to religion or who is of Jewish descent," or more specifically, to paraphrase a professor of Jewish thought who also testified, "How much Jewish solidarity do I owe the 'Feres Mura'?" This is an extremely precise formulation, because it skirts the need for a purely halakhic designation of Jewish status and asks instead whether there might be levels of solidarity owed to people on a variety of different grounds, including not just Jewish descent but possibly even the perception by others that one is Jewish and willing to suffer as a Jew. This was not entirely novel, because the great halakhic decisor Rabbi Moshe Feinstein had already made a similar observation in his 1984 responsum on the Jewishness of Beta Israel as whole, in which he ruled that although he was not sure they were technically Jewish, "they think of themselves as Jews and are perceived by their neighbors as Jews and give up their lives on that basis—we must help them!" (Seeman 1990). This is not just a halakhic frame of thinking but also an assertion of the idea that it is the Jewish people rather than the state who are being called on to decide this question; another way of saying this might be that the nation has certain obligations that may exceed those of the state.

Some participants in the "Feres Mura" dilemma seemed to understand that these categorical negotiations were as much about defining the nature of the Israeli collective as they were about the disposition of some refugees in Addis Ababa, and this is how I understand Rabbi Waldman's adamant declaration to me that "This is *not* a humanitarian issue—it is a Jewish and a national issue!" The refugees seemed to help other Jews crystallize their views on a variety of issues, and this meant that debates about "Feres Mura" were often about many other submerged agendas, like the appropriate role of religion or of rabbis in determining who is a Jew in the national sense of the term. Jewish solidarity theorists tended to be more accepting of "Feres Mura" claims than proponents of the economic refugee model, but this was not a foregone conclusion. At least one witness cited the precedent of medieval Iberian conversos, who sometimes tried to return to Judaism after many years or even generations of life as Christians and faced mixed success in convincing local Jewish communities that they should be accepted as Jews when they did so.[2] Like contemporary Israelis, fifteenth- and sixteenth-century rabbis frankly debated the reasons for conversion as well as for return when they struggled to arrive at a pragmatic moral adjudication of Jewish communal responsibilities toward these individuals.

Ultimately, the Inter-Ministerial Committee adopted a compromise that was destined to entirely please neither the economic refugee theorists nor the advocates of "Jewish solidarity." Immigrant visas would be issued only on a humanitarian basis of family reunification for those who already had first-degree relatives living in Israel. However, those who immigrated would then be encouraged (not required) to undergo a formal "return-to-Judaism" program under the auspices of the Israeli Chief Rabbinate, the graduates of which would be registered as Jews and enabled to bring their first-degree relatives to Israel under family reunification in turn. Those who refused the return to Judaism would still be allowed to stay in the country as full citizens, but they would not be registered as Jews and the special provisions of this compromise involving family reunification would not be applied to them either. The goal was to gradually empty the camp in Addis Ababa without acknowledging that "Feres Mura" were now being recognized as Jews for immigration purposes. Yet by hanging the right to immigrate upon the idea of family reunification rather than directly on the return to Judaism or on residence at the "Feres Mura" compound in Addis Ababa, this compromise ensured that the immigration from Ethiopia would remain essentially open-ended and would not be limited to those who had already left their homes to come to Addis. Indeed, participants in the Addis Ababa program began to complain because people coming from villages might receive their immigrant visas ahead of those who had been waiting in the transit camp for months or years.

For Rabbi Waldman, who administered the return-to-Judaism program on the rabbinate's behalf, the compromise was a qualified success because it retained the link between Jewishness and immigration and tied the question of Jewishness closely to rabbinic adjudication. In defending the concept of the program to a rabbinic audience, he made a three-part argument that worked for a time, although it was later called into question. First, he dismissed the argument made by some other advocates in public settings that "Feres Mura" were simply Jews whose ancestors had assimilated, but never converted to Christianity. The second part of the argument, even more discordant with what some other advocates and almost all of the refugees in Addis Ababa at the time were saying, was that those people who had converted could not be considered forced converts or *anusim*:

> There was [in late nineteenth century Ethiopia] no campaign of extermination [*shmad*] against the Jewish religion, and therefore it does not seem appropriate to define the situation as one of coercion through deadly force. It is known that for a short period the Emperor Yohannes forced conversions, but this coercion ceased with his death (1889), and was forbidden by his successor, the Emperor Menelik II. . . . There have been those over the years who have returned [to Judaism], but many thousands remained Christians despite the entreaties of their kin and the priests of the community. . . . The *Felesmura* therefore do not have the status of *anusim* [forced converts] and are considered to be willing apostates. (Waldman 1996, 257)

This was not a statement that could have been greeted with joy by many "Feres Mura," but Waldman's broader agenda, in this essay written for rabbinic colleagues, was to win continued support for his return-to-Judaism program, first by establishing his own credentials as a rabbinic authority with claims to expertise in Ethiopian history and secondly by framing the problem in a way that clearly upheld the deep rabbinic skepticism and disapproval of apostates.

Rabbi Waldman rarely spoke so bluntly about their history to the people who were enrolled in the return-to-Judaism program, but they understood and acquiesced to his formulation. Indeed, their willingness to do so was central to the third and most important part of his argument, which was that the descendants of "willing apostates" were today nothing other than pliant and pure-hearted religious penitents:

> Members of the Beta Israel community in Addis Ababa have been repeatedly asking from the State of Israel and its representatives over the past five years: "We are Jews. We have abandoned our past. Accept our regret. Guide us in the path of the Torah and commandments. We are prepared to accept upon ourselves all the instructions of the Chief Rabbinate. Please help us to be unified with our families and our brothers in Israel." The solution to their cries, to their suffering, and to their efforts to turn in penitence and to join anew with the Jewish people and the Jewish religion, is a Jewish-human challenge and an obligation to all those who have a Jewish heart beating in their chest; first of all for the halakhic [Jewish law] decision makers in Israel, and particularly the Israeli Chief Rabbinate, who are the fathers of these orphans and the central address for their pleas. (Ibid., 243)

It is telling that Waldman's basis for claims about agency in religious change shifts here from a consideration of broad historical forces and government decrees to a claim of deep personal familiarity with the people he describes simply as "the Beta Israel community in Addis Ababa." The agency of penitents is like pure, transparent water for Waldman, leaving nothing opaque. But these claims are hard to live up to, and the seeds of the return to Judaism's collapse under a weight of disappointment and suspicion may have been sown with just such expectations.

If Waldman's account of religious agency seems implausibly thin, however, we ought to remember the highly polemical context in which they were made. Nor were "Feres Mura" advocates like Waldman the only ones making simplified assertions about "Feres Mura" agency based mainly on impression and surmise. "So long as the dream of *aliyah* [literally, "ascent"] to Israel remained only a dream to the Jews of Ethiopia," write Steven Kaplan and Chaim Rosen in their 1994 entry for the *American Jewish Yearbook*, "the benefits of assuming and maintaining a Christian identity were usually quite obvious. Events from 1977 onward, however, dramatically changed this situation" (Kaplan and Rosen 1994, 68). While nothing in this statement can be called counterfactual, it implicitly reduces the return to Judaism to an instrumental and utilitarian movement without acknowledging the complex of subjective factors that informed individual families' decision to return to Judaism during this period.

The same can be said of the following testimony by a historian before the 1992 inter-ministerial committee:

> [I]t may be put forward that whoever can be clearly identified as belonging to the Falash Mura, has failed in his attempt to become a Christian and merge fully within Christian society. Any attempt to identify additional groups of Falash Mura or to examine the genealogy of Falash Mura members identified until now, will cause additional persons to discover their roots and come out of the closet, in order to get out of Ethiopia and come to Israel. Similarly, establishing institutions and organizing missions to bring people back to Judaism will cause the awakening of new candidates for immigration.[3]

This account is free of the heavily charged moral language ("willing apostasy") deployed by people like Rabbi Waldman, yet it too applies a relatively simple and unitary moral schema to explain the return to Judaism in recent times. The use of such simplifying tropes may be both normal and necessary in the formulation of plausible narratives about the past (see White 1985), but this ought to make us even more careful to account for countervailing evidence where the political consequences of such narratives can be severe.

It would be foolish to deny the powerful material incentives to migrate from Ethiopia today, or the fact that these have had something important to do with the ongoing stream of people who have been seeking to undo their ancestors' conversions to Christianity. Yet we have also seen evidence for long-standing ambivalence on the part of some converts, like those described by Messing long before emigration to Israel had been posed as a live option for Beta Israel. More significant still are the vociferous claims by living men and women that their return to Judaism is part of a sincere ethnic and religious revivalism. Such claims ought not to be dismissed in a cynical or wholesale manner by scholars without real, firsthand investigation of religious experience in the present, just as historians rightly demand firsthand investigation of primary historical sources before authoritative claims about the past can be evaluated. The ambiguities of the return to Judaism simply cannot be explored in any other way.

"You Are *Kayla*!"—Returning to a Place You Have Never Been

Because of the widespread fear that acknowledging any history of estrangement from Judaism would harm refugees' chances of being recognized by Israel, personal narratives about the return to Judaism were not easily shared.

This was often painfully ironic, because such reticence could also easily be interpreted as a failure to achieve the transparent and remorseful attitude expected of penitents. Refugees were torn between Rabbi Waldman's insistence that their religious transformation be made explicit and their own instinctive caution, fueled by warnings from allies or advocates like Avraham Neguse, who founded the "South Wing to Zion" organization specifically to advocate for "Feres Mura." Neguse periodically called on participants in the program to resist not only the term "Feres Mura" but also the weight of self-definition that went along with it. Most refugees who did talk about their return to Judaism did so indirectly or in an episodic way that fell short of extended narrative. It may not have been surprising that one of the people who was most willing to talk about his complicated religious history was also the only one I met who had made a principled decision not to seek to leave Ethiopia.

Tazza Gember's octogenarian brother, Taddesse Yaquob, had rejected the return to Judaism root and branch. Because of his status as one of the last living icons of Beta Israel history in modern times, this was a powerful statement. He was the nephew of Taamrat Emmanuel, who had signed the deed on the Jewish cemetery of Addis Ababa and had become the first principal of the Beta Israel school there. Like Taamrat, Taddesse met Faitlovitch while he was studying at a mission school and was persuaded to accept Jewish patronage instead. He was sent to study in Cairo, but instead of becoming a teacher on his return as Faitlovitch had hoped, he entered the service of the Emperor Haile Selassie, who hoped to modernize his kingdom with the help of such foreign-trained Ethiopians. In 1960 Taddesse became vice minister of agriculture, and in December 1961 he was appointed minister of state in the prime minister's cabinet (Weil 2006). In 1966 he received the title Minister of the Public Service Pension Commission and of the Central Personnel Agency, which he held until Haile Selassie's overthrow by forces of the Communist Dergue in 1974. The Yiddish writer Chaim Shoshke, who visited Ethiopia and met with Beta Israel during the early 1950s (Sohn 2005), described Taddesse as a "practicing Jew" despite his high position (and "black skin"), which only serves to emphasize how his life had become emblematic of the forces pulling at Beta Israel during the early part of the twentieth century. Increased contact with and influence by Western Jews on the one hand combined with growing integration within the Ethiopian state on the other. After the departure of most Beta Israel leaders from Ethiopia during the 1980s and early 1990s, Taddesse was the closest thing to Beta Israel royalty that remained in the country, and his refusal to pursue emigration under the terms set by Israel was especially poignant.

We met in the small gated house (he called it his "villa") that he shared at the time with his middle aged daughter. Already in his eighties in 1993, Taddesse seemed eager to speak about his imprisonment during the Communist years that preceded the fall of the Dergue in 1991. Accused like other government officials of corruption and crimes against the nation, he told me proudly that he had been released when the new regime was unable to prove any charges against him, although it seized his pension, which he was still fighting to reclaim. Despite these bitter reversals, it must be said that Taddesse lived in almost unimaginable wealth compared with many of his relatives and others who had undertaken the return-to-Judaism program. At the "Feres Mura" compound, people still tended to describe him with a certain reverence, notwithstanding the inevitable complaints that he lived in luxury while they starved, or that he had not done enough to help his brethren in their straits. For his own part, Taddesse Yaquob insisted that he had always used his influence and connections to help the Jews of Ethiopia, and that he had served "His Imperial Majesty Haile Selassie" as official representative "on all matters pertaining to the Falasha" during the frequent occasions when his uncle Taamrat was abroad. He bridled when I mentioned that I had met his sister Tazza at the "Feres Mura" compound. It was an open secret at the compound that they did not speak, but he explained that he had broken with her over her decision to risk everything by trying to emigrate to Israel without his advice or consent. More than any other single individual I met, Taddesse Yaquob embodied in his own flesh the contradictions and tragedies of "Feres Mura" history in modern times, including not just his training under Faitlovitch and his ill-fated intimacy with the throne but also his loss of a son who had committed suicide, he said, because he was not fully recognized as a Jew after he moved to Israel.

Unlike any of the villagers and refugees I met in Ethiopia or later in the return-to-Judaism program near Haifa, Taddesse Yaqob was openly proud of his Christian as well as Beta Israel heritage, despite the fact that he identified himself unreservedly as "a Jew in my heart," expressing bewilderment why that should not be enough for the Jewish Agency of Israel. He told me that his maternal grandmother was "half-Falasha" on her father's side, and that she was descended on her mother's side from *Desamatch* nobility, "a family of kings and emperors." His grandfather was a Beta Israel ("a one hundred percent Jew," as he told me in English) who fell in love with his grandmother and "took her by force," then legitimated the union by converting to Christianity to escape reprisal. It is difficult to know exactly what to make of this story. Elopement of love-struck but socially unsuitable young lovers was sometimes described as *t'ilf* or marriage by abduction, allowing families to accept the union while also defending their honor (H. Pankhurst 1992, 102–107) through plausible deniability. While descent and inheritance in highland society were normally ambilineal, drawing upon the kin groups of both parents, it was not uncommon for a child in specific circumstances to identify more strongly with one set of relatives than the other, depending on social or political expediency. In Taddesse Yaquob's case this meant that he would have been more likely to emphasize his Christian rather than Beta Israel heritage, until he encountered Jacques Faitlovitch.

Taddesse was one of the first twenty-five students that Faitlovitch sent abroad to study in Jewish communities outside Ethiopia. Some, like Taamrat Emmanuel and his younger contemporary Yona Bogale, returned to work almost exclusively within a Beta Israel orbit, while Taddesse sought lines of advancement within the burgeoning Ethiopian national context instead. Taddesse portrayed his uncle as growing impatient, over time, with Faitlovitch's insistence on Beta Israel conformation to the ritual practice of Jews outside Ethiopia, but he acknowledged that Taamrat underwent formal immersion like that demanded of "Feres Mura" today. Taddesse viewed the whole matter with distaste. "I am a great admirer of the Bible," he told me in his raspy, pedantic way. "I am a Jew between me and *Elohim* [biblical Hebrew name for God]. Not as a scholar, but as an amateur. Not in order to teach or to preach but in order to protect *Falashas*"; he put a special deep emphasis on that last word. "Jewish between me and *Elohim*" is not a status recognized under the matrilineal requirements of traditional halakhah, nor is "Jewish in my heart" a category recognized by Israeli immigration officials. Yet it conveys a moral coherence that Taddesse Yaqob insisted upon. His self-conscious patronage of Beta Israel remaining in Ethiopia had been interrupted by their eagerness to leave the country and by their willingness to adopt a trope of "returning to Judaism" that he was simply unwilling or unable to share. His nephew gave up an important civil service position in the Ethiopian Ministry of Agriculture in order to go to Israel but was currently languishing with all of the other refugees at the "Feres Mura" compound. "Degu gave up his position," he said disdainfully, "*for nothing.*"

Taddesse asserts that the term "Feres Mura" was probably a corrupted form of "Faras Moqra," whose meaning he can not explain, although he thinks that it may derive from the ancestral Agau language. Indignantly, he also insists that most of Faitlovitch's handpicked students would have been labeled "Feres Mura" by today's standards and complains that he presented a list of all the "Feres Mura" among Faitlovitch's early students to another visiting anthropologist, who failed to publish them; he was not willing to provide such a list again.

Most interesting perhaps, Taddesse suggested that the "Feres Mura" phenomenon might be represented through a series of nonconcentric but partially overlapping circles, with full Jews and full Christians at either end of the chain and "Feres Mura" in the middle. What this means, he says, is that some "Feres Mura" might in fact have identified as Christians, while others underwent merely pro forma conversions and others were better thought of as merely "nonpracticing" Beta Israel. This view is similar to what I heard from other Beta Israel sources, including Kes Imharan in Upper Nazareth, who acknowledged that he thought the term "Feres Mura" included individuals with many different kinds of religious and social history. While Kes Imharan thought that the return-to-Judaism program made good sense as both rehabilitation and "punishment" (Hebrew *'onesh*) for the descendants of converts and apostates, however, Taddesse Yaquob had no patience for those who used the program to try to escape from the implications of their family history. It is more than a little ironic, therefore, that Taddesse himself was an influential and almost mythic figure in the lives of several people who told me about their personal Jewish awakening.

Those who were willing to speak at all about the return to Judaism in their own lives frequently spoke about a dramatic moment in which their family history was laid bare for them. Among the younger generation, leaving home for school was sometimes a moment for coming of age, in which young people were made privy to information about kinship that had been kept from them until that time by protective parents. Mulegeta, a man in his fifties who immigrated to Israel during the 1980s, told me how as a young man he had decided to travel to Addis Ababa to study. His mother told him to seek out his cousin Taddesse Yaquob, who was then an official in Haile Selassie's government. With nostalgia in his voice Mulegeta described the scene:

> When I came to Addis, I went to see Taddesse Yaquob, because my mother said he was our kin. I told him my name and the name of my father, and then he went and brought a list. [I asked, "You mean like a family tree?"] Yes, like a family tree. He found my father's name, and then he pointed at me and said [in Amharic], *Kayla nekh*—you are *Kayla* [with heavy emphasis]. From that time on, I knew I was a Jew.

Kayla is a slightly pejorative term derived from an old Agau word for metalworkers, which has been used in certain regions to refer to Beta Israel since at least the seventeenth century (Quirin 1992, 13; Rosen 1985). Taddesse's use of that term here is not meant to be offensive but conveys a presumption of cultural intimacy (Herzfeld 1997) between the young student and his imperious older relative. It is unlikely in mid-twentieth-century Addis Ababa that *kayla* would otherwise have been spoken to a person's face in polite conversation. A family genealogy kept by an educated and none too traditional relative in the cosmopolitan capital becomes, for a boy raised in a Dembeya region village, a claim for support from local kin, and eventually from a foreign state as well. But there is no evidence to indicate, against Mulegeta's own testimony, that the importance of this revelation was purely instrumental, or that his recovery of an unsuspected yet now valued family history was really motivated just by a quest for material support by a child of the "starving south." On the contrary, this revelation apparently complicated his life in significant ways.

This new information, so casually divulged by a distant relative, had a profound and transformative effect upon Mulegeta. Years later, rather than take his place as an educated teacher or civil servant, he would choose to travel to Israel via the deadly overland route through Sudan; he eventually went to work for the Israeli government helping other Beta Israel (and not only the descendants of converts) emigrate. For him, formal conversion to Judaism in Israel (there was no streamlined return-to-Judaism program at the time) was a distasteful but necessary part of achieving communal recognition for what he already knew without question to be true—"From that time on," he says, "I knew I was a Jew." It is important to note that he never depicts his personal transformation as a moment of spiritual awakening or rebirth, the way missionary converts and contemporary Beta Israel Pentecostals invariably do, but as the natural effect of uncovering something that had always been there, waiting to be discovered. His own five children were being raised as observant Jews in the north of Israel when I met him in 1994, while he worked as an administrator at one of the new programs facilitating "Feres Mura" return to Judaism. The way he described his own journey was also entirely characteristic of other people in the "Feres Mura" community I came to know.

Alem was a fourteen- or fifteen-year-old boy when I met him in Addis Ababa in 1992, a star pupil and an accomplished athlete in the small volunteer circus that NACOEJ sponsored for children at the "Feres Mura" compound. On Sundays they toured the city putting on free performances for children across Addis Ababa, with juggling, tightrope walking, and lots of acrobatics. Alem was a strikingly good acrobat. Our conversations in Ethiopia were mostly about his longing for an immigrant visa and dealing with the poverty and dislocation of life at the "Feres Mura" compound, but later, in Israel, he was willing to speak a little more unguardedly about his personal history. For Alem, the moment of revelation about unsuspected kinship ties coincided with his father's decision to emigrate, as life became untenable for government officials living in their region. Alem remembers fleeing with his younger siblings from running gun battles not long before they left their northern district to come to Addis Ababa. "Five years ago, my father told me one day that we are Jews [he insisted that his father had used the Hebrew word, *yehudi*], and that we were going to go to Israel." On another occasion he told me matter-of-factly, in his broken English, "Now I am only believing in the Jewish faith, but before I was believing in the Christian." Yet just a few months later, when I pointed out the large wooden *mateb,* or Ethiopian cross, that his grandmother wore around her neck in an old family photo, he argued with me heatedly that this was just an Ethiopian cultural rather than a religious symbol, and surprised me by seeming to take genuine offense that I would suggest his grandmother had ever been a Christian. The trope of returning to an original and authentic identity had collapsed for him into the rhetoric of never having left.

The return to Judaism in general, and Alem's story in particular, are about the reconfiguration of social memory rather than the experience of dramatic self-transformation like that described by William James (1958) in his *Varieties of Religious Experience*. James relied heavily on accounts of conversionary experience among Christians, but accounts of the return to Judaism tend to be much more matter-of-fact, without emotional flourish and without perceptions of divine revelation. This does not mean that religious change is perfunctory or lacks meaning for social actors, but that they perceive change as a falling back into place rather than a dramatic new departure. Instead of divine revelation, there is often a revelation of unsuspected family ties.

One older man recounted that while he had been aware of his Beta Israel heritage when he was a schoolboy in Gondar, his classmates had not. "It was not polite to ask a person's place [of origin], or the names of their family, because then you could tell who they were. If they knew who was a Beta Israel, they might say, *buda* ['evil eye']." It was only in retrospect that I realized just how central school was to many of the stories I was hearing. Those who went to a government school often perceived a need to keep their identity as Beta Israel or descendants of Beta Israel secret, or at least to keep it away from the foreground of social relationships. The Ethiopian nationalist project, especially since 1974, had encouraged the creation of public spaces in which separatism along ethnic or religious lines was officially discouraged. Informal divisions and prejudices, however, were something that Beta Israel who tried to "pass" both resented and feared. When I asked one woman why she had never told her children that her own convert parents had been born Beta Israel, she said, "It would be difficult for them in school. People would say *kayla, buda.*" Nor were these pressures faced only by those Beta Israel who had converted or assimilated (Wagaw 1993, 22).

Knowledge of possibly tainted genealogies and religious choices was often kept secret from young children as well as from neighbors, even though such secrets could hardly be kept hermetically. Children growing up in this kind of environment were often protected by their parents from the subtle or merely passive acknowledgment of difference, because anything that made this knowledge too explicit threatened to collapse the delicate equanimity of local social relations. I asked Alem whether he ever missed the friends he left behind in Ethiopia, or thought about going back to them. "No," he answered. "When they found out that I was Beta Israel at school, they cursed me; they said '*buda.*' Since then I haven't spoken with them. I would like to visit, but I would not want to go back there." It is, of course, impossible to know whether Alem's friends and neighbors already knew about his Beta Israel genealogy, but it is more than likely that their elders did. Ethiopia is an intensely origin-conscious society, which is, paradoxically, the reason it is considered so deeply impolite to inquire too directly about a person's origins. The potential for uncovering a potentially compromising piece of information is simply too great—like asking an American acquaintance to see his or her tax return. In retrospect, Alem's baffling discomfiture when I called attention to his grandmother's *mateb* was at least in part a rebuke that I had ignored this fundamental rule of good manners.

The existence of secret knowledge is an absolutely central determinant of the life-world "Feres Mura" inhabit, and one that colors every new social interaction with potential risk. Will they be recognized as "Falasha" among Christians, or as Christian among Beta Israel and foreign Jews? Anxiety about managing appearances and minimizing damage is an absolutely central part of "the picture of what is experienced" for contemporary "Feres Mura" and goes far in making clear why the political context of return to Judaism is such an inextricable part of any ethnography on this subject. The greatest sea change in the experience of those who have come to be known as "Feres Mura" in recent years is precisely that the gaze of fellow Ethiopians, which was once all-important, now vies in importance with the need to manage perceptions by Israeli state policy makers, religious gatekeepers, journalists, and even academics such as myself. Indeed, this helps to explain the sometimes fraught relationship that some academic researchers have maintained with this field of study, in which both researched and researcher implicitly understand that more than simply "the facts" of the case are being negotiated.

Secrets, Lies, and Spoiled Identities

During a trip to Ethiopia, I once sat for twelve hours at the Cairo airport, chatting with fellow passengers. One was an Ethiopian-Israeli returning home to Israel after a visit to the land of his birth, and we discovered in passing that he was also a neighbor of one of my closest informant families in the north of Israel. Once we had discovered this connection, we had a lot to talk about. For reasons I never clearly discovered, he mentioned in passing that one of my old friend's sons was actually the product of a tryst with a *barya* slave in Ethiopia many years before. The fact that such relationships occasionally took place was not surprising, but the discovery that I could have missed this information while composing my kinship charts and spending time with the family for months on end shook my self-confidence. I had no way to verify what I had been told without asking the kinds of questions that one does not lightly ask old friends, so I filed the information away for future inquiry. The first opportunity came a year later, when the occurrence of a household crisis helped to reveal the hidden contours of an underlying social dynamic I had never before suspected. Anthropologists call this processual ethnography (Moore 1987), but it really amounts to seeing through events to the structure that lies beneath.

Teshome was a proud man in his seventies who had led his family through the wilderness of *Derekh Sudan* and continued to rule the family in Israel through force of personality. Recently, though, he had argued with his wife, and she had left him to go live with one of their married daughters instead. "Our father thinks this is still Ethiopia," one of the boys told me, implying that Teshome had treated his wife in ways not thought acceptable in Israel. In fact, most of his seven or eight grown children sided with their mother, although this was expressed mostly in veiled allusions rather than outright hostility. Then one of the siblings told me that they weren't angry with their brother Samuel for siding with his father, since, after all, the woman he called "mother" was really anything but. I had already collected fairly extensive kinship data on this family, and they had not shied away from sharing even potentially embarrassing information, like the fact that their not so distant cousins included people like my "Feres Mura" friends Desta and Rachel, but they had carefully omitted this one important fact. Yet now that it had been revealed, they treated it as casually as could be, although perhaps too this revealed that their conflict with their brother was more severe than anyone was willing to say.

This episode contains an important methodological point, because even though anthropologists correctly maintain that fieldwork is a privileged locus for the generation of culturally and experientially valid data, the truth is that even participant observation remains an artificial construct that can sometimes conceal what it seeks to reveal. Research that relies upon formal interviews, far removed from the contexts of everyday life, is especially susceptible to this kind of distortion, because even information about bread-and-butter issues like kinship is frequently perceived to be a matter of social currency that either does not matter enough to informants in the artificial space of the interview, or else matters too much, and is in either case not accurately revealed. The problem with realizing that one has not always been given the most reliable information is that scholars sometimes take this kind of setback personally or, worse, attribute it to ethical failings on the part of their informants. I was warned by a senior scholar before beginning fieldwork in the Galilee in the late 1980s that I would have little luck in the Ethiopian community because "people will just lie to you." In published scholarship, Shalva Weil (1995b, 2) laments that Ethiopian informants always assume the worst about researchers, who are thought to have come from "the Rabbinate, the Jewish Agency, the police, in fact from anywhere except where she says she originates." "I have found," Weil concludes, "that the suspicion borders on paranoia" (ibid.).

Weil has performed the service of putting into writing something that one frequently hears among Beta Israel researchers. She also supports her argument with citations from some of the most illustrious names in Ethiopian studies: "The Amhara is a master at deception," writes Donald Levine. "With straight face and convincing manner he will relate the most preposterous fiction" (Levine 1965, 250). Levine associates this with the "wax and gold" style of discourse in Ethiopia, and with the "the predilection for employing secret languages, secret formulae, and sharing secrets with friends" (Weil 1995, 3).

Some of Weil's informants, similarly, insisted that interviews be treated like clandestine meetings, responding with the information they thought that she wanted to hear to rather than with what she considered to be true and unbiased information. Other researchers (S. Kaplan and Rosen 1994, 70; Rosen 1994 and 1995) have also described the difficulty of obtaining reliable statistical and genealogical information from Beta Israel. Yet one reads this academic literature nearly in vain for any discussion of the difficult and complex positional realities in which Beta Israel find themselves, or for some analysis of the roles that researchers also play within these social fields. Practically all the major academic scholars of the Beta Israel, including myself, have served at one time or another as government employees, expert witnesses before Knesset committees, or volunteer and professional staff at different kinds of nonprofit organizations. We write opinion pieces for newspapers that deal with immigration policy, and we try to shape public opinion around sensitive issues like ethnic history or the return to Judaism. So when Beta Israel informants assume that researchers are sent by "the Rabbinate, the Jewish Agency, [or] the police" rather than just being interested in the pure quest for knowledge, they are not entirely wrong, and certainly not paranoid.

A more useful way to frame the Ethiopian-Israeli propensity to conceal information might be that both cultural and positional-experiential factors help to define the ways in which privacy is conceived and protected in different settings. "Wax and gold" discourse certainly can predispose Ethiopians to a view of language as multilayered and capable of being used for concealment in a competitive or agonistic social context. But this only forces us to recognize how strategic misinformation can be in a world where knowledge generated benignly in one context may well be used inimically in another. Focusing exclusively on "Ethiopian culture" or on "the Ethiopian personality" risks falsifying the context of our own research practice and places the burden for whatever remains opaque in our accounts squarely on those who can least afford to bear it. One day, after she completed the return-to-Judaism program in Haifa, Rachel told me that an Israeli anthropologist had come to interview her about the price of *teff* (an Ethiopian grain). She wanted to know how much Rachel had to buy each month in order to feed her family. But Rachel told me that she intentionally overestimated her response by a couple of kilos. "I am a woman who knows how to make the *injera* last," she said, "so my family can get by on not very much. But what about someone who doesn't know how to do what I do? Will the government reduce our support if they hear that we can get by on less?" In fact, this fine anthropologist was working on a government-sponsored study, so Rachel's concerns were not entirely out of place.

This attitude to dealing with researchers had relatively little to do with Beta Israel "culture" but almost everything to do with perceptions of risk in a local setting. Steven Kaplan (1999) has argued that Beta Israel who face a veritable onslaught of student and academic researchers as well as bureaucratic interventions have sometimes adopted a strategy of "everyday resistance" that extends so far as cultivating difficulties in learning Hebrew. While I am inclined to think this may be an overstatement, it is the kind of claim that can only be substantiated through a positioned ethnography of the political and cultural-experiential contexts of each encounter. There is a danger, in other words, of substituting an ideologically driven post-Zionist ethnography in the "romance of resistance" (Abu-Lughod 1990) model for the ideologically driven Zionist ethnography that determined an earlier generation of research problems. The focus on secrets and lies within Beta Israel and "Feres Mura" ethnography points to the importance of the state as an interested party to the cultural negotiations in which Ethiopians participate, and it helps to highlight the subtle imbrications of state power and scholarly agendas.

Consider the fascinating case of Azzaj Dinzu Avraham, described by Chaim Rosen (1995), an anthropologist who worked for the Israeli Ministry of Immigrant Absorption. Rosen has conducted significant research in Ethiopia and was well equipped to interpret a letter sent by a family of avowed Christians living in Ethiopia to the Israeli immigration authorities. The family argued in this letter that it should merit immigration rights because of its Jewish lineage and because its father, Azzaj Dinzu Avraham, had worked to "save the Jews in Ethiopia from extermination." Realizing that he could not take this letter at face value, Rosen used oral histories to trace Azzaj Dinzu Avraham to a Beta Israel personality who lived during the reign of Emperor Susenyos, at least 350 years before. The sum of his descendants today would include a huge number of Jews as well as Christians, who might all take a favorable ruling in this case as encouragement that they, too, should seek immigration rights. In his article on this episode, Rosen makes some important points about the polysemy of Beta Israel kinship terms like *zer* (seed), *lijj* (child), and *abbat* (father), which can be applied in a lineal fashion even across many generations of distance between "children" and their distant ancestor. But I am mostly concerned here with the anthropologist's implicit moral and political framing of the incident:

> The author of the letter sent to the Ministry of Absorption was able to speak in terms of *abbatey* [my father] with regard to someone who had lived some fourteen generations earlier. This usage serves as a reminder that for an Ethiopian nothing is more precious than the ability to recall and assert links to remote ancestors, especially where they may have been distinguished historical figures (Hoben, 1973). *What remains unresolved is how anyone can distinguish between a legitimate claim and one made only to further an individual's personal interests, whether to secure a piece of land, or, in the case at hand, to be considered eligible to immigrate to Israel.* (Rosen 1995, 57; emphasis added)

Rosen's frustration when confronted by a need to distinguish between legitimate and illegitimate kinship claims is perfectly reasonable given his institutional position. Yet it must be frankly stated that the question of legitimacy in this context is a bureaucratic rather than an ethnographic concern; its presence here calls attention to the inadequacy of analytic models that focus on Beta Israel culture and society to the exclusion of the bureaucratic taxonomies and sociopolitical institutions of the broader society in which they seek to be embedded. It might even be said that Rosen and other Jewish or Israeli writers are, like me, writing about Beta Israel partly from within the kinship system that they are describing, and that the whole question of legitimacy of kinship claims therefore requires a more reflexive analytic stance.

The state's need to treat kinship as an objective calculus of relatedness and to brand as illegitimate or dishonest the "assert[ion of] links to remote ancestors" makes perfect sense given programmatic goals and limitations of activity by or on behalf of the state. But this assertion is also part of the local moral world whose features ought to be described and assessed rather than taken for granted as a starting place for subsequent research on the culture of Beta Israel. In an otherwise refreshingly open article about what it is like to be a "government anthropologist," Rosen also notes that "attention should be paid to the Ethiopian tendency to correct history or to improve accounts of family lineage if that will further the interests [of the person reporting his or her genealogy]" (Rosen 1994, 128). But is this really an "Ethiopian tendency"? Strategic use of kinship information is a cross-cultural rule rather than an exception (see Bourdieu 1977). Our own social science discourse about fixed cultures may actually serve to mask the fact that negotiations over kinship almost always take place in freighted social and political contexts to which the state itself is an interested party. Azzaj Dinzu Avraham's "children" seem to have understood this, and their appeal to their ancestor's efforts to "save the Jews from extermination" (Rosen's published translation uses the term "Shoah") may be read as implicit—or not so implicit—attempts to link themselves to the community of suffering from which converts are thought to have excluded themselves. Like Taddesse Yaquob, they base their plea on an assertion that they or their ancestor had acted "to protect Falashas," and that this act of classical kinship solidarity ought to trump the complex vagaries of tainted religious genealogy.

Like all citizens, researchers hold their own stakes in the "Feres Mura" dilemma, including their own sense of how government funds and symbolic capital ought to be allocated. It has also been my impression that some scholars resist the threatened dissolution of a pristine "Ethiopian Jewish culture" that has already been constituted as an object of research, while others have become spokespersons for the negative views of "Feres Mura" expressed by their non-convert Beta Israel informants. But one must add to these rationales for negativity the feeling of being misled by potential informants or their advocates in a weighted political field. Anthropologist John Knudsen argues that mistrust between refugees and researchers is endemic to most research settings, because of the unacknowledged political contexts of research on migrant and forced migrant populations:

> Already before the first researchers ask their questions, refugees have passed through several interviews and conversations with several categories of helpers. When the researchers finally arrive, the situation is redefined once more, and the conversation changes. This redefinition may be seen as a survival strategy, and attempt to have as much influence on the definition of self and situation as possible. Like many helpers, the researcher becomes upset and frustrated if met with strategic self-presentation, silence, and withdrawal. The two parties are cast as opponents: the ones asked, in their presentations, the others doing the asking, in their frantic search for valid data. The result may be a *folie a deux*, a double illusion. (1995, 29)

This situation is only exacerbated in Israel, where determinations of migrant agency—in this case, religious agency—are central to the taxonomic business of determining immigrant status. "Why should the refugee trust the researcher," Knudsen asks, "a person whose questions and, even more dangerously, whose interpretations, may represent a threat to their future?" (ibid.).

Anthropologists who work to craft plausible narratives about other people's agency are really just engaging in a more disciplined and specialized version of what participants in social life do all the time; the anthropological gaze mimics the dynamic that is engendered when refugees are interviewed by bureaucratic agencies, or when any two people try to measure each other's motives and honesty in a weighted political and moral context. These encounters are conditioned by all sorts of interpretive habits that include the possibility for misunderstanding and even attribution of bad faith or malevolency, but there is no objective standard from within which different attempts to assess and evaluate agency can all be judged, and this means that certainty is usually only relative. I am in favor of showing disadvantaged groups like "Feres Mura" a measure of what Paul Farmer (1992) once called a "hermeneutics of generosity," which does not mean that what they say must be taken at face value, but that we must be willing to generously consider how the truth of their statements or claims might be evaluated. Farmer's informants in rural Haiti told him that American scientists working for the government had "sent" AIDS to the island, and while this claim cannot really be credited in any literal sense, there are still two ways in which the ethnographer might take it seriously.

The most obvious is that some claims have cultural validity and may open an analytic window upon culture. The importance of ideas about agency and blame in "sent sickness" makes perfect sense in terms of rural Haitian culture, just as the use of "our father" to refer to a distant lineal ancestor might make perfect sense to an Ethiopian. Much more significant, however, is Farmer's argument that people who have been structurally disadvantaged or victimized may have important insights into their own situation that they articulate in ways that are easy for the more privileged to dismiss. Thus, the American government did not send AIDS to Haiti, but Farmer argues strongly that American policies in the region have helped put poor people at risk for different kinds of calamities, including but not limited to AIDS. "Feres Mura" may not be able to assert that their ancestors maintained a literally unbroken chain of fidelity to Judaism, or that their own return to Judaism is uninfluenced by the desire to emigrate to a land of relative plenty, but these claims can be read as more than just lies when we consider the evidence of historical ambivalence about conversion, suffering despite conversion and heartfelt desire to repair the breach in recent decades. Informant claims almost always make more sense when we start from a consideration of what is at stake for them in some local setting than when we start from abstract research questions alone. Generosity means serious consideration of how certain claims might make sense given a particular position in the world, and how counterevidence might be tempered by that realization.

Part of the ethnographic dilemma in any research of this nature lies precisely in deciding which observable signs of agency ought to be given the most weight and which contextual factors should be privileged over others. In and around the "Feres Mura" compound in Addis Ababa, for example, the brightly colored but sometimes misshapen homemade skullcaps (*kippot*) and flapping Jewish prayer fringes (*tzitzit*) were described by the "Feres Mura" themselves as requirements of religion (*haymanot* in Amharic); they were also signs of their stubborn refusal to give up the hope of reunion with the rest of the Beta Israel and other Jews in Israel. Yet they also spoke about these ritual objects as important to the demonstration of their devotion to suspicious outsiders. They understood well, in fact, how these two dimensions to the significance of ritual practice were linked, and the degree to which outsiders remained suspicious of their motives. From their point of view, choosing to dress in a way that made them stand out as both religiously foreign and as probable recipients of foreign aid in the frequently dangerous and impoverished neighborhoods of Addis Ababa was itself an act of commitment to Judaism that should have won them the respect of outsiders. So was the commitment to forgo relatively cheap but nonkosher local meat, or to forgo the possibility of employment on the Sabbath. The problem was that while these were important interpretive signs for Rabbi Waldman and others who supported the return-to-Judaism process, they could also be read simultaneously as signs of cultural and religious inauthenticity by those who already suspected that the program was a sham.

In 1995 Rabbi Waldman produced a short documentary video in both Hebrew and English to be used for fund-raising and advocacy efforts, and this video very much highlighted the religious aspects of life at the "Feres Mura" compound. One scene depicts the participants in the program praying together at the compound's synagogue, chanting in unison as Sephardim often do in their synagogues, but also swaying and bowing like stereotypical Ashkenazi Jews at prayer. Waldman's voice-over narrates the piety of the whole Addis Ababa community, making mention of their daily prayers as well as their observance of "all of the Jewish holidays, including *Yom Ha-Zikaron* and *Yom Ha-Atzma'ut* [Israeli Memorial and Independence days] as well as *Yom Ha-Shoah* [Holocaust Remembrance Day]." This may have been a compelling argument for "Feres Mura" advocates in Israel or in North America who were looking for evidence that these people comported themselves as Jews and as penitents, as well as Zionists, but at the Second Congress for the Study of Ethiopian Jews in Jerusalem, where the film was screened that year, it provoked open hostility and ridicule from many audience members, most of whom were either students or academics. Partly this was because Waldman himself had become a lightning rod of controversy among academics for his outspoken views and assertions of historical expertise (see Waldman 1989 and 1996; the former reviewed by S. Kaplan 1995). Yet several conference participants told me that they simply disapproved, on a deeply visceral level, the inculcation of Ethiopians with what they took to be a predominantly Western form of Jewish practice. Waldman had misgauged his audience, because instead of bearing witness to the signs of pure-hearted penitence among his "returning" Jews, they saw only the manipulations of the Orthodox religious establishment he personified.

I later showed the same film to a group of three hundred Israeli undergraduates in a large introductory anthropology course I was teaching at the Hebrew University. Once again, some of the students were openly troubled, and this became the subject of a conversation about the limits of cultural authenticity. They complained about the imposition of "Ashkenazi" or even "ultra-Orthodox" behavior and practices upon Ethiopians. Yet when I asked them whether they would have objected in the same way to a scene depicting Beta Israel praying in a Moroccan- or a Yemenite-style synagogue (synagogues, it should be pointed out, that would have been equally foreign to the historical experience of Beta Israel in Ethiopia), most acknowledged that they would not. "They are like *mizrahim*" or Eastern Jews, one of the students volunteered, "and it doesn't seem right to see them praying like they are in a *shteibl*" (a small Eastern European synagogue). The truth is that Beta Israel belong to neither of the great cultural and liturgical traditions represented in somewhat oversimplified terms as Ashkenazic and Sephardic—nor even to the catchall category of *'edot ha-mizrah* (sometimes called Eastern or "Oriental" Jews) that includes the descendants of Jews from Arab lands. Like the Benei Israel, or Bombay Jewish community, Beta Israel are outliers to this cultural taxonomy. By any reasonable historical, linguistic, or religious criteria they should be viewed as a group unto themselves, who had little or no ongoing contact over the centuries with Jewish communities outside Ethiopia. Yet it is difficult for them to escape the structured expectations of imagined ethnicity in Israel.

"Feres Mura" frequently are buffeted between different and/or mutually exclusive languages of cultural and religious expectation. In order to fill any of these expectations completely, they must become vulnerable to attacks from other Jewish-Israeli ideological groups, and to potentially devastating portrayals of their choices and lifestyle. For this reason, the return to Judaism must be seen not only as an attempt by certain Israeli and American Jews to craft a ritual response to the charge of historical apostasy, but also as an attempt by descendants of these apostates to manage and navigate the contradictory narratives to which they had been subjected.

In Addis Ababa they had only Rabbi Waldman and a handful of other visitors to please, and this did not change appreciably when an additional transit center was set up in Gondar to the north. But for those who eventually made it to Israel, "returning to Judaism" suddenly took on a more complicated aspect, as the fixing of spoiled identities increasingly came to require the navigation of broader and overlapping—yet not identical—fields of social expectation. "Feres Mura" who thought that arriving in Israel would represent the end of their dilemma and their journey quickly came to understand that in many ways the dilemmas and the journeys had only just begun.

CHAPTER 5

ABSORPTION

The alleged scandal of alterity presupposes the tranquil identity of the same, a freedom sure of itself which is exercised without scruples, and to whom the foreigner brings only constraint and limitation.

—Emmanuel Levinas, *Totality and Infinity*

One of my first visits to the "absorption center" at Neve Carmel was on the day of Tazza Gember's first *tazkar* (memorial feast), in October 1994. *Tazkar* was observed on the fortieth and eightieth days after death in Ethiopia, and up to seven times during the first year, by both Beta Israel and Christians. Observances like these are typically truncated in Israel, but it was a little more than a month since Tazza's death, and a group of older relatives were busy criticizing her grandson, Sintayeho, for holding *tazkar* on the wrong day when I arrived. Others defended him, however, insisting that the important thing to remember was that his mother had achieved the consummation of burial in Israel that all of them had longed for during the dark days of Addis Ababa. Yet, even for them, *tazkar* rites were important. Despite their attenuation in recent decades, many Ethiopians of both religions still describe them as key to entry into the Kingdom of Heaven (Lord 1970, 143; Nordanger 2007). In Ethiopia, the performance of memorial rites by priests was an important source of income for the Church, and Beta Israel *kessotch* also traditionally accepted gifts for their performance. There were only three or four priests living at Neve Carmel, however, and they mostly kept to themselves, still pointedly trying to ignore the "Feres Mura" who had come to dominate the absorption center. As a former Communist functionary, Sintayeho was certainly no ritual expert, but he provided for his family's ritual needs as best he could.

Tazza had been among the first of the Addis Ababa immigrants to arrive in Israel under the family reunification compromise brokered by the Inter-Ministerial Committee in 1992. "Feres Mura" who had first-degree relatives living in Israel were admitted under family reunification statutes, then permitted to undertake a formal return-to-Judaism process and bring their own relatives to Israel in turn. Each month a few buses would arrive from the airport with another group of new immigrants—100, 150, or 200 people, depending on political and other factors. Relatives would meet the buses with tears and shrieks of joy, as well as bundles of used clothing and heavy round stacks of homemade *injera* bread. Each family would be hustled to its new cramped trailer home, and within a very few days the return to Judaism, followed by intensive language and cultural training (*ulpan*), would begin. I circulated widely at Neve Carmel between 1994 and 1996, speaking at length with new immigrants and absorption workers, consuming *injera* and beer at *tazkar* feasts or drinking little cups of black Ethiopian coffee around low tables in rooms suffused by the smell of incense. Eventually, I developed my closest friendships with a few families who represented some of the extremes of life at Neve Carmel, including the family of Tazza's grandson Sintayeho, whom I had already come to know in Ethiopia. It was through their eyes that I tried to understand what the return to Judaism meant for the people who lived it.

On Juggling and Tightrope Walking

Before it was commandeered for the return-to-Judaism program, Neve Carmel had served as an "absorption center" (*merkaz klita*) for previous groups of new immigrants. Such facilities were traditionally located in outlying and depressed areas, but a decision had been made in 1990 to locate more of them near the center of the country, where work and educational opportunities for new immigrants were better (S. Kaplan and Rosen 1994, 81–86). Some absorption centers were conceived as semipermanent facilities for their inhabitants, but Neve Carmel was no more than a trailer park of a few thousand units, set incongruously along the coastal highway linking Haifa with Tel Aviv.

From the windows of the 400 bus that runs to Haifa from Jerusalem, one first passes miles of rocky seacoast and boxy hi-tech facilities for companies like Intel before approaching the tennis courts and well-maintained public beaches that mark the hilly southern suburbs of Haifa at whose foot Neve Carmel sits. Some of the immigrant children made use of those beaches (a child drowned there during my first summer), but their elders rarely did. To the consternation of public planners, older Ethiopian immigrants frequently avoided both beaches and cities located at sea level (like Haifa and Tel Aviv), because of their Ethiopian highlander stereotypes about the disease ridden low-land air (Rosen 1995). But this was not the only area of cultural contestation involving the conundrums of immigration. At a time of growing controversy over the role of immigrants in Israeli society, when affluent communities throughout the country were pushing for the replacement of absorption centers by marinas and lucrative housing developments, it should come as no surprise that the site occupied by Neve Carmel was claimed by the municipality for a new shopping center. The ideological Israel of Zionist ingathering and the new Israel of global consumerism seemed to collide at the entrance to Neve Carmel, where the sounds and smells of a vast Ethiopian village—"my Ethiopia" I used to think of it—pushed the cell-phone culture of central Israel at least temporarily to one side.

A great deal has been written about different aspects of the "absorption" of Ethiopian immigrants in Israel, including their education (Wagaw 1993; Odenheimer 1995), military service (Shabtay 1999), language acquisition (Anteby-Yemini 2004), and gender and family life (Weil 1991; Westheimer and S. Kaplan 1992; Hertzog 1999). I want to focus in this chapter, however, on the special burdens imposed by the return to Judaism on top of all of the other challenges faced by new immigrants. In the morning, "Feres Mura" immigrants would attend special classes led by people like Yitzhak Hadane, the younger brother of Israel's first Ethiopian rabbi (whose own letterhead somewhat grandiosely read "Chief Rabbi of Ethiopian Immigrants"), preparing them with theoretical and practical knowledge for life as religious Jews in Israel—how to identify kosher meat in supermarkets, how to observe the meticulous Sabbath restrictions of rabbinic Judaism, or how to find their way through the Hebrew prayer book. But in the afternoon they would, like other Ethiopian immigrants, also attend classes with social workers on how to live like middle-class Israelis. One such class involved a visit to a "model home" (*bayit le-dugmah*) set up to resemble the dwelling of a nuclear family of Western descent. It included a kitchen table surrounded by four or five tall chairs rather than the low coffee tables surrounded by sofas that were favored by Ethiopian immigrants with many relatives living at close quarters. There was even a series of classes (for women) on how to cook an eggplant, that staple of Israeli cuisine, at the end of which each woman was given an eggplant to take home and practice on—leading to many rotting eggplants around Neve Carmel during the weeks that followed.

For the most part, Ethiopians I knew related to these indoctrinations with good-natured skepticism but kept on doing what they were long accustomed to doing. Uniformly, they purchased low coffee tables instead of kitchen sets and served their fresh black coffee in tiny china cups that they had to travel to the Arab markets to buy, rather than the big mugs and instant coffee that their Israeli Jewish ostensible mentors recommended. Sitting around coffee tables allowed more room for unexpected guests and neighbors to chat or watch television during the long hours of obligatory coffee drinking each day. Coffee was above all a social drink—"part of our culture" (*behalachin* in Amharic) they would often say—and not among the things they were prepared to give up in the name of more perfect "absorption." In matters of everyday life as in religion, immigrants were under pressure to accept changes both subtle and dramatic at practically every step, but this did not mean that they accepted such changes without resistance, and here too ambivalence was a common feature of lived experience.

Tazza Gember's great-grandson Alem was among the brightest of the young students in the return-to-Judaism program when I arrived at Neve Carmel. He said that he was seventeen, but immigrants routinely lied about their ages to gain themselves a few extra years for study before coming of age for the draft at eighteen. In Addis Ababa, Alem had been one of the leading players in Circus Ethiopia, tightrope walking and juggling his way across the capital with other youths who served as cultural ambassadors for the "Feres Mura" while killing time waiting for visas. Alem was a natural athlete who performed with discipline and grace beyond the informal training he had received, and the other boys treated him as a leader. When he arrived in Israel in 1994, he quickly became one of the first of his peers to gain some fluency in Hebrew. With educational challenges looming, his father, Sintayeho, was eager to have me tutor his son, in return for a bed in the trailer set aside for the children and a few meals a week whenever I was at Neve Carmel. We started by swapping lessons in Hebrew and Amharic but quickly became friends and confidants as well. More than anyone, Alem helped me to fathom what I could of the brittle social networks and conduits of shared secrecy that dominated the experience of return to Judaism on a day-to-day basis at the absorption center.

Neve Carmel itself was organized in an expanding grid of identical box trailers, identified only by number. Nevertheless, space took on a highly personalized quality marked by limitations on where people would comfortably walk and who they would talk to. Small clusters of trailers housing no more than five or six related families in close proximity came to be known by the name of the household head with which they were most closely identified. The cluster of trailers in which Alem and some of his cousins lived was thus known by his father's name as *ye-Sintayeho menged,* or "Sintayeho's street." "That is Sintayeho's street," my friend Desta once explained to me, "and I would not go there unless I was invited." After a while, I began to be able to guess at people's friendships and kin relations just by paying attention to who would walk with me down which of the many gravel and dirt paths that made up the absorption center. The extent to which people were sometimes willing to circumscribe their movements in order to avoid walking where they felt they shouldn't was striking.

Divisions among the "Feres Mura" themselves were not the only social divisions at the site, however. Other fault lines that were inscribed upon the social geography of Neve Carmel included those between "Feres Mura" and more veteran immigrants as well as the one that divided all Ethiopians from the much smaller number of immigrants from the former Soviet republic of Georgia, whose clusters of residence were distinguished by the much more expansive way they claimed outside space with small gardens and fences marking off their individual trailers. The two groups barely interacted, and almost never entered one another's areas of residence

In his corner of Neve Carmel, Alem's father Sintayeho was known as *geshe*, an honorific applied to the head of household in Amharic, even though his older brother and father lived there as well. This had something to do with the government position he had held in Ethiopia, which still conveyed prestige in Israel. Like many Ethiopian men who immigrated during that period, Sintayeho often felt that he received less respect than was his due. He tried to continue in the role of patron to his extended family through government connections that he had enjoyed in Ethiopia, but for Israeli officials he was just one more immigrant. His broken Hebrew was better than that of many of his peers, but there was just no way for him to compete with school-going youths like his eldest son.

Alem was strong-willed like his father, and there had been a long history of subtle conflict between the two, rarely breaking the surface but also rarely far from it. Sintayeho had turned Alem out of the house more than once for perceived breaches in the respect due a father, and I was also turned out once as Alem's friend—another imperfectly incorporated young male dependent. It was a Friday night, and Sintayeho had encouraged me to take his boys with me to the synagogue. They usually didn't need much encouragement, because the services were run largely by teenage volunteers from the nearby suburbs who were members of a popular youth group that all the Ethiopian children attended. The services were a mixture of Hebrew and Amharic, mostly following the liturgy that had been prepared for the refugees in Addis Ababa. It had been raining, and we were crowded and sweaty in the echoing prefabricated aluminum of the synagogue with its mud-spattered floors. After services, one committee member made an impassioned speech about the importance of following the dictates of religion (*haymanot*), but the boys were more interested in the presence of girls, and in each other. It was, in other words, a perfectly typical Friday night at Neve Carmel.

When we returned to the trailer, Alem's mother and baby sister were there waiting, but Sintayeho was nowhere to be found. It was not unusual for him to skip services—he had a more cynical edge than practically anyone else I met during fieldwork, and this extended to anything having to do with the return to Judaism. "First we were Jews," he once said to me unprompted. "Then we were Christians. Now we are Jews again." He said it with an ironic smile and a dismissive gesture as if it was all one to him. He liked it when the boys showed an interest in religion, though, partly because he viewed it as acculturation. We waited a few hours before starting the evening meal in his absence, but finally Alem's mother turned to me, as senior male and guest, to offer the blessings over wine and homemade *dabo* (bread) that would allow us all to eat dinner. We talked, ate, and went to bed before Sintayeho returned, but first thing the next morning he began to question me obliquely about what "my people in America" thought about the honor and respect due a father. It was obvious almost immediately that I had blundered. "I was an important man in Ethiopia," he said to me under his breath, "and now look" (he gestured to the trailer around him). It was the kind of mistake that fieldworkers easily make but infrequently write about, and even though his rebuke stung, it also helped me to better appreciate the pressures under which this man functioned. Especially egregious was that I had usurped his position in a ritual context where he already felt irrelevant and undermined. I apologized, but had to move out of his son's quarters for two months and give him the opportunity to make his disapproval of me public for a few weeks before we were finally reconciled. None of this helped his relationship with Alem, though.

Alem's difficulties with his father were not atypical of other Beta Israel families, but they seemed somehow more intense and explosive. They were also exacerbated by the return to Judaism and all of the anxiety for their future that it brought in its wake. On another occasion, Alem told me that my behavior was causing problems in his household. "You must eat whenever I eat," he told me one night when we were alone. "Eat just a little and throw the rest away [if you want to]. . . . Today you didn't eat breakfast." This was confusing. Ethiopian families were frequently suspicious of people who would not eat in their homes because of the implied insult that their food was not ritually pure or that the guest was afraid of being attacked through sorcery or evil eye, but I had enjoyed the hospitality of Sintayeho's household many times, and its members had even come to accept my vegetarian ways, as strange as those first seemed. Had I insulted Alem's mother by not eating enough? Or was I causing them to lose face socially by not taking all of my meals with them? To be sure, I often felt torn by the invitations of many friends, each of whom insisted that I should eat only in their homes, but I thought I had navigated those politics as well as could be expected. Alem said that his mother complained when I didn't eat, but when I pressed him for an explanation he first ignored the question and then told me conspiratorially that she was not, in fact, his mother. For me this was an important revelation, and not one that I thought Alem would make lightly. "My father was married to another woman," he told me. "A Christian woman. She is still in Ethiopia."

Rabbi Waldman (1996) had justified the return-to-Judaism program partly through an argument that no more than 1 percent or so of "Feres Mura" had married people who were of non–Beta Israel heritage, and that the level of genealogical assimilation to non-Jewish society by Beta Israel had been small. Beyond public policy, however, I also knew that Alem could face significant disturbances to his own life if his true parentage became generally known—it would mean, for instance, that he would be required to undergo a full conversion and not just the return-to-Judaism program. He said that Rabbi Waldman did not know who his true birth mother was:

> When we went to . . . you know [he paused to grasp for the Hebrew word for "immersion," then said in Amharic]—*temqat*—some people said [pointing at Sintayeho's current wife], "That's not Alem's mother." So Rabbi Waldman asked my father, "Is that Alem's mother?" He said "Yes," so Rabbi Waldman said, "OK."

Contained in this brief narrative are all the elements of a classic "Feres Mura" dilemma, which I witnessed in different forms throughout fieldwork. Alem refers to *temqat* or baptism in Amharic, when he wants to say immersion in a Jewish *mikveh*, because these two themes had so long been intertwined.

There are also other features of this episode that should claim our attention. Despite Alem's insistence that his mother's identity is a secret, here we find casual onlookers demonstrating that they already know all about his secret genealogy and are ready, for reasons that remain unclear, to call attention to it publicly at an especially sensitive and dangerous moment. Rabbi Waldman may or may not have believed the onlookers, but the question also may have mattered less to him than might be supposed because he had built the return-to-Judaism program with a double fail-safe that ensured minimal rabbinic requirements would be met even in cases where genealogical requirements could not be verified. Although there was a separate, more rigorous and lengthy conversion program set up for immigrants who could not demonstrate Beta Israel descent (or who were related to Beta Israel only through marriage), the return to Judaism itself included the main elements of a full conversion program—immersion, circumcision, and "acceptance of the yoke of the commandments," which meant that any imprecision in Rabbi Waldman's ability to gather accurate genealogical information would not, in his view, invalidate the program. Participants who slipped through without fully satisfying genealogical criteria could still be considered converts after the fact in an imperfect but still acceptable ritual process.

Still puzzled by Alem's story, though, I pushed him to explain what any of this could possibly have had to do with my decision to eat or to skip breakfast that morning. It took a few false starts to make him understand my question, but when he finally did so, the pieces began to fall into place. "She [my father's wife] is not my mother, so when she sees that you are friends with me, or talking to me, she is angry, jealous." I protested: "But she invites me to eat all the time!" "Yes," he said, "but it is not honest. It is our culture. . . . In Ethiopia, whenever I got new clothes, she would say, 'Why did you get new clothes and not my children?' In Ethiopia, nobody helped me; nobody said to me, 'Here, eat.'" I asked him what his father said about all this. "Nothing" was Alem's response. And what about his half-siblings (*gemash wondem* in Amharic) with whom he seemed to get along so well? "Yeah, but you know, it is according to Ethiopian culture—*bahil* [he uses the Amharic word, even though we are speaking in Hebrew]. According to the culture, they don't like me . . . [he pauses]. I like you, so I am telling you the truth." My failure to eat breakfast, in other words, was just an opportunity for the eruption of festering grievances between Alem and his father's wife, which had been brewing since long before they immigrated to Israel. Alem was telling me that my failure to conform to household rhythms had become a trigger for unpleasantness that he fully understood to be rooted elsewhere in "cultural" considerations of jealousy and dissembling.

Overlapping spheres of suspicion and doubt were the wheels within wheels within which life at Neve Carmel turned, suspicion that could only be exacerbated by the concentric way in which membership within families served as a baseline for membership in a religious and national community that also had the power to convey or withhold citizenship. Alem's delicate relationship with his father's wife might cause him problems on all three fronts, and he was nervous that my own anomalous position in the household might make life more difficult for him if I ate (or spoke) out of turn. This meant that the ability to manipulate sensitive family information was an important survival skill—not because of "Ethiopian culture" alone, it is important to emphasize, but because of the political context and hierarchies of power within which people like Alem lived.

In Jerusalem in 1991, I befriended an older woman named Birhane, who had immigrated during Operation Solomon. She and her three grown children had entered the country as Jews, despite the fact that most of their relatives were designated "Feres Mura" and left behind in Addis Ababa. Birhane was in her late forties, though she looked older, and described herself as a widow whose husband had died before she came to Israel. Yet one day her twenty-year-old daughter told me bluntly that her father was really still alive but had chosen to stay in Ethiopia. She also told me that she had made sure the Israeli immigration authorities knew it when they entered the country, no matter what her mother might say. When I asked her why she would contradict her mother that way in front of officials though, her answer was elegant in its brutal simplicity—"We didn't want her to be able to marry again." In Ethiopia, divorce was a relatively informal affair that may well have left no paper trail, whereas Jewish (and by extension Israeli) law requires a very specific kind of writ, called a *get* in Hebrew, which is delivered to the wife by the husband or his agent. When Birhane immigrated as a widow she was leaving open the possibility of later remarriage, but her daughter, by telling officials that Birhane was still married in Ethiopia, had effectively prevented that eventuality. Access to personal kinship information is sometimes a powerful coercive tool wielded precisely by those who are closest (see Knudsen 1995, 26–29), which means that one cannot afford to let one's guard down even among kin, and that a relatively disinterested but trusted outsider can sometimes be valued above all as a special confidant, or *bal nister*—sharer of secrets).

It was as a professional sharer of secrets that I learned that Alem's mother still lives in Ethiopia with several other children, and that Alem would like to visit her (he later did visit—around the year 2000) but has no desire to return there to stay. Sintayeho once described his first wife to me as beautiful but strong-willed, just like her son. In Ethiopia, a child could easily be incorporated into the kin network of the father, but in Israel it was the religious status of the mother alone that counted. By incorporating important elements of the conversion process, the return-to-Judaism program made quiet allowance for the messiness of social life that always resists legal categorization (Moore 1978), and indeed, sought to domesticate these realities. Such flexibility was, however, always held strongly in tension with more rigid and formalistic approaches that characterized other rabbinic and bureaucratic models. Rabbi Waldman was not overly troubled, when I asked him, by the possibility that some irregularities in the program might occur, but policy makers far removed from the field were willing to tolerate the program only insofar as they could maintain the fiction that rigid categorical ideals would be faithfully upheld. Rabbi Waldman's ideal was also certainly one of pure-hearted penitence undertaken by people with unquestioned matrilineal descent from Beta Israel, but his program could tacitly be stretched to incorporate more complicated realities (like the children of Sintayeho's Christian wives) as long as nobody called attention too frequently to cases in which such lenient positions were relied upon. Yet this left the program inherently vulnerable to outside criticism as a result.

One of the most persistent attacks upon the return-to-Judaism program was that participants were insufficiently pious, or that they were "closet missionaries" who practiced Christianity in secret while espousing Judaism for the public benefits it conveyed. Genealogical complications of different kinds were also put forward in partially successful attempts to either shut down the program or ensure its more rigorous application. One of the worst attacks came in 1995, when a girl from Neve Carmel was subjected to deportation proceedings in an unprecedented move by the Israeli government to counter what was perceived as rampant dishonesty and fraud among the immigrants and their supporters. Authorities alleged that a sixteen-year-old girl named Hagit had immigrated under an assumed genealogy, accompanied by people who were not really her parents, and that this should be construed as willful and malevolent misrepresentation worthy of deportation. No one in the "Feres Mura" community really denied that Hagit had immigrated with a relative of her mother's, even though the immigration documents—premised on her first-degree relationship with an Israeli citizen—said she was immigrating with her parents. They failed to understand why the government had decided to make such an issue of it in this case.

For officials, though, more was at stake than a simple violation of some technical rule. Consider the tone, as well as the substance of this statement by a spokesperson for the immigration authorities to the newspaper *Ha'aretz*:

> [She] was a good example of the way in which they try to trick us. We were on to [her] lies very quickly. She is not a poor, pitiable girl [*yalda miskenah*]. It isn't that way. We have to teach them that it is not possible to work on [that is, to fool] the people of Israel. This was a case we were on to from the first moment, and decided to make an issue of it. Everyone tries to fool the people of Israel! Do you know how many reach us, with God knows what identities? For once the State of Israel has to be strong and follow this through to the end. This was a case of trickery and forgery par excellence. The State needs to teach the immigrants not to lie in her face, and not to laugh in her face. Of course, we will honor the High Court's ruling.[1]

No attempt is made here to mask the deep and personalized resentment shown by some officials, which is even put forward as a rationale for state immigration policy. The state and its agents are portrayed as the real victims not so much of material fraud as of being made to play the fool, being laughed at by new immigrants, or turned into what Israelis call a *friar* (a fool or sucker). Someone who follows bureaucratic rules that others shirk can be described as a *friar*, but so can those who fall for tales of suffering and woe that mask attempts to wrest unwarranted sympathy or benefits from the state.

The fear of being seen as a *friar* is a core theme of Israeli popular culture, which one frequently hears about in the contexts of everyday life. But the fear sometimes expressed by officials that they will be made into *friars* by new immigrants can have especially brutal ramifications. Around the time that Hagit's case was wending its way through the Israeli legal system, I learned that another sixteen-year-old girl from Neve Carmel had tried to commit suicide but had been found before she succeeded at hanging herself. I knew this girl peripherally as someone whose parents had died in Ethiopia; she was working hard to take care of several younger siblings without much help from her older brother. The social workers had arranged for her to move into her own trailer after the suicide attempt and had taken the younger children out of her care. When I visited her, she was living by herself in bare surroundings without much furniture, and she told me how much this bothered her. I asked one of the absorption center's social workers about this, but the woman answered me heatedly. "Don't let them work on you. You are being a *friar*. . . . She isn't depressed, even the psychologist said so!" I had my doubts about this confident diagnosis (none of the professionals involved spoke Amharic), but my point in telling this story at the expense of some digression is that even in extremis, Ethiopian immigrants may be made to feel that they are cheats and shirkers in the course of their interactions with agents of the state. No one wants to be considered a *friar*.

Ultimately in Hagit's case, an international child welfare organization won its suit in Israel's High Court to block the deportation, with significant support from mainstream Ethiopian-Israelis like Rahamim Elazar, the Amharic language radio personality who took up her cause. By this time, however, Hagit had already been visited at school by journalists, had her picture and home address published in the newspaper as a criminal, and spent two nights in detention before formal charges had even been brought. It was clear to all that her case was being used to cast aspersions not just upon her family but upon the whole "Feres Mura" community and the return to Judaism they undertook. Some journalists exaggerated the sheer physical rundown of Neve Carmel as a topographic sign of state failure at immigrant screening and absorption, but few if any solicited the experience of Neve Carmel residents in any serious way (see Levi 1995). In the end, the government had chosen a poor test case, because Hagit was young enough to garner sympathy even from sources not normally associated with overt support of the "Feres Mura," and also because many Ethiopians immigrants came to Israel with close kin other than parents. The state's interpretation of malevolent and dishonest agency ("trickery and forgery") in immigration and religious transformation was certainly plausible given their assumptions, but it did not convince crucial observers like the High Court and civil rights groups.

A strong cultural argument could be made that this was at least partly a collision of miscommunication between two mutually unintelligible understandings of kinship and households. Israeli authorities always assumed that the kin relations described by new immigrants—between parents and siblings for example—referred to "real" genealogical or genetic relationships corresponding to the common Western notion of the "nuclear family" known in Hebrew as *mishpachah garinit*. When they asked Ethiopian immigrants about their nuclear families, however, they typically used the Amharic term *beta sab*, which literally means "father's house" and is best understood as the economic and social unit of the "household" rather than as the nuclear family. "The Amharic term *beteseb* [household]," writes anthropologist Allen Hoben (1973, 45), "has no direct reference to kinship ties or to a unit with transgenerational continuity. . . . [F]amilial kinship roles must be analytically distinguished from household roles even though the former frequently serve as recruitment roles for the latter." This is actually a crucial distinction for the interpretation of immigration battles like the ones played out over Hagit at Neve Carmel, because it reminds us that categorical confusion may well have been a factor in generating the widespread anger and recrimination that surrounded the attempt to deport her (see, for example, Gorenberg 1995, 55).

Despite the Israeli preoccupation with kin relations among Ethiopian immigrants, Helen Pankhurst (1992, 17) has gone so far as to claim that "the family unit is rarely mentioned [in the scholarly literature on highland Ethiopia] because it has little operative meaning in the society." While this might be something of an overstatement, Steven Kaplan and Chaim Rosen also note the frustration of immigration officials who found that the kinship categories they used for bureaucratic purposes in Israel were only imperfectly reflected in the lived experience of Beta Israel:

> For the Beta Israel, social life was traditionally organized around the flexible and often overlapping concepts of the extended family (*zamad*) and the household (*beta sa'ab*). *Zamad* is a term whose precise meaning varies according to the circumstances and context. Thus, *zamad* is most frequently used to refer to an extended family (as opposed to strangers), but may also be used to distinguish blood relations from in-laws. In Ethiopia, within the borders of the *zamad*, little attention was paid to the "real" relationships between members. (1994, 71–72)

Israeli absorption workers frequently shared with me their assertion that "in Ethiopia, the family was everything," and backed up this assertion by pointing to the ease with which immigrants rattled off the list of their patrilineal ancestors going back several generations. Yet the assumption that kinship was an important organizing factor in "primitive" societies does not account for the fluidity of households to which Kaplan and Rosen point. "At any given moment," they write, "the precise configurations of the *beta sa'ab* were determined by an assortment of personal preferences and economic needs, and it would change as these changed." As in Hagit's case, "grandparents, uncles or older siblings might function like a child's 'parents,'" and "a person's children might easily include nieces, nephews, stepchildren, and younger siblings" (ibid.).

It would be tempting to conclude with the hackneyed anthropological credo that better cross-cultural communication cures all: that Hagit had made a reasonable cultural choice in identifying her aunt as her mother and that immigration officials simply need to be better educated. Yet I remain cautious for two reasons. One is that this reading implies a level of naïveté among Ethiopian-Israelis that does not accord well with my experience of this community. Although the identification of aunt as mother or of niece as daughter may have made perfectly good sense in cultural terms, Ethiopians are also not slow to understand what Israeli officials are asking of them, and to act defensively when necessary. The second is that the cultural argument fails to appreciate the difficult social and political circumstances in which "Feres Mura" and other immigrants often find themselves. Beyond the false alternatives of malice or cultural innocence, I would like to argue for a more complicated interpretive frame in which the coincidence of great personal need and the moral coherence of native categories combine to make a certain choices—like registering a niece as a child—seem like the strategic and necessary thing to do.

While some of Hagit's neighbors privately made disparaging comments about her family—"they are less Jewish than my family" one neighbor said—they all understood that a loss for Hagit would bode ill for their community as a whole. By contrast, Hagit's young friends and fellow students, like Alem, expressed almost without exception what I took to be honest incredulity that one of their peers could be subjected to the kind of treatment she was subjected to, for no good reason that they could understand. Many of these teenagers, I knew, had already internalized a self-narrative that completely obliterated many of the signal events of the past several years of their lives, including their parents' revelations to them about unsuspected Beta Israel ancestry, their delayed immigration, and even their active participation in the return-to-Judaism program. They maintained not that their return had been sincere, as Rabbi Waldman and others insisted they do, but that there had been nothing in their history to "return" from, and that all of the suspicions or accusations by the immigration authorities were fundamentally grounded in racism (*geza'nut* in Hebrew) rather than religious or cultural concerns. "If they keep on discriminating against Ethiopians," one boy said, completely eliding the "Feres Mura" context of the controversy, "we will have to kill someone." It was an eerie presentiment of the violence that would erupt the following year over accusations that the public health authorities had indeed discriminated against Ethiopians in the politics of donated blood.

These youngsters had internalized a powerful message of the "Feres Mura" advocacy movement. At an educational conference the previous year, I had heard the Ethiopian community leader Avraham Neguse, head of the advocacy organization known as South Wing to Zion, stand up to reprimand a speaker who used the term "Feres Mura" in a public lecture. Neguse thought the refugees should be referred to only as "members of the Beta Israel community who are still in Ethiopia," and he consistently resisted any reference to their history of religious conversion. Careful never to alienate important allies like Rabbi Waldman, Neguse and other community leaders nevertheless insisted that the very use of the term "Feres Mura" was both illegitimate and counterproductive. He never went so far as to denounce the Haifa program, which presumed that "Feres Mura" needed to "return to Judaism," but his refusal to recognize or to use this term usually got him cheers at community strategy sessions involving the residents of Neve Carmel.

For young people like Alem, this situation led to a difficult juggling of disparate realities. They willingly participated in a program whose very existence emphasized a view of their own history that could hardly be held up for self-reflection, let alone public conversation. Although Rabbi Waldman never acknowledged this to me explicitly, I had the distinct sense that he understood this psychological dilemma on some level and softened his message about penitence whenever he addressed Neve Carmel residents. Still, there was no way of eliding the fact that the return-to-Judaism program depended upon a view of participants as "returnees" or penitents in need of some kind of ritual expurgation that many of these participants denied in other contexts. Worse still, from a participant's point of view, was that even this ritual mechanism, which should have erased the signs of a problematic and humiliating history, had also been configured as a bureaucratic event that created official records from which individuals could never really escape. When they sought to marry, to be buried, or to enroll in a religious school, former "Feres Mura" could always be asked to show the certificate of completion that they had received from Rabbi Waldman. Not only bureaucratic encounters, but even meetings with new acquaintances, especially fellow Ethiopians, risked a humiliating exposure once their residence at Neve Carmel—and the implication of being "Feres Mura"—was made explicit. Careful efforts at self-presentation could be ruined in a single moment of carelessness if and when the descendants of converts let down their guard.

Alem coped with this difficult existential situation partly by participating enthusiastically in religious youth groups and after-school activities that gave him contact with sympathetic Israelis who viewed him as a model immigrant. He also constantly sought neutral spaces in which the struggles of the past might be put aside or left behind, however temporarily. Sports were a natural outlet, but even the basketball court at Neve Carmel was not always entirely neutral. It came to be construed as hostile territory for immigrant boys from the former Soviet republics, for example, after some racial remarks the latter had made sparked a fight that the outnumbering Ethiopians inevitably won. More significant, though, was that the Ethiopian boys themselves needed to make some hard decisions about how to reconcile the lessons of the return-to-Judaism program with their passion for games. A few of the most pious chose to refrain from basketball on the Jewish Sabbath and holidays, for example, the way their teachers said they should, but others simply played in their Sabbath clothes or ignored their teachers' advice. For athletic virtuosos like Alem, the *migrash* (basketball court) was an important field of honor on which "Feres Mura" could engage with other Ethiopians and sometimes with white Israelis who visited from the well-heeled suburbs as well. Only once did I witness a near fight between Alem and some older Ethiopian boys from outside Neve Carmel, who pushed him too far on the question of his origins.

Occasionally, Alem and I escaped the oppressive heat of the absorption center to spend an afternoon at nearby Carmel Beach, where he could practice his juggling. One day we met an Israeli juggler, who spent nearly an hour with Alem, exchanging performances. They never traded names, but they agreed to meet the next day at the same time, and Alem spoke with me excitedly that night about his hope that he might learn how to affiliate with the Israeli branch of the International Juggler's Association, which he had been a member of in Ethiopia. The other juggler never showed up, though, and Alem withdrew a little into himself. A month or so later a group of German tourists visited Neve Carmel, and learning of Alem's passion for juggling, they arranged to have some state-of-the-art juggling and circus equipment sent for him and the other veterans of Circus Ethiopia to use. When the American benefactors of the "Feres Mura" from NACOEJ heard about this, they floated the idea of trying to restart Circus Ethiopia as a powerful tool for awareness and public relations in Israel. It would have meant gathering the boys together from the different schools in which they were currently enrolled so that they could study and practice together. I expected Alem to jump at the idea, but instead he and the other boys greeted the proposal coolly, and the donated circus equipment fell into quiet disuse.

In retrospect, of course, their response made perfect sense. As much as they enjoyed the camaraderie of the circus and would have wanted the chance to demonstrate their absolute competence in at least one area of life in their difficult new country, their primary desire at the moment was still to be "absorbed" quickly and quietly with no further public humiliation. They wanted to forget, at least selectively, and to escape the veritable insomnia of constant self-referentiality (see Levinas 1987, 19, 48) imposed upon them by the gatekeepers of national purity. All of those who demanded that "Feres Mura" constantly demonstrate their purity of heart through public penitence missed this basic human point, as did even those advocates who assumed that former "Feres Mura" in Israel would be eager to help call attention to the plight of their fellows who still languished in Ethiopia. Constituting themselves in perpetuity as "Feres Mura" in the new country—even for a noble goal like helping their fellows—was for Alem and his friends, simply more than anybody had a right to ask.

Receiving Jesus

One of the reasons that people like Alem were constantly called upon to demonstrate and affirm their religious position as penitents was the persistent accusation in public media that Neve Carmel was filled with closet Christians (typically referred to as "missionaries," Hebraicized as *misiyonarim*) who had come to Israel in order to evangelize the local Beta Israel population. Such accusations were frequent and came from within the Ethiopian community as well as from outside it. A popular Ethiopian-Israeli radio personality named Rachamim Elazar—the same one who had stood up for Hagit—wrote an essay titled "The Mission in Israel" for the September 1994 issue of the Amharic language magazine *Fana*, published by the largest Ethiopian voluntary organization in the country. Elazar warned Beta Israel against falling for a missionary agenda and portrayed this as a significant danger to the Ethiopian-Israeli community. Similarly, in 1995, the annual *tazkar* ceremony held in Jerusalem for all of the Beta Israel who had perished on their way to Sudan during the 1980s exodus featured Kes Imharan from Upper Nazareth delivering a long sermon on the evils of "the mission." "We came to Jerusalem," Kes Imharan scolded, "because of our religion [*haymanot*]. What does that mean? That means *Orit* [Torah], not the mission!" Imharan had been one of those who supported the controversial immigration of "Feres Mura" (provided they received their appropriate "punishment" of fasting and penitence), and I interpreted his powerful statement against missionary activity in part as an attempt to regain his shaken credibility as a defender of the faith.

This preoccupation with the missionary threat did not, however, stop with the Ethiopian community. I was once approached by a reporter from the newspaper *Yediot;* she wanted to write an exposé for the weekend section about "the missionaries at Neve Carmel." I tried to convince her that this would be a misleading approach, because while there certainly was Christian missionary activity directed at Ethiopians in Israel, there was no particular reason at the time to associate it with the "Feres Mura" or with this particular absorption center outside Haifa. Another way of saying this might be that "Feres Mura" immigrants were much more likely to be the recipients of missionary attention than they were to be its source. Throughout the 1990s and even today, Amharic-language Bibles that include the New Testament are widely distributed to new immigrants by non-Israeli Christian groups that include the contemporary theological descendants of the London Society for the Promotion of Christianity Amongst the Jews. At a bookstore affiliated with this group in the Old City of Jerusalem, I watched in the summer of 2005 while a middle-aged American man came in off the street to request a bag of free Amharic Bibles to distribute among new immigrants. Another Christian Bible shop in Jerusalem specializes in unusual languages spoken mostly by Jewish immigrant groups, like Amharic for Ethiopians or Marathi, the dialect spoken almost exclusively in Israel by Jews from Bombay. On a casual walk down a main street in Haifa during the 1990s, it was not difficult to collect missionary pamphlets in both Amharic and Russian, which were the two main languages spoken by recent immigrants at the time. Indeed, while there are laws on the books against proselytism in Israel, these are typically not enforced.

When I eventually did meet a few Christian believers at Neve Carmel, it happened not by design but through a typically ethnographic kind of serendipity—talking to the right person at the right time. It was a Saturday night when I was waiting for one of the few public pay phones that served the whole absorption center—this was just a few years before the craze of personal cell phones hit Israel. I said a few words in Amharic to the young man standing in front of me in the queue, and he immediately turned to strike up a conversation. His name was Moshe, and he said that had been in Israel since the 1980s—*not* a "Feres

Mura," he emphasized, although he had lived at Neve Carmel ever since his mother immigrated in 1991. Moshe's own absorption center had been located near the coastal resort city of Eilat in the south, and he told me that he later lived in a northern development town. When his mother immigrated he came to live with her, like many young people whose relatives lived at Neve Carmel, because there were more employment opportunities near Haifa. We played a quick game of "Jewish geography," discovered a few common friends in the Ethiopian-Israeli community, and before his turn came to use the phone he had already invited me to visit his mother's trailer the next day "to eat *injera*." This worked out fine, because I was eager for a meal, but I had no way of knowing that the encounter would help to change my understanding of the religious options open to Beta Israel at Neve Carmel.

Moshe and his mother were still sleeping when I knocked on their trailer door the next day at noon, but Moshe emerged, looking disheveled, to invite me inside. He worked nights as a watchman in Haifa he said, and slept late most of the time. The trailer's living area was crammed with more furniture than a new immigrant family typically possessed, including an enormous color television and stereo. There were thick, patterned curtains on all the windows, which kept the room dark but private, even at midday. Moshe apparently slept on a narrow sofa in the living room, and when he disappeared, still disheveled, into the kitchen to get me a glass of water, I took the liberty of admiring a big, leather-bound Amharic Bible he had left sitting on the coffee table. Returning, he asked me if I knew what I was looking at. I read a few words from the Amharic translation of Genesis aloud, and Moshe launched without any preparation at all into a long soliloquy about his faith in Jesus, or as he called him in Hebrew, Yehoshua. It was a highly stylized narrative of suffering and return, which I came to recognize over time from other Pentecostals I interviewed, both inside and outside the Ethiopian community, as the very heart of their belief.

Moshe's life narrative had also changed in some important ways from the night before. He now told me that he had arrived in Israel in 1985 as an adolescent, alone and uncared for. "I was wild. I lived like a dog. You know, I came near to killing a man. And nobody cared about me—I was alone." He went on to describe a personal history of illness and "craziness" that he said doctors were unable to treat. Chronic pain in his head and constant ringing in his ears were accompanied by nearly uncontrollable rage, intravenous drug and alcohol abuse, and deep estrangement from whatever kin or neighbors he might have had living in the country. He remained deliberately vague when I pressed him about his relationship with his family in Ethiopia, and would only say that he had left the Gondar region after a fight with his parents, made his way to Addis Ababa, and eventually managed to leave the country for Israel. His mother immigrated six years later, in 1991, he says, and they met again at Neve Carmel. In the meantime, he had met a (non-Ethiopian) Pentecostal healer in

Eilat, who laid hands on and healed him. "Look at me now!" he proclaims. He is well-spoken and well-dressed, claims to hold down a steady job, and boasts that he no longer uses drugs or visits prostitutes.

Moshe's narrative was similar to what I later heard from other Ethiopian believers in Israel but also, remarkably, to the life stories I had heard from European Pentecostals living on the fringe of the revivifying Jewish community in Krakow in 1992 (see Lehrer 2005), and from South Asian Pentecostals on pilgrimage to the Holy Land in 2003. All of them had emphasized themes of untreatable chronic illness, substance addiction, and sexual promiscuity, interrupted in each case by an act of radical healing and personal transformation that led to newfound stability, independence, and social responsibility. Missionaries in Ethiopia like Henry Stern had certainly portrayed themselves as purveyors of superior medical knowledge and care, and had even sometimes preached healing through faith, but this Pentecostal discourse differed in emphasizing the total transcendence of medical and other kinds of modernizing wisdom through faith. Moshe clearly expressed his contempt for the doctors who could not heal his various chronic conditions. His narrative was unlike others I had heard only in that he clearly blamed the state for his former degradation. He accuses the immigration authorities in particular of failing to meet their responsibilities for his care. "No one cared if I was living or dead," he repeats several times when speaking of his life at the absorption center. I was interested by the assumption (promoted by both Ethiopian and Israeli cultural models) that state authorities should have acted as patrons and substitute kin who could be called on to take an interest in his personal condition.

There were layers to Moshe's narrative that left me unsure of my interpretive footing. In our meeting at the public phone, he had been just another Ethiopian Jewish immigrant struggling to get by, yet when I chanced to pick up and read his Bible, a whole new religious persona came into focus. Then, as we got to know each other, it turned out that even this narrative had been part of a self-consciously formulated attempt to misdirect attention from some of the crucial features of his social world. For one thing, I soon learned that the woman he was living with was not in fact his birth mother, but his "mother in Christ," named Worke, who had introduced him to the faith when he first came to Neve Carmel. Substitutions of "kin in Christ" for "kin of the flesh" have been noted in Pentecostal communities elsewhere in the world (Brodwin 1996, 187), adding one more level of complexity to the problem of incommensurate kinship languages among Ethiopian-Israelis. Moshe described his meeting with Worke as a moment of sudden and momentous personal change: "I was coming [to Neve Carmel] to visit my relatives [holdovers from the Operation Solomon immigration who were still living here]. I saw her, and I looked at her in a certain way, *you know.*" At this point, he pauses for emphasis, and looks at me till I acknowledge that I have understood the sexual innuendo he intended.

1. The London Jewish Society for Promoting Christianity Amongst the Jews mission to the Beta Israel, circa 1860. From *Wanderings Among the Falashas in Abyssinia* by Henry A. Stern.

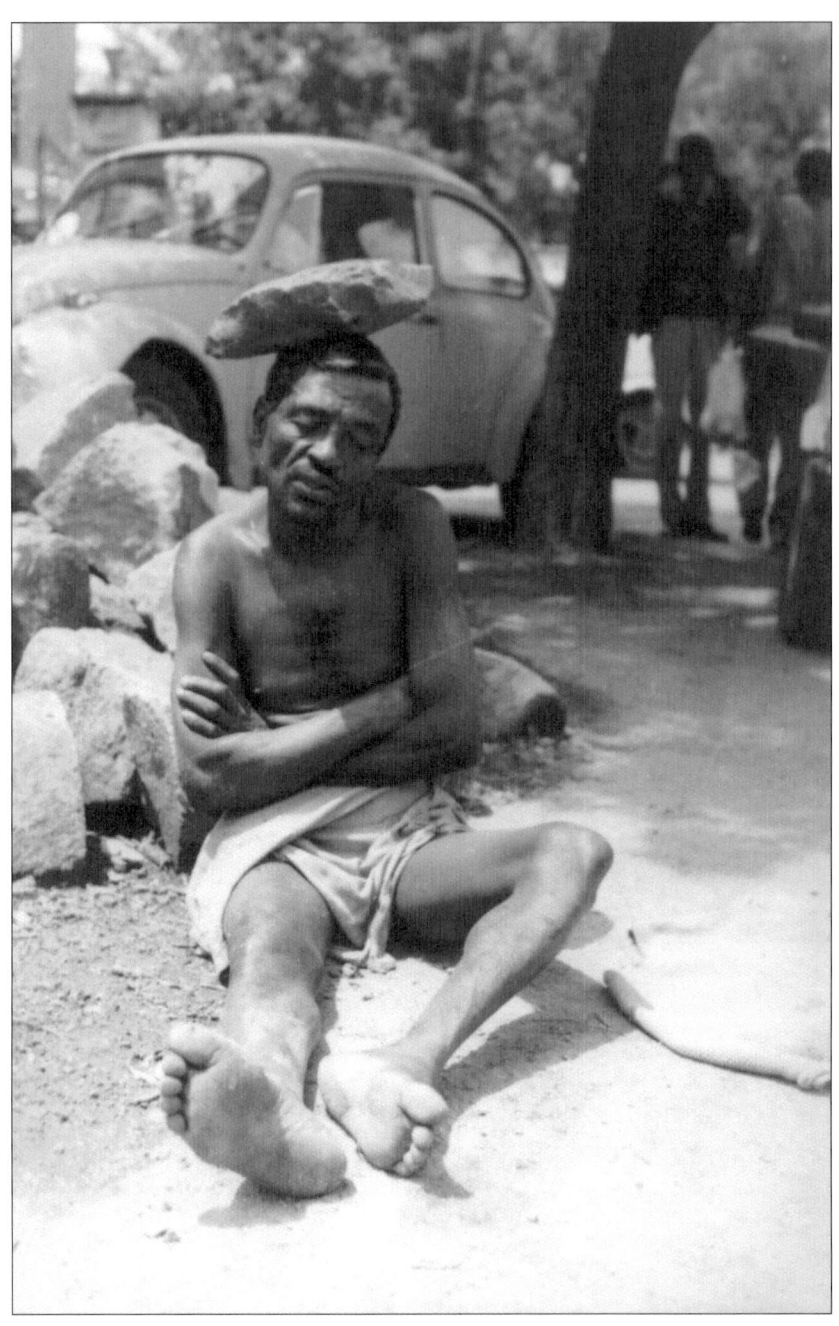
2. A Christian penitent. Courtesy of the author.

3. (left) and 4. (below) Performing in Circus Ethiopia while waiting for a visa. Courtesy of the author.

5. A refugee grave. Courtesy of the author.

6. The Falasha Cemetery. Courtesy of the author.

7. Elders at Neve Carmel. Courtesy of the author.

8. Blood Affair protesters. Courtesy of the author.

9. Re-creation of a Beta Israel village. Courtesy of the author.

"But she did not respond except to tell me that God loves me. Since then, I have no girlfriend." This is a story of radical and instantaneous religious change for the better, the acquisition of newfound moral coherence, and a changed relationship to basic appetites like drink and sex. Indeed, it is not just alcohol and drugs that Moshe claims to have given up entirely since meeting his mother in Christ, but also every other potentially addictive substance including, very significantly, the social drinking of coffee in the Ethiopian manner, which Pentecostals treat as nothing less than an invitation to satanic compulsion.

Working outward from Moshe, I gradually got to know the whole Pentecostal network at Neve Carmel, probably no more than five or six people in total at the time. Worke was the oldest member and apparently the moral center of the group as a whole. She was an extremely heavyset woman, the only truly obese Beta Israel woman I had ever met. The study in sheer physical contrast between her and Moshe, a slim man in his twenties, impressed itself upon me every time I saw them together. At our first meeting she spoke with forceful determination in rapid-fire Amharic, incomprehensibly simultaneous with Moshe's excited Hebrew account. Sometimes they would seem to converge on a point, with him translating or amplifying something she had said, adding further interpolations of his own and making the thread of her narrative even more difficult to follow. Unlike Moshe, Worke sets her illness narrative in northern Ethiopia near Gondar, where she too says that she was afflicted by chronic headaches and by a ringing in her ears that deprived her of sleep for weeks on end. Living alone, she squandered all of her financial resources on spirit healers, or *tankway*, whom she now describes as "servants of Satan." Some Beta Israel Jews in Israel still visit tankway, or pool their resources for trips to renowned healers of different kinds in Ethiopia, but Worke and other Pentecostals I have known always seem to narrow their focus to just one source of legitimate transformative agency—an authorized "believer" or healer—and to relegate almost any other kind of promised healing agency to malignant satanic manipulation. This is true even for the agents of other churches, like Orthodox priests, or the members of "nominal Christian" groups outside the Pentecostal orbit.

On the advice of an Amhara Christian friend, Worke finally visited a Pentecostal healer who had developed something of a local reputation. He miraculously had already foretold and prepared for her coming, and laid hands on her when she arrived, filling her whole body with a profound heat until she swooned. She slept for three days without waking (the Christian symbolism of this time frame should not be ignored), and found when she awoke that the ringing in her ears had finally stopped. Still, she remarks emphatically, the illness will return if her faith in Jesus ever wavers. Moshe breaks in to emphasize just how sick his mother had been before she was healed, wanting me to understand that this was true not just of physical but also moral debilitation. "Her whole body was no good. Now, look how fat [and healthy] she is!" A moment later Moshe interrupted again to tell me, "She was a woman living alone in the city, and you *know* how women manage in the city ... [he pauses] But now she has the Holy Spirit!" Worke herself never implied any sexual undercurrent that I could hear, but she did not correct Moshe, lurching instead to the so-far unmentioned political context in which our interview was taking place. She did not blame the state for her preconversion situation the way Moshe did, but then added defiantly: "We fear no one but God. I don't mind if they want to send me back to Ethiopia!" Following her lead. Moshe asked me not to mention his name in public. "I don't need to reveal myself," he says. "If I had wanted to reveal myself, I could have done so by now." Of course, I agreed to Moshe's request, only to learn in the days ahead that practically everyone at Neve Carmel, including the Israeli administrative staff, already knew all about him and his religious beliefs. Without putting too fine a point on it, Moshe and Worke's neighbors knew that the pair were *Pente* (Pentecostals), if for no other reason than that they were conspicuous in refusing to join their neighbors over coffee.

Coffee is abjured by Pentecostals partly because of widespread Ethiopian practices like offering coffee grounds to the spirits by burying them near the doors of houses or burning incense to the spirits in conjunction with communal drinking (H. Pankhurst 1992, 158–60; Nudelman 1993, 237); some of these practices have continued in Israel (Freeman 1995). More often and more vociferously, though, I was told by Worke and others that coffee drinking was associated with Satan because it led to *sus*, an Amharic term for uncontrollable desire and loss of independent will—the same term that they use for modern drug addiction. Cigarettes, drugs, alcohol, and caffeine are all purveyors of *susenya*, and all are vigorously opposed by Ethiopian Pentecostals who are anxious to establish a realm of freewilled intimacy with God in which to undergo the passivity of receiving Jesus. The fact that many Orthodox Jews in Israel smoke cigarettes, and that alcohol is used in Jewish ritual performances like Kiddush on the Sabbath, strengthened the Pentecostals' assessment of them as weak or immoral. The suffering of addiction is also strongly associated for Pentecostals with a world in which God's power has not been allowed to emerge. The projection of negative human affect onto demonic entities is not uncommon in charismatic Christianity (Csordas 2002 1994), and here addiction is portrayed paradoxically as both the tragic endpoint of unfettered human will and the hijacking of human agency by a malevolent satanic power.

At the same time, coffee drinking is so deeply important to Beta Israel that Pentecostal rejection cannot be understood as anything less than a full-scale attenuation of normal social and kinship ties. Beer is consumed in large quantities, especially by men, at all kinds of life cycle events including *tazkar* and naming feasts, and there are homemade Ethiopian beverages like *tejj* and *talleh* that make their appearance on special occasions. But coffee is consumed as part of the rhythm of everyday life, in small groups of up to a dozen relatives or neighbors who rotate through each other's homes almost every day. In an unpublished report for the Ministry of Absorption of the Government of Israel, anthropologist Chaim Rosen has even suggested that the stability of these coffee-drinking groups should be taken into account by government planners as they go about deciding how many new-immigrant Ethiopians should be settled in any given locale. The traditional "coffee ceremony" is a subject of many Ethiopian government travel posters—the very image of *behalachin*, "our culture" for highlanders—but these Ethiopian-Israeli gatherings are usually more informal, if no less important. They serve as a basis for other kinds of social activities, like the pooling of financial resources through a rotating "credit circle" among friends. Refusing to drink coffee in the house of a particular person might indicate that you suspect them of harboring malice, or even using witchcraft, against you. A university student told me that her mother had died in Ethiopia through *kinet* (jealousy magic) when she drank coffee at the home of an unsuspected rival.[2]

But if refusing to drink coffee at a particular person's home signals suspicion and distrust, the unwillingness to drink coffee anywhere can only be interpreted by other Ethiopians as a generalized malevolence or lack of willingness to share sociality. "They [the other Beta Israel immigrants] say that they don't like us," Moshe told me. His friend Ephraim, also a believer, added, "They mock us, because we don't drink coffee with them." Ephraim acknowledged however that while he refused to drink the fresh-ground *buna* (Amharic for coffee) normally drunk socially in small cups by Ethiopians, he would sometimes start his day with a mug of sweet Israeli Nescafé, consumed alone in his kitchen. For Ephraim, at any rate, it was social rather than physical addiction that counted most strongly. Or perhaps it would be more accurate to say that his perception of *sus* addiction was mediated by a set of cultural attitudes toward the drinking of coffee in social groups. This makes a great deal of sense, because while Pentecostal groups in other parts of the world do not necessarily share the rejection of caffeine products evident here, any Ethiopian religious group seeking to wrest individuals from the close enveloping folds of social pressure and conformity would have had to find some way to remove converts from these powerful networks.

Despite the harsh public rhetoric about the "missionary" threat to Beta Israel life, Pentecostal believers were typically treated as a source of wry amusement or social embarrassment rather than real fear or anger by their local Beta Israel interlocutors. Ephraim's neighbors at Neve Carmel often joked in his presence about his strange religion and sometimes called him "crazy," leaving him tight-lipped and silent. But then they would move on to another topic or just continue to quietly enjoy one another's company. Ephraim said he had received Jesus in Addis Ababa before immigrating, but that no one had asked him about his faith during the immigration process. He was in fact the only member of the "Feres Mura" immigration I met during fieldwork who was openly involved with Christian worship, and he was also one of the very few who told me that he had refrained from participation in the return-to-Judaism program on grounds of religious conscience.

He lived alone in a trailer with heavy curtains on the windows and worked nights just like Moshe. He told me that he preferred to live alone so that he could pray and read the Bible without interruption. He spoke slowly and a little distractedly, as if he suffered from some kind of mild impairment. Neighbors sometimes complained about the strange music (mostly American-made Amharic inspirational videos) emanating from his trailer, and one single mother of five who lived in a nearby trailer made faces of disgust when I mentioned Ephraim's religious practice. Ephraim himself told me that he kept his religion secret from family members and tried to steer conversations away from religious matters when he could, but I was present when an uncle who had already completed the return to Judaism admonished him, shaking his finger and lecturing him about the 'Orit (Amharic for Torah). He smiled while he did it though and gave me the distinct impression that Ephraim's refusal to drink alcohol bothered him almost as much as his unwillingness to participate in Jewish religious practice—the uncle was apparently a bit of a drinker himself.

There was little secrecy surrounding the identities of individual believers at Neve Carmel. When I visited Upper Nazareth in 1996, I learned that Teshome, the patriarch of my adopted family there, was also Worke's cousin, and that this bulwark of Beta Israel piety from the 1985 immigration also knew full well what religious choices his distant kinswoman had made. I let her name drop into conversation on a hunch during a family coffee gathering, provoking mostly raised eyebrows and guarded questions: "How do you know her?" Later, when I was alone with Teshome's wife and her two teenage sons, she told me conspiratorially that "Worke is a Christian, and you shouldn't talk to her." Given the evident embarrassment surrounding the subject, I did not press too much for details, but then she added with a sly laugh that Worke "really isn't *my* relative anyway. She's just related to my husband." After Worke left Neve Carmel for permanent housing in the south of the country while I was away for a few weeks later that year, I asked the absorption center office for her new contact information. "Oh, the missionary," one office worker said, with a smile. There had been a minor furor in 1995 over media reports that the police were under political orders to ignore allegations of illegal missionary activity among Ethiopians, but my impression was that local administrators simply did not view this as the kind of problem that warranted their intervention, no matter what the law might say (Izenberg 1995, 3).

Beta Israel Pentecostals I met inevitably espoused a rhetoric of radical healing and direct experience of divinity. Frequently, I could not help feeling that these were individuals who had been unable on some basic level to navigate the physical and psychosocial demands of religious and national transformation imposed upon them by migration to a new country, and possibly even by the demands of independent life. They were constantly seeking evidence from outside their immediate environs that the religious path they had chosen was the right one, and they were heavily dependent upon supportive material from the United States—pamphlets, books, and audiovisual materials in particular, although contrary to the constant suspicion reflected in media accounts, I never did uncover any evidence that they received direct financial support from foreign Christian groups. One day, Moshe insisted that I come to his trailer to watch a series of videos that were sure, he said, to prove to me the truth of his Christian message. One was a tape of a charismatic Ethiopian preacher from the United States, but another was the Hollywood production of Cecile B. DeMille's *The Ten Commandments*, which Moshe insisted was a demonstration of Scripture's literal veracity. Such episodes left me uncertain about how to evaluate Moshe's frame of mind, but the point of my analysis was never to pass judgment on his personal competence; I needed to understand how the conditions of Beta Israel life were expressed in Pentecostalism as well as in the return to Judaism. Moshe and his friends were the only individuals I met at Neve Carmel who openly espoused or were known to espouse Christianity.

Fieldwork at Neve Carmel required a constant negotiation of my own social and religious position vis-à-vis the field, and nowhere was that truer than in fieldwork among the Pentecostals. Despite my good relations with the handful of individuals who were known among their fellow immigrants as *Pente*, I had to be careful not to spend too much time with them lest I lend unintentional support to the idea that I too was a "missionary," not to be trusted. The believers themselves were willing and even enthusiastic about sharing their beliefs with me, but that was because they viewed this as this as a kind of "witnessing," and I suspected correctly that they would lose interest in me once it became clear to them that I had no interest in converting. Moshe and Ephraim's attitudes toward me began to change soon after they invited me to an Ethiopian-Pentecostal prayer service in Haifa during the winter of 1995. They had been excited about this event because a visiting Ethiopian preacher from the San Francisco Bay area had come to lead services. That night I described part of the experience in my field diary:

Haifa 1995

The apartment is modest and well furnished, unremarkable. It is a long bus ride here from Neve Carmel, and although Ephraim received permission to bring me, I am clearly out of place, whether as a curiosity or a potential threat. Moshe is already waiting. The preacher is from California, and we speak together briefly in English. He is surprised to see me, however, and seems reserved. With the exception of this individual, most of the dozen or so people gathered here are relatives or intimate friends who know each other well. The apartment belongs to a family that has been in Israel for over ten years, and their young children are hustled into the kitchen as the preaching begins ...

The preacher from San Francisco is perspiring and gesturing, holding a Bible in his right hand, speaking more and more quickly, interrupted now and then by the "Amens" of the believers. Then everyone is standing, with eyes on him, and I stand too. People have closed their eyes and stretched out their hands, and each of the worshippers is now uttering a low shriek or cry, increasing in pitch, but without words. A few tremble. The shriek reaches a sudden crescendo, and then it is over, people blinking and looking around at one another. We all sit as *injera* is passed around, and a video of worshippers at a Pentecostal healing service in Ethiopia is played; I have learned to expect a television or video to be playing in the background of every Ethiopian social event, religious or not. Moshe doesn't say anything, but Ephraim demands of me on the way home, "Why aren't you a believer?"

The emotional intensity of the Pentecostal service was quite different from the restrained and bureaucratic ethos of the return to Judaism, and Ephraim had trouble understanding how, after having witnessed this service, I could still refrain from joining in. He began to press me about this more and more frequently over the next several weeks, challenging me to engage in polemics or else join him in his belief.

Ephraim and Moshe made a strong distinction between their Christian faith and their Jewish ethnic or national identity. Like the LJS missionaries of the nineteenth century, they considered Jewishness an important racial and theological category and resisted all assertions that receiving Jesus was tantamount to renouncing Judaism. The visiting preacher from San Francisco told me that he, too, was surprised by this insistence upon Jewishness among Beta Israel Pentecostals, which he had never experienced in the other Pentecostal settings where he had served. "Jews for Jesus used to contact me all the time in America," he told me, "but I used to ignore them. Now after coming here, I am interested in finding out more." Beta Israel Pentecostals were not even typically willing to call themselves Christians, since they associated the term "Christianity" with the Ethiopian Orthodox Church, which they abhor. "Christianity is the worship of Mary, of angels, and of images," Worke told me firmly. "It is idolatry [*'avodah zarah* in Hebrew]. We pray," she says, pointing her index finger upwards to the ceiling, "only to God [*'Elohim*]."

Although neither Worke nor Moshe were designated "Feres Mura," there is at least some anecdotal evidence that Pentecostal converts are frequently drawn from among those who have already converted to Christianity in some form but have become disillusioned with its inherited practices and beliefs. A Pentecostal pilgrim in Jerusalem from predominantly Muslim Malaysia told me that something similar was true of "believers" in her own country, who often converted from Islam to some established church before eventually finding their way to the true faith. Both Worke and Moshe insisted that they were "Jews in their bones" and that their faith constituted "real Judaism." "I went to the synagogue [at Neve Carmel] once," insists Ephraim, "but the people there are serving Satan. They are angry all the time, and the men each have more than one woman. This one has a wife, but then he has another woman on the side.... They are very bad people."

Yet this very insistence upon a notion of "Jewishness" alongside radical conversionary faith in Jesus and the Holy Spirit contained some of the seeds of its own painful contradiction. Moshe, Worke, and Ephraim all talked about the inrush of divine power associated with acts of healing, which they insisted was possible only because of their commitment to keep aloof from compromising social entanglements like the local coffee-drinking group and the satanic power of addictive substances like caffeine. Yet this emphasis on divine healing power meant that suffering and illness of almost any kind could only be attributed to imperfect faith or to the individual's inability to receive divine vitality because of sin. This became a problem for some Beta Israel Pentecostals when it emerged into self-conscious conflict with the idea of modern "Jewishness" as a community of shared suffering, in which religiously committed and secularist Jews both claim a part.

Beta Israel apostates are frequently rejected even by Israelis who describe themselves as secularists precisely because of this perceived abandonment of shared suffering, which is a feature of the local cultural landscape that most immigrants from Ethiopia quickly come to understand. Pentecostal believers with whom I spoke had mixed opinions about whether God would ever sanction the use of medical doctors, but they agreed in principle that illness and suffering come only from sin and that God would heal those who believed. I was sometimes frustrated by Moshe's insistence upon this line of argument and asked him how he could make sense of collective catastrophes like wars or natural disasters, in which who were killed seemed innocent. He became quiet, with no immediate response, but Ephraim had also heard my question and immediately related it to the most painful wound in modern Jewish history:

> You know, I really don't understand. I ask myself this question all the time, and I have looked everywhere for an answer. Especially the *Shoah* [Holocaust]. Why do they always try to kill the Jews? I have even gone to ask a teacher at the university, and everyone, even *he* tells me they don't have an answer. What do you think? This really bothers me.

Pentecostal cosmology is sufficient for Ephraim when it comes to personal illness—especially chronic illness, where medical intervention offers so little comfort anyway—but the Holocaust represents a stumbling block, refractory to his "happy-minded" view (see W. H. James 1958) of the world's moral economy. Such suffering resists his point of contact with an imagined Jewish community that subsumes Beta Israel within a much broader context of Jewishness in Israel and elsewhere. His inability to resolve this contradiction was the only context in which he was willing to acknowledge a degree of ambivalence or confusion about his chosen religious identity.

Ephraim never seemed wholly at ease with his alienation from Beta Israel life. He spoke a great deal about going to America, but continued to put up with the teasing of his neighbors. When they met in their homes each night to drink coffee and eat parched barley (*chollo*) while gossiping about the day's events, Ephraim sat alone and prayed. He said that he was looking actively for a girlfriend so that he could marry, as his friend Moshe did soon after leaving Neve Carmel. "God is great," he said to me in one of our final conversations before he left the absorption center, and I told him that I agreed. Our ability to find some common theological ground was probably one of the only things that allowed our conversations to continue as long as they had. But Ephraim also knew that I did not mean this statement in exactly the same way that he did, and this growing realization came to constitute a rupture that no ethnographic methodology could bridge. There was simply no moment or space in Ephraim's life that he could separate from his preoccupation with receiving Jesus and witnessing that faith for others, and when his zeal met my religious immobility—even masked to some extent by my ethnographic suspension of disbelief—the conversation became frustrating for both of us. It wasn't entirely his doing, of course. Given the strictures of Jewish dietary laws that I observe, I was unable to eat comfortably—although I would have been happy to drink coffee—in his home.

"If You Do That, Where Will They Bury You?"

Including Beta Israel Pentecostals in this study despite the discomfort it will cause some readers helps to illustrate how common existential dilemmas help to shape religious experience across different social positions occasioned by different religious choices. Although Pentecostals are in some ways certainly outliers, their experience represents one prismatic effect of the common dilemmas facing all Beta Israel in modern times. Pentecostals answered the question of kinship with other Jews in the affirmative, but only on their own terms and subject to their own distinctive assumption about religious agency and change. Yet they also paid a price for this distinctiveness not just in a degree of internal ostracism from those who viewed their faith as a betrayal but also from their willingness to forgo some of the material and symbolic benefits of being recognized as Jews in Israel. To the extent that they were open about their religious commitments, Beta Israel Pentecostals would not, for example, be eligible for burial in any of the state-run Jewish cemeteries. There were other options, of course, like the Christian cemetery not far from the absorption center, where crosses decorated with Jewish stars and passages from the New Testament bore witness to a religious reality more complicated than that usually acknowledged as pertaining anywhere outside of Neve Carmel. Many of those buried there must have been Jewish converts to Christianity, or persons of mixed parentage, including immigrants, but this had relatively little appeal to Beta Israel Pentecostals who viewed themselves as Jews rather than Christians.

The vast majority of "Feres Mura" immigrants avoided this problem by agreeing to undergo the return-to-Judaism program, although one older man was reportedly denied burial in a Jewish cemetery because he had refused to join the program, and died while contesting it. He was not a Pentecostal but a "Feres Mura" with veteran Israeli relatives who insisted that the return to Judaism was superfluous and should be resisted. Israeli officials did not portray this as a sanction but as a logical consequence of failing to establish Jewishness, but it was certainly perceived as a sanction—and a strong one—by members of the "Feres Mura" community, equaled only by the denial of the right to bring additional family members from Ethiopia under the family reunification rubric. Although the vast majority of those who arrived in Israel went through the return-to-Judaism program willingly, it is difficult to disaggregate their various reasons for doing so, which certainly included threats such as these. It wasn't the inability to be buried that mattered to the people I knew (cemeteries on secular kibbutzim and other solutions would always be found for those who died outside the program) but the denial of dignity and kinship solidarity that such arrangements implied. The wounds from such indignity suffered by surviving family members could be severe.

Around the time of my first encounters with Moshe and the other Pentecostals, I began taking most of my meals with the family of Desta, a young man who had befriended me in Ethiopia. He was in his twenties and unmarried, spending much of his time with his older sister Rachel and her husband, Meles, who cared for four children and two younger siblings of their own. Desta's family lacked the brittle sensitivity I had come to expect from tensions between Alem and his father, and they welcomed my presence because I had helped to purchase medicine for their youngest son when he was hospitalized in Addis Ababa with what was presumed to be a fatal lung condition. I had been to the grave of Desta's father at the "Falasha Cemetery" in Ethiopia, but only heard in Israel how bitter Desta still was about the circumstances of his father's death and burial in an unmarked refugee's grave.

> When Operation Solomon happened, there was such a *balagan* [Polish-derived Israeli slang for "confusion" or "commotion"]. Everyone was pushing, crowding into the embassy, and I was there with my friend. He said, "Come on!" and pulled me in by the arm. But I said, "How can I go to Israel without my family?" They told us we would go soon, the next day. So I left . . . and my friend went to Israel. But they kept us waiting for four years. One day during the rainy season (*zenab gize* in Amharic) they sent for us from the embassy and told us our turn had come. So it was raining hard, but my father said the time had come, so we went, all of us, with the children, walking in the rain all the way to the embassy. When we got there, they said to us, "Why are you here?" We told them that they had sent for us, but they said it was a mistake, and made us go back in the rain. After that, my father got sick and then he died. When I think about him buried there, in Ethiopia, it makes me angry. I will never forget this, that because of them he could not die in Israel [*ba-aretz* in Hebrew, meaning "in the land"]. I won't forget.

Desta's father avoided the fate of some other "Feres Mura" who perished in Addis Ababa and was buried without incident. But his son blamed the Israeli bureaucrats in charge for the lethal callousness that he believed caused his father's death, preventing him from being buried with dignity in Israel. It was the ultimate rebuff of the kinship logic that Desta said had motivated his family to leave the life they knew and come to Israel in the first place.

Bureaucrats were not the only ostensible kin who often disappointed "Feres Mura" expectations. Before he died, Desta's father commanded his children to memorize his genealogy so that they could find their relatives if and when they finally reached Israel. It happened that one of the most significant of these relatives was my old friend Teshome from Upper Nazareth. It was a measure of Teshome's importance within the Beta Israel community that I so frequently met people who showed an interest in tracing their family connections to him, but in this case the coincidence for me was remarkable—two of my closest friends from the 1985 and 1994 immigrations had turned out to be second or third cousins. When I asked Teshome about this relationship he confirmed it and even helped me to map the family tree that linked him to Desta's grandfather, but added derisively: "Of course they [Desta's family] all went off and became 'Feres Mura.'" Teshome displayed no interest in resuming relations with these distant cousins, although I sensed something other than a theological dispute in his refusal. "When we decided to leave Ethiopia [clandestinely, through Sudan]," his grown daughter told me," there were 'Feres Mura' who informed the Christians we were going."

Beta Israel like Teshome frequently accused "Feres Mura" of disloyalty or betrayal not only for having converted but also for having sided with their enemies at crucial junctures. But this is compounded today by the zero-sum logic that pits one group of immigrants or potential immigrants against others for attention and resources. Once, when I was talking to Teshome's sons about my impending visit to Ethiopia, Avi punctuated his objection to "Feres Mura" immigration by pointing to a fading black-and-white photo of a girl hanging on their living room wall. She was the daughter, he said, of a cousin who had married a Christian man and then died in childbirth, leaving the girl to be raised by her father in his Christian village. I suggested to Avi that this actually made her "Feres Mura" by the current definition, but he adamantly denied this because she had never formally converted to Christianity. He went so far as to argue that the girl's mother didn't know at the time that she was marrying a Christian and that her daughter (the girl in the picture) had tried to leave her father to accompany her cousins to Israel across the dangerous overland route through Sudan in 1985. "When we went on the way to Sudan [that is, to Israel] she ran away from home and came out to go with us. But her father came and brought her back. Soon someone will go back to Ethiopia and get her by force. She is our family, and she has not been able to come here, but now the 'Feres Mura' are coming!" His bitterness was palpable, though he could not explain why he thought that the immigration of "Feres Mura" would delay his own cousin from coming to Israel if she were able. Rachel and Desta expressed interest in their distant relatives but also refrained from pushing to meet them, possibly in order to spare themselves the humiliation of rejection. The only time I ever saw representatives of both Desta and Teshome's families in close proximity (though they did not speak) was at the 1995 funeral of another recent immigrant who had died shortly after arriving in Israel. The man's first wife and children had immigrated ten years earlier and settled in Upper Nazareth, where they were Teshome's neighbors. He and his second wife, however, immigrated as "Feres Mura." I feared that there might be problems with the burial since he had died before completing the return-to-Judaism program, but Rabbi Waldman eulogized him with praise for making the decision to come to Neve Carmel and for recognizing the importance of Jewish education for his children. In this case, having begun the program was as good as having completed it, and he was laid to rest without incident. Although the program made some difficult demands on participants, it was generally the case that appearance of making a sincere attempt to comply was more important than successful completion of any single requirement. This tells us something important about the true meaning of return both for participants and for the agents of the state who facilitated it.

The return-to-Judaism program depended upon the capacity to generate pure hearts, or at least the perception of pure hearts, among its participants. Yet it was at its core a bureaucratic program that invoked repetition and the appeal to ancestral memory much more than the kind of intense religious experiences and clear beliefs that the Pentecostals constantly articulated. It worked best in cases like Alem's or Desta's, where it could be viewed as merely the consummation of a much longer term transformation that had preceded and accompanied immigration. In place of dramatic transformative rituals that anthropologists frequently seek to identify and describe in fieldwork, a series of ritual-bureaucratic acts was required to confirm rather than enact the religious status of new immigrants. This was clear at virtually every step in the extended process to which new immigrants were subject. In November 1995, I followed one cohort of about fifty people through the whole return-to-Judaism process, beginning with a three-month period of intensive classroom education followed by an oral examination. Classes focused on practical rather than theoretical religious issues, with heavy emphasis on liturgy and holidays as well as Sabbath and dietary laws that were by now more or less familiar to "Feres Mura'" and also had strong analogs within the indigenous Beta Israel tradition. Classes were organized to promote the repetition and memorization of information that was considered vital to the ritual competence of Ethiopian-Israelis, but little or no emphasis was placed on either analytic understanding of the laws or spiritual-experiential issues in religious life. At the end of three months, the entire cohort of men and women were examined by a panel of three rabbis who asked very basic questions to the whole group without singling out individuals for more sustained investigation, as is the rule in contemporary Orthodox conversion practice. This was portrayed as a process of penitence rather than true conversion, and it was clear that the intent of the conveners was for all of the individuals involved to be approved. A few days later, the men in the group were informed that the mohel (traditional circumciser) would soon be visiting Neve Carmel.

Ethiopian Christianity has been so closely identified with the practice of male circumcision that the seventeenth-century Jesuit traveler Jerome Lobo (1789/1978, 281, 293) once remarked that "it would not be easy to determine whether Abyssinians are more Jews or Christians." Yet all of the "Feres Mura" undergoing return to Judaism had to undergo one of two forms of circumcision ritual. A smaller number (including Alem, it turned out) had never been circumcised at all, and they were sent to a local hospital where the procedure could be performed under medical supervision. The failure to circumcise was, if anything, evidence that some descendants of converts had been living as something other than pious Christians in Ethiopia. Most of the immigrants had in fact been circumcised in infancy as Christians, however, and for them the problem was that circumcision undertaken without correct religious intentionality is invalid under Jewish law. They were obliged to undergo what the Rabbinate euphemistically called a "symbolic circumcision" (*milah simlit*) or, more technically, *hatafat dam brit* (literally, "drawing the blood of the covenant"), which meant that a drop of blood would have to be drawn from the penis, with proper intentionality, in front of witnesses. The job of the mohel was not just to perform this procedure but also to help witness and validate its completion for the Chief Rabbinate. Despite secularization, circumcision is still close to universal among Jewish males born in Israel, and the circumcision of adult men became increasingly widespread after the mass immigration of Jews from the former Soviet Union during the 1990s (see Yasur-Beit Or 2006; Siegel-Itzkovitch 2008). But the "Feres Mura" case was different because circumcision was enacted collectively for every single immigrant who came to Israel in the context of the return-to-Judaism program.

On the day the mohel arrived, seventy-five men were gathered to meet him. Some were from recent cohorts of the return-to-Judaism program, but there were also Ethiopian immigrants who had arrived in earlier waves but had for one reason or another not been registered as Jews at that time. The ethnographic literature contains many accounts of African tribes in which groups of agemates undergo the ritual and mystery of circumcision together (see V. Turner 1967), but nothing could have prepared me for the bemused, professional, and thoroughly bureaucratic atmosphere in which the Israeli mohel did his work. A heavyset man with a thick beard and dark jacket, he acted with the studied boredom of someone who had done this many times before. Men lined up outside the prefab synagogue building and stepped one by one behind a curtain where the mohel, Rabbi Waldman, and I were all sitting. Some of the men were carrying small boys or infants, and the mohel tried to distract them from glancing at the small, disposable needle in his gloved hand until he was done. Once their pants were pulled down he often managed to accomplish the pinprick (which we had to witness) before a child even noticed, but other times they left the room howling. Participants in the Neve Carmel program didn't seem overly embarrassed or resentful about the procedure, but that was less true of those who had come from outside—people who had been in Israel for years and had little or no personal relationship with Rabbi Waldman. Unlike most of the Neve Carmel residents, these men clearly felt the indignity of their position and were more likely to display their impatience with rolled eyes or veiled comments that neither the rabbi nor the mohel acknowledged hearing.

Hatafat dam brit was performed quickly and without any obvious ritual articulation. There was no liturgy or prayer recited, and as individuals pulled their pants down the mohel kept up a bantering and sometimes humorous running commentary on the quality of their previous circumcisions. It reminded me of nothing more than a professional diamond cutter admiring and critiquing the work of a colleague—"This one must have been circumcised in a village, this one at the hospital. Oh this is a fine job!" There was little or no conversation with the people whose blood was being drawn, who in many cases spoke very little Hebrew anyway. Each man's name was marked off in Rabbi Waldman's notebook as he left, causing me to reflect that the bureaucratic subtext of this encounter was apparently more important to lived experience than any ritual or religious content. In the context of return to Judaism, circumcision and *hatafat dam brit* were not initiation rites in the classic anthropological sense as much as they were rites of submission to state authority, made more complicated by competing and often incommensurate narratives held by competing social and religious factions. Rabbi Waldman's eagerness to save "lost Jews" and bring them home to the Holy Land was constantly juxtaposed with the view of "Feres Mura" primarily as economic refugees, even "missionaries," upon whom the act of return to Judaism could work no magic. Always, there was a sense of working against time, pulling immigrants through the process before some new government policy or diplomatic crisis could intervene, trapping those who were still in Addis Ababa.

Yet the essentially bureaucratic meaning of *hatafat dam brit* and the whole return to Judaism also meant that effort spent in quest of complex ritual symbolism would probably be misplaced, because it was the sheer power of compliance that made the return to Judaism efficacious for those who would accept its mandates. Thick, ethnographic description of the ritual act that focuses on cultural meaning while downplaying the contexts of power within which ritual activities occur would miss the point of ritual processes like those entailed by the return to Judaism, whose articulate, symbolic interpretation is far removed from the consciousness of those undergoing transformation (cf. Asad 1993; Seeman 2004). Asked why they underwent circumcision or drawing of blood, the cynics among Beta Israel immigrants would simply say that this is the price exacted by the state for full citizenship and membership in the Jewish people. The pious would say essentially the same thing, except that they would view it as a price exacted by Jewish law. This impression was reinforced a few days later by the immersion of men and women in the waters of a *mikveh*, which constituted the completion of the return to Judaism for program participants.

It was a chilly, rainy morning when we arrived at the special boarding school for converts where the immersion was scheduled to take place. Almost 150 people disembarked from the buses that had brought us and hustled down the side of a steep hill to the site of the *mikveh*, a small freestanding building with showers and changing rooms. The *mikveh* itself was a small tiled pool sunk into the floor in accordance with ancient specifications and fed by rainwater collected in specially constructed external tanks. Rabbi Waldman was usually happy to have me observe the return-to-Judaism program because he judged me a sympathetic observer, but throughout this process he had also asked me to serve as the third member of his ad hoc *bet din*, or religious court of three adult Jewish men traditionally required to witness each stage of a conversion process. Even without an active role to play, my presence was therefore far from neutral, and this did give me some pause. Even a cursory reading of anthropological literature shows that ethnographers frequently become significant players in local social and political life—handing out medicines, raising money for the construction of clinics, or representing outside forces of business and government. I also knew that some colleagues would view *this* involvement differently, given the controversy surrounding the return-to-Judaism program and "Feres Mura" immigration more generally. But it was and is clear to me that academic researchers have been involved in almost every aspect of Ethiopian Jewish life in Israel, dispersing funds for nonprofit organizations, testifying before powerful government committees, and almost always serving as important patrons for selected clients and friends. Though my decision was not without its complications (I had to work hard to make sure local people did not think I worked for Rabbi Waldman), it is a decision I would make again under similar circumstances.

Immersion turned out to be an intimate procedure. Men and women were first separated by gender, and each group was asked to shower for cleanliness, removing any dirt or other substances (jewelry, cosmetics) that might constitute a *hatzitzah* (separation) between their flesh and the *mikveh*'s purifying water. The women immersed first, in groups of five or six, wearing loose-fitting robes or oversized shirts that allowed the water to circulate underneath. Even a hair remaining above water when they immersed would invalidate the process, and this was one reason that witnesses were required, but the primary reason was that acts of conversion require the witness of a male court of three in traditional halakhah. Most of the women seemed relaxed, although a few giggled as much from the strange experience as from the recognition that they were nearing the end of a long and painful journey. Infants and small girls also had to be immersed in their mother's arms while boys who were sent to await the immersion of the men later that morning. None of these women had been exposed to the vast apologetic literature that exists in both English and Hebrew concerning the spiritual or health benefits of *mikveh* use by women each month, and as far as I could tell they had not been given any kind of intellectual or interpretive justification for why immersion was necessary or should be witnessed by a religious court. A group of women would enter, immerse quickly (some had to be asked to repeat the procedure), then exit back to the changing room. Once all the women had gone through, the same procedure was repeated for the men, except that they immersed naked under the male court's watchful eyes, and with many fewer giggles. Compared to the circumcision and drawing of blood, this was a low-stress affair, treated by most as something to just get over with. After all of the immersions were complete, participants lined up to receive their return-to-Judaism certificates.

After they had been recognized as Jews, immigrants stayed at Neve Carmel for up to two or three years while they continued learning Hebrew, acclimating, and making plans to buy heavily subsidized apartments in different parts of the country. As long as they stayed at Neve Carmel, though, the stigma of being "Feres Mura" was difficult to shake. Israelis in the nearby towns and outlying suburbs had only a vague idea of what Neve Carmel represented, but immigrants sometimes told me they had been harassed on buses or in local schools. It was hard to know when this kind of unpleasantness was really directed more broadly at new immigrants or even specifically at Ethiopians in general rather than "Feres Mura," but I had the sense that diffuse public knowledge of their ancestral involvement with Christianity was part of the mix. The difficulty of their circumstances certainly made even misdirected jibes feel more direct and personal. It was not, however, problems with the *farenge* (whites) that caused former "Feres Mura" the most grief during these early years, but rather the ongoing delicacy in their relations with fellow Beta Israel. Between 1994 and 1996, "Feres Mura" immigrants were never permitted to use the trailer that had been designated a synagogue by the *kessotch* (Beta Israel priests) who had immigrated to Neve Carmel in 1991. The priests held their Sabbath services without much audience or fanfare at dawn on Saturdays in the traditional Ge'ez liturgy. But a second synagogue that had been set up for the "Feres Mura" to use was brimming with activity for public prayer in Hebrew and Amharic three times a day, in addition to classes and youth programs. The priests who lived at Neve Carmel never compromised but other priests from outside Neve Carmel eventually began visiting and treating the "Feres Mura" as Jews.

In 1996 I participated in a Neve Carmel baby-naming ceremony, referred to by many (not just in the "Feres Mura" community) as a *kristena*, or "christening," despite the Christian connotations of that term (see Schwarz 2001). The ceremony was presided over not just by Kes Imharan of Upper Nazareth, who had always shown a degree of sympathy for the plight of "Feres Mura," but also by the fiery and aged Kes Ayellegn of Safed, who had been an early opponent of "Feres Mura" and of the Israeli rabbinic establishment. Both *kessotch* were cordial and respectful of the former "Feres Mura" who were naming their child in accordance with custom on the fortieth day, but they did stop the proceedings at one point to question (and then approve) the parents' choice of name. "Immanuel" is a name with good biblical Hebrew roots (in Isaiah 7:14, it means "God is with us"), but it is sometimes thought to have strong Christian and messianic overtones (see Matthew 1:23) and is especially popular among Protestants. After a short conversation, the priests were satisfied that the Hebrew pronunciation of the name was acceptable, and they allowed the *kristena* to go forward. More and more *kessotch* visited Neve Carmel for life-cycle events like this throughout that year, especially when they could claim some kind of personal or family connection. They were also paid by families for their services.

Ultimately, "Feres Mura" had to contend not just with the daily surveillance and judgment of outsiders like Rabbi Waldman or Kes Ayellegn but with that of their own hypercritical and gossip-prone neighbors. Gossip is a normal part of social life in any small community, but among Ethiopians this sometimes took an especially bitter form because of the constant preoccupation with contested genealogies and religious agency of "Feres Mura" immigrants. Accusations from non-Ethiopians tended to be concerned with the imagined purity of collective cultural and religious identities: "They were Christians when it was convenient to be Christians, and now they are Jews when it is convenient to be Jews!" One relative of new immigrants who visited Neve Carmel told me, "Israelis say that they [the "Feres Mura"] all have AIDS." Accusations that began within the Beta Israel or "Feres Mura" orbit tended by contrast to take on a more personal texture, targeting specific individuals or families along a clear trajectory of local schisms and intimate knowledge of individual families.

On the evening of the Simhat Torah festival in October 1995, residents of Neve Carmel gathered at the "Feres Mura" synagogue for a night of dancing and celebration. It was the conclusion of the fall holiday season, and also the day on which Jewish communities around the world traditionally complete the annual reading of the Torah at the end of Deuteronomy before starting again with Genesis. The circle dancing was boisterous, with hand clapping and singing in both Hebrew and Amharic, Ethiopian immigrants together with members of the local Bnei Akiva youth group. It was one of the rare moments in which the rhetoric of pure-hearted, single-minded immersion in the religious message of the return-to-Judaism program seemed wholly realized. Not everyone from Neve Carmel was present, but those who were seemed on fire with an earnestness I had not seen since Shabbat prayers in Addis Ababa, when everyone present knew that they were staking their future on the idea and practice of a difficult "return." It was more than the slap of cool night air that pulled me out of this reverie when I stepped outside.

An Ethiopian-Israeli man in his thirties or forties approached me directly to strike up a conversation. I had never met him before (he was one of the "veteran" Ethiopians still living at Neve Carmel after several years in the country), and I was not in the mood to talk, but I had learned from experience that offers of conversation could be preludes to important relationships. We made small talk for a few moments, and then he told me why he had sought me out. He wanted to tell me that there were many Ethiopian families that had been torn apart when one spouse became Pentecostal. I waited for the other shoe to drop. He said he had seen me frequenting the trailer of Meles and Rachel (Desta's sister) and wanted me to know ("for my own good") that they were *Pente* missionaries who should not be trusted. I told him I found this hard to believe. Neither Rachel nor her husband attended the Pentecostal services in Haifa, they were never mentioned by other believers, and they participated openly in Ethiopian Jewish rituals, including the social consumption of coffee. This was, moreover, a family I took my meals with at least once each day, and I felt certain that I could not have missed anything so dramatic about their lives. Yet my mysterious interlocutor (he never would identify himself) answered all of my objections with a raised eyebrow and what he considered to be a single, incontrovertible question: Had I seen the car that was often parked near their trailer? How else would they have gotten money for a car, if not from the missionaries? Suddenly, the whole accusation made a great deal more sense.

Investigation revealed that the vehicle parked near their trailer did not in fact belong to Rachel or Meles, but to some veteran Ethiopian-Israelis who had been visiting relatives for a few days at Neve Carmel. Despite the rumor that *Pente* proselytes were well paid for their conversions, I never discovered any evidence during the 1990s to support this claim. The whole pattern of accusation against Rachel and Meles actually reminded me a great deal of the classical witchcraft accusations described in ethnographies of Africa—small-scale societies living close to the edge of economic survival, in which any indication of unusual success by one person or household can easily be thought to come at the expense of others; the subsequent attribution of that success to mysterious and malevolent powers. Anthropologists have shown how closely such accusations are related cross-culturally to patterns of social gossip that mark individuals or small groups off as vectors as jealousy or harm in this kind of setting (Stewart and Strathern 2003). The *content* of traditional East African witchcraft accusation may have been quite different from what I was witnessing at Neve Carmel—the charge that Beta Israel turn themselves into hyenas to eat their Christian neighbors versus the accusation that they lie in wait as missionaries to harm their fellow Jews—but the *structure* of the accusation was eerily the same. It would have been easy to dismiss the accusation altogether, especially given the smell of alcohol upon the accuser, but this would have been a mistake. It was not the first time I was reminded of the uncomfortable kinship between certain kinds of ethnographic research and police work. Both rely upon the uncovering and analysis of morally charged data (that is, "secrets") that our informants might prefer to protect from outsiders.

It took a few weeks to find an opportunity to raise the issue without hurting my friends. We were drinking coffee late one night by ourselves, so I asked Rachel and Meles what they knew about Pentecostals at Neve Carmel. Despite my precautions, they immediately surmised that I had been hearing the rumors about them. They became visibly and uncharacteristically agitated as they complained about the atmosphere of lies and accusations that had poisoned their lives at Neve Carmel, and confided in me that they were making a push to raise money to leave the absorption center for permanent housing much sooner than most of their relatives because of it. They spoke powerfully about their desire to make a fresh start in some place where they would have only a few Ethiopian neighbors and where the burden of stigma they carried as "Feres Mura" might finally be relieved. They told me they thought they knew who was spreading the rumors about them and attributed it to jealousy because of their education and relative success at acclimating to life in Israel. That explanation didn't really settle anything, but it was certainly plausible, and it confirmed my own suspicions and observations. I apologized for bringing up such a painful subject and wished them luck in moving. Within just a few weeks in fact, they announced that they had indeed found a small apartment they could afford near the center of the country and asked for my help with the logistics and short-term expenses of moving. They were the first of the families I had met in Addis Ababa who left the absorption center for life on their own, and their departure signified a kind of closure and moving on for me as well.

One day while they were packing their belongings for the move, however, Rachel returned on her own accord to our conversation about the gossip against them at Neve Carmel. We were alone in her trailer with some of the younger children, and for just a moment I had the distinctive feeling that all of the defensive masks born of desperation had finally fallen. We had seen each other through some difficult times over the previous few years, including the serious illnesses of her children, the desperate waiting time in Addis Ababa, and the disappointed euphoria of reaching Israel and completing the return to Judaism only to discover that new hurdles for acceptance remained. She reminded me about our conversation concerning Pentecostals at Neve Carmel, and then paused, possibly uncertain. This was the first time she had directly addressed the whole question of religious history and change unprompted:

> I have eaten many things during my lifetime, but we are Jews. It was our grandfather who made a mistake [in becoming a Christian], not us, so why won't people just leave us alone! One time, Rabbi Waldman came to our *caravan* [trailer home]. He pointed his finger and said, "I know you are *Pente*." But I told him it was not true, and got very angry. Some time later, he came back to apologize. But from that day, I said I would not go into his synagogue. My husband goes, but I will not go there.

This alimentary metaphor ("I have eaten many things") was somehow more poignant and direct than almost anything I had heard since the beginning of my research into the "Feres Mura" dilemma several years before. It was an acknowledgement of religious heterogeneity and change, framed not in the frequently misleading language of theology and belief favored by scholars and bureaucrats but in the much more ethnographically vivid language of consumption and literal bodily incorporation of the changing circumstances and choices that help to make up a life. "I have eaten many things" meant not just "I have eaten forbidden foods" (possibly an oblique reference to life in the past as a Christian); it was also an expression of the profound estrangement she had experienced in both worlds and the ironic, somewhat critical perspective she had on each of them.

Rachel was defiant in relation to the return to Judaism and its never-ending suspicion and surveillance. She insisted that her family's decision to adopt Judaism and Jewish-Israeli nationality were sincere. She also said that Rabbi Waldman had acknowledged his mistake in accusing them—had it been a fishing expedition on his part?—but she refused to let him off the hook so easily. Rachel's religious and social reality cannot easily be encompassed by the totalizing descriptions of most commentators on the "Feres Mura" dilemma. We have yet to pioneer a descriptive language that can make sense both of her definite long-term shift in sense of self-orientation and religious commitment and her ongoing ambivalence about many of the demands that these changes imposed upon her. All of her children were being sent to religious Jewish schools and continued to maintain a level of traditional Jewish observance even after they left Neve Carmel. But Rachel and her family were far from the pliant and self-effacing penitents that defenders of the return-to-Judaism program sometimes portrayed. She seemed at this moment to really want me to understand the delicate balance she sought. When her girls were told at school that they should only wear dresses, never pants, in accordance with Orthodox standards of modesty, her oldest daughter complained. Rachel acknowledged the school's education message, then added, "But if she wants to wear pants, I cannot tell her not to. That is something she will have to decide. What can I do?"

Her attitude was not so different from that of many other Israeli families I knew who sent their children to state-sponsored religious schools yet describe themselves as *masorti* ("traditional") or might even describe themselves as *dati* ("Orthodox"), but nevertheless reserve the right to question or disregard some of the things that educators and rabbis insist upon (cf. Kedem 1995; Sharot 1995). The dilemma for "Feres Mura" was that they were constantly being judged on the basis of such subtle signs of disaffection, in ways that could be debilitating. A group of boys flinging off their knitted *kippot* (skullcaps) when they descend from the bus after a day of classes is a primordial scene repeated in many Israeli towns every day, but at Neve Carmel it led one anthropologist I knew to wonder aloud whether the whole return to Judaism at Neve Carmel might really be a sham. People like Rachel were subtly aware of these symbolic transactions, which could have powerful repercussions for themselves and their children. It made the return to Judaism into an exhausting and often demoralizing process, but there was nothing to do about it but weather the storm and hope for better things.

Rachel's admission to having "eaten many things" is only the external facade of what Durkheim (1982) once called a "social fact." It acquires analytic relevance only through the ethnographer's willingness to embed it in some more-or-less plausible account of human agency and constraint, which is what the whole "Feres Mura" dilemma is really about. What critics of ethnography sometimes decry as anecdotalism is really just the attempt to build up a picture of what is experienced or undergone in some concrete local setting through the collection of multiple tableaus upon a common scene. Drawing from multiple different sources and subject positions—formal interviews with both immigrants and social workers, as well as informal conversations at public telephones and media accounts of contemporary controversies, for example—is a way of building up a structure of plausibility for the story that the ethnographer would like to tell. There really is no substitute for this meandering process, least of all the reduction of people's lived experience to a single set of formal interviews or experience-distant statistical and historical analyses. Yet this recognition imposes a heavy burden upon scholars who understand that some particular emplotment of other people's lives and motivation might help to generate even more constraint and limitation in a particular social setting. Will some reader conclude that Rachel's family was in fact hiding something that should disqualify their assertions of Jewishness, or will readers respond to the complexity of motivation and of circumstance (to the picture of what is experienced) with a new sympathy and appreciation for just how imperfect religious and bureaucratic categories can be?

It is tempting to try to protect informants like Rachel by adopting what Ernst Gellner once called a "ventriloquist" model of anthropology, in which the ethnographer substitutes his or her own interpretation for the lived experiences of informants. Gellner did not mean it as a compliment, and I take this to be one of the most trenchant critiques of the kind of anthropology that I am advocating. The desire to protect informants by closing off certain avenues of interpretation, and to protect oneself by making the data seem more self-explanatory and incontrovertible than the fieldwork experience actually indicates, is very real. The attempt to pierce behind the obfuscating mask of shared "culture" to the human stories that lie beneath can leave an ethnographic account appearing underdetermined, in the sense that the researcher is left just like any other social actor, struggling to make sense of partial clues and "wax and gold" style indirection (sometimes even misdirection) while attempting to construct a plausible narrative about why people do what they do. The appeal of ventriloquism is that it allows the writer to counter possibly unpalatable conclusions by stacking the decks against readers through a rhetorical conceit of social scientific certainty. But the problem is that both analytic honesty and concern for the inviolable humanity of informants pushes in precisely the opposite direction, to the acknowledgment of what remains opaque or indeterminate in the experience of other people.

One day over lunch, shortly before she and her family left Neve Carmel for good, Rachel told me about a seemingly trivial experience that nevertheless shook her—and that shook me when she told me about it—to the core. Like other Ethiopian women living in Israel (with the exception of Pentecostals),

Rachel was accustomed to drinking strong, freshly ground coffee with her friends and relatives for hours at a time, and as often as three times a day. But she had learned in the return-to-Judaism program that it was prohibited to cook or to cultivate fire on the Sabbath, and that this extended to heating water for coffee. For some Beta Israel women, caffeine-deprivation headaches on the holy day were a way of life. Orthodox Jews outside of Neve Carmel have developed ways to observe the Sabbath and feed their addiction too, by using electric coffee urns that can keep water heated all Sabbath long, or by placing already brewed coffee on a hotplate. But for immigrants like Rachel, this was simply unfamiliar. Like Karaites, traditional Beta Israel society had prohibited the use of fire on the Sabbath even if it had been kindled beforehand, so observant Beta Israel in Ethiopia simply ate cold foods on the Sabbath. This frequently continues even in Israel today, as there was no Ethiopian custom (as there was in Europe for example) dealing with how to keep food warm for the Sabbath day. Even in Israel technological solutions like electric urns or hotplates were considered too expensive by many new immigrants.

Rachel confided in me that on one recent Sabbath she had been so tired from all of her work, and her headache had gotten so bad, that she steeled herself to violate Jewish law by making a cup of tea in the privacy of her own kitchen (the smell of coffee would have roused the neighbors). As she went about her preparations, though, she was interrupted by her attentive nine-year-old son, Avraham:

> He said to me, *Innate* ["my mother" in Amharic], "If you do that, where will they bury you?" When I heard that, I wanted to cry. I told it to my husband when he came home, and the very next day he went out and bought us a *plata* [Hebrew for "electric hotplate"] even though it cost seventy shekels [about twenty-three U.S. dollars]!

Given their family history and unresolved grief over the burial of Rachel's father in the "Falasha Cemetery" of Addis Ababa, Avraham's question could not have been more poignant or insightful. He was only nine, but he understood the dangers involved. Would violating the Sabbath entail his mother's expulsion retroactively from the return-to-Judaism program, and if it did, where could she be buried? The fears and vulnerabilities of an entire community were summed up in that question. Rachel wept when she told the story, and I came near to weeping when I heard it.

Yet the question remains. Should this episode be read as evidence that the instrumental reading of the return to Judaism was ultimately correct? I do not presume to plumb the hearts and minds of all the people who shared their lives with me at Neve Carmel, or to guarantee the purity of heart that both Kierkegaard and Rabbi Waldman describe. In truth, I find that discourse to be as deeply flawed and misleading as its counterpart in the assertion of malevolent or dishonest motivation common to many academic and bureaucratic accounts. And I remain wary, too, of the possibility that religious agency may shift with time and circumstance, so that motivation which was once more nearly instrumental may become less so as religious changes take root in the structure of a person's life. However they begin, transformations like those undergone by "Feres Mura" are not in the end so easily reducible to just a single register of explanation. Rachel's account and the emotions it aroused for her—regret, ambivalence, and an upwelling of love for her son—are the irreducible core of what it means to be human.

In the end, Avraham's fear and Rachel's decision are as unfathomable to the theological language of pure hearts as they are refractory to the ungenerous hermeneutics of suspicion and accusation. But this means that they also remain to some degree opaque to any analysis that has been schooled in these alternatives. Personally, I prefer to read this story as a powerful reminder of what can be at stake for individuals in a simple yet culturally ramified act like making a cup of coffee or tea at the wrong time and place in the uncertain "Feres Mura" universe. Rachel could have responded to her son's question in many different ways, but she chose in this case to rethink her action and reaffirm one of the most important authenticating rituals of traditional Jewish life. She undertook, that is, to refrain from making coffee on the Sabbath.

CHAPTER 6

BLOOD AND TERROR

> They have spilled their blood like water round about Jerusalem, and there is none to bury it; we have become a taunt to our neighbors, a scorn and derision to those round about us. How long, Lord?
>
> —Psalm 79 (recited during afternoon prayers at Neve Carmel on February 25, 1996, after the suicide bombings of two buses in Jerusalem and Ashkelon)

Not all events that were of ethnographic import to the main themes of this book took place within the "Feres Mura" community alone, or in the microcosm of local social relations at Neve Carmel. On a Friday in late January 1996, an investigative report in the daily newspaper *Ma'ariv* broke a story that changed the whole discourse on immigration and cultural authenticity in fundamental and unexpected ways. A journalist revealed publicly for the first time that the Israeli blood bank administered by *Magen David Adom* (Red Star of David—Israel's equivalent of the Red Cross) had been routinely destroying blood donations made by Ethiopian-Israelis. Blood bank and Ministry of Health officials were quick to announce that they had acted to protect the public blood supply from contamination by high rates of infectious disease among Ethiopian immigrants including hepatitis and malaria, but especially HIV-AB. Most Ethiopians were unimpressed. By Saturday night I had received a call from Desta telling me that a large demonstration was being planned for the following Monday. I had no idea how large or how violent the demonstration would ultimately be, or how crucial a turning point it would turn out to be in the lives of Ethiopian-Israelis. Nor did I understand at first how critical this series of events would be in further undermining—and redefining—the position of "Feres Mura" immigrants and their kin who still remained in Ethiopia. I failed to suspect at the time just how quickly the Blood Affair, as it came to be known (*parashat ha-dam* in Hebrew) would come to be interpreted in light of the violent maelstrom that was soon to engulf Israeli society as a whole.

Grief and a Stone Thrower's Rage

"Of course I threw rocks! Don't you realize they are killing us?" The speaker was a woman in her late twenties, studying for a professional degree. Most of the stone throwers, from what I could see, were men, but her response was not atypical. Between 8,000 and 10,000 demonstrators had converged on the offices of the prime minister in Jerusalem. A permit had been issued for only 850, and despite newspaper predictions that thousands of angry protesters would arrive, the police were clearly unprepared for the scale of the event. Officers later attributed their failure to call for reinforcements to the belief that there was no need to do so, because "they knew the Ethiopians to be a quiet and retiring community" (*Yediot Aharonot*, January 29, 1996, p. 2). That passive stereotype was one of the Blood Affair's first casualties. By sundown, at least sixty-one people had been injured seriously enough to require medical attention. Forty-one of these were members of the police and security services, Among the worst injuries were those suffered by a police officer who lost an eye and a young demonstrator whose skull was cracked by an errant stone. Despite the potential for lethal harm however, it is an ethnographic fact of some importance that no one was killed.

I am mindful of the pitfalls in describing an event like the Blood Affair. Renato Rosaldo (1989) wrote that he understood for the first time, in the wake of his wife's tragic death during fieldwork, why his informants had always resisted the imputation by anthropologists of "deeper" symbolic realities behind what they described as relatively straightforward expressions of grief and rage. When the former headhunters among whom he worked told him that they took the heads of their enemies in response to anger and personal loss, his initial reaction had been to seek the abstract cultural logic and symbolism that would neatly explain such practices, until his own experience taught him what loss could do. It is difficult to parse the rage of Ethiopian-Israelis who threw rocks at police or who wept in public over the humiliating rejection of their blood from the public blood supply, and it would be a fallacy of cultural analysis to reduce that outrage and humiliation to some mechanical reaction to the transgression of cultural boundaries. Culture does not by itself determine how a community will respond to provocation, how it will interpret its history and social experience, or how contingencies of time and place will coalesce in a potentially bloody course of action, and this is why experience-oriented ethnography tends to complicate rather than simplify the story of human agency in local settings. There was too much at stake for too many individuals, too much unsettling rage and shifting ambivalence over time, for any neatly packaged analytic or explanatory model to bear the whole weight of interpretation, and although it erupted in just a moment, the Blood Affair took on several different kinds of meaning as it unfolded over time.

January 28, 1996

It is 10 a.m., outside the offices of the Prime Minister in Jerusalem, and it is obvious that this will not be a demonstration like all the others. Thousands of Ethiopian-Israelis line the streets and cover the steep rock-bank which faces the building. What first catches my eye is a row of older women, in their white shammas and colorful kerchiefs over graying hair. They are slowly shaking their fists in the direction of the government building. Already the faces of government workers can be seen lining the windows. Until today, the well-known icon of Ethiopian protest had been the silent sit-in waged at the offices of the Chief Rabbinate [against the need for "symbolic conversion"] in 1985.

Everyone is here, representatives of every family with whom I am in contact. During the course of the day, I meet Yossie, Alem, and two of Teshome's young daughters. . . . They have come from Upper Nazareth and from the immigrant "absorption center" near Haifa, by public transportation and in buses chartered by the Ethiopian "umbrella organization" chaired by Addisu Messele. Students have taken off from school, soldiers have left their bases without leave. This is one of those jarring moments in which people whom I have come to know in very different settings suddenly come together as representatives of a small community in a small country. They are carrying placards in Hebrew and English with messages like "One People, One Blood," "We are Jews Like You," "Stop the Racist Apartheid," "Our Blood is Also Red," and "We Will Not Allow Our Blood to go Ownerless." Many boys are wearing wool ski-hats reminiscent of African-American fashions, while others sport knitted yarmulkes. Some also display the Ethiopian national colors. In an unusual gesture, a group of monks from the Ethiopian Orthodox Church in Jerusalem have come bearing an Ethiopian flag in an effort to make common cause. On the other hand, there are not many white faces in the crowd—a handful of anthropologists and long time political activists, reporters, a few sympathetic members of religious youth groups, and some secular teenagers with their Ethiopian friends or sweethearts. Sometimes these visible outsiders are challenged to justify their presence here. It is young Ethiopian men with hand-held megaphones who are directing the crowd, and this is their day.

Within an hour of my arrival the demonstrators have forced their way past police and soldiers into the inner parking lot of the offices of the Prime Minister. Another fence still separates them from the entrance to the building. At a point not visible to me, a group of people have tried to force the fence and we are all pushed back with short blasts of water. An old man, dripping and laughing, says "Bring on the gas!" and those of us who are nearby chuckle.

Even the police seem to be laughing as a couple of young girls, shrieking, dodge to avoid the water. Then, off to my left, a stone goes sailing toward the police. More stones. Other demonstrators are yelling at the stone-throwers to stop. Police charge with batons. Choked by tear gas, we run with closed eyes, accompanied by the sound of stones bouncing off of parked cars. . . . Later, while picking ourselves up off the grass, coughing, an older man to my right extends his hand with a look of sympathy. But from the young man to my left, I hear the startled and angry question: "What are we, Arabs?" The crowd begins to regroup. I go to search for people I know.

Ownerless Blood

One of the most popular slogans chanted at the demonstration was *lo nitan dameinu hefker*, "We will not allow our blood to go ownerless [or to be abandoned]" an elegant condensation of several important messages that protesters had come to bear. On its most explicit level, *lo nitan dameinu hefker* meant simply that the secret destruction of Ethiopian blood donations would no longer be tolerated.[1] "Our blood will not be treated as if it were ownerless," however, meant by extension that Ethiopian-Israelis would no longer tolerate being treated as if they were less than full and capable masters of their own bodies, charged with the responsible disposition of their own blood (and, undeniably in the context of HIV, their own sexuality), just like other adult citizens. Repeatedly, in the context of this demonstration, the insult of having been lied to by public health officials vied in importance for Ethiopian-Israelis with the insult of having had their blood donations summarily rejected, or "spilt" in the evocative though inaccurate imagery of public protest.

"Ownerless" blood is a highly charged metaphor in Israel, as the Ethiopian-Israelis who deployed that language well knew. The Hebrew world *hefker*, which I have translated here as "ownerless," implies not just lack of legal ownership but also wildness, irresponsibility (including sexual promiscuity), and abandonment (Alcalay 1965, 565). *Shetah hefker* is, literally, "no-man's land" in modern Hebrew, and property that has been declared *hefker* by its owners is free for the taking. Allowing a child to go *hefker* means abandoning parental responsibility, with a strong implication that the child will come to lawlessness as a result. But *dam hefker*, or ownerless blood, relates in mainstream Israeli-Jewish discourse to the cry of the defenseless victim whose blood has no avenger. A victim's blood is free for the taking, in the sense that no killer will be brought to justice. The phrase *dam yehudi hefker* (ownerless or abandoned Jewish blood) has become a potent shorthand expression for pervasive physical insecurity, evoking the Holocaust and contemporary political violence in a potent and easily recognizable semantic network (see B. J. Good 1994). This is the sense in which "ownerless blood" is sometimes deployed in nationalist rhetoric as evidence for the overwhelming moral imperative to establish and defend a majority Jewish nation-state. Around the time of the Ethiopian protest, I attended a right-wing nationalist demonstration in the Old City of Jerusalem, where a small group calling itself the Temple Mount Faithful screamed that allowing the Temple Mount (Haram Al-Sharif in Arabic) to remain in Muslim hands was tantamount to a "continuation of Hitler" and a situation of *dam yehudi hefker*. They probably had never heard about a group of Jewish partisans who took vengeance on German targets in Lublin after World War II, calling themselves by the acronym DIN (Hebrew for "judgment"), which also means "the Blood of Israel Avenges" (Lang 1996).

By insisting that they would refuse to allow their blood to be treated as if it were ownerless, Ethiopian-Israeli protesters were able to stake an ironic claim on Jewish historical memory, portraying themselves as the Jewish victims of an implacable outside enemy. In chapter 1 I showed just how pervasive the use of Holocaust imagery could be in conversations about the Jewishness of "Feres Mura," and the appearance of prominent Holocaust imagery at this demonstration was also a strong, early sign that questions of Jewish historical memory were of primary importance. I saw placards held by young Ethiopians reading "Remember what Hitler did!" and "Stop the second Holocaust!" One youth could be heard shouting through the din, "I thought that this people learned something fifty years ago—this is a second *Shoah* [Holocaust]!" Later, outside the fray, my friend Emebet, a "Feres Mura" immigrant who had been to Poland on a government-sponsored Jewish heritage trip, echoed the same slogan over falafel and hummus at the central bus station in Tel Aviv.

For me, the comparison between public health policies banning the use of immigrant blood and Nazi genocide was troubling, to say the least. During the chaos of the demonstration, I mustered the courage to ask one young man with a placard what he meant by invoking the Holocaust, and he told me that for him, this was really a protest against racism. Yet when a persistent foreign journalist who had overheard our conversation began to ask leading questions about racism in Israel, he refused to repeat that assertion. Certain accusations, apparently, were still meant for local ears only. After the reporter left he told me that he was a recently deactivated soldier who had given blood "every day" while he was in the army, and that this only exacerbated his sense of betrayal when he learned that his gift of blood had been so contemptuously discarded. While only a small percentage of Ethiopian immigrants had ever tried to donate blood in the years before the Blood Affair (it was still considered dangerous by many Ethiopians to give up their life's blood), it is worth mentioning that the majority of those who did so were members of army units who came to blood bank stations together with other soldiers and rolled up their sleeves in camaraderie with their friends; one-third of all blood donations in Israel are collected on army bases (Navon et al. 1996,11). This indeed was one of the justifications later offered by officials for the ill-fated policy of secrecy on the part of the blood bank, citing concerns that Ethiopian soldiers would have felt themselves stigmatized by their units had they been turned away at donor stations. Such explanations did not, however, prevent expressions of extreme anger from the people officials were ostensibly trying to protect.

When I approached a group of twenty-something demonstrators to ask what they meant by shouting comparisons between the Blood Affair and the Holocaust, I heard one young woman call out in agreement with me, "Let's not talk about that!" but she was ignored. I have always found that a stance of respectful disagreement served me well, when necessary, in dealing with my Ethiopian-Israeli friends and interlocutors, but invoking that stance amidst teargas and flying stones may have been a little injudicious. A woman I recognized from the university, said to me, "We have all come here today because it hurts so much." "In the stomach it hurts." Then some of her large male friends gave me to understand that further questions were unwelcome, and Desta, who had appeared by my side as if out of nowhere, pulled me back into the crowd, muttering excuses for me in Amharic as we went. How did we always seem to find each other at crucial moments? He did not, in any case, come to my aid later when a group of teenage girls, seeing a *farenge* face in the crowd, took the time to pause in their smashing of parked car windows to mock, "What are you doing here, pig-eater!" My attempt at a polite response in Amharic was not enough to deter them from repeating, "You all eat pigs!" This time, Desta just laughed. Despite the occasional hostility to a white face, this crowd was actually filled with friends who would pause to say hello and catch up on one another's lives before moving back into the fray.

Desta's presence at the demonstration with many others from Neve Carmel was one of the signs that relations between "Feres Mura" and other Ethiopian-Israelis were already being renegotiated in light of the Blood Affair. For some Ethiopians, religious divisions within the community now seemed to pale by comparison with the looming crisis between Ethiopians and the rest of country. Soon enough the "Feres Mura" issue would come to complicate the Blood Affair in unexpected ways but for now the simple presence of so many "Feres Mura" at the demonstration bespoke a different and perhaps longer-term trend. Within the Ethiopian-Israeli community, the Blood Affair became an occasion for publicly reformulating social boundaries and renegotiating the basis of imagined belonging in the Israeli body politic away from traditional Beta Israel preoccupations with religious fidelity and pure lineage toward a more politically articulate pan-Ethiopian sense of belonging. Violence played an important though often neglected role in this rethinking.

"Sweet Ethiopians"

Violence was far from incidental to the conduct of the Blood Affair protest. Many protesters longed to break apart the stereotype of Ethiopian passivity or gentleness in the face of provocation—related for them to the idea of being a *friar*—even though they displayed some ambivalence about how best to accomplish this aim. A demonstrator in his twenties began to chant "Death to Racists! Death to [Minister of Health] Ephraim Sneh!" One of his colleagues seized the megaphone to explain that he had *really* meant "death to *racism*." In the wake of Prime Minister Yitzhak Rabin's assassination earlier that year, even much lesser expressions had led to arrests and charges of incitement to violence in other contexts. In this case, however, the police refused to intervene, and the chant was soon picked up again with only slight variation up and down the line: "Death to Racists! Ephraim Sneh is a racist!"

In another corner, a young man with a megaphone was calling out "We are as Jewish as the Yemenites, and more Jewish than the Russians!" When Haitians in the United States demonstrated against American blood-screening policies in the early 1990s, one of their chants had been "Let's fight AIDS, not nationality" (Farmer 1992), but here it was clear that national membership was precisely what was at stake for many protesters. The Blood Affair was understood by most Ethiopian-Israelis as a direct attack on their membership in the "imagined community" (Anderson 1991), a violent repudiation that called for violence in return. Yet this violence was not without ambivalence, because one of its primary messages was that its purveyors should be included within the national collective. A group of young men with a megaphone who had begun to chant "Shame on the state!" (*bushah la-medinah*) were called together in a huddle with protest leaders, after which they changed their chant to "Shame on the government!" (*bushah la-memshalah*), which sounded less offensive to patriotic norms. The day was characterized by modulated verbal and physical violence from the demonstrators, who steered clear of certain red lines. While demonstrators came well prepared with sticks and clubs, for example, no one used firearms despite their wide accessibility and the fact that some of the protesters were themselves serving in the Israeli army.

I heard the young man who had been threatening Minister of Health Ephraim Sneh a few moments before yelling through his megaphone, "They all think of us as 'sweet Ethiopians' [*etyopim nehmadim*]! Today we have come to show them a different face.... If it takes violence, then we will use violence. We will raise them up another Uzi Meshullam!" Meshullam was the notorious leader of a Yemenite Jewish underground that had made the so-called stolen Yemenite children into a cornerstone of its confrontational ethnic and religious politics throughout the years that had preceded the Blood Affair. In May of 1994, Meshullam and forty armed followers barricaded themselves into a house to demand a government inquiry into long-standing allegations that Yemenite children by the hundreds had been "stolen" from new immigrants by public health authorities during the 1950s, then sold for adoption after their parents were told that they had died in hospital. According to one version of this accusation, the children were actually sold or given away to childless Ashkenazi Holocaust survivors—a powerful expression of ethnic resentment over the privileged place occupied by the Holocaust in Israeli public life. At the time of the Blood Affair, Meshullam and several followers were serving prison terms, but a series of long articles about him and his movement in the press had brought renewed public attention to his allegations. Many Yemenites in particular continued to consider him a folk hero. Ethiopian-Israeli demonstrators appropriated these images of suffering by another ethnic minority less out of solidarity with them than as a vehicle for the expression of their own particular outrage. Different ways of talking about violence and grief were, in fact, key to the rhetorical reconfiguration of ethnicity and nationhood that accompanied the Blood Affair from its outset, and may well have determined its agenda for organizers. Viewed in this way, the symbolic appropriation of Holocaust suffering or of Yemenite anger at Israel's ruling elites was more than an effective political maneuver—it was also an exploration of divergent possibilities for the configuration of self in a national state context (see Gabriel1992; Good and Good 1988).

An important component of these imagined configurations was the new willingness to threaten violence as a tool of self-representation. For many Ethiopian-Israelis, the threat or promise of violence and rage in response to wrongs suffered entailed a powerful, if ambivalent, sense of liberation, and the ability to talk openly for the first time about troubling inconsistencies in the texture of national belonging:

> You can't argue with emotion. I took part yesterday in the demonstration outside the Prime Minister's office. I am Ethiopian. Black. This was a demonstration of blacks. We never imagined ourselves in such a difficult situation. Jews against Jews, blacks against whites, and ultimately we are all Jews. Only a simpleton would believe that the "Blood Bank Affair" was the main issue. This was a powerful explosion of emotions. Ten thousand extremely angry people are a terrifying image of great power. For a long time we have been quiet. This time I saw people weeping, angry, opening up. (*Ma'ariv*, January 29, 1996, p. 1; newspaper excerpts translated from Hebrew by the author)

Maski Shibaru-Sivan, an Ethiopian-Israel actress who was in her twenties at the time, here invokes an identity as "black" that had not previously been affirmed in public by many Beta Israel. Traditional Beta Israel had in fact self-consciously described themselves as light or "red" (*kai*) skinned, to differentiate themselves from black Africans (Salamon 1995). Shibaru-Sivan is careful, however, to couch this claim in a frame of shared Jewishness, lest she be misunderstood. Despite appearances, she argues, donated blood was not the main issue of the protest, which really grew from a set of broader grievances that allowed the rejection of blood donations to be experienced by Ethiopian-Israelis as just "one more thing" (see Farmer 1992).

One demonstration organizer with whom I spoke later that day echoed Shibaru-Sivan's sentiment when he described the blood donations scandal as merely "the straw that broke the camel's back." Yet Shibaru-Sivan, who had immigrated during the mid-1980s and achieved some success as a television actress, was unusually articulate in this regard and asked questions about HIV that were not publicly articulated by most others in the Ethiopian-Israeli community:

> We will not be satisfied with an investigatory panel into the events concerning the blood bank. We are demanding treatment of the real problems: education at an appropriate level, a substantial change in the way our soldiers are treated, and equal treatment by the Ministry of Health. We will not accept the publication of new surveys and statistics concerning the numbers of AIDS carriers in the Ethiopian community as long as not even one additional person has been tested from among the general population, or among immigrants from the former Soviet Union, from Brazil, from France, or from any other part of the enlightened world where AIDS can be found. We will demand the publication of full statistics not only for homosexuals and Ethiopians, but for society in general. (*Ma'ariv*, January 29, 1996, p. 1)

It is clear that the cultural significance of blood matters relatively little in this account compared with the experience of inequality across a spectrum of different settings—education, the army, and the public health establishment—that together created the context in which the Blood Affair could explode in the way it did. Like demonstration organizers, Shibaru-Sivan also demanded an investigation into the recent suicides of several Ethiopian soldiers serving in the Israel Defense Forces; these suicides were widely attributed within the immigrant community to discrimination and racial or ethnic slurs by fellow soldiers or commanders, and they were a source of great agitation in the community at the time (cf. S. Kaplan and Rosen 1994, 105–106).[2]

Most striking for me was the way in which this actress understood the explosion of emotion and violence as marking something new about the way Ethiopian-Israelis had begun to conceptualize their relations with the State of Israel, with other Jewish ethnic groups, and with "the Jewish people" broadly conceived. Her ambivalence about that violence was itself essential to the story she was trying to tell, because it demonstrated the limits of how far Ethiopian-Israelis were willing to go in their realignment of group narrative:

> What happened yesterday was not preventable. It pains me that police officers were wounded at the demonstration, and I wish them a speedy recovery. It is too bad that this happened, but it must be understood that this was the outcome of an impossible reality, according to which the Ethiopian community has not been "heard" until today, and relations with it have not been conducted in a proper manner. . . . I hope that from now on people will be more attentive and will display more understanding of the problems facing the Ethiopian community. And I hope that there will never, never again be a need for another demonstration of this kind. (*Ma'ariv*, January 29, 1996, p. 1)

Justifying and disavowing violence simultaneously, Shibaru-Sivan wishes a speedy recovery to police officers who may have been injured. For their part, police refrained from public criticism of the Ethiopian community, and one of the most seriously wounded officers later made a point of publicly disavowing any grudge against demonstrators from his hospital bed. Despite demonstrations of rage and social rupture, both parties to the violence made a point of expressing their concern for one another's welfare as well as their implicit commitment to avoid any irreparable breach of national solidarity.

Addisu Messele, the chairman of the Ethiopian-Israeli umbrella organization that had organized the demonstration, returned from an emergency meeting with Acting Prime Minister Shimon Peres some five hours after the demonstration had begun to declare the protest a success, telling demonstrators that Peres had agreed to the establishment of a public investigatory commission to consider all of the issues that they had raised. "We have accomplished in one day," he told the exhausted but still restless crowd, "what it took the Yemenites forty years to accomplish!" He framed the demonstration as a coming of age for former immigrants, now tested in the core of Israeli politics—no more would they be seen as "sweet" and acquiescent subjects whose blood itself could be freely disposed of by the state. Messele himself managed to leverage his leadership of the protest into an important public role: soon after this meeting with Shimon Peres he was promoted by Peres for a position on the Labor Party list for Knesset, as Peres struggled—without much success, it turned out—to garner support from traditionally right-leaning groups like Ethiopians in his looming confrontation with the Likud Party chair, Benjamin Netanyahu.

I have no reason to question Messele's sincerity as a protest leader—his grief over the Blood Affair seemed quite real. But it is also important to understand that he worked hard to transform this protest into an occasion for the consolidation of a recognizably Israeli form of public political discourse, one compatible with the mainstream narratives of the state even where it was harshly critical of certain policies. Although his tenure in parliament lasted only one term (he publicly accused party chairman Ehud Barak of racism when his slot was given to a Russian immigrant candidate before the next election),

Messele's success demonstrates the potential benefit of a strategy that builds on familiar rhetorical devices and themes. He served not only as a protest leader at the demonstration but also as a translator for government representatives like Minister of Immigrant Absorption Yair Tzaban who were called to the scene. In this extraordinarily powerful mediative position, Messele was able to manage the flow of imagery and information to both sides. Yet Messele's relatively conventional rhetorical strategy was not the only option available to Ethiopian-Israelis, and a consideration of more radical options that were adopted by some others leads inexorably beyond the protest itself to the complicated ethnographic field of which it was a part.

Contexts of Violence

On the morning following the Jerusalem demonstration, one major newspaper (*Yediot Aharonot*, January 29, 1996, p. 3) carried an article with a headline that screamed "Like Gaza During the Intifada!" The majority of the casualties, as I have mentioned, were members of the security forces who had tried to contain the demonstration. One officer was reported to have wondered aloud, "What happened to the quiet Ethiopians? Even on the worst days in Gaza during the Intifada we didn't see scenes so difficult as those the Ethiopians prepared for us today in Jerusalem" (ibid.). Aryeh Amit, the Jerusalem police commander, likewise commented that "since the days of the Intifada, I don't remember such a range of stones and clubs" (*Ha'aretz*, January 29, 1991, p. 1). One ranking member of the police establishment later confided in me that he had not been surprised by the violence of the demonstrators per se—as an officer, he had intervened in violent domestic disturbances within the Ethiopian immigrant community before—but by the fact that this was the first time that "violence had been directed against us, the representatives of the State."[3] It was the perceived directionality of violence on both sides, rather than merely its intensity, that provoked critical reflections by many participants in the events of the day, including many Ethiopian-Israelis. "While we are actually not as unfailingly patient, gentle, and long-suffering as people suppose," wrote Solomon Ezra (a distant relative of Desta and Rachel) in an opinion piece for the *Jerusalem Post* (Ezra 1996), "we do not turn violently against those to whom we owe our education, our homes, and even our lives. But recently we did just that. Why?"

Both police and demonstrators mobilized images from the first Palestinian Intifada of 1987–1990 in order to describe and cast aspersions on the violence exercised by the other side, like the young man described at the beginning of this chapter, who picked himself up after being tear gassed to ask bitterly, "What are we, Arabs?" The very possibility of this question reveals something significant about local knowledge presumptions (see Geertz 1983) concerning the legitimate uses of force and its limitations. Each side to the conflict complained that the other had behaved as if this had really been an episode of the Palestinian Intifada, a clash with external enemies, rather than a civil dispute between fellow citizens. Once given voice, however, these associations can be highly multivocal. The following commentary, written by Palestinian-Israeli journalist Riad Ali for the Hebrew daily *Davar Rishon*, deserves extended consideration:

> *Palestinians and Ethiopians in Israel: "We are Kindred"*
>
> When I was watching the demonstration of the Ethiopians on television and witnessed the outbreak of their rage, I could not help but compare our situation to theirs. . . . The scenes were the same: police, clubs, tear gas, water hoses and lots of violence. Only the actors were different, and instead of police confronting Arabs, they were now confronting Ethiopians. It was exactly 20 years ago—in 1976—that the Arab masses in Israel answered the call of their leaders and demonstrated their rage with a fury that then, too, astonished the country. That day, later to be known as Land Day, the Arabs came out to demonstrate the issue of land expropriations. . . . Both of us, the Arabs and the Ethiopians, have felt on our own flesh and in the most humiliating way possible, the difference between theory and practice. In theory, we are all equal citizens of the state. . . . They are the blacks among the Jews and we are the country's Arabs! They are "HIV carriers," and we are the victims of "hereditary knife-wielders syndrome." . . . They are forced to prove their Jewish identity, which was obliterated after they were flown to Israel from Addis Ababa in a grueling journey. We are forced daily to atone for our original sin: not having abandoned our homeland with the coming of the white Jews.[4]

This is a solution to the question of kinship that not even Jacques Faitlovitch could have imagined, because it envisions Beta Israel making common cause with Palestinian Arabs against the claims of Zionist Jewish solidarity at the heart of the "ingathering of exiles" paradigm. This was not the first time that Ethiopian-Israelis had been invoked as emblems for the success or failure of the Jewish state (see Dominguez 1989), but it was the first direct appeal by a Palestinian-Israeli citizen to a popular Hebrew readership. Ali later achieved notoriety when he was arrested by the Palestinian Authority for criticizing its president, Yassir Arafat, and then escaping back to Israeli jurisdiction. Here, though, he asks Ethiopian-Israelis to identify their own struggle with the difficult situation faced by Israeli Arabs—a different context than most Ethiopian-Israelis chose to emphasize.

The similarity between Ethiopian and Palestinian Israelis to which Ali points is indexed in terms of violence levied or suffered in interactions with the apparatus of the state, and by emotional qualifiers like "rage" and "wrath" (*za'am*). These are also key terms for other kinds of ethnic and state politics in

Israel (Gabriel 1992), and are embedded in official discourse as justifications for violence against external enemies, especially when nonmilitary targets may be involved. Several months after the Blood Affair took shape, Shimon Peres launched the 'Invei Zaʿam (Grapes of Wrath) operation into Hezbollah-controlled southern Lebanon, deliberately driving thousand of Lebanese civilians from their homes in an effort to force Lebanese authorities to take responsibility for preventing cross-border attacks by Hezbollah guerillas. The language of fury is mobilized in the name of state power and in opposition to it, in response to perceived victimization on all sides, and in service of ethnic and national identities that are fostered by state hegemony as well as those, like Palestinian nationalism(s) and confrontational Jewish ethnic affiliations, that seek to locate themselves in the state's porous symbolic borderlands. "Rage" and "fury," with their associated naturalization of violence, repeatedly serve as the intelligible fault lines along which groups seek to establish the contours of collective identification in Israel (cf. Good and Good 1988).

It may not be surprising that most Beta Israel failed to answer Riad Ali's call. In his bid to establish a rhetorical identity between the two groups, Ali refers to both Ethiopians and Arabs as having been displaced by the Zionist state but references only to the "coming of the white Jews," suppressing recognition that most Ethiopians came to Israel as eager participants in the Jewish national project and are little different from "white Jews" in this regard. Although he writes that claims against Ethiopians as HIV carriers and against Arabs as knife wielders are both expressions of entrenched state racism, he also positions himself as a citizen demanding the fulfillment of the state's egalitarian ideology. As groups defined by their victimization, he implies, both Palestinian-Israelis and Ethiopian-Israelis are entitled to demand their rights from the state by force. Several months before the Blood Affair, when Druze military officers in the IDF staged a violent protest that forced Prime Minister Yitzhak Rabin to be evacuated from his office by helicopter, I remember clearly that few commentators, including the prime minister himself, asserted that the Druze had been wrong to press their demands in this way. Officials and citizens alike seemed inclined to accept that violence could sometimes be accepted within certain well-defined but never stated limits. Like Ethiopians, but unlike most Palestinian-Israelis, Druze officers were perceived as loyal participants in the national project, voicing frustration over inequities that even the prime minister described as intolerable, yet somehow beyond his control. This is not to say that violent protests achieved their goals for change in either case, but they did succeed in calling national attention to the problem and were not perceived as completely illegitimate even by those in power. A media poll conducted during the week of the Blood Affair revealed that 40 percent of the 440 citizens polled were willing to justify the blood bank's policy toward Ethiopian donations, while 38 percent opposed it, and nearly half said they understood the Ethiopian community's violent response (*Yediot Aharanot*, January 31, 1996, p. 9).

Palestinians' and Ethiopians' occasional appropriation of one another as icons of suffering and violence was also complicated on the level of daily interactions, where both groups needed to orient themselves in relation to one another as well as the state. Dominant political and social science models of protest movements rarely investigate this level of ethnographic complexity, but I believe it is crucial to a proper understanding of the Blood Affair, because it helps to illustrate how responses to the Blood Affair were selected from a broad repertoire of possibilities, not all of which could be realized simultaneously. The explosion of violence and the interpretive flurry that took place in its aftermath allowed Ethiopian-Israelis to project certain options for self-configuration into bold relief, while closing off others. For "Feres Mura," as for other Ethiopian-Israelis, this was a particularly sensitive moment because it opened questions to public view that had been quietly sidelined in recent years—questions like the proper relationship of Beta Israel to other Jews, and to the state. The humiliating airing of communal secrets that precipitated the Blood Affair was not related primarily to high rates of HIV infection in my view, but to the painfully unfinished business of answering the question of kinship between Beta Israel and other Jews.

Inconstant Nationhood

On a Saturday night in autumn 1995, a brawl broke out between Jewish and Arab youths at a local dance club in the northern Israeli city of Upper Nazareth, where I had conducted significant fieldwork. I was staying with good friends, and it was nearly 1 a.m. when a group of boys, most of them around army age or slightly younger, came home from their Saturday night excursion, laughing and joking among themselves. From the way they told the story, it was clear that they had been more than impartial bystanders. "The Arabs just come here looking for fights; they always do," offered Avi, and the rest of his friends agreed. I never did get the details of what had actually transpired at the club, but when I asked them whether they had also joined in the fight themselves, I was more than a little surprised by the answer: "It was just between Jews and Arabs. Both sides leave us alone." This was not like anything I had remembered hearing before, and I was trying hard not to sound overly curious. "Aren't you Jews?" I asked. But the only answer I got was a disinterested teenage shoulder shrug and the very Israeli retort, "*Ani yode'ah* [Do I know]"? I took it to mean that they were not willing to deal with the question in the terms I had asked it.

None of these boys seemed especially troubled by the implication that they might not be viewed in this context as Jews, even though I knew from experience that such would be fighting words in almost any other context. Brawls in the dance club are apparently not infrequent, and although these young men all attended religious high schools, served with due enthusiasm in the Israeli military, and tended to vote for center-right political parties like Likud, they also did not feel called upon to take part in the informal but culturally patterned and gendered violence of Jews and Arabs in this local setting. They did tell me that they were troubled because some Ethiopian-Israeli girls had been "ruined" by dating Arabs they met at the club (*hen netkalkelu*), although I later learned that at least one of the boys himself had a girlfriend whose Arabic ancestry was first betrayed to me only by a slight accent in her spoken Hebrew. Upper Nazareth is one of the few truly mixed Jewish-Arab towns in the Galilee (Rabinowitz 1997), but this does not mean relationships are simple or without conflict.

Sensitized by this encounter, I began to notice comparable patterns of relationship and ambivalence in other settings. Several weeks after the Blood Affair had been revealed to the public, I sat in a trailer home at Neve Carmel with an immigrant from Operation Solomon who had come to visit his own new-immigrant relatives at the absorption center. He was in his twenties and did not wear any identifiable sign of religious affiliation. Two other relatives were also visiting that day; both were men in their forties, who had come to Israel during the 1980s, and wore knitted *kippot* that identified them as at least "traditional" in local religious terms. The conversation between all three visitors turned to politics when their host went to the kitchen to get coffee. Benjamin Netanyahu had recently won his short-lived place in the prime minister's office, and both older men were eager to defend a Likud-oriented political platform that evinced deep skepticism of the Oslo Accords signed by Yassir Arafat and Yitzchak Rabin five years earlier. The younger visitor began to argue that the Labor Party had been right to enter into accords with the PLO despite the wave of suicide bombings that had recently begun to rock the country; he suggested that despite the setbacks, these accords might one day lead to peace. This kind of fraught but informal debate takes place constantly in Israel during an election year, and all three men were defending positions that were well within the mainstream of Israeli public opinion. Yet it soon became clear that the two older men were making an assumption that something uniquely Ethiopian was at stake here as well.

"Don't think that just because you're an Ethiopian that you'll be safe," they admonished the younger man, "just because they don't bother us, just because they [the Palestinians] think we're *miskenim* [pitiable sufferers]." "Look," the younger man replied, "if they [the Palestinians] want to curse, I can curse; if they want to fight, I can fight; if they want to make peace, I can go with them for peace." He denied, in other words, the inference that his political sympathies had been influenced by a sense of exclusion *as an Ethiopian* from threats of violence directed at other Jews, or that his political views were incompatible with loyalty to an exclusively Israeli and Jewish politics of self. Conversations of this kind are simply not reducible to the language of geopolitics on the one hand or reified categories of culture and identity on the other; they express the shifting and contested grounds of being-in-the-world across a broad experiential field in which terrorist attacks or the threat of attacks may be crucial in one context, yet eclipsed by the immediacy of blood "spilled" at donor stations or a local bar fight in another. Bureaucratic habits of thought require fixed "identities" that should remain constant in different contexts and whose shifting from one context to another cannot help but inspire accusations of inconstancy or dishonesty. Leaving such habits behind is the first step in achieving a more precise and compelling account of lived experience in real local moral worlds.

Informal conversations between individuals with differently constructed political and religious commitments begin to reveal something about the everyday contestation that goes into the making of national and religious selves, the different ways in which Ethiopians are sometimes able to think of themselves as "belonging to" the category "Israeli," for example, or "Jewish." In some contexts, Ethiopian-Israelis may be conscious of falling into the interstices of national identity such that neither "Jews" nor "Arabs" expect them to join a dance club brawl fought along ethnic lines. Yet these same young men might be called upon (or call upon one another) in other contexts to affirm their loyalty to an unproblematized construct of Israeli Jewishness. Such subtle, positioned exchanges affirm nationhood even while revealing its inconstant texture, laying bare the sometimes painful possibility that cultural and personal intimacies will be revealed to onlookers. The Ethiopian-Israeli community is unable to exercise control over how it will ultimately be perceived by outsiders and may not even be able to exercise much influence over the self-perceptions of its own members, who are both constrained and enabled by local settings—like a dance club in a mixed Jewish-Arab development town on Israel's northern periphery—to see things in unexpected ways. The inconstant texture of nationhood was precisely what was brought into painful public scrutiny by the events of the Blood Affair, and that this may be why it managed to arouse and sustain the passions that it did, notwithstanding the pull of even more pressing and bloody political events.

One People, One Blood

On Friday, February 16, 1996, a Norwegian newspaper cited by the *Jerusalem Post* reported a speech allegedly made by Palestinian Authority President Yassir Arafat to Arab diplomats in Stockholm on January 30, just two days after the fiery Jerusalem demonstration:

Arafat said he expects civil war to erupt in Israel, in which Russian immigrants, "half of whom are Christians or Moslems," will fight for "a united Palestinian state." He also asserted that the "so-called Ethiopian Jews" are Moslems. . . . Outlining his strategy, he said, "The PLO will now concentrate on splitting Israel psychologically . . . If the Jews can import all kinds of Ethiopians, Russians, Uzbekians, and Ukranians as Jews, we can import all kinds of Arabs."

On the same day that accounts of this speech began to appear in the Israeli press, I showed a copy of the partial transcript to a group of teenagers with whom I had stayed up late into the night at Neve Carmel, talking about life. A few of the boys laughed when I read them Arafat's comment about "so-called Ethiopian Jews," but Ashagre was indignant: "He's right! For sure he's right! You know why? It's because this is a racist country. They don't want to accept us here." Later, when Ashagre left, another boy said to me, "Don't pay attention to what Ashagre said about Arafat. We don't really feel that way." It was clear to me from long acquaintance that Ashagre's outbursts about racism often needed to be taken with a grain of salt—he would refuse to study for school exams for example, and then accuse the teachers of racism when his grades declined—yet both the outburst and the discomfort it aroused among his peers were signs that something of deeper collective import was being negotiated.

On the morning of Sunday, February 25, two civilian buses were blown to pieces almost simultaneously in Jerusalem and Ashkelon by suicide bombers associated with the Palestinian Hamas organization; more than twenty people were killed. It was the beginning of a long and bloody campaign that accompanied the Israeli elections that year. At Neve Carmel, I spent the whole morning with Rachel and Meles and their family in front of the television that dominated their cramped immigrants' trailer home, weeping and silent in turns as we watched the horrific scenes repeating themselves with almost hypnotic regularity: frantic women searching hospital emergency rooms for loved ones, young men from the ultra-Orthodox volunteer organization ZAKA (Identification and Rescue), also known as the True Kindness Society, hunting through the wreckage of the buses (as well as in nearby trees and the windows of buildings) for human remains or even pools of blood that could still be collected for burial. There were exclamations of grief and rage by politicians from across the political spectrum, some of them playing to cameras against the backdrop of charred and mangled passenger buses. There is a certain public choreography to the aftermath of a terror attack in Israel, with assigned and well-known roles played by emergency workers, politicians, and members of the media who have almost always seen these events before. We were transfixed by the images that saddened and angered us as they played across the screen.

As the day wore on however, images of the carnage were supplemented by a seemingly endless variety of analysis and commentary. In a television studio, one newscaster asked an official of the blood bank who was sitting with him whether he thought that people would now begin resuming large-scale blood donations in light of the tragedy. It was a cryptic remark, except that news had been spreading ever since the Blood Affair that donations had been falling under the pressure of Ethiopian accusations of blood bank racism. The official replied that he hoped this would be the case, but he did not elaborate, and the matter was never to my knowledge raised in public again. Nor did my Ethiopian friends in the room exchange any comment among themselves about this brief and oblique reference to their own recent political trauma. Donor stations around the country were soon flooded again to beyond capacity, just as Ethiopian criticism of the blood bank seemed to evaporate with the first news of the attacks. If anything, expressions of the desire to give blood began to vie with anger and rejection of the blood donation regime. "After the attacks," argued one community leader, "we need to be able to *give*: it isn't enough just to receive." The blood bank is not just a symbol of national unity in Israel; through the exchange of precious and inalienable gifts (see Bourdieu 1977, 191–192), it is a privileged site of its physical enactment (cf. Sapolsky 1989). Especially in a time of war, the bank is widely perceived as a resource for the whole national collective, and as such it is both difficult and impolitic to criticize.

Blood spilled on the streets of Ashkelon and Jerusalem on that day in late February was only the prelude to a campaign that claimed over fifty lives in its first week, putting many Ethiopian-Israelis into an impossible emotional and existential bind. Blood spilled by terrorists was experienced as a call to the affirmation of shared peoplehood in suffering, while the rejected donations "spilled" at blood donor stations were understood as a prima facie refutation of those claims. Angry performances of rejection, including acts of violence and indexed references to Palestinians, the Intifada, and antistate Jewish undergrounds like that of Uzi Meshullam, were rendered suddenly intolerable by force of events and by a felt demand for identification with terror victims. These are not simple matters to render ethnographically, and few ethnographies of contemporary Israel have in fact attempted to do so, despite the absolute centrality of terror, political violence, and responses to terror within the "picture of what is experienced" in daily life (see Willen 2007). There may be many reasons for this, not least of which is the desire to maintain an impression of scholarly distance and the difficulty of doing so when the ethnographic field is of "overbearing practical relevance" (Kleinman and Kleinman 1991) to the anthropologist's own lived experience. There is also the very real anxiety of being misunderstood—of having one's own experience of fear and loss reduced to the simplistic and inflammatory images of international newscasts, or being subject to the politicized judgment of colleagues whose connection to the events is wholly incommensurate with one's own. Yet there is no help for it. Ethnography can only help to complicate our simplistic moral and political narratives when we turn it toward the whole social and experiential field in which life happens, and the Blood Affair cannot easily be separated from the broader contexts of violence in which it was rhetorically embedded.

Toward afternoon on the day of the first bombings, I was sitting in front of the television at Rachel and Meles's trailer when their distant cousin Mulegeta stopped by, and I think all of us were glad of the distraction. Mulegeta was a frequent visitor at Neve Carmel because he worked for the immigrant absorption authorities and was often at the site on business. He had come to Israel in the 1980s (I described his return to Judaism in chapter 4) and was something of a success story for the new immigrants. His children attended good religious schools and he was usually well dressed, with a cap on his head in deference to religious tradition. I knew him as a solid and unexcitable type who sometimes had interesting insights to share, so after we exchanged pleasantries and gazed for a while at the carnage on television, I pulled out the newspaper clipping of Arafat's speech from Norway and asked him what he thought about "so-called Ethiopian Jews" really being Muslims—I was surprised by his vehemence. "That's true!" he said, shaking his finger at me and speaking quickly, with anger. "Do you want to know why? I'll tell you—in Ethiopia they didn't want us, and here they won't have us either. Someone who isn't wanted at the church and can't go to the synagogue, what is he—he's a Muslim!" This was a replay of Ashagre's outburst, but from an individual whose views were not so easily dismissed by his peers. For me it was a moment in which the disparate threads of ethnographic inquiry suddenly converged in an unsuspected confluence of inconstant nationhood, blood, and the "Feres Mura" dilemma:

> They have been throwing away our blood because they don't want us here. But I don't care what they think any more. They are going to tell us to drop our pants [for circumcision], even old men! [he makes a dismissive gesture]. The Torah says to circumcise once, at age eight days, not twice.... They have a rabbi who is dead and they say he is the Messiah [a reference to the Habad movement whose leader died in 1994, and who had opposed Beta Israel claims to Jewishness]—is that what the Torah says? That is just idolatry! I know who I am, and if someone doesn't accept me, I don't care about them. I have children and that is what I tell them also.

Suddenly Mulegeta paused, deflated, as if he had just run out of steam. He allowed his gaze to rest again for a little while upon the images of devastation that were still playing on the television in the corner, then reached forward in his chair to touch my knee. "I am sorry," he said sadly. "I don't really mean all that. I am just so upset." And then, pointing to the television screen, "*That's what I am upset about....* They are just killing us." Conversation resumed, but Mulegeta was quiet for a while and apologized again before he left. Violence enters the intimate spaces of daily life in Israel and *changes* them, deflecting the well-directed rage and social protests of migrants. Blood will have its out.

I made my way to the makeshift synagogue at the heart of the absorption center, where a strategy session for an upcoming demonstration about the pace of "Feres Mura" immigration was being led by Avraham Neguse and Rabbi Waldman. The tone of the meeting was not like that of the Blood Affair—there were perhaps a hundred people gathered, and their attitude was one of quiet determination. Before the meeting was called to order, Rabbi Waldman called for afternoon prayers, which he opened with a moment of silence for the victims of the attacks in Jerusalem and Ashkelon, followed by a responsive reading from Psalms: *They have spilled their blood like water round about Jerusalem, and there is none to bury it.* Was anyone there struck, I wondered, by the visceral impact of those words chanted only a month after the Jerusalem demonstration? I never learned, because it seemed somehow inappropriate at the moment to ask. The chanting continued with a not so subtle repetition of sentiments I had been hearing all month in different settings related to the inconstant nationhood of Ethiopians as well as terror in public transportation: *We have become a taunt to our neighbors, a scorn and derision to those round about us. How long, Lord*? (Psalm 79:3–5).

AIDS, IMMIGRATION AND THE POLITICS OF EXCLUSION

The investigatory commission established by Acting Prime Minister Shimon Peres under former Israeli President Yitzhak Navon was less than what Addisu Messele had promised protesters on the day of the demonstration. It lacked the power of subpoena, was conducted only partly in open hearings, and limited itself in practice to an investigation of the blood issue, narrowly defined. There was no significant exploration of religious issues, alleged discrimination in education, or the problem of suicide among Ethiopian soldiers in the IDF. Instead, the commission worked to blame the explosion of emotions on Ethiopian culture's allegedly special relationship with blood, and to blame the increasing disease burden among Ethiopian-Israelis upon the immigration of "Feres Mura" to the near exclusion of other factors.

These interpretive acts were already in evidence to some degree at the demonstration itself, despite the participation of so many post-1991 immigrants in the Blood Affair protest. When Addisu Messele returned from his hastily arranged meeting with Shimon Peres on the day of the protest, he first announced that an investigative commission would soon be convened, and declared that the demonstration had been a great success. He also remarked, apparently as a way of calming the crowd, that he had been assured the government did not really believe all Ethiopian blood was tainted, but that public health concerns were focused primarily on the newcomers from Addis Ababa. Whether that claim did in fact originate with Shimon Peres and his entourage, it was a powerful rhetorical device that allowed some Ethiopian-Israelis to save face in the eyes of outsiders. Beta Israel elders and religious leaders who were called upon to testify before the Navon Commission argued repeatedly that the stigma of infectious disease should not fall upon their communities, because *their* blood was pure of contaminating contact with outsiders. One of the most revered and senior Beta Israel priests in Israel, Kes Ayellegn, testified that true Ethiopian Jews had pure and disease-free blood because they had kept themselves separate from Christians in Ethiopia—which obviously could not be said about the "Feres Mura." Ayellegn and many others understood the exclusion of Ethiopian-Israeli blood through the logic of kinship rather than public health, which is to say that it had little to do with abstract gradations of risk for infectious disease and everything to do with the question of kinship and rejection of Christianity.

Many Israelis insisted that Ethiopians were only protesting because they misunderstood the nature of risk assessment in public health, but the truth is that this focus on religious and ethnic purity and on "Feres Mura" immigration allowed Ethiopians as well as Israelis to deflect attention from a number of more troubling and potentially explosive issues. How, for example, was HIV being transmitted among Ethiopians in Israel, and why had authorities failed to develop or even discuss a comprehensive plan for its prevention? There is no debating that HIV infection increased among the post-1991 immigrants relative to previous groups, but the significance to be attributed to that fact was open to question. Statistics collected by the Navon Commission show that 1,439 samples collected at random from immigrants evacuated from Sudanese refugee camps in 1984–85 all tested negative for HIV antibodies, though they did show high rates of malaria and hepatitis, which inspired the initial policy to reject Ethiopian blood donations even before AIDS had emerged as a threat clearly recognized by public health authorities. By 1991, however, AIDS had emerged as a frightening global pandemic, and this time all new immigrants were subject to blood tests, which revealed that between 1 and 2 percent of new immigrants over the age of nine tested positive for HIV. This represented only between 150 and 300 individuals, but it revolutionized the epidemiology—and politics—of HIV-AIDS in Israel. It was the first time, almost overnight, that the HIV-AB strain of the virus common in Africa became prevalent in Israel, and it changed the profile of typical victims from intravenous drug users and men who had unprotected sex with other men to large numbers of heterosexuals, including women. Although Ethiopians made up less than 1 percent of the total population at the time, they took up half the beds at Israel's primary AIDS hospice, and doctors assumed that for every case of HIV infection they knew about at any given time, one more awaited discovery.⁵ Although absolute numbers were never large, the percentages, given Israel's previous history with the disease, were enormous, and the cultural implications uncertain.

By 1994, when the return-to-Judaism program opened in Haifa, the public health situation in Ethiopia had deteriorated considerably. With refugees spending three years or more in Addis Ababa and HIV rates soaring across the Horn of Africa, it is unsurprising that the HIV-positive rate among new immigrants reached 5.8 percent, or 31 out of 534 new immigrants. By 1996, at the time of Blood Affair, around 8 percent (14 out of 175 new immigrants) had tested positive for HIV (Navon et al. 1996, 9). The overall rate of infection for all Ethiopian-Israelis at this time was 2.8 percent for men and 1.6 percent for women, compared to 4.0 percent for intravenous drug users and 0.0002 percent for the general population (ibid., 8). It is fair to note, however, that no comparable data exist for other Israeli ethnic groups, because only Ethiopians were tested en masse upon their arrival in the country. It must also be stated very plainly that while rates of infection among those arriving from Ethiopia continued to rise, no data at all existed during this period concerning vectors of infection among those already in Israel, where infection was also on the rise. When I asked an AIDS specialist who spoke at an academic conference how he knew that veteran immigrants were being infected primarily by "Feres Mura," he said it was "just logical," but ignored other factors, like the growth in Ethiopian-Israeli tourism to Ethiopia during this period. It was actually known that men traveling to Ethiopia might well become vectors of infection, and one airline was even persuaded for a brief time to distribute AIDS educational materials on its flights from Tel Aviv. Ethiopian-Israeli community leaders complained about the unfair stigma, though, and the policy was quietly dropped. "In our culture," Sintayeho told once me, "a man does not sleep in an empty bed when he travels." Whether or not men returning from Ethiopia became significant vectors of infection, the fact is that many individuals who never left Israel were infected during the 1990s, giving the problem a distinctly local context that the Navon Commission largely ignored.

Although he was not cited in the final report, Addis Messele gave public testimony to the Navon Commission that he thought the "Feres Mura" waiting in Addis Ababa should be brought to Israel more quickly, before the rate of HIV infection among the refugees could climb any higher. Yet the secretary of his Ethiopian umbrella organization, Shlomo Mola (today one of two Ethiopian Knesset members), was quoted as objecting to further immigration because "Five hundred HIV carriers [among Ethiopian-Israelis] are enough." Messele, in turn, responded that Mola "has always been opposed to [the 'Feres Mura'] because they are Christians" (Tsur and Siegel 1996).

Open and sometimes bitter arguments frequently erupted between expert witnesses and members of the Navon Commission regarding the advisability of HIV-linked restrictions on immigration. At one extreme, Addisu Messele argued that "these people [the 'Feres Mura'] are our families and we are very concerned about them." Most medical witnesses emphasized that restrictions on immigration were not, in their view, the best or most credible way to fight AIDS in Israel or the Ethiopian-Israeli community. Yet commission member Dr. Eliezer Rachmilevitch, the controversial head of Hadassah Hospital's hematology unit, repeatedly emphasized during his questioning of witnesses that he was scandalized by the continued immigration of people who had been identified as members of a group at high risk for HIV infection and whose claims to Israeli citizenship were not even formally based on Jewish nationality. When one witness pointed out that disease-based restrictions on immigration had never been applied by Israel to Jewish communities at risk of persecution in the Diaspora, Rachmilevitch made it clear that this was not in his view a Jewish community. It became something of a game for me to predict how he would hammer individual witnesses until he elicited statements that seemed to support this point of view.

The commission's final report makes little or no mention of the politically explosive topic of "Feres Mura" immigration, but when Minister of Health Ephraim Sneh testified toward the end of public hearings, he was explicitly charged by the commission chair, Yitzhak Navon, to clarify, in consultation with the government, what ought to constitute official policy on the immigration of seropositive individuals and high-risk groups. A letter to the minister of health signed by all of the active members of the Navon Commission on December 1, 1996, includes a single sentence calling "for the closure of the camp in Addis Ababa," with no discussion of the implications such a step might have for the health and welfare of those being supported there. Official attitudes resonate strongly here with the local-knowledge presumptions of traditionalists like Kes Ayellegn, who also chose to represent the HIV-AIDS problem as a crisis of social and religious boundaries. The sad irony is that these attempts at exclusion of "Feres Mura" served over the long run not to prevent immigration—although they may have delayed it—but to deflect public attention from all of the issues of exclusion and inequality that were raised not only by the Blood Affair protest but by the social and medical realities that preceded it.

Honor, Blood, and the Problem of Culture

Although the reality of AIDS in Israel was configured in public discourse as a disease of immigration, the policy on Ethiopian blood donations was applied without exception to those who had spent decades in the country and even those who had been born in Israel. To be fair, ethnic exclusion of donors was common practice in the United States until protests during the early 1990s forced a fundamental rethinking of how potential donors should be screened, based on high-risk behaviors rather than social identities (Farmer 1992). Far more damning, therefore, is the fact that while the rationale for discarding Ethiopian blood shifted radically between 1984 and 1996, from a concern with malaria and hepatitis to the fear of the devastating AIDS pandemic, public health policy remained static and to all appearances unexamined during this whole period (see Navon et al. 1996, 21–22, 32, 36). Cosmetic changes were introduced, so that blood samples originally marked "Ethiopian Immigrant" were later changed to read "For Research Purposes Only" (ibid., 15–16), but the Navon Commission discovered no record of any conversation or meeting at the blood bank or Ministry of Health to discuss the changing epidemiology of AIDS in the country, or the need to undertake a proactive campaign of prevention within the Ethiopian enclave. Blood bank chairman Dr. Amnon Ben-David testified that the failure to reconsider earlier policies was the result of an organizational culture in which certain kinds of questions simply were not asked:

> This whole issue of written material and documents came practically to expression, and we dealt with it, only once [the Blood Affair] had exploded; until then, we did not search for one piece of paper or another. The matter [concerning treatment of Ethiopian donors and donations] was clear. It passed from generation to generation in the blood bank. (Ibid., 35).

This issue is arguably far more important than the question of whether Ethiopians were unfairly excluded from the blood pool, because it speaks to the much broader question of how cultural attitudes and assumptions about kinship on the part of public health authorities may have helped to define Ethiopian-Israelis primarily as vectors of risk rather than citizens whose devastating burden of illness required attention in its own right. Individuals were treated and cared for, but the bureaucratic production of indifference (see Herzfeld 1992) ensured that no one in the public health sector took responsibility for meeting this health challenge to a group that was implicitly defined as peripheral to the body politic.

Public health officials made a plausible argument that their policy of secrecy in relation to Ethiopian blood donations had been designed to protect Ethiopians from the kind of stigma suffered by groups like Haitians in New York during the early 1990s (Farmer 1992). But this policy opened them to an even more devastating critique by Anatmar Hillel, a social worker who was the sole Ethiopian-Israeli representative on the Navon Commission. Her dissenting opinion was appended to the majority's official report:

> I am of the opinion that the policy of hiding the facts regarding the number of AIDS carriers among the immigrants of Operation Solomon, even if it was done from good and pure intentions, was a mistake. I am of the opinion that the policy of silence prevented, after the fact, serious treatment of AIDS carriers. I see in this negligence a kind of fatalistic attitude, whereby this group was abandoned [*hafkarah*] to its fate, and a lack of commensurate understanding that hiding from this disease and from its bearers . . . would be likely to lead to the spread of the disease beyond the boundaries of the infected group. (Navon et al. 1996, 38)

Hillel claimed that the practical effect of the secret policy was to inhibit authorities from responding to the situation of Ethiopian-Israelis with the urgency their situation required. Supporting her contention was the fact that a culturally sensitive AIDS education program had already been created during the early 1990s by an interdisciplinary public health and anthropological team but was left largely unimplemented because of shortfalls in funding (see Chemtov, Rosen, Shtarkshall and Soskolne 1993; Etzioni, Pollack, and Ben-Ishai 1994). It was not the *hafkarah* (abandonment) of blood that cried out from this episode, as Hillel correctly noted, but the apparent *hafkarah* of the community whose illness burden continued to worsen.

Former president Navon periodically reminded those assembled for semipublic hearings that the blood bank had enacted all of its policies for the defense of Israeli society, "*including* Ethiopians" (his emphasis). He also concluded the commission's official report by affirming: "[I]t is unnecessary to emphasize that the full integration of Ethiopian immigrants touches on the basis of the mission of the State of Israel, and serves as a supreme test for it" (Navon et al. 1996, 47). Yet he pointedly failed to acknowledge the culturally conditioned bureaucratic indifference that the commission's own research had brought to light. The Commission's final report takes its cue from Navon's breathtaking assertion—one that is impossible even in principle to verify—that officials acted purely on the basis of "objective medical considerations . . . without any trace of racism" toward Ethiopian immigrants (ibid., 19–20). While the commission was willing to critique discrete policies that had been adopted (the policy of secrecy, for example), it was ultimately unwilling to examine the structural issues that fostered neglect by the public health establishment or the broad and variegated experiences that led most Ethiopian-Israelis to interpret the blood policy as just one more instance of racial prejudice—a final and shocking "no" to the question of kinship that had been posed by Henry Stern and Jacques Faitlovitch over a century before. Like the "Feres Mura" dilemma, in other words, it turns out that the Blood Affair was really a battle over constructions of agency and motivation, although in this case it was the agency of policy makers and implementers that received most public attention.

Once it had rejected by simple fiat the charge of racism leveled at state agents, the Navon Commission went to work framing the Ethiopian conflict with public health authorities as one between rationality and culture, or between objective medical science and fraught Beta Israel emotionalism. Some form of this frame was invoked at almost every hearing and was often the premise of questions posed to witnesses. While public health officials and Ethiopian-Israelis both tended to describe donated blood as a "gift," for example, it quickly became obvious that they differed strongly on the implications of that designation. Several officials who testified expressed bafflement and incredulity over the outrage directed at them for secretly rejecting Ethiopian blood donations. "I have to say that I was shocked by the anger," one blood bank official told the commission. "I thought that people give us their blood as a gift, to use as we see fit. The anger really surprised me." To which an Ethiopian witness later responded:

> How would you feel if someone took the gifts you gave them time after time and threw them into the garbage? Which do you think would be better, to take a gift and then throw it into the garbage, or else to say, "I don't want to accept your gift"? Of course it would be better to tell [the truth] than to accept [a gift] and then throw it away!

For this witness, donated blood was a gift in the classic anthropological sense, a medium of privileged exchange in which giving and receiving are an invitation to kinship and mutual obligation. For poor immigrants who almost always found themselves on the receiving end of gifts by the state—welfare, housing subsidies, even "rescue" from Ethiopia—the gift of blood offered a rare opportunity for reciprocity; its secret rejection by paternalistic authorities could only serve to shame and infantilize them beyond toleration.

Recognition of the different gift logics at play in this exchange could well have been used to open a window upon the painful asymmetry of Beta Israel relations with the state and its representatives, or the troubled nature of economic and power relations that contributed to a generalized perception of grievance by many Ethiopian-Israelis. Even an open and honest conversation about the incommensurability of cultures might have proven useful if it had been conducted with a degree of critical self-reflection on the part of non-Ethiopian participants rather than attributing all the "culture" to Ethiopians and all the rationality to Israeli public health experts. Assertions by young Ethiopian protest leaders that "the blood is our identity" (*ha-dam zeh zehut shelanu*) or "throwing out our blood is like throwing out our identity" (*zorkim et ha-zehut shelanu*) were not probed for evidence of what other policies or experiences might lie behind this fear of identity loss in a migrant population. Instead, they were offered as evidence of a purely mechanistic understanding of political violence, as if the transgression of some abstract cultural taboo involving blood had led automatically to the throwing of stones.

When another Ethiopian witness cited the Amharic expression *dematchin nefsatchew*, which means literally "our blood is our soul," Rachmilevitch waved him impatiently to silence while translating the expression into its correct biblical Hebrew idiom, *ha-dam hu ha-nefesh*—which also means the "the blood is the life" (Deuteronomy 12:23)—implying that these testimonies held no revelation for him. "Yes," the Sephardic delegate to the commission reassured him before he could cut the witness off again, "but [that is true] for them [Ethiopians] even more than it is for us [Israelis]." Ethiopians were portrayed as suffering from a surfeit of culture and emotion, which might serve to excuse their violence but not to force a rethinking of basic Israeli policy. When the same witness testified that "for us [Ethiopian-Israelis], honor is more important than life," this led not to a discussion of the contexts in which the rejection of donated blood could come to be seen as a kind of deep humiliation, but to another rehearsal of dehistoricized argumentation about the "importance of blood in Ethiopian culture," which served only to dislocate contemporary social conflict onto an imaginary landscape of unchanging tradition. Acculturation to Israeli society would inevitably tend to prevent such incidents in the future, according to this logic, because the locus of conflict was not Israel but the rapidly receding and inaccessible Ethiopian past.

This reticence is no accident. Mainstream (Ashkenazi) Jewish discourse in Israel frequently relegates the discussion of "honor" (*kavod* in Hebrew) to the non-Western or cultural other. As is true elsewhere in the Western world (Wikan 2002), honor can sometimes even be claimed as a cultural defense for murders of women by men in the Arab or Druze—and sometimes Ethiopian but almost never Ashkenazi Jewish—sectors (see Ginat 1987; Hasan 2002). Honor has also become a major trope of the "peace process" discourse, which often has asserted that talks between Israelis and Palestinians must be based on the presumption that Israelis are concerned about rational strategic interests, while Palestinians have an emotional, honor-driven agenda. Elsewhere (Seeman 2005b), I have shown how some Jewish extremists make use of this very dichotomy to shock listeners and defend their own violence against Arabs as the reclamation of the honor concept for Jews and for Israel. Yet this honor-driven discourse, which can be used to excuse or defend violence in both intimate and explicitly political contexts, also resonates with a discourse on primitivity and race. Testimony by Ethiopian witnesses about the importance of honor may have been intended to provide context and elicit sympathy for violent political activity, but it was also clearly and explicitly juxtaposed with the cool rationality and absence of emotional engagement by state agents who presented themselves as the representatives and defenders of science. While they expressed bafflement and regret over Ethiopian reactions, public health officials were by and large freed from any public demand for serious self-reflection about the depths of the failure that the Blood Affair had revealed. Addisu Messele made one of his more astute observations when I cornered him one afternoon during a break in the Navon Commission hearings: "They [the members of the Commission] are constantly trying to define the issue as public health versus the honor of the Ethiopian community," he said, "and I am trying to say that this is a mistake—it wasn't honor that brought us out there. This is about public health versus the social problem, not public health versus honor." And later: "They need to understand that we don't live in a clinic" (see Kleinman and Seeman 1998).

It is difficult in this context not to sympathize with the American anthropologist Edward Sapir (1957, 200–201), who noted with dismay in 1932 that the "distributive locus" of culture in anthropological writing tended to reify its object. "Cultures," he wrote, are merely abstracted configurations of idea and action patterns" that tend to distract anthropologists from "the configuration of experience . . . in the life of the [specific] person being appealed to." These were outlandish and almost inassimilable ideas in the anthropology of the 1930s, when "culture" was still a radical and uncertain notion struggling to undo the intellectual and moral damage caused by generations of "race science" and institutionalized racism. Anthropologists of the Beta Israel like Salamon (1993) and Anteby (1997, 1999) are no doubt correct to emphasize the importance of blood as a cultural marker in understanding the response of Ethiopians to a blood bank policy that they perceived as exclusionary. In Ethiopia, Beta Israel had distinguished themselves from Christians through an elaborate symbolic language of blood sacrifice, menstrual taboos, and prohibitions on the consumption of blood, all of which had been challenged or made impossible to continue in Israel. Yet this can hardly be credited for the whole panoply of emotional and violent expressions that characterized the Blood Affair unless we also find ways to account for the undertow of social commentary, accounts of personal humiliation and collective political frustration that tell a more complicated story. The offense against honor occasioned by spilled blood makes sense only when it is located within the context of historical contingency and lived experience in which the question of kinship became a raw wound for Beta Israel, now exposed to view. "It is not the concept of culture [itself] which is subtly misleading," Sapir notes, so much as "the metaphysical locus to which culture is generally assigned" (1985 [1937], 509).

It was the "metaphysical locus" attributed to culture by bureaucrats and apologists for the state more than any other single factor that helped to frustrate adequate assessment of the Blood Affair by obfuscating what was really being negotiated in blood on the streets of Jerusalem. For "Feres Mura" who bore the brunt of AIDS-related blame, the focus on Beta Israel culture worked implicitly to reinforce their vulnerability as outsiders, or worse. "The product of science," writes Mary Douglas, "its knowledge, is made into a resource for claims and counter claims about how citizenship is to be defined.... So long as the class at risk can be kept in the margins, the public concern to pay for the research and the welfare of the victims will be the weaker" (1992, 114). How else can I make sense of the fact that while Ethiopian Jewish "culture" was given consistent lip service during the Navon Commission hearings ("their culture drove them to protest"), the committee's final report restricted itself to two "cultural" documents that obscured far more than they revealed about the proximate context of the explosion? One was a short collection of traditional Beta Israel prayers that seemed to have been chosen for its similarity to parts of the normative Hebrew liturgy and was clearly appended in order to pacify Beta Israel by asserting their legitimacy as Jews.

Even more troubling was the astounding appendix 4, which consisted of a half-page excerpt from a published Hebrew translation of Beta Israel folktales. The excerpt chosen was about a group of medieval Beta Israel women whose husbands had been killed in war and were now being dragged away in shackles by the conquering Christian army. The women "signal to one another through glances, recite the Shema Yisrael prayer and then pull on their chains, dragging themselves and the king's soldiers with them down into the abyss" (Navon et al. 1996, 53). The heroism of many Beta Israel men and women during periods of religious or political persecution in historical Ethiopia is not at all in question here, and we may forgive the anachronism of having the women recite a prayer that was closely associated with martyrdom in Talmudic and later rabbinic Judaism but to all accounts unknown within the Ethiopian context. Yet we are entitled nevertheless to ask whether the tenor of the commission's report would have been appreciably different if it had concluded not with a fanciful account of sixteenth-century martyrdom but with the founding of the "Falasha cemetery" in Addis Ababa by change agents like the onetime mission student Taamrat Emmanuel. Or if it had described the dilemma faced by Ethiopian-Israeli youths allowed—or required?—to remain on the sidelines of a nightclub brawl because it was "just between Jews and Arabs," neither of whom claimed Beta Israel for this purpose as their own. Either choice would have entailed a painful recognition of the inconstant nationhood that the report of the Navon Commission was committed to obscure.

By declaring Ethiopian culture and attitudes about blood to be the main problems underlying the Blood Affair, this commission ensured that more fundamental questions about the functioning of the public health services, the broad grievances of the Ethiopian community, and the grounds of belonging within Israeli society would receive no more than peremptory attention. The commission made some reasonable recommendations about increasing budgets for AIDS education and prevention within the Ethiopian community, discontinuing secretive policies, and changing the kinds of screening questions to be asked of potential donors (Seeman 1999c). They did not, however, succeed in establishing a chain of responsibility for the decisions of the blood bank, or in addressing any of the other grievances expressed by Ethiopian-Israelis. Nor had they succeeded in articulating a clear and compelling narrative for why the Ethiopian-Israeli community had reacted so fiercely. They scapegoated "Feres Mura," reified culture, and tried to deny lived experience its due.

CHAPTER 7

THE "FERES MURA" DILEMMA

> But Africa is not only a geographical expression; it is also a metaphysical landscape; it is in fact a view of the world and of the whole cosmos perceived from a particular position. This is as close to the brink of chaos as I dare proceed. As for who an African novelist is, it is partly a matter of passports, of individual volition and particularly of seeing from that perspective.... Being an African, like being a Jew, carries certain penalties—as well as certain benefits, of course. But perhaps more penalties than benefits. Ben-Gurion once said: If someone wants to be a Jew, that's enough for me. We could say the same thing about being an African.
>
> —Chinua Achebe, *Hopes and Impediments*

When the Nigerian writer Chinua Achebe (1988) sat down to compose an essay on the question "Who is an African novelist?" it is not surprising that he was drawn to its cognate question, "Who is a Jew?" Like David Ben-Gurion, Achebe was writing in a context of postcolonial statehood, transnational migration, and anxiety over the identities—bureaucratic, national, and religious—that the new social order had helped to shape. I find this intervention by an African novelist useful because of the way in which it reminds us that questions of belonging and kinship are universal as well as culturally specific, and rarely as simple as bureaucratic taxonomies would have us believe. It is an ethnographic rather than a bureaucratic perspective that points to "passports, individual volition and . . . seeing the world from that perspective" as constituents of who we come to be in the world. And even though Achebe concludes on a note of radical volition ("If someone wants to be a Jew, that's enough for me"), he also calls attention to what some philosophers and anthropologists have referred to as the "thrownness" or *Geworfenheit* of social existence (see Jackson 1995, 1998)—the quality of responding to an external world which is given to us rather than chosen. The German word itself, drawn from onetime National Socialist Heidegger's phenomenological lexicon, cannot help but draw attention to the penalties and benefits—but mostly penalties, as Achebe correctly notes—of being a Jew.

When, as an ethnographer, I confront the questions "who is a Jew?" or even "who is an Ethiopian Jew?" I prefer to invoke a more conditional set of responses than many readers will find satisfying, because this is truer to the social reality that anthropologists are given to describe. Bureaucrats, rabbis, and others may frequently be called upon to make categorical determinations that have real consequence in the lives of individuals and communities, but it is crucial to witness how such interpretive decisions are conditioned by time and circumstance, by cultural factors, and by the politics of local moral worlds in which they take place. I find it useful to think of the "Feres Mura" dilemma as just one instantiation of the kinship question posed to all Beta Israel over the past 150 years and to view the question of kinship in the context of ongoing controversy over "who is a Jew?" in modern times.

The Rise and Fall of the Return to Judaism

Riding on a bus between Tel Aviv and Jerusalem in 1997, just a few months after the Blood Affair had subsided from public consciousness, I sat next to an Ethiopian woman who had been my student in an anthropology course the year before. Despite the months that had passed, she said that the predominant emotion among her friends was still one of smoldering anger at what they believed almost without exception to have been an expression of government-sponsored racism toward their community. She had broken up with her white boyfriend after the episode, not because of anything he had said or done, but just because the rupture and hurt of the Blood Affair made many people her age want to turn inward and away from the integrationist model emphasized by immigrants from an earlier period. She told me about a friend's wedding to a white Israeli that had been held at Heikhal Shlomo, the seat of Israel's Chief Rabbinate in Jerusalem, not long after the demonstration. The wedding went on as planned, she said, except that the bride's family were upset and would not dance. "Look what they did to us!" she portrayed them as saying to one another. It was my impression that this kind of response was far from atypical. Nervous media accounts began to surface suggesting that the popularity of reggae and rap music among Ethiopian-Israeli teens (see Shabtay 2001, 2003) should be interpreted as a failure of Israel's absorption and integration efforts, even though non-Ethiopian youth in Israel are also drawn to Western music of different kinds.[1] Partly because of their newness and partly because of their mystique as members of lost biblical tribes,

Ethiopians sometimes seem to be treated as icons of a Zionist purity to which other groups are not equally subject.

None of this directly seemed to affect my friends from Neve Carmel. Rachel and Meles settled in a city in central Israel; they were soon followed by Desta and their other siblings, while Alem went off to boarding school when his father—who was now partially blind—resettled in a northern development town. A new center for the return-to-Judaism program had been established at an absorption center in the north of the country, and even though Neve Carmel still retained some of its population and even received a few new immigrants, it gradually began to feel like a ghost town, filled increasingly by empty trailer homes. People rarely talked about the Blood Affair, but it became part of the understood background of social life. Before the elections in 1996, Acting Prime Minister Shimon Peres staged a "reconciliation ceremony" to which hundreds of Ethiopian schoolchildren were bused at the government's expense. "They came to our school," a student later told me, "and said that there was a bus to take us to Jerusalem, so we went—we didn't ask exactly what it was all about." Probably expecting a close election, Peres also promoted Addisu Messele for Knesset as part of a strategy to woo even small numbers of voters from groups like the Ethiopians, who had traditionally voted heavily for the Likud. When Messele came to Neve Carmel to campaign for Labor in 1996, however, he was greeted by flying stones because of his perceived ambivalence about the "Feres Mura" issue and his statements at the Jerusalem demonstration linking immigrants from Addis Ababa with AIDS.

Peres lost the election to Benjamin "Bibi" Netanyahu after having been declared the winner before all the votes were counted, but Messele had his seat in Knesset, and continued to promote the party. He visited Neve Carmel again in 1997 to urge common cause between all the different Ethiopian factions in the country, including the "Feres Mura." The proximate reason for his visit was conveyed by a bizarre headline from a March 5, 1997, article by Iris Krauss in the daily *Ha'aretz*:

> *National Health Fund Decides to Reduce Activity [of its clinic] at Trailer Park Due to Increase there in People with AIDS-Illness*
>
> The [National Health] Fund has decided to reduce the activity of its clinic at the site, at which 2,500 Ethiopians live, since the number of AIDS patients and carriers is high and the care for them is expensive. The number of carriers and patients at the site is more than 60, average for a city of 100,000 residents.

Health care in Israel is partially socialized, but it is divided among several different state-funded "health funds" or HMOs that are permitted to compete with each other by offering different "baskets" of health services. For convenience, all the Ethiopian immigrants had been enrolled when they arrived in the country in the Kupat Holim Le'umit, or National Health Fund, with the understanding that they could eventually transfer to other funds once they left the absorption centers. In the meantime however, Le'umit held a monopoly over Neve Carmel residents that proved to be a mixed blessing for the HMO once costs related to HIV became apparent. Officers claimed that the state had failed to reimburse the fund and argued that they preferred to "scatter" the afflicted Ethiopians across several different HMOs that would share the burden more equitably. They did not, however, comment on what arrangements might be made to guarantee unbroken medical access to new immigrants. "The purpose of the Fund is to fill the need for health services," argued its chairman, "but on an economic basis." He added that "one of the characteristics of these blessed waves of immigration [the phrase sounds more sincere in Hebrew than it does in translation] is the round of severe illnesses" that had forced the National Health Fund to withdraw its services.

Residents tried to draw attention to their situation by announcing that they would refuse to send their children to school until a solution was found, and by organizing a series of public protests against Le'umit. Relations between Neve Carmel residents and the clinic had been strained to begin with for a variety of reasons, including the fact that a few of the doctors who had been assigned to Neve Carmel were themselves Russian immigrants who didn't get on with the Ethiopians, sometimes accusing them of malingering when they asked for sick notes. Despite relatively good access to health care, researchers have shown that Ethiopian-Israelis in general were dissatisfied with their doctors as well as with their own health, due to cultural misunderstandings, unrealistic expectations, and the fact that some doctors took it upon themselves to "teach" their patients in a paternalistic way about everything from correct naming practices to parenting techniques during medical encounters (Reiff 1999; Reiff, Zakut, and Weingarten 1999). "When we were in Ethiopia, we thought there would be no sickness in Israel," my friend Yossie lamented, "but now look at us!" He complained that his mother could not get X-rays or pills as often as she wanted for her chronic pains and headaches, and he blamed this situation on doctors' lack of compassion. Even a problematic clinic was better than no clinic at all though, and the prospect of AIDS patients losing their local health services even temporarily was frightening.

Addisu Messele took the opportunity of this crisis to focus and reframe his message toward the graduates of the return-to-Judaism program at Neve Carmel:

> The struggle here is the struggle of the whole 'edah [that is, the whole Ethiopian community]. No one denies that there is a problem of AIDS amongst the 'edah, and especially among the Felesmura. But the 'edah has been made responsible for the AIDS illness in the State of Israel! Medical care of the sick

does not need to be the problem of the Ethiopians, but of the government of Israel. It makes no difference to me which fund takes care of Ethiopians, but the National Health Fund is acting in a racist manner and attempting to link the disease to Ethiopian Jews. (Krauss 1997, 5a)

This may have been the first time that a major Ethiopian-Israeli communal leader had reached out to "Feres Mura" as equals. He did not foreswear the use of the term "Felesmura" as Avraham Neguse and his allies had been demanding, but the community could forgive a lot to someone who undertook to represent them in a respectful way. The Blood Affair may have failed to engender common cause between Ethiopians and Palestinians, but it did at least help Ethiopians start making common cause with one another. Messele's repeated use of the term 'edah (ethnic community) in this context was telling.

Virginia Dominguez (1989) has shown that Israelis use the term 'edah with great selectivity as a marker of social and political boundaries. It is normally applied only to Jewish ethnic groups of Eastern or "Oriental" (*mizrahi*) origin, so that there is said to be a Moroccan 'edah and a Yemenite 'edah—all of these collectively are frequently referred to as "Oriental" communities or 'edot ha-mizrah—but there is no Russian 'edah and no Polish one. Palestinians and members of other Arab states are also rarely described in terms of their membership in an 'edah, but the Druze minority, which holds Israeli citizenship and serves in the military, frequently is. Since their immigration, Ethiopian-Israelis have described themselves and been described by others as the Ethiopian 'edah, (*ha-'edah ha- 'etiyopit*), implying that they are a recognized Jewish ethnic group who have more in common with Kurdish or Tunisian Jews than with Germans or North Americans. While the designation has its drawbacks in the orientalization of non-Western groups, its benefits included a secure and recognized place in the Israeli social fabric. Neve Carmel residents did not stone Messele this time, even though his motivations remained suspect. In his own conflicted approach to the problem, he had confirmed "Feres Mura" integration even while challenging their continued immigration. After a trip to Ethiopia in 1998, he himself argued that those who still remained in Ethiopia were Christians who should not be brought to Israel, and he debated Avraham Neguse to that effect on the evening news.

Ultimately, the clinic at Neve Carmel remained open under public pressure, but other developments were more ominous. As I mentioned in the last chapter, members of the Navon Commission sent a letter to Prime Minister Bibi Netanyahu calling for the closure of the transit camp in Addis Ababa, and Netanyahu is rumored to have received the letter sympathetically. He declared "Feres Mura" immigration complete in 1998, despite the fact that a new influx from the countryside had already raised official estimates of those seeking to immigrate to between ten and thirty thousand (Bard 2002, 193). At the same time, religious challenges to the efficacy of the return-to-Judaism program had begun to gather steam. In a letter to the Ministerial Committee on the Felesmura dated 14 Heshvan 5757 (October 31, 1996), Chief Sephardic Rabbi Eliyahu Bakshi-Doron effectively delegitimized the program by casting doubt on Rabbi Waldman's assurances that only those people with clear Jewish genealogy would be included in the program and would almost all become observant Orthodox Jews. He also questioned Waldman's assertion that the immigrants "seek with all their strength to return to Judaism," and framed the return to Judaism as a conversionary rather than penitential program, with the much higher demand for "pure hearts" and commitment for self-transformation that this entailed. "Because of various rumors and because of requests that we speed the process and consider means to return [the "Feres Mura"] to Judaism in Addis Ababa, we [the Chief Rabbinate] have decided to investigate the matter closely."

It is not clear what kind of investigation the chief rabbi had in mind. No representative from the rabbinate made any attempt to speak in depth with members of the "Feres Mura" community, to investigate their lived experience, or to employ the services of researchers who had the capacity to do so. Like so many aspects of the "Feres Mura" dilemma, and as Rabbi Bakshi-Doron himself acknowledged, this process was strongly driven by "rumor." I had the strong impression, furthermore, that some of those rumors were coming from inside Neve Carmel, from teachers and others who were dissatisfied with the level of piety and single-mindedness that their new immigrant charges demonstrated. For Bakshi-Doron this translated into a series of harsh accusations:

> It has become clear that the genealogies [of the "Feres Mura"] are not clear, and that since there is no registration of who was a Jew [in the past], the investigations and clarifications [conducted by Rabbi Waldman] are not trustworthy. In accordance with the terms of the Law of Return, those who return to Judaism in Israel then draw after them many non-Jews who [also] come to the country. The return to Judaism of a not insubstantial number [of these immigrants] is insincere, and they arrive in Israel even though they do not know, and do not observe the commandments, and undergo an expedited process which is no conversion at all.

The chief rabbi's portrayal of immigrants' religious lives seems impressionistic at best—there is no attempt to define "insincerity"—but the unequivocal depiction of the program as a failed process of conversion is what ultimately sealed its fate, because while the weight of Orthodox religious tradition is to show flexibility to penitents ("so as not to lock the door before those who return") there is also strong precedent for discouraging converts, whose intentional purity must be demonstrated through fidelity to the commandments over time. Although he would later reverse himself, Addisu Messele used Bakshi Doron's letter as an opportunity to portray himself once more as a defender of the "Feres Mura." The chief rabbi, he said, was acting on the basis of faulty information and bowing to political pressure. Then, as a member of the parliamentary opposition: "The current government wants to leave the Felesmura in Ethiopia," but should "operate according to the decision reached [in 1992] by the ministerial commission, which recognized that the Felesmura are entitled to immigrate" (Sa'ar 1996, 1a).

Bakshi-Doron's unprecedented attack on the return to Judaism was premised on a basic instability of the program, which had been sold to its supporters and sponsors on the basis of an improbable demand for purity of heart: a crystalline transparency of motive and agency that goes "all the way down." The appearance of clouded motives inaccessible to observers (or of apparent instrumentalism on the part of new immigrants) was immediately branded as delegitimating insincerity. This is not because the new immigrants were considered to be worse than anybody else, it is important to note, but precisely because they were in some fundamental sense the same as everybody else, although expectations for them as true converts or at best descendants of apostates, were set much higher. Even though he had never been to Neve Carmel, Bakshi-Doron was responding in part to the unsettling social and religious dynamics at the absorption center, which can be thought of as a microcosm of all of the tensions and spiritual antinomies that characterized Israeli society at the time.

One apparently minor but actually quite potent example of this problem involved a secular athletics instructor from Tel Aviv who objected to the religious restrictions on programming at Neve Carmel. He was an older man with many years of experience in immigrant absorption, but he regularly came into conflict with the young, religious women assigned to the absorption center through the IDF teachers' corps or the religiously oriented national service program (*sherut le'umi*) that some young women chose in lieu of army service. These were almost without exception hardworking and idealistic women, who were loved by immigrant children and appreciated by their parents, but they were also painfully young and in many cases exposed for the first time to the realities of life outside their close-knit religious communities. They viewed themselves as the primary spiritual and educational resources for Neve Carmel residents and took umbrage at the athletic instructor's cavalier attitude toward religion. When he set what they thought was a bad example for immigrants by ignoring religious restrictions or carrying on personal relationships that they thought were inappropriate, they agitated for his removal from the post. Even though the attempt failed, their persistent complaints about the religious atmosphere at Neve Carmel began to trickle up through parents and friends—and in at least one case to a family neighbor who was a well-placed Knesset member in the National Religious Party. The painful thing for me about the miniature *kulturkampf* unfolding at Neve Carmel was that both sides cared deeply about the individual immigrants they had come to know, yet frequently lacked the moral imagination to comprehend how their inability to find common ground was adding to the enormous pressures and difficulties faced by new immigrants—including adolescents like Alem, who were constantly under pressure to choose sides.

Almost inevitably, religious educators who had been sold on the discourse of pure hearts were disappointed to discover a more complex reality in which immigrants willed many things, including some that were incompatible with the religious messages they were being taught. I asked a twenty-five-year-old Ethiopian-Israeli educator who taught in the program what he thought about his pupils:

> You tell me—what did you expect? I am disappointed. I thought, these people, they should be making an effort to show that they are religious, that they really are models, if they want to make up for the past, of their grandparents becoming Christians. But it's not always that way. I see what goes on. They are just like everyone else.

He remained committed to the return to Judaism, but some of his non-Ethiopian colleagues became disillusioned and convinced that their students' failure to conform fully to expectations constituted a kind of dishonesty, or even a personal affront. The hermeneutics of suspicion was nothing new to the "Feres Mura" dilemma, but the extension of that hermeneutic to the very people responsible for keeping the return to Judaism running on a day-to-day basis became a very real problem. It was also especially difficult for defenders of the program to defuse because it was so unspecific.

One of my reasons for focusing analytically on both the public health and religious contexts of exclusion in this book is that doubts in one sphere inevitably reinforced doubts in the other and may also have served as structural parallels. Rabbis, physicians, and public health officials were each configured as state-authorized experts in the assessment of risks requiring management on the public's behalf. The risk of infectious disease is incontrovertible enough, but we have already seen how perceptions of danger were also conditioned by assumptions about the national or religious affiliation of those who were framed as vectors of risk. It is, in fact, unclear to me whether such strong public health claims against the immigration of a perceived high-risk group could effectively have been made unless pervasive values of ethnic and religious solidarity had already been breached. Many, though by no means all, Israelis portrayed the danger of *hitbolelut* (assimilation), which in this case really means inappropriate genealogical mixing or exogamy, as every bit as real as that from HIV. My argument is that rabbis and public health officials fill similar kinds of structural roles in Israel that are implicitly understood as equivalent by many public actors. The Blood Affair protest against public health officials resembled the Ethiopians' 1985 protest against the Chief Rabbinate (S. Kaplan 1987) in that both cases involved challenges to state-authorized experts and gatekeepers in which the government asserted its support for the immigrants while in fact resisting all challenges to the status quo. The irony is that because of the vagaries of the Israeli political system, Shimon Peres was the prime minister called upon to balance immigrants, experts, and public opinion in both cases.

Despite this parallel, one way in which rabbinic authority has actually trumped public health concerns was that as long as religious concerns about the "Feres Mura" were held at bay through assertions of Jewishness and the return to Judaism, other problems could be more or less managed by immigration advocates. Yet once Rabbi Bakshi-Doron decided to use his authority to end "Feres Mura" immigration, he wielded that authority to greater effect than public health authorities ever did:

> [We] have decided that the categorization of the Felesmura as Jews according to the criteria which have been in use until now is not to be relied upon. Without further information and further certification [by the Rabbinate], they are not to be viewed as former Jews . . . and if those who arrive in Israel wish to enter Judaism, they will have to pass through a process of conversion . . . just like any other non-Jew who seeks to convert. We have instructed the Division on Religious Conversions of the Ministry of Religions not to register conversions of the Felesmura who have returned to Judaism in the current manner.

This was undoubtedly the worst crisis that the project of "Feres Mura" immigration and rehabilitation had faced so far, because it represented the collapse of the return-to-Judaism program under its own weight of doubt, suspicion, and unmet expectations. "Feres Mura" and their advocates predictably (and to some extent correctly) pointed to the political machinations of their enemies to explain what had happened—for example, the "rumors" cited in Bakshi-Doron's letter—but they rarely noted to what extent this outcome had been the foreseeable and perhaps even inevitable result of the decision to operate under a banner of pure-hearts discourse in circumstances that left very little room for the transparency and single-mindedness that this framework had always presumed.

The "Feres Mura" Dilemma and the Jewish Question

Together, the Blood Affair and the "Feres Mura" dilemma help to illustrate not just how raw the question of kinship remains for many Beta Israel—descendants of converts or not—even today, but also how difficult and open-ended the question has remained for Israeli society as a whole. One of the only non-Jewish anthropologists ever to conduct significant rescarch on Israeli Jewish society, Virginia Dominguez (1989), has argued that questions of kinship posed to Ethiopian immigrants during the 1980s were also implicitly questions about the boundaries and contours of the unfinished Jewish Israeli collective. She shows through a close reading of popular discourse and news media how the ambivalent cultural conversations surrounding Ethiopian difference in Israel—racial, religious, and cultural difference—were actually elements in an anxiety-ridden and open-ended conversion about the social construction of Israeli Jewishness itself. When Israelis discussed the "primitivity" of Ethiopian immigrants (as insulting as that designation now seems) they were also, not surprisingly, trying to negotiate their own ambivalence about how close they were culturally to the "primitive" developing world, and working to build an ongoing consensus about what it means to be a Jew or an Israeli.

This analysis is undoubtedly correct, and helps to turn a necessary spotlight onto the culture of the "absorbing" society, which is still far from common in the burgeoning cottage industry of "Ethiopian Jewry studies." Yet there is one area in which it may be worthwhile to push back against Dominguez's analysis. Although Dominguez acknowledges that "few groups of people have as long standing and continuous a claim to peoplehood as do Jews" (1989, 90), she also appears to be impatient with the whole notion of collective identity, which she subjects to a strong social constructivist critique. To put the matter plainly, she writes that collective identities, like those that define national or ethnic attachment, are always to some degree contested and negotiated and should really be viewed as "funny fictions" that call for analytic deconstruction. The cultural anxiety provoked in Israel by Ethiopian immigration ought to convince us that ideas like "peoplehood" lack the self-evident, "really-real" quality that should be attributed only to face-to-face relations between people on a local scale.

The assertion that individuals have an ontological priority over groups and group attachments is a complex and important notion that Dominguez uses to advance her moral and political as well as analytic agenda. She is baffled, she writes, that "so much power struggle should focus on the *rights* of peoples—not just individuals—and so little attention be paid explicitly to the semiotic contradictions of peoplehood" (ibid., 191). This is a real-world dilemma that has only intensified in the tiny strip of contested land known as Israel and Palestine since Dominguez wrote: "For over a century now, nationalists have invoked peoplehood as the fundamental justification and rationale for their demand for political independence" (ibid.). This is indeed part of the underlying connection between modern Zionism and the "question of kinship" formulated by people like Henry Stern and Jacques Faitlovitch, who were each in their own way concerned with the Jewish people's return to Zion in modern times. What these men described as a set of relations grounded in nature and race,

Dominguez calls a funny fiction, which, given the excesses of extreme nationalism, are really not so funny after all. Yet Dominguez's argument is both right and wrong, for reasons that must occupy us for a few moments in the context of the "Feres Mura" dilemma.

The academic trope of "invented traditions" (Hobsbawm and Ranger 1992) has had a powerful and generative effect upon many fields of study. We now know that "traditional Ethiopian-Jewish figurines," sold mostly to Western Jewish visitors in Ethiopia and now popular in Israel, were actually invented with the help of a sympathetic supporter who wanted to help impoverished Beta Israel near Gondar by developing a local tourist industry (S. Kaplan and Rosen 1993, 1996; Rosen 1994). My hesitation is not with the constructed nature of traditions and identities, therefore, which this book also documents to a considerable degree, but with the implication of lightness or insubstantiality—of a lack of ontological heft—that scholars sometimes seem to ascribe to the objects of their study, despite the anger or pain that this ethos of "debunking" often provokes (Briggs 1996). The texture of Israeli Jewish nationhood is an inconstant, negotiated thing, at least where Ethiopian-Israelis are concerned, but this hardly means that it is experienced as the play of free will and voluntarism that constructivist models imply. The anxiety over being buried among one's people, which has emerged as an organizing theme of this whole ethnography, imbues lived experience with a degree of moral urgency and "overbearing practical relevance" (Kleinman and Kleinman 1991) that ought to give us pause. Despite inconstancy, the visceral substantiality of belonging pertains not just to a set of local face-to-face relations but also to a privileged engagement with others that takes place across time and circumstance. Indeed, there is no clear empirical or ethnographic reason to suggest that face-to-face relations have any more ontological solidity in this context than the pull of kinship and collective identities do.

The whole debate around constructed and primordial identities may be misplaced in experiential terms, because belonging and kinship are experienced as both fixed *and* contingent, given and chosen in social life. Beta Israel today do recognize the possibility of radical alienation from Jewishness through conversion or assimilation, but they also sometimes experience powerful or overbearing moral compulsions to avoid these as betrayals of who and what they really are. The idea of "return" is without question one of the most powerful tropes of modern Jewish religious experience. There are even those who speculate that important aspects of early modern Judaism were shaped in subtle and direct ways by the need to respond to the crisis of apostasy and return raised by Iberian conversos returning to Judaism in places like Safed, where new forms of religiosity were being forgerd and propogated (see Magid 2005; Fine 2003). It is difficult now to know how familiar the trope of return would have been to Beta Israel before they enjoyed substantial contact with Europeans starting in the 1860s, but there are some indications that this theme already resonated to some degree through episodes like Abba Mahari's fateful 1861 march to the Holy Land.

The involvement of the State of Israel in promoting the idea of return is not surprising, given its complex relationship with Jewish cultural and religious paradigms and its de facto status as the gatekeeper to *'eretz yisra'el*—the biblical promise of the land that Beta Israel frequently referred to in Amharic simply as "Jerusalem." The emergence of a practical geopolitical locus for the idea of return in modern times cannot be underestimated, nor would it have been underestimated by many classical Zionist thinkers. But the relationship between Zion as the imagined center of Jewish national and religious consciousness transcends narrow policy considerations like expanding the state's population, or settling the West Bank, that some foreign critics of the Ethiopian immigration have cited, in my opinion incorrectly (see Spector 2005, 18, 91, 170–171), as fundamental to the push for "Feres Mura" immigration. Despite political and other complications such as Jewish cosmopolitanism and diaspora nationalisms, the rise of secularism, and the rejection of the modern state by some religious groups, the return to Zion remains a feature of the cosmological landscape of modern Jewishness even for those who reject or modify it, and in this it has important but imperfect parallels in other settings.

Gauri Viswanathan (1998) has described the development of programs to "reconvert" Indian Muslims to their allegedly primordial Hindu identity, framed not as proselytism but as realignment of the disturbed cosmic and political order. Like Israelis involved in the return to Judaism, these Hindu nationalists aim to show that conversions to Islam over a long period of time were forced and invalid, leaving a submerged Hindu identity that is recoverable, despite the appearance of change over long periods. There is a close connection between this contestation of souls and the contestation of holy sites that are also treated as primordially Hindu despite subsequent histories of Muslim use. Viswanathan argues that the sometimes violent conflicts that ensue are hardly soluble through resolutions of fact alone (was there really a Hindu temple beneath the mosque at Ayodha?) because incommensurate historical narratives have been generated in the struggle for power. The Israeli parallel may even be more complicated because it involves not just holy sites and the disposition of converts but also ongoing struggles about the imposition and/or recovery of Hebrew histories and place names across the whole landscape of places where Jews and Arabs both have lived (Benvenisti 2000). This is not, in other words, an issue limited to confessedly religious contexts or social actors—it is embedded in complicated ways throughout the whole cultural construct of the modern Jewish national project. Returning Christian "Feres Mura" to Jerusalem is, for supporters, an act of kindness and a rehabilitation of what is most real about the social world.

When modern Jews talk about Judaism as a primordial ethnicity or as a kind of nationhood (the discourse on Jewish race has diminished appreciably in the West since the Holocaust), part of what they mean is that Jewishness is conveyed through genealogy and embodied connection with the ancestors even more than it is through religious or theological commitments that many contemporary Jews do not share. This is one of the reasons that conversion to Judaism has become such a fraught issue over the last decades, with different secular and religious bodies (the American Reform Movement, the High Court of Israel, and the Orthodox Chief Rabbinate of Israel, to name just a few) all struggling to define what conversion might mean in this context. Can a person become a Jew without accepting all the ritual and theological burdens of classical Judaism? By extension, can a person remain a Jew without any connection to Judaism as a religion? And if so, what about the substitution of some other form of religious commitment alongside ethnic Jewishness? In Poland I once had the unnerving experience of trying to explain to a fervent Pentecostal missionary why most Jews think that Christianity contradicts Judaism in a way that Marxism—even atheism—does not. She was a venerable old matriarch who had spent a few months in Auschwitz as a Polish political prisoner during the war, and now she wanted to know why so many Jews objected to her current plans to teach Christianity to Jewish children from the former Soviet bloc: "Doesn't Christianity have more in common with Judaism than Marxism does?" On some level her logic was impeccable, but the fact remains that while only a few hypertraditionalists impugn the basic Jewishness of Jewish Marxists and committed secularists of other kinds, conversion to Christianity is considered by almost every Jewish group today to constitute an ultimate betrayal and contradiction. We have already seen how this strong feature of modern Judaism led to rejection and turmoil for the descendants of Beta Israel converts who sought to reassert their Jewishness, yet it is paradoxically that same primordial, inalienable conception of Jewishness that the act of return promises to uncover. The obvious paradox is that Jewishness, which is beyond individual choice and volition, must be chosen willingly by former converts or their descendants.

Various proposals have been made in recent years, with different levels of seriousness, for the creation of a kind of secular conversion to Jewishness without Judaism that would allow people to join the Jewish national project without religious barriers and encumbrances (see Beilin 1999; Bayme et al. 2000; Ilan 2007). None of these has gone very far, and all have met strong opposition from those who think that Judaism and Jewishness must somehow go hand in hand. Standards and conceptions also differ widely today among the different branches of religiously oriented Jewry, from the predominant Orthodox demand for ongoing, practical observance of the commandments to a variety of much looser and more flexible requirements in other settings. Yet here too, one of the most pressing issues has been to define how much weight should be given to "national" or ethnic commitments among potential converts. Some scholars have argued that even within classical Orthodoxy there is precedent for allowing the conversion of people whose religious commitment to the performance of the commandments was less than ideal as long as they committed to joining the Jewish people, and they argue that these precedents—contested though they always were—should be adapted to contemporary conversion policy in Israel (Zohar and Sagi 1994; Sinclair 1992). It is telling that there is no parallel tradition of accepting converts on the basis of religious sentiment alone without full presumed commitment to all of the "penalties and benefits," as Achebe would say, that this choice entails. "Your people shall be my people" note Zohar and Sagi, precedes "your God shall be my God" (Ruth 1:16). Converts, as the sociologist of Judaism Sylvia Barak-Fishman once remarked, are expected to become ethnic Jews.

One of the reasons that the return to Judaism generates so much anxiety in Israel is that, like conversion, it evokes debate over the relationship between religious and ethnic bases of national belonging, which are often closely related to the tension between agency and constraint in the formulation of contemporary Jewishness. Conversion, like "return," can be understood as a ritual attempt to overcome the sense of radical and threatening choice upon which decisions to affiliate as a Jew rely by cultivating an experience of social and metaphysical rootedness—"a view of the world and of the whole cosmos perceived from a particular position." Thrownness and choice, or agency and constraint, are among the fundamental axes of human experience across time and culture (Jackson 1998, 2005; Archer 2000), but the ways in which they interact with, support, or undercut one another may be as variable as the lived settings in which humans struggle and live. Ritual attempts to reconcile them, like the return to Judaism for descendants of Beta Israel converts, are always vulnerable to collapse when either agency or rootedness are called into question by circumstances or by juxtaposition to the opposing principle. The more "Feres Mura" claimed an essential and unchanging Jewishness, the more their commitment to real religious change was undermined by the taint of historical apostasy, but the claim to be essentially converts would have undermined their claim to be in Israel as descendants of Jews. Conceiving the "Feres Mura" dilemma in this way does not yield any neat sociological model, but it does allow for the description of lived experience across a variety of different social fields and for a less politically overdetermined conversation about the different ways in which "Feres Mura" themselves have come to conceive their options and inescapable contradictions in modern times.

The "Feres Mura" dilemma is unlikely to be resolved in any definitive way as long as Jews in Israel and elsewhere remain as deeply divided as they are today about matters of religion and state. Although temporarily devastating, not even

R. Bakshi-Doron's determined attack managed to put the return to Judaism to rest, and this illustrates something important about the way the "Feres Mura" question has been embedded in, yet is also distinct from, larger conflicts in Israel about conversion and "who is a Jew." Bakshi-Doron's withdrawal of authorization for the return-to-Judaism program was related at least loosely to the growing polarization of views on conversion that has pitted the chief rabbis more and more against other sectors of the Israeli public in recent years. It cannot be accidental that his attack on the return to Judaism came precisely during a period of increasingly harsh attacks on the Rabbinate's conversion policy, including High Court rulings that circumscribed the Rabbinate's power to determine the personal status of non-Orthodox immigrant converts. The delegitimization of the return-to-Judaism program must also be viewed within the context of the Rabbinate's struggle to ensure its own legitimacy in the face of an increasingly strong exertion of influence by Haredi (ultra-Orthodox) rabbis and politicians who reject more flexible precedents that some previous Israeli chief rabbis have adopted when dealing with situations of mass immigration. Circling the wagons on many fronts, it is not surprising that the return to Judaism administered by Rabbi Waldman came to seem like an intolerable dilution of standards just at a time when the heightening of barriers was called for.

Bakshi-Doron was succeeded in 2003 by Rabbi Shlomo Amar, who has been an even more vociferous defender of the Chief Rabbinate's traditional prerogative over conversions and determinations of personal status in Israel. In 2005, he took the unprecedented step of announcing that the Chief Rabbinate would no longer automatically accept the conversions performed by Orthodox rabbis in North America unless those rabbis submitted to a series of reforms including the centralization of American conversions in a handful of regional rabbinical courts staffed by rabbis acceptable to the Chief Rabbinate. The legal and philosophical parameters of this ongoing dispute are beyond the scope of my discussion, but it is fascinating to note that while ratcheting up the controversy over conversions on almost every other front, Rabbi Amar actually reversed Rabbi Bakshi-Doron on the "Feres Mura" issue, going so far as to say that he hoped "millions" of new immigrants from Ethiopia would come to Israel under the return-to-Judaism rubric (Sela 2008). One cynical Ethiopian told me he thought the reason Ethiopians were being exempted from harsher standards in conversion was that the rabbis didn't expect their daughters to marry one, but in this case it is more plausible to acknowledge that Rabbi Amar was the protégé of former Sephardic Chief Rabbi Ovadiah Yosef, whose ruling on the Jewishness of Beta Israel in 1973 set the stage for their eventual immigration to Israel (Seeman 1991; Corinaldi 1998). Rabbi Yosef wrote a letter in 2002 affirming that "Feres Mura" were Jews who had converted to Christianity under duress and also calling for them to be brought back to Judaism in an expedited way. Rabbi Amar himself visited Ethiopia to observe the situation and wrote upon his return that "Feres Mura" were "full Jews [*yehudim gemurim*]" who should be brought to Israel—though they must still convert "from the side of stringency."[2] The parameters of the return-to-Judaism program are somewhat stricter than they were under Rabbi Waldman's original plan: individuals now study for a full year before being examined by a rabbinical court, and more care is reportedly taken to distinguish between returning Jews and those whose Beta Israel lineage is suspect, but this is a striking example of how individual policy makers can isolate the "Feres Mura" dilemma from other controversies when they choose to.

Rabbi Amar's election as chief rabbi in 2003 corresponded with a period of increasingly vociferous pressure not just from the families of "Feres Mura" in Israel but also from major organs of the American Jewish community to accelerate and thus bring this immigration to a close. Orthodox (but not ultra-Orthodox), Conservative, and Reform denominations in the United States have all issued declarations of strong support for the immigration of Beta Israel remaining in Ethiopia. It is not my intention to recount the whole story of rabbinic and political intrigue that has accompanied the "Feres Mura" dilemma over the past two decades (though I hope that someone else will undertake to write that story), but merely to highlight some of those events that have direct analytic import to the themes that have been central to this book. One of the important developments of recent years has been the emergence of a gap between the ways in which American and Israeli Jews have approached the "Feres Mura" dilemma on a practical and ideological level. The North American Conference on Ethiopian Jews continued to finance and run the transit center in Addis Ababa until it left amid controversy in 2005, and it is still active to the north in Gondar as well as in the arena of policy and public relations in both North America and Israel (Heilman 2005). Yet where NACOEJ had once been perceived as an outlier in the consensus among major North American Jewish groups with respect to the "Feres Mura" dilemma, it gradually seemed to capture mainstream support on this issue, much to the consternation of some Israeli officials.

Possibly the most telling sign of the shift in discourse has been the willingness of mainstream American Jewish groups to take issue with Israelis publicly on what might previously have been seen as internal matters of immigration policy. In 2006, American Jews raised $70 million in what they thought was a coordinated effort with the Israeli government to facilitate the rapid immigration of people seeking immigration visas in Ethiopia. A rare public row ensued when Israel failed to raise the number of immigration visas it issued to "Feres Mura."

Ethiopians, US Jews Join Forces to Protest New Falashmura Policy

The United Jewish Communities of North America yesterday issued an unusual statement accusing the Israeli government of reneging on its promises, in view of the Finance Ministry's intention to reduce the monthly quota of Ethiopian immigrants from 300 to 150. . . . A delegation of American Jewish community leaders visited Israel about two months ago and raised tough questions about the government's failure to increase the monthly immigration quota to 600 after asking them for money to that end. "Already then they couldn't understand this. What will we tell them now?" the senior UJC [United Jewish Communities] official in Israel said. "We're dealing with a deep problem of trust here. This will exact a price. The next time we come to ask them for money, they might think twice." (Sinai and Sanbetu 2006)

American groups have sometimes implied that Israeli foot-dragging on this immigration is an expression of racism, but a more analytically nuanced formulation would be that it is an expression of the same uncertainty over the question of kinship that has characterized nearly all Jewish responses (including American ones) until recently. The gradual acceptance of a NACOEJ-like position by the United Jewish Communities of North America did not take into account that in Israel, where stakes were higher than in North America, opinion has continued to be mixed and volatile.

In the summer of 2007, Minister of the Interior Meir Shitreet tried to galvanize public opinion to emend the Law of Return to withhold automatic citizenship from immigrant converts in order to remove the temptation of mass conversion by groups like the "Feres Mura." "Who needs them?" he was reported to say. "They are all Christians. We need to take care of the future of Israel and this immigration will never finish" (Butcher 2007). To which the indefatigable Avraham Neguse replied, "These people are our blood, our flesh, and our bones" (ibid.). Neguse demanded that Shitreet retract his comments and warned the Moroccan-born politician not to "forget where he came from" (Eglash 2007). But Shitreet's proposal also outraged American groups who viewed it as an attack on the legitimacy of their own converted members as well as a shot across the bow in the ongoing wars of Jewish legitimacy between themselves and Israel's religious establishment. Shitreet was not deterred. "No one should go looking for any lost tribes," he warned, "because I won't let them in any more. We have enough problems in Israel. Let them go to America" (ibid.). He accused "Feres Mura" advocates of making a living off the continued immigration and added that Israel should focus on "becoming a real state and not acting as a committee for the Jewish people" (ibid.). Which begs the question of what a "real state" is meant to be and how it differs from a committee for the Jewish people.

Shitreet's comments were not made in a vacuum. They echo cultural and political struggles in other areas—the High Court's recent ruling that the semi-governmental Jewish Agency may no longer develop land held in trust solely for Jewish settlement to the exclusion of other citizens; increasing limitations placed on the Chief Rabbinate's ability to block non-Orthodox converts from being recognized by the state registrar as Jews; and challenges to the Law of Return from groups who have grown uncomfortable with Israel's encouragement of Jewish immigration from the Diaspora. What all of these controversies have in common is the testing and in some cases transcendence of the ethno-religious claim of shared nationhood upon which the state was founded (see Joppke and Rosenhek 2002; Joppke 2005). Proposed in more and less radical forms, and greeted by some with moral conviction and others with distaste or alarm, the gradual disengagement of the state from the myths of its founding—ingathering of the exiles, defense of threatened Jewish communities, and furtherance of the Jewish people's historical destiny—have provoked a crisis within Zionism and perhaps more broadly, within the self conceptions of many Israelis and Jews elsewhere.

Shitreet's position was not an argument for the radical rejection of Israel's identity as a Jewish state. It was, however, a rejection of the close identification between classical Zionist motifs and contemporary state priorities. He had positioned himself as a contender for future high office, and he pitched his critique in populist rather than philosophical terms as a complaint about American Jews asking Israelis to bear the long-term social and economic costs of their Zionist fantasies. Dismissing humanitarian concerns, Shitreet called on American Jews who were concerned about the ongoing plight of "Feres Mura" in Ethiopia to "take them to America" if they want care for them. "I haven't seen them take even one Ethiopian to America and in the meantime, Israel is the only country to get Ethiopians. And we accept them with open hearts" (Egash 2007). Shitreet's political and ideological opponents clearly understood the deeper import of this argument. "We will continue our fight for the right of every Jew to make aliya," proclaimed Avraham Neguse. "Israel is the home for all Jews" (ibid.). Sally Falk Moore (1987) has called attention to the fact that state governments are rarely if ever unitary agents acting in accordance with a specific ideological or political agenda, but nowhere is this more obvious than in contemporary Israel. Minister of Immigrant Absorption Yaakov Edery (from Ehud Olmert's ruling Kadima Party) argued, "The conversion of non-Jews is both a national and strategic mission, and is vital to the future of the State of Israel. We have to enable citizens who are interested in converting to fully integrate with the nation and Israeli society" (Egash 2007).

This is precisely where contested cosmologies of Jewish nationhood meet realpolitik and the contingencies of modern Jewish-Israeli life. Enormous changes have been wrought in the fabric of Israeli society by the confluence of national mythologies of ingathering and the collapse of Communism, which caused millions of people in the impoverished former Soviet bloc and Ethiopia to seek redemption in the relatively prosperous West, which, amazingly, now includes Israel. But these processes are not always smooth, and the ensuing public controversies do not map neatly onto the received cultural antimonies of "religious and secular" or "left and right" in Israeli public discourse. Individuals like Shlomo Amar, Meir Shitreet, or Menahem Waldman invoke a variety of different cultural templates strategically in light of circumstance, ideological proclivity, and perceived political interest of the moment. Is the conversion of religiously problematic new immigrants a "national and strategic mission" because it ensures that the ideal of a Jewish and democratic state can be maintained for the foreseeable future, or is it an attack on the authenticity of religious conversion because it forces the state to recognize converts who do not meet the high standards of Jewish law? Constructs like "Jewish state" or "return to Judaism" are all evidently "funny fictions," but they are also expressions of powerful culturally inflected sentiments and profound ethical commitments over time. Despite the importance of political context, such commitments cannot be reduced or deconstructed out of the local moral universe. In the world of Foucalt and Goffman, at any rate, it is difficult to say that the ontological status of the individual is any more easily assured than that of the meaningful collectives to which such individuals claim fervently to belong. Whether Israel is a real state or whether the Jews are a real people are questions I think can only be adjudicated by those who live such realities and whose lives are shaped by them.

I hesitated to publish this book for a long time as I waited for the drama and controversy over "Feres Mura" immigration to recede, but it has not done so. In the summer of 2008, Israel's Housing Minister Ze'ev Boim implied that American "Feres Mura" activists were guilty of racism because they raised money for Russian Jews to settle in the United States, but demanded that Israel take responsibility for settling the Ethiopians (Rettig et al. 2008). Yet Knesset member Michael Eitan, who sponsored legislation to speed the immigration of nine thousand people remaining in Gondar, retorted that, in his view, "Israel did not have the right to exist if it tried to prevent the aliya [immigration] of Jews in distress" (ibid.). I do not know how often the elected officials of other nations rhetorically question the grounds of existence of the states that they serve, but this was not a particularly unusual or shocking comment in Israel, where the very telos of the state is subject to regular probing and rancorous public debate. Some will argue that this illustrates the instability of the Jewish national project or constitutes an argument for its reformulation in terms more familiar from the United States or European democracies. Yet for me it is hard not to feel that this bears witness to a hopeful set of continuities or resonances between contemporary Israel, its status as a vehicle of Jewish national aspirations, and the ethical impulse of prophetic insistence on values that transcend immediate national interest. The "Feres Mura" dilemma has encouraged difficult and painful probing of Israel's priorities and purposes. One could only wish that the conversation were conducted in a way that shed rather more light than heat and allowed immigrant experience to emerge in its own right rather than using immigrants and potential immigrants primarily as ciphers for the political positions of others.

In the end, no ethnography can tell Israeli society how it ought to define Jewishness or Judaism, or how those determinations ought to influence immigration and other policies. For all of its many virtues, there is no reason to suppose that an American model of radical separation between church and state is the only reasonable one for an aspiring democracy to adopt, and there is also, emphatically, no reason to think that such a model would necessarily have offered a better solution to the "Feres Mura" dilemma. The very premise of Ethiopian Jewish immigration to Israel has been based upon an assertion of ethno-religious kinship that imposes obligations of moral solidarity and makes the "Feres Mura" dilemma impossible for Israelis to ignore. The same set of forces that made the descendants of Beta Israel converts vulnerable were also the ones that made the state and many of its citizens accept a sometimes grudging responsibility for their welfare. Not every claim to mass immigration can be honored by a small sovereign state, and the potential for discovery of lost tribes willing either to convert or to assert their ancient, recovered Judaism is today almost limitless. Yet my personal intuition is that any attempt to sever the question of kinship entirely from the question of citizenship and mutual responsibility in Israel today would constitute a collapse of one of the most fundamental categories of Jewishness remaining to us. Israel faces many difficult challenges in meeting its responsibilities to its non-Jewish and Palestinian citizens for protection, material support, and the ability to build meaningful symbolic communities of different kinds (cf. Rouhana 1997). But it should not be assumed that the modern state, which is premised above all on the notion of geographical continuity as an expression of community between those who live within the state's borders, nullifies entirely the older covenantal notion of continuity and shared responsibility across time (Elazar 1987).

This means that Shitreet and others are correct, that the embroilment of the State of Israel in the fate of Jews outside the country, including even contested Jews like the "Feres Mura," distinguishes it from dominant models of statehood in the world today. But whether that means the relationship should be severed does not necessarily follow and is a weighty question that has never really received the devoted and self-conscious attention it deserves. From the earliest debates over "Feres Mura" immigration in 1992, it has been clear that this matter far transcends any merely pragmatic consideration of state resources and geopolitical interests, and that Beta Israel converts are once again forcing

Jews in Israel and outside it—as they did in the late nineteenth century—to try to come to terms with what Jewishness entails in a rapidly changing world. It is our inability to do so in a coherent way, and the competing, often conflicted forces of political and religious groups far from Ethiopia, that keep transit camps filled with displaced people in Gondar and immigrants struggling in places like Haifa or Jerusalem to contend with the explosive consequences of inconstant nationhood described in this book.

As an individual, it should be clear that I am sympathetic though not entirely uncritical of the basic claims of Jewish connection and desire to return to Judaism that have been made and will no doubt continue to be made by and on behalf of "Feres Mura." Having missed the historic opportunity to bring all of those who probably came to Addis Ababa with tacit Israeli encouragement in 1991 (a mere three thousand or so beyond those who were actually airlifted), the establishment of camps to support those who remained was a humanitarian necessity that inevitably encouraged and continues to encourage more people to emerge from the countryside brandishing claims to Jewishness. Whether that was a positive development is a long-term political, philosophical and theological question that cannot be answered ethnographically. One thing is clear, however: the genie cannot be put back into the bottle. The return-to-Judaism program has remained the path of least resistance for almost everyone, as long as immigrants continue to be willing to undergo it and the Rabbinate continues to be willing to certify it. Once one of those conditions finally breaks down, the controversy will erupt with renewed force and vigor. This has often been compared with the much larger immigration of many who are not recognized as Jews from the former Soviet Union, and while I cannot engage in a full comparison of the two issues here, one important difference is that in principle, the question in the Soviet case is the immigration of individuals who may lack the status of halakhic Jews along with others who possess it, whereas here the issue has been framed as the immigration of a whole community that is said to lack that status in a way that is culturally more difficult to ignore. Despite controversy and painful delays, my view of the trajectory so far has been that because of the return to Judaism, "Feres Mura" have a clearer and more certain path to citizenship and recognized Jewishness than other contested immigrant groups. Yet their level of need and the desperation of their preimmigration situation are also in most cases much greater.

While American Jews, Israelis, and now Ethiopian-Israelis are all struggling to figure out where they stand on the most basic issues raised by this dilemma, such as the meaning of Jewishness and its relationship to Israeli national conceptions or the ability of decisions in the here and now to efface the taint of secular or religious apostasy, we ought also be more sensitive to the complexities of lived experience that evade simplistic formulations. The strong cultural representation of suffering in both Jewish and Israeli self-understanding needs to be balanced by the understanding that individuals and groups are always more than ciphers or symbolic representations for positions in the culture wars, and that a humane stance requires somehow making space not just for difference but also for the painful coexistence of conflicting ideals within a single cultural space. Holders of the Jewish authenticity paradigm must by now have learned that the state cannot uniformly enforce its cultural and religious mandates and may collapse if it tries. But if the state is not just a "committee for the Jewish people" that does not free it from the burdens of history, the question of kinship, or the responsibility to serve as the vehicle of Jewish national or religious aspirations in our time. However these cultural and philosophical agendas are resolved, we ought to commit ourselves to care for the immediate needs of those who are most vulnerable to our indecision.

Moral Experience, Religious Transformation, and the Ethnographic Opaque

The death and resurrection of the return-to-Judaism program at the end of the 1990s did not have much immediate effect on the lives of those who had already completed the program and left Neve Carmel. From a formal bureaucratic point of view they were now better off than the descendants of unconverted Beta Israel who had refused the Rabbinate's demand for "conversion from the side of stringency" and had frequently been issued identity cards listing their nationality as "Ethiopian" rather than "Jewish." This formal advantage was not always matched in lived experience however, because former "Feres Mura" might at almost any moment be subject to informal stigma and suspicion from non-Ethiopians as well as fellow Beta Israel. Many individuals took steps to avoid this eventuality by moving to neighborhoods that did not have large, previously existing Ethiopian communities. Rachel and Meles used their subsidized government mortgage to buy a small three-bedroom apartment in a dull housing project abutting a prosperous old Israeli neighborhood and a burgeoning, mostly North American immigrant enclave. They were preceded by Argentine and elderly Russian immigrants and by some poor native Israeli families. On the day they took residence, a neighbor's children stood in the front yard taunting "Falasha, Falasha," but Rachel confronted them saying, "We are all Jews here, so why are you doing that?" and their mother quietly hushed them.

Despite Rachel and Meles's plans to the contrary, their new neighborhood quickly began to fill with former Neve Carmel residents, starting with Rachel's own mother and siblings. After the closing of Neve Carmel, new residents also came from the other absorption centers that had been set up to accommodate the return to Judaism, like Givat Ha-Matos in Jerusalem, Hatzrot Yosaf in the north, or Mevasseret in the Jerusalem–Tel Aviv corridor. Even today relations with most of their non-Ethiopian neighbors are cordial rather than intimate, and there have been tensions. A neighbor from upstairs pulled me aside to complain about the sharp smell of Ethiopian cooking coming from Rachel's apartment, and her brother Desta had to adopt his most reasonable tones to avoid conflict with an irate neighbor who objected to the loud voices of all his nephews and nieces running up and down the stairs on a Friday night while the adults gathered at his apartment for the sabbath. Some incidents also took on the special tones of interethnic immigrant conflict, like the time Rachel's sister fought physically with a Russian immigrant while she was running for local office.

In 2005 the affluent American neighbors began to complain that their children's bicycles were being stolen by Ethiopian kids, and by 2008 their complaints had escalated to charges of scary playground violence perpetrated by Ethiopian teenagers. At first, veterans of Neve Carmel like Desta agreed that the Ethiopian were at fault in their worsening relations with their neighbors, but they blamed the problem indignantly upon the "newcomers" (*hadashim*) who had come to Israel after 1997 and only recently purchased apartments in the city. "They aren't like us," someone said, over *injera* and spicy beans on a lazy Shabbat afternoon. "The children are wild, they lack culture." This provoked a brief but spirited conversation among Desta's many cousins and siblings, until one of his older brothers punctuated the exchange by telling me that he didn't think these newcomers were Jews at all. It was striking to hear such claims from people who only a few years ago had been deeply entrenched in their own pitched battles over authenticity and public perception. During a visit in 2008, when I asked my friends at a family gathering whether the aliyah ought to continue, Tamrat, who works in a local factory, said "No! I think it is enough already!" and was set upon by his brother-in-law for speaking so cavalierly about other peoples' relatives. The willingness of some former "Feres Mura" to criticize newcomers was only a little surprising to me, because it indicates, among other things, that they had grown comfortable enough as Israelis to claim the structural high ground over even newer newcomers. Like many of their own predecessors, some of my friends were concerned that the new immigrants—portrayed as less cultured and less Jewish—would affect their own standing in Israeli public perception. They may have been right.

Among Ethiopian Israelis who are not "Feres Mura," the vociferous debate over public policy and social legitimacy of the new immigrants has continued on the Internet and blogosphere among younger people and has generated some interesting new collaborations. Traditional Beta Israel priests (*kessotch* or *kessim* in the Hebraicized form) and a small but growing number of Ethiopian rabbis, trained and ordained in Israel, have very different visions of religious legitimacy and practice, but they made common cause in October of 2007 to oppose the continuation of "Feres Mura" immigration. A conference in Rehovoth entitled "Defeating the Manifestation of the [Christian] Mission within the Community" was reportedly attended by hundreds of people:

> The *keisim* and rabbis called for establishing new rules for bringing Ethiopian Jews to Israel, maintaining that in recent years many of the Falshamura in Israel have resorted to Christianity and built missions in Jaffa, Jerusalem, and Rehovot, as a result of their difficult financial situation. . . . Conference participants elected a *keisim*-led committee that will map out the various missions in each city and prepare a list of missionaries, which they will transfer to the Interior Ministry, requesting that they be barred from marrying or being buried in a Jewish cemetery. In addition, the committee will formulate a position paper on potential future Falashmura aliyah. "The missionaries persecuted us in Ethiopia, and [we must] not permit them to persecute us in the Holy Land," said the conference participants.

Despite very real and understandable angst within the Ethiopian community about the targeting of their youth by Protestant missionary groups (one such group had noticably increased its presence in the areas of the transit camps in Addis Ababa and Gondar), and the attempt to marshall traditional tactics like the denial of burial plots to converts, it is unclear to me that this protest had any realistic hope of making more than a rhetorical contribution. In 2006, Rabbi Izhak Zagai, the "chief rabbi" of the Ethiopian community in Rehovot (other ethnic groups are not generally said to have local chief rabbis) wrote a letter to the mayor of his town warning that "[p]eople here are threatening to resort to extreme measures, such as blowing up the missionary headquarters with gas tanks" (see also Wagner 2006). Yet while there have in fact been a number of violent attacks on Christian missionary and "Messianic Jewish" groups in Israel over the past two years, none of these have specifically involved Ethiopian missionaries or assailants.

Indeed, the specter of increased activity by Christian missionary groups has been one of the most consistent themes of opposition to the "Feres Mura" immigration since its inception, especially when "missionaries" and "Feres Mura" are treated as almost interchangeable terms. In chapter 5, I argued that this fear was grossly exaggerated, given the reality of life at Neve Carmel during the period of my fieldwork. One of the changes that has taken place since then has been the gradual merging and flexible interaction between small Ethiopian Pentecostal prayer groups like the one I described in Haifa and "white" Jewish messianic groups that derive their inspiration and practical support from North American evangelicals. This synergy, which is the subject of a separate ethnographic study in progress, builds on some of the earliest themes in the Beta Israel–missionary encounter described in chapter 2. It is premised, for example, on the indelible and theologically significant character of Jews as the chosen people, which leads many members of these groups to deny any implication that they are Christians, despite Trinitarian and other classical Christian beliefs. I have noticed that such groups seem to have grown both more numerous and more comfortable with their public personae in Israel over the last few years, taking out advertisements in Israeli newspapers and generally becoming more assertive of their right to operate openly in Israeli society. When someone left an explosive package on the doorstep of a Messianic community leader in Jerusalem in 2008, community members were quite outspoken in their criticism of the police handling of the case (Ha'aretz staff 2008).

While Moshe and his "mother in Christ" (see chapter 5) are still actively involved in the Pentecostal/Messianic community, a few other members of the Neve Carmel community have also joined in the years since they left the absorption center. This is still a relatively marginal phenomenon, but it will take more dedicated ethnographic research to demonstrate its parameters within the Beta Israel or "Feres Mura," communities. It is not, in any case, a religious movement driven by Ethiopians or by "Feres Mura," though Ethiopians do participate alongside Russians, some Palestinians, and native Israeli Jews. Perhaps it is ironic that those who become messianic or Pentecostal are invariably those who speak most clearly and resolutely about the religious significance of Israel, the importance of rejecting customs associated with Ethiopian Orthodox Christianity, and the centrality of the Hebrew Bible (as well as the New Testament) to their religious lives. The family of one twenty-something believer I spoke with was unhappy about the change he had undergone but they were not quick to exclude him from the circle of kinship. It is more often the Messianic believers, in fact, who seek separation from their families as part of their own quest for religious purity and ideological coherence. "You may have noticed that I have been kind of estranged from my family," Avi told me. "How can I just sit around with them all day talking and drinking coffee—do you know what kind of gossip they talk about?" He preferred to meet with his companions to read the Bible—Daniel and Job were particular favorites—or to listen to religious music from the United States and Ethiopia.

Unlike Moshe and Ephraim, Avi gave every appearance of being well adjusted and goal oriented. He held down a good job and had a girlfriend; he was poised and quietly at home in his own skin. Like the Protestant missionaries who came to Ethiopia 150 years ago, he invoked a lexicon of faith and intentional purity that was simply not commensurate with anything I had heard from pious Beta Israel inside or out of the return-to-Judaism program. His juxtaposition of evangelical piety with clipped Israeli slang could sometimes prove unnerving. When a Palestinian construction worker used his bulldozer to attack a bus and run over some civilian cars on a busy Jerusalem street one hot summer day in 2008, Avi explained to me that this was part of Satan's work because no one simply wakes up in the morning and decides to commit such an act without satanic compulsion. When I demurred—satanic compulsion has never been a big part of my own religious outlook—he launched into an account of Satan's fall from grace, "him and his whole *jamma*," using the Israeli-Arabic slang for a gang or disreputable fraternity.

For me this conjured boys on a street corner rather than metaphysical evil, but he meant it to include the relatively benign *zar* spirits to whom Ethiopians still make offerings of coffee and incense when the occasion arises but that Pentecostals view as demonic powers. This is not dissimilar from the ways Pentecostals talk in other African settings (Kileyesus 2006), but his eagerness to describe all of this to me in such a direct Israeli idiom made me realize how much the direct explication of religious ideas and experience had been missing from most of my fieldwork in and around the return to Judaism. Most Beta Israel, including "Feres Mura" that I know, simply do not narrate their religious worlds in such an intense and articulate way, and this is a theme to which I will need to return as I draw this ethnography to a close.

I have argued in this book that the return to Judaism was intended as a ritual-bureaucratic system for the transformation of apostates into penitents, nominal Christians into Jews. In this regard it can probably be described as a qualified success. While proponents and observers of the program were often disappointed that so many participants fell short of the single-minded religious devotion that they felt they had been promised by its advocates, the fact is that nearly all of the participants I encountered during fieldwork succeeded in recasting themselves in the Ethiopian-Jewish mold. Their levels of ongoing ritual observance have varied as I assumed they would and have often seemed to be dependent upon what kinds of neighborhoods and social networks the participants settled into once they left Neve Carmel. One family described sending their children to a religious school for two years before becoming disheartened with the low level of education in that school and transferring to a local secular school—with expected results for their children's religious outlook going forward. But the civil religion of these immigrants is, with the exception of a few self-conscious Pentecostals like Avi, an Israeli-Jewish civil religion, in its distinctive Ethiopian-Israeli form. Former "Feres Mura" may attend Sigd and observe *tazkar* rites for the dead along with the Ethiopian immigrants who preceded them, but they also celebrate Israeli Independence Day and the Memorial Day for fallen soldiers. The Sabbath that they recognize, even in the breach, is without exception a Jewish-Israeli rather than a Christian Ethiopian Sabbath, and the liturgical calendar that defines their everyday lifeworld today is, even for those who are not especially punctilious about religion, a Jewish Israeli one. These are not transcendent "religious experiences" of the kind Pentecostals love to describe, or of the kind that some critics of the return-to-Judaism program seem to require. However, these observances, together with a sense of shared history or destiny and some limited ritual or liturgical practice (attending synagogue on the holidays or sharing Sabbath dinner with one's family), are what constitute Jewishness for the majority of contemporary Israelis, whom sociologists say cannot be described as either strictly religious or wholly secular (Leibman 1997; Leibman and Katz 1997). There is no sense in denying that the return to Judaism has not generated the pure hearts and strict Orthodoxy that some have promised or demanded, but it did succeed in helping to generate the conditions for new forms of moral experience as Jews in Israel—no more or less, by and large, than the majority of their neighbors in towns like Bet Shemesh, Kiryat Malachi, or Talpiot Mizrah. Whether that is sufficient for the descendants of people designated apostates is not, of course, an ethnographic question, but a cultural and philosophical one.

One of the underlying features of the "Feres Mura" dilemma has been the inability of Israelis and other Jews to agree upon a single characterization of religious experience and transformation among Beta Israel converts or their descendants. In most cases, debates have focused on privileged moments of religious change—the moment of apostasy to Christianity or of return to Judaism—that are treated as starkly definitive and binary, either purely religious or completely instrumental. We have seen what kinds of methodological and epistemological quandaries and contradictions this generates, although no one has really suggested a better approach. This is not a problem unique to Israeli politics, however, or to the "Feres Mura" case, although here the freighted political context and the human costs of political uncertainty make the matter seem more pressing. Rita Smith Kipp's (1995) ethnography of Indonesian converts to Protestantism also emphasizes the inadequacy of models that put too much emphasis on moments of religious origin or the unique experiences that underlie them. "Approaches that focus too exclusively on the individual's religious experience," she writes, miss the potential social and personal impact of any decision to change religious allegiance" even when the initial transformation may have been little more than nominal:

> Similarly, accounts that reduce conversion to affiliation and its short term benefits, or those that depict only the social predispositions and consequences of this act, undervalue the religious implications of what has happened, or more precisely, what may happen. Many colonial-era Karo Christians were baptized as young men and women seeking access to mission schools but came to interpret their lives through a new faith. (878)

Her theoretical intervention tries to shift attention from the suspicious assessment of agency at the moment of conversion and toward the gradual unfolding of those decisions in the lifeworld of converts over time. Rachel tried to tell me something similar in her insistence that she is a Jew despite eating many things during the course of her life, but this is not the kind of claim that state agencies are well equipped to hear. Veena Das (1990, 1994, 2006) has written movingly about the plight of women trapped or abducted on the wrong side of the border during the partition of India and Pakistan in the late 1940s who have more recently been victimized by forced repatriation, without consideration for the family and religious attachments they may have developed over many years on the "wrong" side of the border. Like women in the Hindu and Muslim contexts of South Asia, "Feres Mura" have become ciphers in contests over the shape of Israeli Jewishness, in which "the religious implications of what has happened, or more precisely, what may happen" too often disappear beneath a collapsing weight of speculation about what has already happened.

Thomas Trautmann has traced anthropology's fascination with moments of origin to nineteenth-century historical philology's promise "to recover a vanished past from vestiges unconsciously preserved in living languages, discoverable only to those who could decipher the signs" (1987, 73). This promise led early anthropology to a false literalism in the study of kinship categories of the people they studied, since it was assumed that such categories yielded primarily archaeological information about lost forms of social organization. In literary contexts, "deciphering the signs" has frequently meant that semantics "gives way to an abstract lexicalism, and the unfounded supposition is made that the meanings of words, of terms . . . and of statements are univocal and can therefore be uncovered *once their origin has been exposed*" (Al-Azmeh 1993, 135; see also Seeman 1998). I have argued throughout this book that the "Feres Mura" dilemma is in many ways a crisis of interpretive paradigms applied by rabbis, bureaucrats, and even academic scholars to the study of religious change, based in the "unfounded supposition" that the meaning of conversion can be defined once its origin has been exposed. The deciphering of codes is in the end a mechanical process that stands in opposition to the kinds of expansive skills and intuitive choices exercised by readers of literary texts, who must interpret rather than decode. For me, the "Feres Mura" dilemma constitutes a failure of interpretation under the cultural imperative to decipher hidden signs of spoiled agency and false kinship claims. Decoding and the hermeneutics of suspicion are attractive to bureaucrats as well as scholars because interpretation, unlike deciphering, remains open-ended and contingent. Not every reading can be defended, but there is almost always more than one plausible construction of agency in the text, or in life. There is something opaque about religious experience that frustrates the certainty of received taxonomies; we seek a false but comforting certainty by deciphering rather than interpreting the expressions of agency that stand behind religious change—and therein lies the whole dilemma of "Feres Mura" claims.

There is no way to escape the eventuality of gaps in meaning, misunderstanding or misdirection, and simple contingency of interpretation in human affairs. "It is at this point," writes Alfred Schutz, "that the complicated relation of the social sciences to their subject becomes evident" (1967, 9). Schutz, who struggled to combine Weber's concern with cultural meaning and Husserl's phenomenology, understood that there is no direct access to lived experience in social science that is not mediated, to some degree, by language and positionality, and by the interpretation of what has come before. More than that, he understood that experience is, even from the point of view of the experiencing subject, also an interpretive act, struggling as we do to make pragmatic sense out of our own motivations and those of others in the social world, and to incorporate previous experience into the stories we tell ourselves about ourselves.

The important and frequently overlooked corollary of this realization is that the specialized methodological tools of the social scientist exist on a continuum with the everyday interpretive strategies of people who must always struggle to imperfectly assess the agency and motivations of those they come into contact with, and who also frequently work to interpret or to reinterpret their own experiences over time. Although social scientists and other social beings frequently miss this fact, they are almost always engaged in a contingent set of interpretive practices that yield a mixture of error, uncertainty, and (when we are careful or lucky) good-enough assessments of the social world. I have tried in this book to highlight the contingency of interpretation not because of any postmodernist theoretical conceit, but because this recognition has important analytical and ethical implications for the world we study. It leads me to avoid absolutist statements about the experiences and motivations of other people, and to come clean to the best of my ability about why I have interpreted the "Feres Mura" dilemma in the ways that I have. I have argued much greater caution in the way we translate claims about the quality of religious experience into the language of state policy. The obligation to do no harm and to humanly represent that which is human is more than an ethical imperative of anthropological research, in my view; it is also fundamental to the possibility of valid knowledge about those topics around which the "Feres Mura" dilemma has turned.

The ethnography of human experience has sometimes made exaggerated claims about its access to the lived and embodied subjectivity of other people. But how many of us can say, in the course of our own lives, that we have fully plumbed the depths even of those closest to us, and how would they respond if we made such claims in public? Ethnographers have a great deal in common with novelists and writers of fiction in their attempts to represent a world completely enough that the reader can make an intellectual and intuitive leap to embrace another way of being. Yet, unlike writers and readers of fiction, we are also constrained—in a powerful and morally invigorating way—by the fact that the worlds we describe have lives that continue to grow beyond our texts and, with increasing frequency, to talk back. "Living in the world," writes Schutz, "we live with others and for others, orienting our lives to them. In experiencing them as *others*, as contemporaries and fellow creatures, as predecessors and successors, by joining with them in common activity and work, influencing them and being influenced by them in turn—in doing these things we *understand* the behavior of others and assume that they understand ours" (ibid.) Participant observation—by which I mean living intimately and in conjunction with strangers—is not just another research tool or a discrete methodology of one branch of the social sciences. In its best and broadest understanding, which includes both formal methodology and a whole ethos of engaged interaction with other beings, it is a necessary condition for the very possibility of understanding.

It is difficult to draw this ethnography to a close. I have intentionally refrained from discussing the ongoing and difficult conditions of people still waiting in Ethiopia and the experience of the most recent groups of immigrants returning to Judaism in Israel. These are the subjects of ongoing research by myself and other scholars (Goodman 2008a 2008b; Cohen 2006; Shabtay 2007) and deserve much more extended treatment than I can offer here. But I would like to share a few words about just a few of the people whose willngness to share their lives with me has opened a window onto the return to Judaism and so much more. I cannot promise that they will like everything I have written here, but I offer this book with humility to a better understanding of the forces that have helped shape their lives so far.

Alem left Neve Carmel on an upward trajectory with his acceptance to an elite boarding school. He later contacted me in the United States for financial help after his father finally cut him off financially, presumably because he was intimidated by his son's newfound mastery and success. We corresponded a few times and spoke by telephone, but eventually I heard that he had dropped out of school and gone off to work in the port of Eilat. When he saved up enough money he traveled to Ethiopia for an extended visit to his mother. While he did eventually return to pick up the thread of his life in Israel, he never went back to school so far as I know, and he lost contact with many of our mutual friends. Returning to Ethiopia as expatriate tourists had become popular among all strata of Beta Israel society during those years, and some had turned it into a business opportunity by carrying cloth or spices back to Israel for the immigrant market. Such trips took on special meaning for many former "Feres Mura," however, because of the importance of the kinship and other ties that they maintained with those who remained in the land of their birth. Some of my non–"Feres Mura" friends began returning to Ethiopia in the late 1990s and early 2000s to seek healing for chronic illnesses from famous rural spirit healers known as *tankway*, but others, like Ageru Kassa (1998), returned to volunteer at the NACOEJ compound before it was closed in 2005, and to work as an educator and public ambassador for those who were still struggling to come to Israel. Other Ethiopians returned to their villages in Gondar to pay local villagers for the upkeep of their families' graves. A sad and strange report holds that Christian Ethiopians in some areas have been digging up Beta Israel graves for their bones—the receptacles of Jewishness—which are still sometimes said to hold magical or prophylactic powers (Sanbetu 2005).

Meanwhile, in Israel, Desta married into a Beer Sheba family who had immigrated during Operation Solomon. I had only to tell my taxi driver at the central bus station in Tel Aviv that I was invited to an Ethiopian wedding and he knew just where to take me. I was one of the only white faces among 650 guests, so the bride's family can be excused for thinking I was part of the waitstaff and asking for beers. The religious portions of the wedding were conducted by an Ethiopian rabbi, entirely in the Israeli Orthodox style, and while ubiquitous Israeli schnitzel was served, the music and dancing resembled any Ethiopian nightclub in Addis Ababa or Washington, DC. Weddings I had attended in Israel during the 1980s had almost always had a village feel. They were held outdoors in courtyards or local activity centers; the women guests all cooked and the festivities were accompanied by a few hand instruments and clapping. By contrast, Desta employed a well-paid Ethiopian deejay who focused on hits from cosmopolitan Addis Ababa and occasionally even traveled to Ethiopia to contract new songs from popular singers there. This kind of music is now de rigueur for sophisticated young Beta Israel, who have, paradoxically, adopted pan-Ethiopian culture as they have become Israeli, keyed to the latest trends not just of Addis but also of the Ethiopian diaspora in places like Atlanta or Berlin. Desta's wedding was a performance of success and conspicuous consumption for people who only a few years before had been impoverished refugees, and it was good to watch them celebrate—and to celebrate with them. But Desta made a point of pulling me aside during the festivities to remind me quietly of his sadness that his father still lay in an unmarked grave in the "Falasha cemetery" in Addis Ababa—not just that he had failed to live to see this day, but also that he had died, in Desta's view, for no reason, denied the honor that had been his due.

Almost all Ethiopian-Israelis can tell stories of loss and unresolved grief that are related to their time of migration. A new memorial has recently been established in Jerusalem for those who died on the long road to Sudan during the 1980s, and this has become the center of an important commemoration every year on the day that Jewish Israelis celebrate the reunification of Jerusalem after 1967—Jerusalem Day. For returnees to Judaism who did not trek to Sudan but who faced their own barriers and sometimes insurmountable odds, these feelings of grief may be complicated by unresolved anger toward the government and others that they hold responsible for their humiliation. When I asked Desta at a family gathering in 2005 whether coming to Israel had been worth all the turmoil he and his family had undergone, he affirmed without question that he had now fulfilled his father's dream and was at peace with himself for that.

Yet when I repeated the question at our next meeting in 2008, he expressed bitter cynicism about incidents of racism he said he had witnessed at work, like a comment by a coworker that he would never work for an Ethiopian supervisor. I heard similar expressions from other successful men his age during my visit, and I suspect this relates to immigrants in their thirties coming to feel that their financial and career success in Israel had plateaued. Desta and his family are willing to reminisce about the return to Judaism and their time in Addis Ababa or Neve Carmel, but typically only when prompted. When I told him that my book on the "Feres Mura" dilemma had been accepted for publication, he smiled mischievously and asked me not to put his picture on the cover.

Both of Desta's sisters lost their husbands to illness shortly after completing the return to Judaism and leaving Neve Carmel. Meles spent a few months in and out of an infectious disease unit with tuberculosis but died despite treatment. Rachel chose not to remarry and has taken on the role of family matriarch instead. Before the disaster, she had had aspirations to find work as a teacher, but now she helps her siblings care for their children and watches others achieve careers while she stays closer to home, wears traditional clothing, and begins to take on the features and mannerisms of her own mother. She has managed well enough, and the government will continue paying her mortgage until her youngest child leaves home (it is unclear to me what she is supposed to do then), but there is a sadness in her eyes that does not go away, and a quietude. She does not like talking about her husband's death, but Desta told me that some people in the family attribute his illness to grief and frustration about not being able to arrange an immigrant visa for his sister who is in Ethiopia. A couple of years after Meles's death Rachel spent a month visiting her husband's family in Addis Ababa and looked better to me somehow when she returned. During a private moment over coffee, she showed me a photo album from her trip. There were no more than a handful of pictures of the people she had traveled to see, but there were almost a dozen photos of the "Falasha cemetery" where I had first met her family. I find it difficult to express the sadness mixed with gratification and even pride for her that I felt when she showed me the pictures of her father's refurbished grave. It was enclosed now in a kind of white gazebo with a latched door, adorned with flowers and a picture of her father—a duplicate of the one that adorned the wall of her apartment in Israel. For a little while the conversation grew quiet as we gazed at the photos and talked about what had been involved in doing this small but momentous thing for her family. We had come full circle, she and I.

NOTES

CHAPTER 2 — THE QUESTION OF KINSHIP

1. Rev. Alex McCaul, "The Duty and Method of Bearing Good Tidings to Zion," *LJS Annual Sermon* (London, April 21, 1841), 25. The London Society was founded under Anglican auspices in 1809 with only a single missionary. By the time of the Ethiopian mission in 1861, however, it boasted "29 ordained missionaries, 26 unordained missionary agents, 61 colporteurs, scripture readers, school masters and mistresses, etc., the greater part of them Christianized Jews, distributed in 39 work stations in Europe, Asia and Africa." It was devoted to "declaring the Messiahship of Jesus to the Jew first and also to the non-Jew," to "encouraging the Hebrew/Messianic Jewish movement," "teaching the Church its Jewish roots," and "encouraging the physical restoration of the Jewish people to the . . . Land of Israel" (see Low 1861).

2. For an account of conversion by several *debteroch* including the celebrated Beru, see *Jewish Intelligence*, July 1, 1861, 190–191.

3. Charles James was Lord Bishop of London. The quote is from "God's Ancient People, Cast Not Away" *LJS Annual Sermon* (London, May 4, 1843), 25.

CHAPTER 3 — PURITY OF HEART

1. Steven Kaplan's account (1992b, 130–132), which suggests that the boy's parents rather than his uncle acquiesced in this punishment, should probably be emended in light of *Jewish Record* accounts in April-May 1863, pp. 13–14.

2. See *Oswald Rufeisen v. Minister of the Interior*, H.C. 72/62, P.D. 16, 2424, and Law of Return (Amendment no. 2) 5730-1970, Sec. 4B.

3. Based on a Hebrew translation of Taamrat's letter to Mr. Charles Isaacson of New York on November 30, 1935.

CHAPTER 4 — RETURNING TO JUDAISM

Daniel Levi (Miguel) de Barrios was a seventeenth-century "crypto-Jew" living in Spain, who returned to Judaism after moving to Amsterdam. His sonnet "Words of a Penitent Sinner," from which this line is taken, begins: "Lord, not with tears shall I wash clean the stain/ That robs my soul of sunlight from thy face." The entire sonnet is cited and translated by Yosef Kaplan (1989a, 330).

1. Testimony to the Ministerial Committee on the Subject of the Falash Mura, December 31, 1992, document B-2134.
2. Ibid., document B-2141.
3. Ibid., document B-2134-.

CHAPTER 5 — ABSORPTION

1. Levi 1995, 14. I have altered the original quote only to delete the name of the girl in question. Although it is part of the public record, I do not wish to make it any more accessible to the merely curious. She has suffered enough from unwanted attention.
2. For a parallel account of the fear of poisoning through commensality, see Uni Wikan (1990). Wikan, of course, also uses this example to bring home her point that anthropologists need to consider the perception of risk experienced by their informants, and not just their cultural patterns and beliefs.

CHAPTER 6 — BLOOD AND TERROR

1. Ethiopian blood was not, of course, discarded on the spot, as some media reports implied (Navon et al. 1996). All samples were tested for HIV antibodies and then autoclaved before disposal. Samples from especially rare blood types were also exempted from the demand for automatic destruction.
2. For one account of reactions to an unexplained suicide by an Ethiopian-Israeli soldier, see Winkler 1997, 16.
3. This was not in fact, strictly true. In 1995, for instance, stone throwing and tear gas caused injury to three police officers and three Ethiopian-Israelis at a demonstration over allegedly substandard housing for new immigrants near Netanya. In contrast to the Jerusalem demonstration, the Netanya demonstration involved only a few dozen protesters, who were met by an unusually large contingent of Border Police, prompting an investigation about why so many officers had been sent. See the *Jerusalem Post,* August 18, 1995, "City Lights" section, p. 1. Also see S. Kaplan and Rosen 1994, 75, 109.
4. This essay was originally published in Hebrew in the daily newspaper *Davar Rishon*, February 1, 1996. The translation is from an excerpt that appeared in the magazine *News from Within* 12, no. 2 (February 1996): 18.
5. Testimony given on May 11, 1996, by Dr. Z. Ben-Ishai, head of the Committee on AIDS at Rambam Medical Center. In 1996 there were known to be 1,386 seropositive individuals in Israel, with Ben-Ishai estimating that this translated into 2,500–3,000 actual cases (see Navon et al. 1996, 7–8).

CHAPTER 7 — THE "FERES MURA" DILEMMA

1. This trend has continued. See Ben Lynfield, "In Israel, Distress Signals from Ethiopians," *Christian Science Monitor,* May 22, 2002, p. 16; Irit Avrahami and Omer Barak, "African Israelis/Ethiopian Jews Reject Israeli Society as it has Rejected Them," *Haaretz* (online), January 14, 2005; Omer Barak and Idit Avrahami, "Ethiopian Youth Dance in Ashkelon but Dream of Harlem," *Haaretz* (online), January 12, 2005.
2. Letter from Chief Rabbi Shlomo Amar to Prime Minister Ariel Sharon, 21 Iyyar 5763 [May 29, 2003], *Haaretz* (online), May 29, 2003.

REFERENCES

Abbink, Jon. 1985. "An Ethiopian Jewish 'Missionary' as Culture Broker." *Israel Social Science Research* 3:21–32.
———. 1986. "Two Amharic Letters by the Falasha Leader Tamrat Emmanuel." *Journal of the Royal Asiatic Society*: 190–200.
———. 1990. "The Enigma of Beta Esra'el Ethnogenesis: An Anthro-Historical Study." *Cahiers d'Etudes Africaines* 120:397–449.
Abir, Mordechai. 1968. *Ethiopia: The Era of the Princes*. London: Longmans, Green.
Abu-Lughod, Lila. 1990. "The Romance of Resistance: Tracing Transformations of Power Through Bedouin Women." *American Ethnologist* 17:41–55.
———. 1991. "Writing Against Culture." In *Recapturing Anthropology: Working in the Present*, ed. Richard Fox, 137–162. Santa Fe, NM: School of American Research Press.
Achebe, Chinua. 1988. *Hopes and Impediments: Selected Essays*. New York: Doubleday.
Al-Azmeh, Aziz. 1993. *Islams and Modernities*. New York: Verso.
Albert, Phyllis Cohen. 1982. "Ethnic and Jewish Solidarity in Nineteenth Century France." In *Mystics, Philosophers and Politicians*, ed. Jehuda Reinharz and Daniel Swetschinski, 249–274. Durham, N.C.: Duke University Press.
Alcalay, Reuben. 1965. *The Complete English-Hebrew Dictionary*. Hartford, CT: Prayer Book Press.
Anderson, Benedict. 1991. *Imagined Communities*. New York: Verso.
Anteby, Lisa. 1995. "Rituals of Birth and Death: The Construction of Identity for Ethiopian Jews." *Israel Social Science Research* 10 (2):41–54.
———. 1996. "Voies de l'integration, voix de la tradition: itineraires socio-culturels et pratiques de communication parmi les juifs ethiopiens en Israel." Ph.D. diss., Sorbonne, Paris.
———. 1997. "Blood, Identity and Integration: Reflections on the Ethiopian Jews in Israel." In *Ethiopia in Broader Perspective, Papers of the XIIIth International Conference of Ethiopian Studies*, ed. Katsuyoshi Fukui, Eisei Kurimoto, and Masayoshi Shigeta, 262–283. Kyoto: Shokado Book Sellers.

———. 1999. "There's Blood in the House: Negotiating Female Rituals of Purity among Ethiopian Jews in Israel." In *Women and Water: Menstruation in Jewish Life and Law*, ed. Rahel R. Wasserfall, 166–186. Hanover, NH: Brandeis University Press.

Anteby-Yemini, Lisa. 2004. *Les Juifs éthiopiens en Israel: les paradoxes du paradis*. Paris: CNRS éditions.

Archer, Margaret S. 2000. *Being Human: The Problem of Agency*. Cambridge: Cambridge University Press.

Aretxaga, Begoña. 1995. "Dirty Protest: Symbolic Overdetermination and Ethnic Violence." *Ethos* 23 (2):123–148.

Asad, Talal. 1993. *Genealogies of Religion: Discipline and Reasons of Power in Christianity and Islam*. Baltimore: Johns Hopkins University Press.

Ashkenazi, Michael. 1988. "Political Organization and Resources Among Ethiopian Immigrants." *Social Science Information* 27:371–389.

Ashkenazi, Michael, and Alex Weingrod, eds. 1987. *Ethiopian Jews and Israel*. New Brunswick, NJ: Transaction Books.

Astuti, Rita. 1995. "'The Vezo Are Not a Kind of People': Identity, Difference and 'Ethnicity' Among a Fishing People of Western Madagascar." *American Ethnologist* 22:464–482.

Azoulay, Katya. 1997. *Black, Jewish and Interracial*. Durham, NC: Duke University Press.

Baldwin, James. 1962. *The Fire Next Time*. New York: Vintage International.

Bard, Mitchell Geoffrey. 2002. *From Tragedy to Triumph: The Politics Behind the Rescue of Ethiopian Jewry*. Westbury, CT: Praeger.

Barnes, Andrew E. 1997. "Aryanizing Projects: African Collaborators and Colonial Transcripts." *Comparative Studies of South Asia, Africa, and the Middle East* 17:46–61.

Bayer, Ronald, Carol Levine, and Susan M. Wolf. 1989. "HIV Antibody Screening: An Ethical Framework for Evaluating Proposed Programs." In *The AIDS Epidemic: Private Right and the Public Interest*, ed. Padraig O'Malley, 173–187. Boston: Beacon Press.

Bayme, Steven. 2000. "Round Table on Yossie Beilin's *Death of the American Uncle*," *Israel Studies* 5:348–354.

Behar, Ruth. 1996. *The Vulnerable Observer: Anthropology that Breaks Your Heart*. Boston: Beacon Press.

Beilin, Yossie. 1999. *Death of the American Uncle*. [In Hebrew.] Tel Aviv: Yedioth Aharonoth.

Benbassa, Esther, ed. 1995. *Haim Nahum: A Sephardic Chief Rabbi in Politics, 1892–1923*. Trans. Miriam Kochan. Tuscaloosea and London: University of Alabama Press.

BenEzer, Gadi. 1992. *Kemo Or ba-Kad: 'Aliyatam u-Kelitatam shel Yehude Etyopyah* [Like Light in a Jug: Migration and Absorption of Ethiopian Jews]. Jerusalem: Reuben Mass.

———. 2002. *The Ethiopian Jewish Exodus: Narratives of the Migration Journey to Israel 1977–1985*. London and New York: Routledge.

Ben-Dor, Shoshana. 1985. "The Holy Places of Ethiopian Jewry." [In Hebrew.] *Pe'amim* 22:32–52.

———. 1987. "The Journey to Eretz Israel: The Story of Abba Mahari." [In Hebrew.] *Pe'amim* 33:5–31.

———. 1994. "The Ties Between the Jews of Ethiopia and the Emperor Tewodros." [In Hebrew.] *Pe'amim* 58:67–85.

Benjamin, Walter. 1968. *Illuminations*. Trans. Harry Zohn. New York: Schocken.
Benvenisti, Meron. 2000. *Sacred Landscape: The Buried History of the Holy Land Since 1948*. Berkeley: University of California Press.
Berry, LaVerle. 1979. "Factions and Coalitions during the Gonder Period, 1630–1755." In *Proceedings of the Fifth International Conference on Ethiopian Studies, Session B* (1978), ed. R. L. Hess, 431–444. Chicago: Office of Publications Services, University of Illinois at Chicago Circle.
Bourdieu, Pierre. 1977. *Outline of a Theory of Practice*. Trans. Richard Nice. Cambridge: Cambridge University Press.
———. 1980. *The Logic of Practice*. Trans. Richard Nice. Stanford, CA: Stanford University Press.
Boyarin, Jonathan. 1992. *Storm from Paradise: The Politics of Jewish Memory*. Minneapolis: University of Minnesota Press.
Bratlinger, Patrick. 1985. "Victorians and Africans: The Genealogy of the Myth of the Dark Continent." In *"Race," Writing, and Difference*, ed. Louis Henry Gates Jr., 185–222. Chicago: University of Chicago Press.
Brhane, Meskerem. 2000. "The Road 'Back' to Judaism: Rumors and the Politics of Conversion." Unpublished manuscript.
Briggs, Charles L. 1996. "The Politics of Discursive Authority in Research on the 'Invention of Tradition.'" *Cultural Anthropology* 11 (4): 435–469.
Brodkin, Karen. 1999. *How Jews Became White Folks and What that Says About Race in America*. New Brunswick, NJ: Rutgers University press.
Brodwin, Paul. 1996. *Medicine and Morality in Haiti*. Cambridge: Cambridge University Press.
Buckser, Andrew, and Stephen D. Glazier. 2003. *The Anthropology of Religious Conversion*. Lanham, MD.: Rowman & Littlefield.
Butcher, Jim. 2007. "Israeli Minister in Racism Row." *Telegraph* United Kingdom). August 4.
Carlebach, Elisheva. 2001. *Divided Souls: Converts from Judaism in Germany 1500–1750*. New Haven, CT: Yale University Press.
Chemtob, Daniel, Iris Kalka, and Yossef Fassberg. 1990. "Research Note: Blood Drawing and Hepatitis B—The Case of Ethiopian Jews in Israel." *Sociology of Health and Illness* 12 (2): 216–226.
Chemtov, D., H. Rosen, R. Shtarkshall, and V. Soskolne. 1993. "A Culturally Specific Educational Program to Reduce the Risk of HIV and HBV Transmission Among Ethiopian Immigrants to Israel: A Preliminary Report on Training Veteran Immigrants as Health Educators." *Israel Journal of Medical Science* 29:437–442.
Cohen, Ravit. 2006. "Waiting on their Way: The 'Seed of Israel' Community in a Gondar Transit Camp." [In Hebrew]. Master's thesis, The Hebrew University of Jerusalem.
Cohler-Esses, Lawrence. 1998. "Help on the Way for Falash Mura?" *Jewish Week*. September 25, p. 37.
Comaroff, Jean. 1993. "The Diseased Heart of Africa: Medicine, Colonialism, and the Black Body." In *Knowledge, Power and Practice: The Anthropology of Medicine and Everyday Life*, ed. Shirley Lindenbaum and Margaret Lock, 305–329. Berkeley: University of California Press.
Comaroff, Jean, and John Comaroff. 1991. *Of Revelation and Revolution: Christianity, Colonialism and Consciousness in South Africa*. Chicago: University of Chicago Press.

Corinaldi, Michael. 1988. *Yahadut Etyopya: Zehut u-Masoret* [Ethiopian Jewry: Identity and Tradition]. Jerusalem: Reuben Mass.

———. 1998. *Jewish Identity: The Case of Ethiopian Jewry.* Jerusalem: Magnes Press, The Hebrew University.

Cox, Harvey. 1995. *Fire From Heaven: The Rise of Pentecostal Sprituality and the Reshaping of Religion in the Twenty-First Century.* New York: Addison-Wesley.

Crummey, Donald. 1969. "Tewodoros as Reformer and Modernizer." *Journal of African History* 10 (3): 457–469.

———. 1972. *Priests and Politicians: Protestant and Catholic Missions in Orthodox Ethiopia 1830–1868.* London: Clarendon.

———. 1975. "Society and Ethnicity in the Politics of Christian Ethiopia During the Zamana Masafant." *International Journal of African Historical Studies* 8 (2): 266–278.

———. 1983. "Family and Property Amongst the Amhara Nobility." *Journal of African History* 24:207–220.

Csordas, Thomas J. 1990. "Embodiment as a Paradigm for Anthropology." *Ethos* 18:5–47.

———. 1994. *The Sacred Self: A Cultural Phenomenology of Charismatic Healing.* Berkeley: University of California Press.

———. 2002. *Body/Meaning/Healing.* New York: Palgrave Macmillan.

Danahay, Martin A. 1993. *A Community of One: Masculine Autobiography and Autonomy in Nineteenth Century Britain.* Albany: State University of New York Press.

Daniel, Valentine E., and John Christian Knudsen. 1995. "Introduction." In *Mistrusting Refugees*, ed. Daniel E. Valentine and John Chr. Knudsen, 1–12. Berkeley: University of California Press.

Das, Veena. 1990. *Mirrors of Violence: Communities, Riots, and Survivors in South Asia.* Delhi: Oxford University Press.

———. 1994. "Moral Orientations to Suffering: Legitimation, Power, and Healing." In *Health and Social Change in International Perspective*, ed. Lincoln C. Chen, Arthur Kleinman, and Nora C. Ware, 139–167. Boston: Harvard School of Public Health.

———. 1995. *Critical Events: An Anthropological Perspective on Contemporary India.* Delhi: Oxford University Press.

———. 2006. *Life and Words: Violence and the Descent into the Ordinary.* Berkeley: University of California Press.

Desjarlais, Robert. 1992. *Body and Emotion: The Aesthetics of Illness and Healing in the Nepal Himalayas.* Philadelphia: University of Pennsylvania Press.

———. 1994. "Struggling Along: The Possibilities for Experience among the Homeless Mentally Ill." *American Anthropologist* 96 (4): 886–901.

———. 1995. "On the Vagaries of Bodies." *Culture, Medicine and Psychiatry* 19:207–215.

Diamond, James Arthur. 2002. *Maimonides and the Hermeneutics of Concealment.* Albany: State University of New York.

Dominguez, Virginia. 1989. *People as Subject, People as Object: Selfhood and Peoplehood in Contemporary Israel.* Madison: University of Wisconsin Press.

Douglas, Mary. 1966. *Purity and Danger: An Analysis of the Concepts of Pollution and Taboo.* New York: Ark Paperbacks.

———. 1982. *Natural Symbols: Explorations in Cosmology.* New York: Pantheon Books.

———. 1992. *Risk and Blame*. New York: Routledge.
Douglas, Mary, and Aaron Wildavsky. 1982. *Risk and Culture*. Berkeley: University of California Press.
Durkheim, Emile. 1982. *Rules of Sociological Method*. Ed. Steven Lukes. Trans. W. D. Halls. New York: The Free Press.
Eglash, Ruth. 2007. "Ethiopians Slam Shitreet's Comments." *Jerusalem Post* (online). August 2.
Elazar, Daniel, ed. 1987. *Kinship and Consent: The Jewish Political Tradition and its Contemporary Uses*. Washington, DC: American Free Press.
Emmanuel, Taamrat. 1994. "The School for Falasha Children in Ethiopia at the Time of the Italian Invasion." [In Hebrew.] *Pe'amim* 58:98–103.
Etzioni, A, S. Pollack, and Z. Ben-Ishai. 1994. "Prevention Program of HIV Infection in Ethiopian New Immigrants to Israel." *Acta Paediatrica*. Suppl. 400:22–24.
Evans-Pritchard, E.E. 1951. *Kinship and Marriage among the Nuer*. Oxford, UK: Clarendon Press.
Ezra, Solomon. 1996. "A Wrenching Breach of Faith." *Jerusalem Post*. February 16.
Faitlovitch, Jaques. 1928. *The Falashas*. Philadelphia: Jewish Publication Society of America.
Farmer, Paul. 1992. *AIDS and Accusation: Haiti and the Geography of Blame*. Berkeley: University of California Press.
Feldman, Micha. 1998. *Yetsi'at Etyopya* [Ethiopian Exodus]. Jerusalem: ha-Sokhnut ha-Yehudit le-Erets-Yisra'el.
Fine, Lawrence. 2003. *Physician of the Soul, Healer of the Cosmos: Isaac Luria and his Kabbalistic Fellowship*. Stanford, CA: Stanford University Press.
Flad, J. M. 1869. *The Falashas (Jews) of Abyssinia*. Trans. S. P. Goodhart. London: William Macintosh.
Fram, Edward. 1996. "Perception and Reception of Repentant Apostates in Medieval Ashkenaz and Premodern Poland." *AJS Review* 21 (2): 299–339.
Freeman, Dena. 1995. "The Importance of Coffee for the Social Health of the Beta Israel." Paper delivered at the Second International Conference of the Society for the Study of Ethiopian Jewry, Jerusalem.
Gabriel, Ayala. 1992. "Grief and Rage: Collective Emotions in the Politics of Peace and the Politics of Gender in Israel." *Culture, Medicine and Psychiatry* 16 (3): 311–335.
Gamst, Frederick C. 1969. *The Qemant: A Pagan-Hebraic Peasantry of Ethiopia*. Prospect Heights, IL: Waveland Press.
Gartenhaus, Jacob. 1979. *Famous Hebrew Christians*. Grand Rapids, MI: Baker Book House.
Geertz, Clifford. 1973. "Religion as a Cultural System." In *The Interpretation of Cultures; Selected Essays*, 87–124. New York: Basic Books.
———. 1983. *Local Knowledge: Further Essays in Interpretive Anthropology*. New York: Basic Books.
Gidney, W. T. 1900. *At Home and Abroad: A Description of Missions to Jews in Great Britain and on the Continent*. London: London Society for Promoting Christianity Amongst the Jews.
———. 1914. *Missions to Jews: A Handbook of Reasons, Facts, and Figures*. London: London Society for Promoting Christianity Amongst the Jews.
Gilman, Sander. 1991. *The Jew's Body*. New York: Routledge.

Ginat, Joseph. 1987. *Blood Disputes among Bedouin and Rural Arabs in Israel.* Pittsburgh, PA: University of Pittsburgh Press.

Goldberg, Harvey. 1997. "Gravesites and Memorials of Libyan Jews: Alternative Versions of the Sacralization of Space in Judaism." In *Grasping Land: Space and Place in Contemporary Israeli Discourse and Experience,* ed. Ayal Ben-Ari and Yoram Bilu, 47–60. Albany: State University of New York Press.

Goldstein, Eric L. 2006. *The Price of Whiteness: Jews, Race and American Identity.* Princeton, NJ: Princeton University Press.

Good, Byron J. 1994. *Medicine, Rationality and Experience: An Anthropological Perspective.* Lewis Henry Morgan Lectures. Cambridge: Cambridge University Press.

Good, Mary Jo Delvecchio, and Byron J. Good. 1988. "Ritual, the State and the Transformation of Emotional Discourse in Iranian Society." *Culture, Medicine and Psychiatry* 12:43–63.

Goode, F. 1835. "Christ, the Glory of Israel." *LJS Annual Sermon.* London. May 7.

Goodman, Yehuda C. 2008a. "Converting Immigrants: Citizenship, Governmentality and Religionization in Israel During the 2000s." [In Hebrew.] In *Citizenship Gaps in Israel,* ed. Y. Yonah and A. Kemp, 207–238. Jerusalem and Tel Aviv: Van Leer Institute and Kibbutz Hameuhad.

———. 2008b. "Citizenship, Modernity and Belief in the Nation-State: Racializaiton and De-racializaiton in Converting 'Russian' and 'Ethiopian' Immigrants in Israel." [In Hebrew.] In *Racism in Israel,* ed. Yehouda. Shenhav and Yossi Yonah, 381–415. Jerusalem and Tel Aviv: Van Leer Institute and Kibbutz Hameuhad.

Goody, Jack. 1976. *Production and Reproduction.* Cambridge: Cambridge University Press.

Gorenberg, Gershom. 1995. "Fear of Flooding." *Jerusalem Report.* July 27, p. 55

Grinfeld, Itzhak. 1986. "Jews in Addis Ababa: Beginnings of the Jewish Community Until the Italian Occupation." In *Ethiopian Studies: Proceedings of the Sixth International Conference,* Tel Aviv, 14–17 April 1980, ed. Gideon Goldenberg, 251–259. Rotterdam: A. A. Balkema.

Grossman, David. 1991. Op-ed. "The Spark and the Flute." *New York Times.* May 21.

Haaretz staff. 2008. "Incidents Suggest Rise in Violence Between Haredim, Messianic Jews." *Haaretz* (online). March 24.

Halévy, Joseph. 1877. *Travels in Abyssinia.* Trans. James Picciotto. London: Society of Hebrew Literature.

Haley, Bruce. 1978. *The Healthy Body and Victorian Culture.* Cambridge, MA: Harvard University Press.

Handelman, Don, and Lea Shamgar-Handelman. 1997. "The Presence of Absence: The Memorialism of National Death in Israel." In *Grasping Land: Space and Place in Contemporary Israeli Discourse and Experience,* ed. Eyal Ben-Ari and Yoram Bilu, 85–128. Albany: State University of New York Press.

Hasan, Manar. 2002. "The Politics of Honor: Patriarchy, the State and the Murder of Women in the Name of Family Honor." *Journal of Israeli History* 21 (1): 1–37.

Hastings, Adrian. 1994. *The Church in Africa: 1450–1950.* Oxford, UK: Clarendon Press.

Hefner, Robert W. 1993. "World Building and the Rationality of Conversion." In *Conversion to Christianity: Historical and Anthropological Perspectives on a Great Transformation,* ed. Robert W. Hefner, 3–46. Berkeley: University of California Press.

Heilman, Uriel. 2005. "JDC: Emergency Funds to Falash Mura." *Jerusalem Post* (online). July 7.

Henty, G. A. 1868. *The March to Magdala*. London: Tinsley Brothers.

Herbert, Eugenia W. 1993. *Iron, Gender, and Power: Rituals of Transformation in African Societies*. Bloomington: Indiana University Press.

Hertzog, Esther. 1999. *Immigrants and Bureaucrats: Ethiopians in an Israeli Absorption Center*. New York: Berghahn Books.

Herzfeld, Michael. 1992. *The Social Production of Indifference: Exploring the Symbolic Roots of Western Bureaucracy*. Chicago: University of Chicago Press.

———. 1997. *Cultural Intimacy: Social Poetics in the Nation-State*. New York: Routledge.

Hoben, Allan. 1970. "Social Stratification in Traditional Amhara Society." In *Social Stratification in Africa*, ed. Arthur Tuden and Leonard Plotnicov, 187–223. New York: Free Press.

———. 1973. *Land Tenure Among the Amhara of Ethiopia: The Dynamics of Cognatic Descent*. Chicago: University of Chicago Press.

Hobsbawm, Eric, and Terence Ranger, eds. 1992. *The Invention of Tradition*. Cambridge: Cambridge University Press.

Hodes, Richard. 1995. "Traditional Illness Complaints of Ethiopian Jews." Paper presented at the Second International Congress on the Study of Ethiopian Jews, Jerusalem.

Holcomb, Bonnie K., and Sisai Ibssa. 1990. *The Invention of Ethiopia: The Making of a Dependent Colonial State in Northeast Africa*. Trenton, NJ: Red Sea Press.

Husserl, Edmund. 1970. *The Crisis of European Sciences and Transcendental Phenomenology*. Evanston, IL: Northwestern University Press.

Ilan, Shachar. 2007. "Knesset Set to Launch Caucus for Secular Conversion." *Haaretz* (online). February 12.

Isaac, Ephraim. 1995. "The Significance of Food in Hebraic-African Thought and the Role of Fasting in the Ethiopian Church." In *Asceticism*, ed. Vincent L. Wimbush and Richard Valantasis, 329–342. Oxford, UK: Oxford University Press.

Izenberg, Dan. 1995. "Missionaries Active Among Ethiopian Immigrants." *Jerusalem Post*. January 5, p. 3.

Jackson, Michael. 1989. *Paths Toward a Clearing*. Bloomington: Indiana University Press.

———. 1995. *At Home in the World*. Durham, NC: Duke University Press.

———. 1996. "Introduction: Phenomenology, Radical Empiricism, and Anthropological Critique." In *Things as They Are: New Directions in Phenomenological Anthropology*, ed. Michael Jackson, 1–51. Bloomington: Indiana University Press.

———. 1998. *Minima Ethnographiaca: Intersubjectivity and the Anthropological Project*. Chicago: University of Chicago Press.

———. 2005. *Existential Anthropology: Events, Exigencies and Effects*. New York: Berghahn Books.

James, Wendy. 1990. "Kings, Commoners, and the Ethnographic Imagination in Sudan and Ethiopia." In *Localizing Strategies: Regional Traditions of Ethnographic Writing*, ed. Richard Fardon, 96–136. Washington, DC: Smithsonian Institution Press.

James, William Henry. 1958. *The Varieties of Religious Experience*. New York: American Library of World Literature.

Joppke, Christian. 2005. *Selecting by Origin: Ethnic Immigration and the Liberal State*. Cambridge: Harvard University Press.

Joppke, Christian, and Zeev Rosenhek. 2002. "Contesting Ethnic Immigration: Germany and Israel Compared." *European Journal of Sociology* 43:301–35.

Kahn, Susan Martha. 2003. *Reproducing Jews: A Cultural Account of Assisted Conception in Israel*. Durham, NC: Duke University Press.

Kaplan, Steven. 1984. *The Monastic Holy Man and the Christianization of Early Solomonic Ethiopia*. Wiesbaden, Germany: Franz Steiner.

———. 1986. "History and Typology: The Africanization of Missionary Christianity." *Journal of Religion in Africa* 16 (3): 166–186.

———. 1987. "The Beta Israel (Falasha) Encounter With Protestant Missionaries: 1860–1905." *Jewish Social Studies* 49 (1): 27–42.

———. 1988a. "'Falasha' Religion: Ancient Judaism or Evolving Ethiopian Tradition?" Review article of *Music, Ritual, and Falasha History* by Kay Kaufman Shelemay. *Jewish Quarterly Review* 79 (1): 49–65.

———. 1988b. "The Beta Israel and the Rabbinate: Law, Politics, and Ritual." *Social Science Information* 28 (3): 357–370.

———. 1992a. "Indigenous Categories and the Study of World Religions in Ethiopia: The Case of the Beta Israel." *Journal of Religion in Africa* 22 (3): 208–221.

———. 1992b. *The Beta Israel (Falasha) in Ethiopia*. New York: New York University Press.

———. 1994a. "Joseph Halévy: A Journey to Ethiopia to Discover the Falashas." [In Hebrew.] *Pe'amim* 58:5–66.

———. 1994b. "On Changes in the Study of Ethiopian Jewry." [In Hebrew.] *Pe'amim* 58:137–150.

———. 1994. "The School for Falasha Children in Ethiopia at the Time of the Italian Invasion." [In Hebrew.] *Pe'amim* 58:98–103.

———. 1995. "History, *Halakha* and Identity: The Beta Israel and World Jewry." *Israel Social Science Research* 10 (2): 13–24.

———. 1999a. "Can the Ethiopian Change His Skin? The Beta Israel (Ethiopian Jews) and Radical Discourse." *African Affairs* 98:535–550.

———. 1999b. "Everyday Resistance and the Study of Ethiopian Jews." In *The Beta Israel in Ethiopia and Israel: Studies on Ethiopian Jews*, ed. Tudor Parfitt and Emanuela Trevisan Semi, 113–127. London: Curzon.

Kaplan, Steven, and Chaim Rosen. 1993. "Ethiopian Immigrants in Israel: Between Preservation of Culture and Invention of Tradition." *Journal of Jewish Sociology* 35 (1): 35–48.

———. 1994. "The Immigration and Absorption of Ethiopian Jews in Israel." In *American Jewish Yearbook, 1994*, ed. David Singer, 59–109. New York: American Jewish Committee.

———. 1996. "Created in their Own Image: A Comment on Beta Israel Figurines." *Cahiers d'Études Africaines* 141–142:171–182.

Kaplan, Steven, and Shoshana Ben-Dor, eds. 1988. *Yehude Etyopyah: Bibliographia Mu'eret* [Ethiopian Jewry: An Annotated Bibliography]. Jerusalem: Ben-Zvi Institute.

Kaplan, Yosef. 1989a. *From Christianity to Judaism: The Story of Isaac Orobio de Castro*. Trans. Raphael Loewe. Oxford, UK: Oxford University Press.

———. 1989b. "Patterns of Assimilation in Spanish Converso Society in the 15th–17th Centuries." [In Hebrew.] In Yosef Kaplan and Menahem Stern, *Hitbolelut u-ṭemi'ah*:

hemshekhiyut u-temurah be-tarbut ha-'amim uve-Yiśra'el, 157–172. Jerusalem: Merkaz Zalman Shazar le-toldot Yiśra'el.

Kassa, Ageru. 1998. "The Black Jews Describe to Their Fellow White Jews About the Hardship and Suffering They Have Had to Face." Unpublished manuscript, p. 35.

Kedem, Peri. 1995. "Dimensions of Jewish Religiosity." In *Religion in Israel*, ed. Shlomo Deshen, Charles S. Liebman, and Moshe Shokeid, 33–59. New Brunswick, NJ: Transaction Books.

Kessler, David, and Tudor Parfitt. 1985. "The Falashas: The Jews of Ethiopia." *Minority Rights Group Report* no. 67. London: Minority Rights Group.

Kierkegaard, Søren. 1956. *Purity of Heart is to Will One Thing*. Trans. Douglas van Steere. New York: Harper and Row.

Kileyesus, Abebe. 2006. "Cosmologies in Collision: Pentecostal Conversion and Christian Cults in Asmara." *African Studies Review* 49:75–92.

Kipp, Rita Smith. 1995. "Conversion by Affiliation: The History of the Karo Batak Protestant Church." *American Ethnologist* 22 (4): 868–82.

Kleinman, Arthur. 1995. *Writing at the Margin: Discourse between Anthropology and Medicine*. Berkeley: University of California Press.

———. 1997. "'Everything that Really Matters': Social Suffering, Subjectivity, and the Remaking of Human Experience in a Disordering World." *Harvard Theological Review* 90, no. 3 (July): 315–335.

———. 2006. *What Really Matters: Living a Moral Life Amidst Uncertainty and Danger*. New York: Oxford University Press.

Kleinman, Arthur, and Joan Kleinman. 1991. "Suffering and its Professional Transformation: Toward an Ethnography of Interpersonal Experience." *Culture, Medicine and Psychiatry* 5 (3): 275–301.

———. 1994. "How Bodies Remember: Social Memory and Bodily Experience of Criticism, Resistance, and Delegitimation Following China's Cultural Revolution." *New Literary History* 25 (1): 707–732.

Kleinman, Arthur, and Don Seeman. 2000. "The Personal Experience of Illness." In *The Handbook of Social Studies in Health and Medicine*, ed. Gary Albrecht, Ray Fitzpatrick, and Susan Scrimshaw. London: Sage.

Knudsen, John Christian. 1995. "When Trust is on Trial: Negotiating Refugee Narratives." In *Mistrusting Refugees*, ed. Valentine E. Daniel and John Chr. Knudsen, 13–35. Berkeley: University of California Press.

Krauss, Iris. 1997. *Ha'aretz*. March 5, p. 5a.

Kushner, Arlene, and Amy Kalina. 1986. *Falasha No More: An Ethiopian Jewish Child Comes Home*. New York: Shapolsky Books.

Lang, Berel. 1996. "Holocaust Memory and Revenge: The Presence of the Past." *Jewish Social Studies* 2 (2): 1–20.

Lapidoth, Moshe and Gali Aharonowitz. 2004. "Tattoo Removal among Ethiopian Jews in Israel: Tradition Faces Technology." *Journal of the American Academy of Dermatology* 51 (6): 906–909.

Lehrer, Erica T. 2005. "'Shoah Business,' 'Holocaust Culture,' and the Repair of the World in 'Post-Jewish' Poland: A Quest for Ethnography, Empathy, and the Ethnic Self After Genocide." Ph.D. diss., University of Michigan.

Leibman, Charles S. 1997. "Reconceptualizing the Culture Conflict among Israeli Jews." *Israel Studies* 2 (2): 172–189.

Leibman, Charles S., and Elihu Katz, eds. 1997. *The Jewishness of Israelis: Responses to the Guttman Report*. Albany: State University of New York.

Leibman, Charles [S.], and Bernard Susser. 1997. "The Forgotten Center: Traditional Jewishness in Israel." *Modern Judaism* 17:211–220.

Leslau, Wolf. 1947. "A Falasha Religious Dispute." *American Academy for Jewish Research Proceedings* 15–16:71–95.

———. 1949. "The Black Jews of Ethiopia: An Expedition to the Falasha." *Commentary* 7:216–224.

———. 1951. *Falasha Anthology*. New Haven, CT: Yale University Press

———. 1975. "Taamrat Emmanuel's Notes of Falasha Monks and Holy Places." In *Salo Wittmayer Barron Jubilee Volume*, 623–637. Jerusalem: American Academy of Jewish Research.

Levi, Gidon. 1995. "Her Journey with her Aunt." *Musaf Haaretz*. August 9.

Lévi-Strauss, Claude. 1966. *The Savage Mind*. Chicago: University of Chicago Press.

Levinas, Emmanuel. 1987. *Time and the Other*. Trans. Richard A. Cohen. Pittsburgh, PA: Duquesne University Press.

Levine, Donald. 1965. *Wax and Gold: Tradition and Innovation in Ethiopian Culture*. Chicago: University of Chicago Press.

———. 1974. *Greater Ethiopia: The Evolution of a Multi-Ethnic Society*. Chicago: University of Chicago.

Lienhardt, Godfrey. 1961. *Divinity and Experience: The Religion of the Dinka*. New York: Oxford University Press.

Lobo, Jerome. 1789/1978. *A Voyage to Abyssinia*. Trans. Samuel Johnson. New York: AMS Press.

Lord, Edith. 1970. *Cultural Patterns of Ethiopia: Queen of Sheba's Heirs*. Washington D.C.: Acropolis Books.

Low, Samuel. 1861. *The Charities of London*. London: Samson, Low, Son and Marston, Milton House, Ludgate Hill.

Madan, T.N. 1975. "On Living Intimately with Strangers." In *Encounter and Experience: Personal Accounts of Fieldwork*, ed. André Béteille and T.N. Madan, 131–156. Honolulu: University of Hawaii Press.

Magid, Shaul. 2005. "The Politics of (Un)Conversion: The "Mixed Multitude" ('Erev Rav) as Conversos in Rabbi Hayyim Vital's 'Ets Ha-Da'at Tov." *Jewish Quarterly Review* 95:625–666.

Malkii, Liisa H. 1992. "National Geographic: Rooting of Peoples and the Territorialization of National Identity Among Scholars and Refugees." *Cultural Anthropology* 7 (1): 24–44.

———. 1995. *Purity and Exile: National Cosmology Among Hutu Refugees in Tanzania*. Chicago: University of Chicago Press.

Mann, Jonathan, Daniel J. M. Tarantola, and Thomas W. Netter. *AIDS in the World: A Global Report*. Cambridge, MA: Harvard University Press, 1992.

Markowitz, Fran, Sara Helman, and Dafna Shir-Vertesh. 2003. "Soul Citizenship: The Black Hebrews and the State of Israel." *American Anthropologist* 105:301–312.

Martensen, Robert L. 1995. "Alienation and the Production of Strangers: Western Medical Epistemology and the Architectonics of the Body, and Historical Perspective." *Culture, Medicine and Psychiatry* 19:141–182.

Marcus, George. 1995. "Ethnography In/Of the World System: The Emergence of Multi-Sited Ethnography." *Annual Review of Anthropology* 24: 95–117.

Marcus, Harold G. 1994. *A History of Ethiopia*. Berkeley: University of California Press.

Marrus, Michael Robert. 1971. *The Politics of Assimilation: A Study of the French Jewish Community at the Time of the Dreyfus Affair*. Oxford, UK: Clarendon Press.

Mauss, Marcel. 1979. "Body Techniques." In *Sociology and Psychology: Essays*, trans. Ben Brewster, 95–123. London: Routledge & Kegan Paul.

Messing, Simon D. 1956. "Journey to the Falashas, Ethiopia's Black Jews." *Commentary* 22 (July–December): 28–40.

———. 1957. "The Highland-Plateau Amhara of Ethiopia." Ph.D. diss., University of Pennsylvania.

———. 1982. *The Story of the Falashas: "Black Jews" of Ethiopia*. Brooklyn, NY: Balshon Printing and Offset.

Meyer, Birgit. 1995. "African Pentecostal Churches, Satan, and the Dissociation from Tradition." Paper presented at the symposium "Religious Revitalization and Syncretism in Africa and the Americas." 94th Annual Meeting of the American Anthropological Association, Washington, DC, November 15–19.

Moore, Sally Falk. 1978. *Law as Process: An Anthropological Approach*. Boston: Routledge and Kegan Paul.

———. 1987. "Explaining the Present: Theoretical Dilemmas in Processual Ethnography." *American Ethnologist* 14 (4): 727–736.

Motzen, Chaim. 1998. "Report on the Falash Mura in Addis Ababa." New York: American Joint Distribution Committee.

Nahoum, Haim. 1908. "The Mission to the Falashas (interview)." *Jewish Chronicle*, August 7, p. 14.

Navon, Yitzhak, et al. 1996. "Report of the Commission for Investigation of the Affair Concerning Ethiopian Immigrants' Blood Donations Affair." In Hebrew.] Jerusalem: Government of the State of Israel.

Netanyahu, Binyamin. 1995. *Makom tahat ha-shemesh: maavako shel 'am Yisrael le-'atsmaut, le-vitahon ule-shalom* [A Place Under the Sun: Israel's Struggle for Independence, Security and Peace]. Tel Aviv: Yedi'ot Aharonot.

Nordanger, Dag. 2007. "Discourses of Loss and Bereavement in Tigray, Ethiopia." *Culture, Medicine and Psychiatry* 31 (2): 173–194.

Nudelman, A. 1993. "The Importance of Traditional Healing for Ethiopian Immigrants in Israel." *Collegium Antropologicum* 17 (2): 233–239.

Odenheimer, Micha. 1995. "How Israel's Educational System is Failing Ethiopian Immigrant Youth." Report of the Israel Association for Ethiopian Jews, Jerusalem.

Oppenheimer, Gerald. 1988. "In the Eye of the Storm: The Epidemiological Construction of AIDS." In *AIDS: The Burdens of History*, ed. Elizabeth Fee and Daniel M. Fox, 267–292. Berkeley: University of California Press.

Ortner, Sherry B. 1984. "Theory in Anthropology Since the Sixties." *Comparative Studies in Society and History* 26:126–166.

Pankhurst, Alula. 1994. "Reflections on Pilgrimages in Ethiopia." In *New Trends in Ethiopian Studies: Ethiopia 94—Papers of the 12th International Conference of Ethiopian Studies, Michigan State University, 5–10 September 1994*, ed. Harold G. Marcus and Grover Hudson, 933–953. Lawrenceville, NJ: Red Sea Press.

Pankhurst, Helen. 1992. *Gender, Development and Identity: An Ethiopian Study*. London: Zed.
Pankhurst, Richard. 1990. *An Introduction to the Medical History of Ethiopia*. Trenton, NJ: The Red Sea Press.
———. 1995. "The Béta Esra'él (Falashas) in their Ethiopian Setting." *Israel Social Science Research* 10 (2): 1–24.
Payne, Eric. 1972. *Ethiopian Jews: The Story of a Mission*. London: Olive Press.
Pliskin, Karen L. 1987. *Silent Boundaries: Cultural Constraints on Sickness and Diagnosis of Iranians in Israel*. New Haven, CT: Yale University Press.
Proudfoot, Wayne. 1985. *Religious Experience*. Berkeley: University of California Press.
Quirin, James Arthur. 1992. *The Evolution of the Ethiopian Jews: A History of the Beta Israel (Falasha) to 1920*. Philadelphia: University of Pennsylvania Press.
Rabinowitz, Dan. 1997. *Overlooking Nazareth: The Ethnography of Exclusion in Galilee*. Cambridge: Cambridge University Press.
Rambo, Lewis R. 1993. *Understanding Religious Conversion*. New Haven, CT: Yale University Press.
Ranger, Terence. 1993. "The Local and the Global in Southern African Religious History." In *Conversion to Christianity: Historical and Anthropological Perspectives on a Great Transformation*, ed. Robert W. Hefner, 65–98. Berkeley: University of California Press.
Reiff, Marian. 1999. "Sickness and Medicine: Perceptions of Ethiopian Immigrants and their Doctors in Israel." In *The Beta Israel in Ethiopia and Israel: Studies on Ethiopian Jews*, ed. Tudor Parfitt and Emanuela Trevisan Semi, 275–284. London: Curzon.
Reiff, Marian, Havah Zakut, and Michael Weingarten. 1999. "Immigration and Medicine: Illness and Treatment Perceptions of Ethiopian Immigrants and their Doctors in Israel." *American Journal of Public Health* 89 (12): 1814–1818.
Reminick, Ronald. 1974. "The Evil Eye Belief Among the Amhara of Ethiopia." *Ethnology* 13:279–92.
Rettig, Haviv, Rebecca Anna Stoil, and Ruth Eglash. 2008 "Boim: US Jews Won't Accept Felashmura." *Jerusalem Post* (online). July 23.
Rosaldo, Renato. 1989. "Grief and a Headhunter's Rage." In *Culture and Truth: The Remaking of Social Analysis*, 1–24. Boston: Beacon Press.
Rosen, Chaim. 1985. "Falasha, Kayla, Beta Israel? Ethnographic Observations on the Names for the Jews of Ethiopia." [In Hebrew.] *Pe'amim* 33:53–58.
———. 1989. "Ethiopian Jews in Israel: Review and Prospectus." Report. June.
———. 1994. "The Use of Genealogy Among Beta Israel: On the Image of an Historical Hero in Literature and Oral Traditions." [In Hebrew.] *Pe'amim* 58:120–128.
———. 1995. "Working as a Government Anthropologist Among Ethiopian Jews in Israel." *Israel Social Science Research* 10 (2): 55–68.
Rouhana, Nadime. 1997. *Palestinian Citizens in an Ethnic Jewish State: Identities in Conflict*. New Haven, CT: Yale University Press.
Rubenson, Sven. 1966. *King of Kings, Tewodros of Ethiopia*. Addis Ababa: Haile Sellassie I University.
Sa'ar, Rali. 1996. "Rabbi Bakshi-Doron Instructs Stoppage of the Return of Felesmura to Judaism in an Accelerated Program." *Ha'aretz*. October 31, p. 1a.
Salamon, Hagar. 1987. "Journeys as a Means of Communication Among Beta Israel in Ethiopia. " [In Hebrew.] *Pe'amim* 33:5–30.

———. 1993. "Blood Between the Beta Israel and their Christian Neighbors in Ethiopia: Key Symbols in an Intergroup Context." [In Hebrew.] *Jerusalem Studies in Jewish Folklore* 16:117–134.

———. 1994. "Between Ethnicity and Religiosity: Internal Group Aspects of Conversion Among the Beta Israel in Ethiopia." [In Hebrew.] *Pe'amim* 58:104–119.

———. 1995. "Reflections of Ethiopian Cultural Patterns on the Beta Israel Absorption in Israel: The '*Barya*' Case." In *Between Africa and Zion: Proceedings of the First International Congress of the Society for the Study of Ethiopian Jewry*, ed. Steven Kaplan, Tudor Parfitt, and Emanuela Trevisan Semi, 126–30. Jerusalem: Ben-Zvi Institute.

———. 1999. *The Hyena People: Ethiopian Jews in Christian Ethiopia*. Berkeley: University of California Press.

Salamon, Hagar, and Steven Kaplan, eds. 1998. *Yehude Etyopyah: Bibliographia Mu'eret 5748–5758* [Ethiopian Jewry: An Annotated Bibliography 1988–1997]. Jerusalem: Ben-Zvi Institute.

Sanbetu, Ayanawu Farada. 2005. "Locals Damage Jewish Graves in Ethiopia Believing Bones Lucky." *Haaretz* (online). October 24.

———. 2007. "Ethiopian Leaders Hold a Conference for 'Defeating the Christian Mission in Israel.'" *Haaretz* (online). February 6.

Sapir, Edward. 1957. "The Emergence of the Concept of Personality in the Study of Cultures." In *Culture, Language, and Personality: Selected Essays*, ed. David G. Mandelbaum, 590–597. Berkeley: University of California Press.

———. 1985. "Cultural Anthropology and Psychiatry" (1932). In *Selected Writings in Language, Personality and Culture*, ed. David G. Mandelbaum, 509–521. Berkeley: University of California Press.

Sapolsky, Harvey M. 1989. "AIDS, Blood Banking, and the Bonds of Community." *Daedalus* 118 (3): 145–163.

Schindler, Ruben, and David Ribner. 1997. *The Trauma of Transition: The Psycho-Social Cost of Ethiopian Immigration to Israel*. Aldershot, England, and Brookfield, VT: Avebury.

Schneider, David M. 1995. *A Critique of the Study of Kinship*. Ann Arbor: University of Michigan Press.

Schoenberger, Michele. 1975. "The Falasha of Ethiopia: An Ethnographic Study." Ph.D. diss., Cambridge University.

Schutz, Alfred. 1967. *The Phenomenology of the Social World*. Chicago: Northwestern University Press.

———. 1970. *On Phenomenology and Social Relations: Selected Writings*. Chicago: University of Chicago Press.

Schutz, Alfred, and Thomas Luckmann. 1989. *The Structures of the Life-World*. Vol. 2. Trans. Richard M. Zaner and David J. Parent. Evanston, Il: Northwestern University Press.

Schwarz, Tanya. 2001. *Ethiopian Jewish Immigrants in Israel: The Homeland Postponed*. Richmond, UK: Curzon.

Scott, James C. 1990. *Domination and the Arts of Resistance: Hidden Transcripts*. New Haven, CT: Yale University Press.

Seeman, Don. 1990. "Images of Continuity: Religious and Social Change Among Ethiopian Jews in Israel." Bachelor's thesis, Harvard University.

———. 1991. "Ethnographers, Rabbis and Jewish Epistemology: The Case of the Ethiopian Jews." *Tradition* 25 (4): 13–29.

———. 1998. "'Where Is Sarah Your Wife': Cultural Poetics of Gender and Nationhood in the Hebrew Bible." *Harvard Theological Review* 91 (2): 103–125.

———. 1999a. "Subjectivity, Culture, Life-World: An Appraisal." *Transcultural Psychiatry* 36 (4): 437–445.

———. 1999b. "'One People, One Blood': Public Health, Political Violence, and HIV in an Ethiopian-Israeli Setting." *Culture, Medicine and Psychiatry* 23:159–195.

———. 1999c. "All in the Family: Kinship as a Paradigm for the Ethnography of Beta Israel." In *The Beta Israel in Ethiopia and Israel: Studies on Ethiopian Jews*, ed. Tudor Parfitt and Emanuela Trevisan Semi, 94–112. London: Curzon.

———. 2000. "Bodies and Narratives: The Question of Kinship in the Beta Israel-European Encounter (1860–1920)." *Journal of Religion in Africa* 30 (1): 86–120.

———. 2003. "Agency, Bureaucracy and Religious Conversion: Ethiopian 'Feleshmura' Immigrants to Israel." In *The Anthropology of Religious Conversion*, ed. Andrew S. Buckser and Steven Glazier, 29–42. London: Rowman and Littlefield.

———. 2004. "Otherwise than Meaning: On the Generosity of Ritual." *Social Analysis* 48 (2): 55–71.

———. 2005a. "Ritual Practice and Its Discontents." In *A Companion to Psychological Anthropology*, ed. Conerly Casey and Robert B. Edgerton, 358–73. Malden, MA, and Oxford: Blackwell.

———. 2005b. "Violence, Ethics and Divine Honor in Modern Jewish Thought." *Journal of the American Academy of Religion* 73 (4): 1–32.

———. 2008. "Honoring the Divine as Virtue and Practice in Maimonides." *Journal of Jewish Thought and Philosophy* 16 (2).

Sela, Neta. 2008. "Chief Rabbi" Bring all of Falash Mura to Israel," *Ynet News.com*. January 16.

Shabtay, Malka. 1999. *"Hakhi aḥi": masaʿ ha-zehut shel ḥayalim ʿolim me-Etyopyah*. [In Hebrew.] Tel Aviv: Tsʿerikover.

———. 2001. *Between Reggae and Rap: The Integration Challenge of Ethiopian Youths in Israel*. [In Hebrew.] Tel Aviv: Tcherikover.

———. 2003. "'RaGap': Music and Identity among Young Ethiopians in Israel." *Critical Arts* 17 (1–2): 93–105.

———. 2007. *Ethiopian Jews from the Seed of Beta Israel*. Ma'aleh Edumim: The Jewish Agency.

Shaki, Avner H. 1978. *Mi-hu yehudi be-dine medinat Yiśraʾel* [Who is a Jew in the laws of the State of Israel]. Jerusalem: ha-Makhon le-heker ha-mishpahah ve dine ha-mishpahah be-Yiśraʾel.

Sharot, Stephen. 1995. "Sociological Analyses of Religion." *Religion in Israel*, ed. Shlomo Deshen, Charles S. Liebman, and Moshe Shokeid, 19–32. New Brunswick, NJ: Transaction Books.

Shelemay, Kay Kaufman. 1989. *Music, Ritual, and Falasha History*. 2nd ed. East Lansing: University of Michigan Press.

———. 1991. *A Song of Longing: An Ethiopian Journey*. Chicago: University of Illinois Press.

———. 1992. "The Musician and Transmission of Religious Tradition: The Multiple Roles of the Ethiopian *DABTARRA*." *Journal of Religion in Africa* 22 (3): 242–260.

Shillington, Kevin. 1987. "Culture, Not History." Review of *Body of Power, Spirit of Resistance: The Culture and History of a South African People* by Jean Comaroff. *Journal of African History* 28 (2): 321–322.

Shore, Cris, and Susan Wright, eds. 1997. *Anthropology of Policy: Critical Perspectives on Governance and Power*. New York: Routledge.

Siegel-Itzkovitch, Judy. 2008. "Third of FSU Immigrants Avoid Circumcision." *Jerusalem Post* (online). October 7.

Sinai, Ruth, and Ayanawo Fareda Sanbetu. 2006. "Ethiopians, US Jews Join Forces to Protest New Falashmura Policy." *Haaretz* (online). September 10.

Sinclair, Daniel B. 1992. "Trends in Rabbinic Policy in Relation to Insincere Conversions in Post-Emancipation Responsa." *Diné Israel* 16:46–70.

Soloveitchik, Joseph B. 1968. "Kol Dodi Dofek [The Voice of My Beloved Knocks]." In *Ish ha-Emunah*, 65–106. Jerusalem: Mosad ha-Rav Kook.

———. 2000. *Fate and Destiny: From Holocaust to the State of Israel*. Hoboken, NJ: Ktav.

Sohn, Sigrid. 2005. "A 'Yiddish Journey' to Ethiopia: Chaim Shoshkes's Book *DURKH UMBAKANTE LENDER*." In *Materia Guidaica: Rivista dell'associazione italiana per lo studio del giudaismo* X/2: 365–373.

Spector, Stephen. 2005. *Operation Solomon: The Daring Rescue of the Ethiopian Jews*. Oxford: Oxford University Press.

Stern, Henry A. 1862/1968. *Wanderings Among the Falasha in Abyssinia*. London: Frank Cass.

———. 1869. *The Captive Missionary: Being an Account of the Country and People of Abyssinia*. London: Cassell, Petter, and Galpin.

Stewart, Pamela J., and Andrew Strathern. 2003. *Witchcraft, Sorcery, Rumors and Gossip*. Cambridge: Cambridge University Press.

Stocking, George W., Jr. 1986. "Introduction." In *Malinowski, Rivers, Benedict and Others*, ed. G.W. Stocking, Jr. Madison: University of Wisconsin Press.

Strathern, Marilyn. 1992. *Reproducing the Future: Anthropology, Kinship, and the New Reproductive Technologies*. Manchester, UK: Routledge.

Summerfield, Daniel. 1997. "From Falashas to Ethiopian Jews: The External Influences for Change c. 1860–1960." Doctoral diss., University of London.

———. 2003. *From Falashas to Ethiopian Jews: The External Influences for Change c. 1860–1960*. London and New York: RoutledgeCurzon.

Taddesse, Takkele. 1994. "Do the Amhara Exist as a Distinct Ethnic Group?" In *New Trends in Ethiopian Studies: Ethiopia 94—Papers of the 12th International Conference of Ethiopian Studies, Michigan State University, 5–10 September 1994*, ed. Harold G. Marcus and Grover Hudson, 168–187. Lawrenceville, NJ: Red Sea Press.

Tamrat, Taddesse. 1972. *Church and State in Ethiopia, 1270–1527*. London: Oxford University Press.

———. 1988. "Processes of Ethnic Interaction and Integration in Ethiopian History: The Case of the Agaw." *Journal of African History* 29 (1): 5–18.

Taylor, Charles. 1985. *Human Agency and Language: Philosophical Papers I*. Cambridge: Cambridge University Press.

Thompson, Larry. 1998. "The Last Jews in Ethiopia." *Refugees International Report*.

Trautmann, Thomas R. 1987. *Lewis Henry Morgan and the Invention of Kinship*. Berkeley: University of California Press.

Trevisan Semi, Emanuela. 1985. "The Beta Israel: From Purity to Impurity." *Jewish Journal of Sociology* 27:103–114.

———. 1994. "The Educational Activity of Jacques Faitlovitch in Ethiopia (1904–1924)." [In Hebrew.] *Pe'amim* 58:86–97.

———. 1995. "The Dainelli and Viterbo Missions among the Falashas (1936–37)." In *Between Africa and Zion: Proceedings of the First International Congress of the Society for the Study of Ethiopian Jewry*, ed. Steven Kaplan, Tudor Parfitt, and Emanuela Trevisan Semi, 72–79. Jerusalem: Ben-Zvi Institute.

———. 2002. "The Conversion of the Beta Israel in Ethiopia: A Reversible 'Rite of Passage.'" *Journal of Modern Jewish Studies* 1 (1): 90–103.

———. 2005. "Ethiopian Jews in Europe: Taamrat Emmanuel in Italy and Makonnen Levi in England." In *Jews of Ethiopia: Birth of an Elite*, ed. Tudor Parfitt and Emmanuela Trevisan Semi, 74–100. New York: Routlege.

———. 2007. *Jacques Faitlovitch and the Jews of Ethiopia*. London: Daniel Valentine.

Trilling, Lionel. 2006. *Sincerity and Authenticity*. Rev. ed. Cambridge, MA: Harvard University Press.

Tsur, Bathsheva, and Judy Siegel. 1996. "Ethiopian Leaders Divided Over Bringing Falash Mura Here." *Jerusalem Post*. October 18.

Turner, Bryan S. 1980. "The Body and Religion: Towards an Alliance of Medical Sociology and Sociology of Religion." *Annual Review of the Social Sciences of Religion* 4:247–284.

Turner, Victor. 1967. *The Forest of Symbols: Aspects of Ndembu Ritual*. Ithaca, NY: Cornell University Press.

Ullendorff, Edward. 1965. *The Ethiopians: An Introduction to Country and People*. London: Oxford University Press.

———. 1967. *Ethiopia and the Bible*. London: Oxford University Press.

Vail, Leroy. 1989. "Introduction: Ethnicity in Southern African History." In *The Creation of Tribalism in Southern Africa*, ed. Leroy Vail, 1–19. London: James Currey.

Viswanathan, Gauri. 1998. *Outside the Fold: Conversion, Modernity, and Belief*. Princeton, NJ: Princeton University Press.

Wagaw, Teshome G. 1993. *For Our Soul: Ethiopian Jews in Israel*. Detroit: Wayne State University Press.

Wagner, Matthew. "Ethiopians Fight Christian Proseletyzers." *Haaretz* (online). October 18.

Waldman, Menahem. 1989. *Me-'ever le-nahare Kush: Yehude Etyopyah yeha-'am ha-Yehudi* [Beyond the Rivers of Ethiopia: The Jews of Ethiopia and the Jewish People]. Tel Aviv: Israel Ministry of Defense.

———. 1996. "The Return to Judaism of the 'Felasmura.'" [In Hebrew.] *Tehumin* 16:243–272.

Weber, Max. 1946. "Class, Status, Party." In *From Max Weber: Essays in Sociology*, ed. H. H. Gerth and C. Wright Mills. Oxford: Oxford University Press.

———. 1963. *Sociology of Religion*. Trans. Ephraim Fischoff. Boston: Beacon Press.

Weil, Shalva. 1991. *Ethiopian One-Parent Families in Israel* (Hebrew). Jerusalem: Hebrew University of Jerusalem.

———. 1995a. "Collective Designations and Collective Identity Among Ethiopian Jews." *Israel Social Science Research* 10 (2): 25–40.

———. 1995b. "'It is Futile to Trust in Man': Methodological Difficulties in Studying Non-Mainstream Populations with Reference to Ethiopian Jews in Israel." *Human Organization* 54 (1): 1–9.

———. 2005. "Abraham Adgeh: The Perfect English Gentleman." In *Jews of Ethiopia: Birth of an Elite*, ed. Tudor Parfitt and Emmanuela Trevisan Semi, 101. New York: Routledge.

———. 2006. "Tadesse Yacob of Cairo and Addis Abeba." *International Journal of Ethiopian Studies* 2 (1 and 2): 233–243.

Werbner, Richard. 1997. "The Suffering Body: Passion and Ritual Allegory in Christian Encounters." *Journal of Southern African Studies* 23:311–324.

Westheimer, Ruth, and Steven Kaplan. 1992. *Surviving Salvation: The Ethiopian Jewish Family in Transition*. New York: New York University Press.

White, Hayden V. 1985. *Tropics of Discourse: Essays in Cultural Criticism*. Baltimore, MD: Johns Hopkins University Press.

Wikan, Unni. 1988. "Bereavement and Loss in Two Muslim Communities: Egypt and Bali Compared." *Social Science Medicine* 27 (5): 451–460.

———. 1990. *Managing Turbulent Hearts: A Balinese Formula for Living*. Chicago: University of Chicago Press.

———. 2002. *Generous Betrayal: Politics of Culture in the New Europe*. Chicago: University of Chicago Press.

Willen, Sarah S. 2007. "'Flesh of Our Flesh'? Terror and Mourning at the Boundaries of the Israeli Body Politic." In *Transnational Migration to Israel in Global Comparative Context*, ed. S. Willen, 159–184. Lanham, MD: Lexington Books.

Wimbush, Vincent L., and Richard Valantasis. 1995. "Introduction." In *Asceticism*, ed. Vincent L. Wimbush and Richard Valantasis, xix–xxxiii. New York: Oxford University Press.

Winkler, Yehudit. 1997. "Something Bad Happened at Night." *Ha'aretz*. January 3, p. 16.

Wittgenstein, Ludwig. 1980. *Remarks on the Philosophy of Psychology*. Trans. G. E. M. Anscomb. Oxford: University of Chicago Press.

Yasur-Beit Or, Meital. 2006. "Israel Teaches WHO about Circumcision." *YNET*. November 28.

Young, Allan. 1973. "Medical Beliefs and Practices of Begemder Amhara." Ph.D. diss., University of Pennsylvania.

———. 1975. "Magic as a Quasi-Profession: The Organization of Magic and Magical Healing Among Amhara." *Ethnology* 14:245–265.

———. 1977. "Order, Analogy, and Efficacy in Ethiopian Medical Divination." *Culture, Medicine, and Psychiatry* 1:183–199.

Yuval, Israel J. 1993. "Vengeance and Damnation, Blood and Defamation: From Jewish Martyrdom to Blood Libel Accusations." [In Hebrew.] *Zion* 58 (1): 33–90.

Zewde, Bahru. 1991. *A History of Modern Ethiopia, 1855–1974*. London: J. Currey.

Zohar, Tzvi, and Avraham Sagi. 1994. *Giyur ve-Zehut Yehudit* [Conversion and Jewish Identity]. Jerusalem: Mossad Bialik.

INDEX

AAEJ. *See* American Association for Ethiopian Jews
Aberja, village of, 30
absorption: balancing efforts, 110–123; burial issues, 109, 134–149; centers (*see* immigration, absorption centers); described, 109–110; Pentecostal efforts, 123–134; problems of, 6. *See also* Judaism, return to—program
Abyssinia, 53, 77, 79, 138
Achebe, Chinua, 180–181
addiction, drug, 126–127, 171
Addis Ababa: death in, 12–15; "Falasha Cemetery," 15–21, 94, 178; "Falasha school," 80–81; Feres Mura community, 84–87; Jewish Community of, 16; refugees to, 30, 171, 182, 200; transit camp, 184, 195
Adenite Jews. *See* Judaism, Adenite Jews
aesthetic tattooing, 35
Agau dialect, 43
agency, questions of, 24, 85–93, 207
AIDS, 158, 169–172, 182
airlift. *See* Operation Solomon
AIU. *See* Alliance Israélite Universelle
alcohol, use of, 128, 144
Alem, Ain, 67
Alexander, Michael Solomon, 47
Ali, Riad, 161–162
Alliance Israélite Universelle (AIU), 17, 54–55, 57–59
Amar, Shlomo, 194, 198
ambivalence in religious conversion, 68–73

American Association for Ethiopian Jews (AAEJ), 57, 87
American Jewish Congress, 59
American Jewish Yearbook, 92
American Pro-Falasha Committee, 80
"Amharization," process of, 43–44
Amit, Aryeh, 160
amulet writing, 51
Anglicans, 42
Annual Sermon (James), 53
Anteby, Lisa, 177
anusim, 22–24, 27
Arafat, Yassir, 161, 164, 165–166, 168
asceticism, 46–50
Ashkenazi Jews. *See* Judaism, Ashkenazi Jews
Ateke, village of, 30
attenqun, 44
avoidance rules, 44–45
Avraham, Azzaj Dinzu, 103–104
Ayellegn, Kes, 142, 170, 172

baby-naming ceremony. See *kristena*
Bakshi-Doron, Eliyahu, 185–186, 188, 194
baptism. See *temqat*
Barak, Ehud, 159
Barak-Fishman, Sylvia, 193
barya, 28, 72, 79
bath, ritual. See *mikveh*
Beer Sheba, 210–211
Beleta, Gochu, 66, 67–68
Ben-David, Amnon, 173
Ben-Gurion, David, 180
Beru ("native agent"), 51

Beta Israel: absorption, problems of, 6; airlift (*see* Operation Solomon); allegiance to kin, 3; ascetic and monastic character of, 45–46; bodily recognition, 53; in Ethiopian context, 42–47; fasting, 46; generic doubt, issues of, 89; heritage of, 2 (*see also* kinship, rules of); historical context, 6; joint cemetery, creation of, 18; language (*see* language); missionary attention, 17, 50–61, 62–68, 123–149; occupations (*see* occupational caste group); relationship between European Jews, 62; religious and cultural structures, 45; self-perception, 1; social relations with Christians, 69; social separation, 44; "splintering of," 63; term described, 8. See also "Feres Mura"
beta sab. See nuclear family
beteseb. See nuclear family
Bet Shemesh, 206
Bible, Amharic, 124–125
"black," identity as, 157–158
"The Black Jews Describe to their Fellow White Jews About the Hardship and Suffering They Have Had to Face" (Kassa), 39
blacksmiths, 44, 69, 79, 97. See also occupational caste group
blood: donated, 3, 167 (*see also* Blood Affair); "drawing the blood of the covenant" (see *hatafat dam brit*); as "gift," 175; ownerless, 153–155
Blood Affair, 3, 70, 150–179, 181–182, 184, 188, 214n 1 (chap. 6)
"the Blood of Israel Avenges." *See* DIN
body piercing, 36
Bogale, Yona, 78, 96
Boim, Ze'ev, 198
bones, issues of, 71–72, 74, 210
Brhane, Meskerem, 6
Brhane, Zimna, 30–31
Bronkhurst (missionary), 50
buda, 44–45, 99
burial, issues of, 12–21, 26, 35, 39–40, 85, 109, 134–149, 190

cemeteries. *See* burial, issues of
chewa, 72
Chewahit, village of, 30
Chilga, village of, 30
christening, 142
Christianity: charismatic, 128; conversion to, 2, 24; Ethiopian, 138; Ethiopian Orthodox, 15, 132, 152, 204; Jewish perception of, 192; Karo Christians, 206; Orthodox Christians, 44–46, 52; Pentecostal Christians, 9, 17, 50–61, 62–68, 98, 123–149, 203–205; religious and cultural structures, 45; social relations with Beta Israel, 69
Church Missionary Society (CMS), 47, 80
cigarettes, use of, 128
circumcision, 138–139, 141
Circus Ethiopia, 112, 123
CMS. *See* Church Missionary Society
codes, deciphering of, 207
coffee: ceremony, 129, 205; social drinking of, 127–129, 133, 143, 148–149
Cohen, Ravit, 6
Combes, E., 44
Commentary, 59
communion. *See* Eucharist
Communism, collapse of, 198
Conservative Jews. *See* Judaism, Conservative Jews
conversion: aesthetics of, 47–50; Dembeya, as center of, 48; forced vs. voluntary, 3, 23–24; incomplete, 14; magical-religious transformation, 70; quest for "purity of heart," 62–83; "symbolic," 70. *See also* Judaism, return to—program
Coptic Amhara Abyssinians, 77, 78
"covenant of fate." *See* suffering, shared
craniometry, 58
cross: display of, 79; Ethiopian, 98; sign of the, 25, 35
Crummey, Donald, 43
culture: "brokers," 17; Christianity–Beta Israel proximity, 45; context of, 6; honor and blood, 172–179; nature of, 5

Das, Veena, 206–207
Davar Rishon, 161
deacons, 51
debteroch. *See* deacons
Dembeya region, 30, 48, 65, 77, 97
DeMille, Cecil B., 131
Derekh Sudan, 22, 32, 100
the Dergue, 14, 94–95
Diaspora, Jewish, 18, 42, 80, 172, 197
dietary laws, 88, 138
DIN, 154
discipline, application of, 87–88
disease: immigration restrictions, 172; infectious, 150, 169–170, 187; stereotypes, 110; untreatable, 126–127
displacement, 1
divination, 51
divorce, 116

INDEX 235

Dominguez, Virginia, 184, 189–190
double entendres, 74–75
double-mindedness religious conversion, 68–73, 82
doubt, spheres of, 116
Douglas, Mary, 32, 178
drug use. *See* addiction, drug
Druze military officers, 162
duplicity, religious, 88
Durkheim, Emile, 146

Eastern Jews. *See* Judaism, Eastern Jews
economic refugees. *See* refugees, economic
economic salvation, 4
Edery, Yaakov, 197
education issues, immigration, 111
Eilat, proximity to absorption center, 125
Eitan, Michael, 198
Elazar, Rahamim, 119, 123–124
Emmanuel, Taamrat, 78: activist, 16–17, 96; on older groups of converts, 80–81; promised return to Jerusalem, 79; signatory to cemetery purchase, 16, 94, 178
Entebee, raid on, 21
Era of the Princes, 42–43, 44, 45
Ethiopian Christianity. *See* Christianity, Ethiopian
Ethiopian evangelicals, 41
Ethiopian-Israeli, term described, 9. *See also* Beta Israel
Ethiopian Jews. *See* Beta Israel; Feres Mura
Ethiopian Orthodox. *See* Christianity, Ethiopian Orthodox
Ethiopians, characteristics of, 156–160
ethnography: described, 5; lived experiences, 2, 3, 5, 7, 36, 37; opaqueness of, 201–209; personal narratives, 4, 93–100; processual, 100; subjectivity of, 13–14
Eucharist: ideology of, 45; sacrament of, 69
European Jews. *See* Judaism, European Jews
evangelists. *See* Beta Israel, missionary attention
evil eye, 68, 69. See also *buda*
exclusion, politics of, 3, 7, 169–172
"experience," use of term, 33–34
experience-near ethnographic approach, 4
experiencing subject, phenomenology of, 4
"experiment," use of term, 33
Ezra, Solomon, 160

Faitlovitch, Jacques: association with Emmanuel, 94; Beta Israel/international Jewry connections, activist for, 16–17; conversion practices, 76–77, 80, 96; kinship, questions of, 57–59, 62, 161, 174, 189; signatory to cemetery purchase, 16
Falasha, term described, 8, 15–16. *See also* Beta Israel
"Falasha Marranos," 78
Falasha No More (Kushner and Kalina), 15–16
Falasha she-hemir et-dato, use of term, 24
family: life, 111; relations, 119; reunification, 91, 110
Fana, 123
Fanta, Kindy, 65–66
"Faras Moqra," term described, 9, 96. *See also* "Feres Mura"
Farmer, Paul, 105–106
fasting, 46, 124
Feinstein, Moshe, 90
Felasmukra, designation of term, 24
"Felasha-mora," use of term, 24. *See also* Feres Mura
"Felashmura," use of term, 24. *See also* Feres Mura
"Felasmura," use of term, 24. *See also* Feres Mura
"Feres Mura": advocacy movement message, 121; ancestors of, 2; burial (*see* burial, issues of); challenges, special, 6; designation of, 13; divisions among, 112–113; double exclusion, 3; exclusion, politics of, 7; forced eviction of, 86; forced vs. voluntary conversion, 3; framing, 21–30; generic doubt, issues of, 89; immigration and bones, issues of, 72; immigration conditions, 1; immigration policy toward, 3–4, 23; Israel's religious establishment and, 3–4; Jewishness of, 23, 188–201; Judaism, return to (*see* Judaism, return to—program); left behind in airlift, 14, 19; lived experiences, 2; population statistics, 5–6; public health practice toward, 3–4; religious experience, questions of, 14; self-perception, 1; social experience of, 14; studies of, 6; term described, 9–10, 96–97; view of, 5–6. *See also* Beta Israel
Flad, J. M., 46, 49, 51, 54, 64
Foucalt, Michel, 198
French Alliance Israélite Universelle, 49
friar, use of term, 118–119, 156

Gaza, 160–161
Geertz, Clifford, 6
Gellner, Ernst, 147
Gember, Tazza, 84–85, 94, 109–110, 112
genealogy: complications of, 117–118; purity, 89, 98–100
gender biases, 66, 111
generic doubt, issues of, 89
Gentiles, structural opposition of, 24
Gidney, T. L., 64
Gidney, W. T., 54
Givat Ha-Matos, 201
Gobat, Samuel, 47
Goffman, Erving, 198
Gondar Province, Ethiopia: Beta Israel center, 80–81; burials in, 209–210; language, 43; transit camp, 32, 108, 195, 198, 200
Goode, F., 53
Goodman, Yehuda C., 6
gossip, 143–145
Grapes of Wrath. *See* 'Invei Za'am
Grinfeld, Izhak, 16
Grossman, David, 21, 38
Gudareff refugee camp, 22, 32

Ha'aretz, 182
Hadane, Yitzhak, 111
Hadassah Hospital, 172
Haifa, Israel, 5, 110, 125, 200
Halévy, Joseph, 17, 49, 54–59, 77
halakha/Jewish Law, 25, 92, 96, 138, 140, 141, 148, 198
Hamas, 166
Hana, Abba Gabra, 75
hands, laying on of, 46
Hatzrot Yosaf, 201
hatafat dam brit, 138–141
havvayah, 34
healing: forms of, 51; rhetoric of, 130; sites, 67
health care, 182–184
health consequences of ascetic practice, 49
Hebrew University, 5, 107
hedonism and asceticism, 50
Heidegger, Martin, 181
Heisenberg effect, 7
hepatitis, 170, 173
Herzfeld, Michael, 76
Herzl, Theodore, 19
Hezbollah, 162
Hillel, Anatmar, 173–174
Hindu identity, 191

Hitler, Adolf, 154
HIV, 158, 161–163, 170, 172
Hoben, Allan, 48
holidays, importance of, 88, 109, 138
Holocaust, 38, 39, 55, 153–155, 157
honor, blood and culture, 172–179
housing, demonstration on, 214n 3 (chap. 6)
human experience, nature of, 5
Husserl, Edmund, 4, 36, 207–208
hyenas, transformation into, 45, 69, 144

Iberian conversions, 22–23
identities, spoiled, 100–108
Identification and Rescue. *See* ZAKA
IDF. *See* Israel, Defense Forces
IJDC. *See* International Joint Distribution Committee
illness. *See* disease
Imharan, Kes, 27, 28, 96–97, 124, 142
immersion, procedure of, 141
immigration: absorption centers, 5, 22, 103, 109–111, 125, 186–187, 200; AIDS and politics of exclusion, 169–172; bones, issues of, 72; conditions of, 1; controversy over, 110; disease-based restrictions, 172; education issues, 111; eligibility, 28, 73; gender and family life, 111; language acquisition, 111; lived experiences and, 5; military service, issue of, 111; motivations, questions of, 89; policy, 3–4, 23, 85, 87, 117–118, 195; problems of, 6, 10; recent immigrants, 202–203
impurity, suffering, 30–40
India, partitioning of, 207
Indonesian coverts, 206
information, obtaining reliable, 101–102
Inter-Ministerial Committee, 89–90, 109
International Joint Distribution Committee (IJDC), 86
International Juggler's Association, 123
interpretive sociology of meaning, 4
Intifada, 160
'Invei Za'am, 162
iron smiths. *See* blacksmiths
Ishanaw, Debterah, 67–68
Israel: adjustment to life in, 6; Beta Israel airlift (*see* Operation Solomon); bureaucratic view of Ethiopians, 3; Defense Forces (IDF), 158, 162, 169, 186; determination/measurement of belonging, 2; Ethiopian Jews in (*see* Beta Israel); identification of Jews of the Diaspora, 80; middle class, 111;

Ministry of Immigrant Absorption, 103, 129, 160, 197; Palestinians in, 161–162; religious establishment policies, 3–4

Jackson, Michael, 3
James, Charles, 53
James, William, 33, 99
Jember, Melki, 30–31, 32
Jenda, village of, 77
Jerusalem, 5, 201
Jerusalem Day, 210
Jerusalem Post, 160, 165
Jewish Missionary Intelligence, 74
Jewish solidarity, 90–91
Jewish Week, 86
"Jews for Jesus," 132
Joint Distribution Committee, 87
Judaism: Adenite Jews, 18, 88; Ashkenazi Jews, 107, 157, 176; Conservative Jews, 195; Eastern Jews, 107; European Jews, 62, 184; Kurdish Jews, 184; national distinctiveness, 54; North American Jews, 184; Oriental Jews, 107; Orthodox Jews, 128, 195; racial distinctiveness, 53–61, 62; Reformed Jews, 195; religious distinctiveness, 53–55; return to—program, 1–2, 6, 7, 24, 27, 82, 84–108, 111, 114–115, 117, 122, 181–188, 185–186, 193–195, 200–201, 202–209 (*see also* absorption); Sephardic Jews, 107; Soviet Union Jews, 200; structural opposition of, 24; Tunisian Jews, 184; ultra-Orthodox Jews, 107

Kalina, Amy, 15–16
Kaplan, Steven, 42, 44–45, 70, 92, 102–103, 120
Karo Christians. *See* Christians, Karo
Kassa, Ageru, 39–40, 209
Kayla, 97
Kemant, 43
kessotch, 27
Kierkegaard, Søren, 62, 81, 82, 148
"kin in Christ," use of term, 126
"kin of the flesh," use of term, 126
kinship: according to the flesh, 52–61; assertion of, 38, 85; calculus of relatedness, 103–104; claims to shared—, 31–32; logic of, 170; network of, 117; question of, 41–61, 62, 117–118, 161, 163, 174, 189; rules of, 3; stories of, 12–13; strategic use of—information, 103–105, 207; understanding of, 119–120

Kipp, Rita Smith, 206
Kiryat Malachi, 206
Kleinman, Arthur, 3
Knesset committees, 102, 159, 182, 186, 198
Knudsen, John, 105
Krakow, Jewish community in, 126
Krauss, Iris, 182
kristena, 142
Kugler, Christian, 47
Kupat Holim Le'umit. *See* National Health Fund
Kurdish Jews. *See* Judaism, Kurdish Jews
Kushner, Arlene, 15–16

Labor Party, 159, 164, 182
Lake Tana, 77
Land Day, 161
language: adoption of Amharic, 43; Beta Israel, 43; codes, deciphering of, 207–208; double entendres, 74–75; hidden meanings, 74; immigration and—, 111; living, 207; wordplays, 74–75
Law of Return, 2, 35, 196. *See also* Judaism, return to—program
Le'umit. *See* National Health Fund
Leslau, Wolf, 59–60
Levine, Donald, 46, 101
Lévi-Strauss, Claude, 27, 38
lies, 100–108
Likud party, 159, 164, 182
linguistic contexts, 6
liturgy, emphasis on, 138
lived experience. *See* ethnography, lived experiences
LJS. *See* London Jewish Society
Lobo, Jerome, 46, 138
London Jewish Society (LJS), 42–43, 50–52, 64, 77
London Society for the Promotion of Christianity Amongst the Jews, 42, 47, 53–54, 124, 132. *See also* London Jewish Society
loss, perceptions of, 32
lovers of Mary. *See maryam wodet*
lycanthropy-sorcery, 79

Ma'ariv, 150
Madan, T. N., 5
Magdalah, 52
Magen David, 35
Magen David Adom, 150
"magical" transformations, 69
Mahari, Abba, 48–51
Maimonides, Moses, 75

malaria, 170, 173
malevolent transformation, 68–73
Malki, Kes, 27, 28, 82
marriage by abduction. See *t'ilf*
martyrdom, 65
Marxism, 192
Maryam Wodedoch, 78. See also *Maryam Wodet*
Maryam Wodet, 24, 78, 79
mateb, 98, 100
matrilineal line, genealogic purity of, 89
meat, eating, 45
medical services: dissatisfaction with, 32; knowledge of, 126. See also public health practice
medical tattooing, 35
Meheret, Kes, 27, 82
Mekuriaw, Tigest, 12–15, 18, 20, 29, 32
memorial feast. See *tazkar*
Menassie, Abba, 49
Menelik, emperor, 91
Menelik Hospital, 12, 20
Mengistu, Hailie Mariam, 18–19, 87
Meshullam, Uzi, 156–157, 167
Messele, Addisu, 152, 159–160, 169, 171–172, 177, 182–186
Messing, Simon, 17, 77–80, 93
metalworkers. See blacksmiths
Mevasseret, 201
mikveh, 70–71, 115, 140
military service: blood donations, 154–155; discrimination in, 158; immigration and, 111; suicides of Ethiopian soldiers, 158, 169
mishpachah garinit. See nuclear family
missionaries. See Beta Israel, missionary attention
"The Mission in Israel" (Elazar), 123
mistrust. See trust, issues of
mitnatzrim, 23–24
Mola, Shlomo, 171
monasticism, institution of, 45
Moore, Sally Falk, 197
moral experience, 201–209
"mother in Christ," use of term, 126
music, 181, 210
Muslims, 15, 78, 165–166, 168, 191

NACOEJ. See North American Conference on Ethiopian Jews
Nahum, Haim, 58–59
Napier, Lord, 52
nation, issues of: inconstant nationhood, 163–165; national belonging, 193;

national distinctiveness, 54; national identity, 35
National Health Fund, 183
National Religious Party, 186
native agent, 51, 67–68
Navon, Yitzhak, 169, 172, 174
Navon Commission, 170–175, 177–178, 184
Neguse, Avraham, 72, 88, 94, 121, 169, 184, 196–197
Neguse, Debterah, 51–52, 65, 67
Netanyahu, Benjamin, 159, 164, 182, 184
Neve Carmel absorption center, 109–111, 125
New York Times, 21, 38
NGOs, 17, 18
nisayon-experience, 34
non-governmental organizations. See NGOs
North American Conference on Ethiopian Jews (NACOEJ), 36–37: administration of "return to Judaism" program, 85–89; circus sponsorship, 98, 123; encouragement to "Feres Mura," 19, 30, 57; kinship, questions of, 196; operation of Addis Ababa transit center, 39, 195
North American Jews. See Judaism, North American Jews
nuclear family, 119
Numeiri, Muhammad Ja'far, 22
Nuremberg law, 2

occupational caste group, 43–44
Operation Moses, 22, 33
Operation Solomon: aftermath of, 30, 33, 84; AIDS immigrants, 174; confusion during, 136; historic airlift, 14, 18–22, 25, 86; Law of Return during—, 35; references to immigrants, 38, 116
oral histories, 103
Oriental Jews. See Judaism, Oriental Jews
Orthodox Christians. See Christianity, Orthodox Christians
Orthodox Church. See Christianity, Ethiopian Orthodox
Orthodox Jews. See Judaism, Orthodox Jews
Oslo Accords, 164
Ottoman Empire, 58
"ownerless" blood. See blood, ownerless

Pakistan, partitioning of, 207
Palestinian Arabs, 161

INDEX

Palestinian Liberation Organization (PLO), 164
Pankhurst, Helen, 120
parashat ha-dam. See Blood Affair
participant observation, artificial construct, 101
patronage, claims to, 31–32
penitence salvation, 4, 86, 122, 124–134
Pentecostal Christianity. *See* Christianity, Pentecostal Christians
Peres, Simon, 159, 162, 169–170, 182, 188
phenomenology, 4, 24, 208
pilgrimage sites, 46, 67
plausible narratives, 4
PLO. *See* Palestinian Liberation Organization
potters, 44, 69, 79. *See also* occupational caste group
poverty, 1, 44, 85
"Pro-Falasha Committees," 57
Protestant missionaries, 41
public health practices, 3–4, 170, 173, 178
punishment, burdens of, 2, 124–134
purity: quest for "purity of heart," 62–83, 86, 137–138, 148–149; religious and ethnic, 170; rites, 20–21; themes of, 32

Quirin, James, 43, 44, 45, 62–63
Qozmos (monk), 45
Quokora, village of, 30
Qwara region, 45–46

Rabin, Yitzhak, 156, 162, 164
Rachmilevitch, Eliezer, 172, 176
racial issues: American "Feres Mura" activists, 198; blood, 167 (*see also* Blood Affair); ideologies of, 59, 211; immigrant authorities and—, 121; immigrant blood, 154 (*see also* Blood Affair); institutionalized racism, 177; in military service, 158; race science, 177; racial animus, 28–29; racial distinctiveness, 53–61, 62; state racism, 162, 181
"reconciliation ceremony," 182
Reform Jews. *See* Judaism, Reformed Jews
refugees: camps, 22 (*see also* immigration, absorption centers); economic refugee, 3, 14, 24, 89; graves of, 18; trust, issues of, 29, 105. *See also* immigration
Refugees International Report, 39, 86
Rehovot, Ethiopian community in, 203
religious issues: aesthetic and moral dimensions, 50; backsliding, 88; change (*see* conversion); Christianity–Beta Israel proximity, 45; gatekeeping, 6; identity, 35, 90; religious distinctiveness, 53–55; religious prestige competition, 44; subjectivity, 13; tattooing (*see* tattooing); transformations, 201–209 (*see also* Judaism, return to—program)
religious teachers, 186–187
researchers, dealing with, 101–103, 105
ritual: conceptions of, 60; contesting, 50–52; rectification, 26–28, 193; significance of, 106, 205
Rosaldo, Renato, 151
Rosen, Chaim, 92, 103–104, 120, 129
Russian Jews, 156, 166, 184, 198

Sabbath, observance of, 79, 138, 148–149, 205
saints, 46
Salamon, Hagar, 9, 24, 28, 68–69, 72, 76–77, 80, 177
Sanbatu, Debteroch, 67–68
Sapir, Edward, 177
Schutz, Alfred, 4, 36–37, 207–209
science, issues of bodily practices, 59
Scripture, interpretation of, 75
Second Congress for the Study of Ethiopian Jews in Jerusalem, 107
secrecy, public health policies, 173, 178
secret knowledge, 100–108, 115–117, 130
secularism, rise of, 191
Seeman, Don, 6, 33, 70, 73, 82, 90, 140, 176, 177, 179, 194, 207
Selassie, Haile, 94–95, 97
semana worke, 74
"sent sickness," 105–106
Sephardic Jews. *See* Judaism, Sephardic Jews
sexual promiscuity, themes of, 126–127
Shabtay, Malka, 6
shared suffering. *See* suffering, shared
Shelemay, Kay Kaufman, 45, 51
sherut le'umi, 186
Shibaru-Sivan, Maski, 157–159
Shitreet, Meir, 196–199
Shoshke, Chaim, 94
sickness, feelings of, 32
Sigd festival, 41, 205
sign of the cross. *See* cross, sign of the
Six Day War, 21
Sneh, Ephraim, 156, 172
social life: divisions of, 112–113; gossip, 143–145; integration issues, 6; nature of, 5; youth activities, 122, 163–164
social memory, 98–99

social ostracism, 44
social relations, 69
sociology of meaning, 4
South Asian Pentecostals, 126
"South Wing to Zion," 94, 121
Soviet Union Jews. See Judaism, Soviet Union Jews
spirit healer. See *tankway*
sports and youth activities, 122
Stern, Henry Aaron, 126: autobiography, 74; conversion practices, 47–50, 63–67, 76, 80, 82; kinsmen, question of, 52–61, 62, 174, 189; ritual, contesting, 50–52
Sudan refugee camps, 1, 10
suffering: impurity, 30–40; shared, 26; themes of, 32
suicide, 65–66, 158, 169
supernatural terms, social separation, 44
Susenyos, emperor, 42, 103
suspicion, spheres of, 116, 121, 207

taharah, 12
Talpiot Mizrah, 206
Tamisier, M., 44
tankway, 127, 209
tattooing, 25, 34–36
Taylor, Charles, 4
tazkar, 109–110, 124, 205
Tel-Aviv, 84, 110, 201
Temple Mount, 154
Temple Mount Faithful, 154
temqat, 69–70, 115
The Ten Commandments, 131
terminology, conflict over, 24
Tessema, Gobeze Besuneh, 39–40
tevilah, 70–71
Tewodoros II, emperor, 42, 52, 65–66
Tigrean rebels, 19
t'ilf, 95
tourism, growth of, 171, 190
Trautmann, Thomas, 207
trauma, perceptions of, 32
Travels to Abyssinia (Halévy), 55
Trinitarianism, 45, 204
True Kindness Society. See ZAKA
trust, issues of, 29, 57, 105
tuberculosis, 211
Tunisian Jews. See Judaism, Tunisian Jews
Tzaban, Yair, 160

UJC. See United Jewish Communities

ultra-Orthodox Jews. See Judaism, ultra-Orthodox Jews
United Jewish Communities (UJC), 196

Varieties of Religious Experience (James), 99
"ventriloquist" model of anthropology, 147
Victorian era and moral balance, 49–50
violence: contexts of, 160–163 (*see also* Blood Affair); self-representation tool, 157; structural, 68; use of, 44
Viswanathan, Gauri, 191

Waldman, R. Menahem: kinship, issues of, 94, 121, 185; return to Judaism program, 85–86, 88, 90–93, 114–115, 117, 122, 139–142, 145–146, 148, 169, 194, 195, 198; on ritual rectification, 26, 106–108
Wanderings in Abyssinia (Stern), 48
Wanzagie, healing spring, 48, 67
Washington, Booker T., 59
"wax and gold" style indirection, 74–83, 147
Weber, Max, 4, 36, 207
Wedaje, Abba, 45
Weil, Shalva, 101–102
Werbner, Richard, 60
Western Wall, 41
Wikan, Unni, 3
witchcraft, accusations of, 68, 144
Wittgenstein, Ludwig, 40
women: hair, 79; separation during menstruation, 45
wordplays, 74–75
World War II, 38, 86

Yaquob, Taddesse, 78, 94–97, 104
Yaqob, Zara, 35
Yediot, 124
Yemenite children, stolen, 156–157
Yeshaq, emperor, 16, 43
Yosef, Ovadiah, 194–195

Zagai, Izhak, 203
ZAKA, 166
zamad, 120
zemana mesafent. See Era of the Princes
Zepin, George, 59
Zimbabwe, 19
Zionist Jewish solidarity, 161

ABOUT THE AUTHOR

DON SEEMAN is associate professor in the Department of Religion and the Tam Institute of Jewish Studies at Emory University. A social and medical anthropologist, he is also the author of numerous studies in Jewish thought, ritual theory, and the ethnography of contemporary Israel.